Evolution of the Market Process

From the outset, the Austrian and Swedish schools of thought within economics have shared a common thread, thereby creating a generation of close connections between the main thinkers from each tradition. This volume is the first attempt at focusing on this interesting theme in economics.

Topics covered in this impressive volume include market process theory, technological change and capital theory. With contributions from a wide variety of scholars including Axel Leijonhufvud, Harald Hagemann and Lars Magnusson, *Evolution of the Market Process* provides an important contribution to an intriguing debate.

Academics and students with an interest in these two schools of thought will find this book to be a valuable asset, while those with an interest in economics generally will also see this as an important addition to their reading lists.

Michel Bellet is Professor of Economics at the University Jean Monnet of Saint-Etienne, France. **Sandye Gloria-Palermo** is Professor of Economics at the University of the French West-Indies, Guadeloupe. **Abdallah Zouache** is Associate Professor at the University Jean Monnet of Saint-Etienne, France.

Routledge studies in the history of economics

Evolution of the Market Process

Austrian and Swedish economics

**Edited by Michel Bellet,
Sandye Gloria-Palermo and
Abdallah Zouache**

Routledge
Taylor & Francis Group

LONDON AND NEW YORK

First published 2005
by Routledge
2 Park Square, Milton Park, Abingdon, Oxon OX14 4RN

Simultaneously published in the USA and Canada
by Routledge
270 Madison Ave, New York, NY 10016

Routledge is an imprint of the Taylor & Francis Group

Typeset in Perpetua by Wearset Ltd, Boldon, Tyne and Wear
Printed and bound in Great Britain by MPG Books Ltd, Bodmin

British Library Cataloguing in Publication Data
A catalogue record for this book is available from the British Library

Library of Congress Cataloging in Publication Data
A catalog record for this book has been requested.

ISBN 0-415-31683-9

Contents

Contributors

Michel Bellet is Professor of Economics at the University Jean Monnet of Saint-Etienne, France. He is the co-editor (with C. L'Harmet) of *Industry, Space and Competition: The Contribution of Economists of the Past* (Cheltenham: Edgar Elgar, 1998). He has published several articles in the field of the history of political economy in *History of Economic Ideas, Revue d'économie politique*.

Peter J. Boettke is the Deputy Director of the James M. Buchanan Center for Political Economy and Professor of Economics, George Mason University, Fairfax, Virginia, USA. He is the editor of the *Review of Austrian Economics*. He has published a number of books, for example, *Calculation and Coordination: Essays on Socialism and Transitional Political Economy* (Routledge, 2001) and also many articles in *Journal of the History of Economic Thought, History of Political Economy, Journal of Economic Perspectives, Market Process, Critical Review, Public Choice, American Journal of Economics and Sociology, and Cultural Dynamics*.

Mauro Boianovsky is currently Professor of History of Economic Thought and Monetary Economics at the Universidade of Brasilia, Brazil. He has published many articles in *History of Political Economy, European Journal of the History of Economic Thought, Cambridge Journal of Economics, the American Journal of Economics and Sociology, and Journal of the History of Economic Thought*. He has also contributed to a number of collected volumes. He is the winner of the *Best Article Award* (History of Economics Society, 1999) and the *Prize for Best Article* (Brazilian Economic Association, 1996 and 1998).

Benny Carlson is Associate Professor in the Department of Economic History at the University of Lund, Sweden. His main interest is the history of economic ideas, especially the spread of ideas, in particular in the balance between State and market. His work covers the following fields: Swedish economic liberals' view of the State; German *Katheder* and State socialism; American institutionalism; welfare capitalism; deregulation and welfare reform. He has published several books, and several articles in the *Journal of*

History of Economic Thought, and *European Journal of the History of Economic Thought*.

Christopher J. Coyne is a Research Fellow at the James M. Buchanan Center for Political Economy at George Mason University in Fairfax, Virginia, USA. His fields of interest are: Austrian economics, political economy and new institutional economics. His entry on 'Friedrich Hayek (1899–1992)' (co-authored with Peter Boettke) is forthcoming in the *Dictionary of Modern American Philosophers*, edited by Dan Krier and Jean Van Delinder (Thoemmes Press).

Jean Magnan de Bornier is currently Professor of Economics at the University of Aix-Marseille III, France. He previously taught at the Universities of Rouen (1974–83) and Dijon (1984–90). His main research interests are the history of political economy, with publications mainly on the Austrian School of economics and law and economics as applied to industrial organisation.

Jacques Durieu is Associate Professor in the Department of Economics at the University Jean Monnet of Sainte-Etienne, France. His fields of interests include game theory and the history of economic thought. He has published articles in *Games and Economic Behavior, International Journal of Game Theory* and *Economic Theory*.

Ragip Ege is Professor of Economics at the University Louis Pasteur, Strasbourg, France. His article, 'La valeur chez Marx: construction d'un objet analytique', is forthcoming in a special issue of the French journal *Economies et Sociétés*.

Sandye Gloria-Palermo is Professor of Economics at the University of the French West Indies, in Guadeloupe, France. She specialises in the works of the Austrian School of Economics. She is the author of an anthology, *Modern Austrian Economics*, 3 vols (Pickering and Chatto Publishers), a book, *The Evolution of Austrian Economics: From Menger to Lachmann* (Routledge), and of various papers in international reviews.

Harald Hagemann is Professor of Economic Theory at the University of Hoheinheim, Stuttgart. His main areas of research are: macroeconomic theory and policy, technological change and employment, growth and structural change and history of economic thought. He is managing editor of the *Journal of Structural Change and Economic Dynamics* and member of the editorial board of the *European Journal of the History of Economic Thought*. He has published many articles on Austrian Economics and has edited several books on history of economic thought, notably *The Legacy of Hicks* (with O. Hamouda).

Gilles Jacoud is Professor of Economics at the University Jean Monnet of Saint-Etienne, France. He is the author of several books and articles on money and banking and on the history of economic thought.

Olivier Jenn-Treyer is a Researcher Fellow at the University of Paris XII, and member of PHARE (University of Paris 1), France.

Lars Jonung is Research Adviser at DG ECFIN, the European Commission, Brussels, since September 2000 dealing with macroeconomic issues. He was previously Professor of Economics at the Stockholm School of Economics. His research is focused on monetary and fiscal policies, particularly on the policy of the Riksbank, on monetary unions and exchange rate arrangements, on inflationary expectations and perceptions, business cycle issues, and on the history of economic thought. He served as chief economic adviser to Prime Minister Carl Bildt in 1992–94. Jonung has published several books, *The Stockholm School of Economics Revisited* (1991), *Lessons for EMU from the History of Monetary Unions* (with M.D. Bordo), and *Bertil Ohlin: A Centennial Celebration, 1899–1999* (with R. Findlay and M. Lundahl, co-editors).

Axel Leijonhufvud is Professor of Monetary Theory and Policy at the University of Trento, Italy, and Professor Emeritus at the University of California at Los Angeles, USA. He is a specialist in several fields, including the evolution of modern macroeconomics, the transformation of socialist systems, monetary theory, European economic history, and computable economics. He has published many articles in *American Economic Review*, *Journal of Economic Literature*, *Swedish Journal of Economics*, *Oxford Economic Papers*, *European Journal of the History of Economic Thought*, *Journal of Economic Methodology*, *Southern Economic Journal*, and many books. He has also contributed to a number of collected volumes.

Lars Magnusson is Professor and Chairman of the Department of Economic History, Uppsala, and Research Director at the National Institute for Working Life, Stockholm, Sweden. He is the author of *Mercantilism: The Shaping of an Economic Language* (Routledge, 1994) and *An Economic History of Sweden* (Routledge, 2000).

Robert Nadeau is Professor of Philosophy in the Department of Philosophy at the Université du Québec à Montréal. His general field of research is philosophy of social sciences but he specialises in comparative epistemology and methodology of economics. He has edited or co-edited many books and special issues of different journals in this area. He contributed to the *Handbook of Economic Methodology* (1998), edited by John B. Davis, D. Wade Hands and Uskali Mäki, with an article on 'Spontaneous Order'. He is currently finishing a book on *Hayek and the Refutation of Socialism*.

Giulio Palermo is researcher in Political Economy at the University of Brescia, Italy. He has worked on the socialist calculation debate and the relations between Austrian economics, new institutional economics and Marxism. He has published a book (Manifestolibri) and some articles in international journals such as *Cambridge Journal of Economics*, *Journal of Economic Issues*, *Review of Political Economy* and *History of Economic Ideas*.

Dominique Torre is Professor of Economics at the University of Nice Sophia Antipolis, France, and member of LEM-CNRS-UNSA. His research interests include monetary economics, internet economics and the history of economic thought.

Elise Tosi is Professor of Economics at the Euro American Institute of Technology (groupe CERAM) and a member of LEM-CNRS (Nice-Sophia Antipolis), France.

Hans-Michael Trautwein is Professor of International Economics at the University of Oldenburg, Germany. He has published numerous articles on international economics, monetary theory and the history of economic thought in the *Canadian Journal of Economics*, *History of Political Economy*, *The Journal of Economic Surveys*, *Weltwirtschaf tliches Archiv*, and other journals.

Carlo Zappia is Associate Professor of Economics at the University of Siena, Italy. His research deals with the historical and methodological aspects of interaction in a complex environment. In particular, he is interested in the Austrian approach to the interaction among individual agents. He has published articles in *Journal of the History of Economic Thought*, *European Journal of the History of Economic Thought* and the *History of Economic Ideas*.

Abdallah Zouache is Associate Professor of Economics at the University of Jean Monnet of Saint-Etienne, France. His research interest includes the question of coordination, the history of macroeconomics monetary policy rules and the new neoclassical synthesis. He has published several articles on the history of economic thought in *Louvain Economic Review*, and *L'Actualité Economique*, and *History of Economic Ideas*.

Preface

This collection of essays is the result of an international workshop organised by the CREUSET, the economics research centre of the University of Saint-Etienne, France, in March 2002 on the relationship between the Austrian and the Swedish Schools of economics. The idea of holding this workshop was conceived as an attempt to make explicit the array of analytical connections that exists between the leaders of these two traditions, connections that we had become aware of due to the internal seminars or informal discussions in our research department.

Our research centre gives the history of thought a place of its own in the definition of its research policy. Not only do we think that the history of economic analysis is a fascinating subject, but, as economists, we are also aware that we cannot escape from our past. We have much to gain from analysing the way in which our predecessors came up with their ideas and theories. The workshop was an attempt to show that the ideas of Menger and Wicksell are still alive.

From the end of the nineteenth century, the Austrian and Swedish traditions developed along similar lines. From the outset, these two traditions shared a common critical view with the expanding Walrasian paradigm, thereby creating for each new generation close connections between these authors: between Böhm-Bawerk, Mises and Wieser, on the one hand, and Wicksell on the other hand, and later on, between Hayek and the Stockholm School of the 1930s (especially Myrdal).

Overview of the book

The contributions here focus on an original topic, namely, the meeting of Austrian economics with Swedish economics (Leijonhufvud, Coyne and Boettke).

Previously, Austrian economics has had a revival in different areas but this was not really the case as far as Swedish economics is concerned. We think that the great cross-fertilisation of ideas between both traditions (especially in the 1920s and the 1930s) is still valid today. It is our expectation that this book will pave the way for new developments aimed at a mutual enrichment of both traditions. In particular, one of our aims is to bring back into favour the crucial role of Swedish economists in the development of economic ideas and economic policies (Carlson and Jonung, Magnusson).

This book offers the opportunity to discuss this common evolution and to emphasise the similarities and differences between both traditions on shared fundamental topics such as money and business cycle theory (Boianovsky, and Hagemann, Trautwein, Bellet and Zouache, Torre and Tosi), capital theory (Jenn-Treyer, De Bornier, Gloria-Palermo and Palermo), the role of expectations (Zappia, Bellet and Durieu, Jacoud) and the nature of their methodology (Ege, Nadeau).

Acknowledgements

The editors wish to thank all the participants in the workshop for their enthusiasm and commitment to this challenge, in particular, Axel Leijonhufvud for his availability. We are also grateful to the members of the CREUSET organising staff, especially Sylvie Grenier, Lise Causse and Régine Bufferne.

Acknowledgements are also due to the Regional Council of Rhône-Alpes and the local Council of Saint-Etienne Métropole for their assistance with the publication of this volume.

Michel Bellet
Sandye Gloria-Palermo
Abdallah Zouache

Part I
The meeting of Austrian and Swedish economics

1   The metamorphoses of neoclassical economics

Axel Leijonhufvud

Introduction

Between the two world wars, there were still distinct traditions or 'schools' in economics. But interaction by correspondence and travel between the various centers of learning was increasing and there was a widespread expectation that the various traditions were merging into a unified international neoclassical discipline, perhaps even a science. With the exception, perhaps, of the relationship between the London School of Economics and Cambridge, there was in or around 1930, as yet little sense of controversial opposition between the various traditions but instead more of an appreciation of what they could learn from each other.

In or around 1930, it would, moreover, have been a reasonable expectation that this unified international economics not only would incorporate the main teachings of the Austrian and the related Swedish traditions but also that it was likely to develop in directions defined by the work then being done by the younger generation of Austrians and Swedes. Everyone acknowledged that the Lausanne School had demonstrated better than anyone else how 'everything depended upon everything else' but it had little influence on the research actually being done in those years. Similarly, everyone had to know their Marshall but the Marshallian tradition was not the main source of the problems and questions that interested economists at that time.

So what happened? The Stockholm School died out and today is largely forgotten. The Austrian School survived as a small minority, isolated and neglected by the mainstream, and devoted to the purification and preservation of uniquely Austrian tenets. Marshallian cost-curves kept a foothold in undergraduate textbooks but hardly anyone did Marshallian research. All three ended up, as it were, 'marginalized'.

The standard answer to the question of what happened is that the Keynesian revolution won out over the Austrians and Swedes in macroeconomics and, I suppose, that the Hicks–Samuelson mathematization of theory in effect did the same in microeconomics. I have no objection to that answer except that it does not explain *how* or *why* this all came about.

The 'great transformation' of neoclassical economics

My own interest in this question has a macroeconomic motivation in that I want to understand the developments in general economic theory that have eventually left us with the microfoundations of macroeconomics that were in force in the 1980s and 1990s. As I see it, the evolution of macroeconomics in the twentieth century has to a large extent been driven by a shift in the understanding of what would constitute appropriate microfoundations. This shift has occurred in several stages which, taken together, have wrought a 'great transformation' of neoclassical economics.

It is perhaps best to make clear from the outset that I am not referring to the mathematization of neoclassical economics, since economists of an Austrian persuasion often blame that for what they consider wrong with economics, and since the Stockholm School was at least skeptical about the usefulness of mathematical formalisms.[1] But it is not the formalization of economic theory *per se* or the evolution of successive formalisms that are at stake. It is our understanding of what even the most elemental formalism *means* that has changed. If there is a methodological lesson in the story that I will try to tell, it is *not* that we should refrain from formalizing economic theory but simply that being 'rigorous' in this particular way has not prevented a very drastic shift in how economists understand the core of neoclassical economics.

I will not be able to trace all the stages in the 'great transformation' that I am talking about. Nor can I claim that 'reasons of space' are my only handicap. What follows should be understood as attempting a sweeping generalization to make sense of a long and complex historical process. It will have the deficiencies of all such sweeping generalizations. I must leave it to a later occasion – and most probably to other people – to document who, among earlier economists, it truly fits and to whose thought it does violence.

I will proceed by first describing where we have ended up and then go back and attempt a sketch of where we started from. This should provide a firmer idea of what I mean when I refer to this transformation of understanding. Then, I will attempt to describe some of the stages of the process and to indicate at least how and why the Austrians and the Swedes decided not to 'go along' with the majority of our profession.

Turn of the century: modern microfoundations

Optimality at individual and competitive equilibrium at aggregate levels are the hallmarks of modern theory. It is largely the meanings attached to 'optimality' or 'maximization', to 'equilibrium' and to 'competition' that will be our concern in what follows. They are context-dependent and the conceptual context has not always been the same as the one in force in recent years. At the end of the century, the common understanding may be summarized as follows.

Individual agent level

- Observed behavior is understood as the exercise of *choice*.
- Choice is represented formally in terms of constrained optimization.
- For the optimization problem to have a determinate solution, the agent has to know his opportunity set in all its dimensions (for example, all prices, present and future).
- The solution is a *plan*. For the plan to explain *observed behavior*, the information defining the agent's opportunity set must be objectively true. Uncertainty about the future can be present only in the form of objectively known stochastic distributions (also, of course, the agent must be able to calculate the optimum).

Market and system level

- If this behavior description is to apply to *all* agents, the system must be represented as *in equilibrium*. If observed actions are to be interpreted as realizations of optimal plans, the state of the system must be such that all plans are *consistent* with one another.
- If all actions always have to be apprehended as part of objectively optimal plans, 'disequilibrium' is a meaningless term and 'equilibrium' is a superfluous term.
- In a temporal context, the economy is seen as following an *intertemporal equilibrium* trajectory, conceptually predetermined by the reconciliation of all individual plans. Agents have to know (the probability distributions of) future equilibrium prices in order to formulate their optimal plans.
- This means that everyone's choices have to be reconciled *before* anyone's choice can be made. The process by which this reconciliation takes place cannot be described within the context of the model.
- The logical contradiction can be avoided by assuming rational expectations, that is, it is supposed that past experience enables agents accurately to predict the stochastic distributions of future prices. The learning whereby agents distill rational expectations from experience cannot be described within the context of the model.
- Further experience is worthless to agents. Shocks to the system never violate the probability distributions that agents take as known. Barreling down the intertemporal equilibrium path, no one learns anything they did not know to begin with.

The present-day intertemporal competitive general equilibrium (ICGE) theory is the end-product of a gradual but profound change in our understanding of what neoclassical economics was all about.

In the past few years, of course, there have been attempts to break out of this conception in macroeconomic models of learning and, in particular, in the theory of repeated games. Perhaps, there is now hope that this most recent focus on issues of learning and expectations formation will in effect revive the older conception of what neoclassical economics once entailed. But here I am concerned with the long transition from this early neoclassical economics to modern ICGE.

Founding fathers

The economists of the British classical school (including Marx) sought to deduce the 'laws of motion' of the economy. In spirit, their doctrines were 'magnificent dynamics', as Baumol once characterized them. But they lacked, of course, the mathematical tools to formally analyze the dynamics of their system. Presuming (without proof) that the system must go to a point attractor, they were able to analyze its 'dismal' *stationary state*.

The neoclassical system builders similarly conceived of both optima and equilibria as steady-states of individual and collective adaptive processes respectively. This, I would argue, was what they all meant when they referred to the characteristic neoclassical constructions as *static theory*.

Individual agent level

Early marginalist writers might explain, for example, that utility maximization of the consumer would require that the expression

$$MU_1/p_1 = MU_2/p_2 = \ldots MU_n/p_n$$

be satisfied. But they did *not* obtain this condition by formulating and solving a constrained optimization decision problem. Instead, they would demonstrate that if the condition were violated, the consumer 'could do better' by very simple rearrangement of his or her purchases. Thus, the optimality conditions for individual agents were understood as rest states of unspecified adaptive processes. As such, they were often referred to as 'equilibria' of the household or of the firm.

Market level

Similarly, market equilibria were thought of as the rest-states of interactive processes driven by profit or loss on the margin and by excess demand or supply. Consider, for example, how Keynes in trying to trace the bias in favor of *laissez-*

faire described how economists think. In part, 'because they have been biased by the traditions of the subject', he says:

> they have begun by assuming a state of affairs where the ideal distribution of productive resources can be brought about through individuals *acting indepen-dently by the method of trial and error* in such a way that those individuals who move in the right direction *will destroy by competition* those who move in the wrong direction.
>
> (Keynes 1926, section III, italics added)

This is very different, surely, from arguing that the representative agent has cor-rectly solved the economy's dynamic programming problem defined by the deep parameters of preferences and productivity and that, consequently, the govern-ment should leave him or her alone.

The modern theory takes an entirely fantastic notion of human rationality and projects it by construction into an image of how the economy functions. The older neoclassical conception, voiced by Keynes – albeit with critical intent – was that interaction within a framework of market institutions imposed a measure of rationality on market participants.

Competition

The theory of perfect competition started out as an inquiry into the question under what conditions rates of return would be equalized across all industries in the long run stationary state. Again, the analysis concerned the end-state of adap-tive processes. As J.B. Clark put it (quoted by E. Lundberg 1930: 13), 'however stormy may be the ocean, there is an ideal level surface projecting itself through the waves, and the actual surface of the turbulent water fluctuates about it'.

Again, a different conception from the model in which all agents face paramet-ric prices *ex ante* all the time. Moreover, the older conception was one of a 'rival-rous process' (as in Keynes's quote above), not the measure-theoretic one of independence of actions stemming from everyone's atomistic insignificance in the market.[2]

Marshall

It is instructive at this stage to use that other loser in the competition for theo-retical influence on twentieth-century theory, Alfred Marshall, as an example and briefly to contrast his mode of theory construction with that of Walras, the retro-spective winner.

Walras drew his diagrams with price on the horizontal, quantity on the verti-cal axis. The first stage in his analysis was finding the agent's optimal choice of quantity, given the price, $q^d(p)$ and $q^s(p)$. The second stage was aggregation at given prices and the third, the market clearing equilibrium.[3]

Marshall drew quantity on the horizontal, price on the vertical axis. He too obeyed mathematical convention because he began by defining the agent's demand-price and supply-price, given the quantity, $p^d(q)$ and $p^s(q)$. A demand price is defined as the *maximum* price a consumer would pay and the supply price as the *minimum* price a supplier would accept for a given quantity. These, then, are upper and lower boundaries of sets. They are most *definitely not* the result of some constrained optimization experiment. Marshall does not start from maximization. That is the most important contrast to draw.

Marshallian agents act on simple decision rules. I will refer to them as 'Marshall's laws of motion'. Agents are constantly adapting to a changing environment. The basic behavior propositions may be put as follows:

> For the consumer – if demand price exceeds market price, increase consumption; in the opposite case, cut back.

> For the middleman – if inventory turnover slows down, reduce prices to both customers and suppliers; in the opposite case, raise them.

> For the producer – if supply price exceeds the price realized, reduce output; in the opposite case, expand. And, if profits are above normal (given the interest rate), accumulate more productive capital, etc.

These are simple gradient climbing rules. Reliance on them explains, I believe, Marshall's motto for his *Principles*: 'Natura non facit saltum' and his oft-repeated references to this 'continuity principle'. While Marshall's agents obviously do not possess the *substantive rationality* assumed in modern economics, they may be accorded a measure of *procedural rationality* in environments where continuity and convexity can both be assumed.

The laws of motion are best thought of as governed by feedback. The producer, for example, obeys a difference equation of the form:

$$q_{t+1} = h[s(q_t) - p^*_t] + q_t$$

where the expression in brackets measures the difference between his supply price for the quantity he *did* produce and the price actually *received*. Note that these values are *ex post*. Feedback rules are backward-looking, based on the evaluation of immediate past performance.[4]

Marshall's starting point, then, is what today we call *agent-based* modeling: a multitude of heterogeneous agents interacting on the basis of simple behavior rules. But the complex non-linear dynamics which such models normally exhibit neither he nor anyone else in his time could possible handle (imagine all his laws of motion in operation in thousands of markets, at the same time and with different speeds and lags!). He tamed the complex dynamics by assuming (i) a strong ranking of the various adjustment speeds; and (ii) that each of the thus separated processes would converge directly on a point attractor. Thus, his characteristic hierarchy of equilibria – for the market day, the short run, and the long run – has, of course, no counterpart in modern ICGE theory. At each level, Marshall's concept of equilibrium is *constancy* of an observable variable as opposed to *consistency* of the plans of all participants.[5]

In a previous paper (Leijonhufvud 1998), I have explained how Keynes, working strictly from within this Marshallian tradition, discovered that Marshall's 'laws of motion' did not necessarily converge on a full employment equilibrium but that a more general theory was required. This earlier paper also tries to explain why Marshall and Keynes seem theoretically incompetent to the point of unintelligibility to 'modern' readers.

Competition

George Stigler, in his famous essay 'Perfect Competition, Historically Contemplated' (1957), noted with some puzzlement that Alfred Marshall did not seem to have contributed at all to the development of the concept of 'perfect competition'.[6] The reason why he did not stems from the manner in which he built his supply and demand models. The usual interpretation has Marshall obtaining his supply functions from aggregating the maximizing output choices of firms in the now usual way. This would obviously be inconsistent with my assertion that his firms only obey a simple law of motion.

In my interpretation, Marshall obtains his agent-based short-run industry equilibrium first. It is a state where, in the aggregate, the corresponding laws of motion have ceased to operate. Having obtained this equilibrium, he then asks: what would be true of a 'representative firm' when the aggregate output of the industry shows no change? His answer is that a firm that is representative of the dynamic behavior of the industry would see no incentive to change its own output either. And that would be the case if its marginal and average cost equaled price. But these are the standard first-order conditions for an optimum. When written out formally, the model seems indistinguishable from an *ex ante* neo-Walrasian construction.

Two things are worth noting about this. First, Marshall, in effect, reversed the usual order of constructing the partial equilibrium model. Instead of going from individual optimization through aggregation to industry equilibrium, he went via market equilibrium to the optimality conditions for the representative firm. And there is no *ex ante* aggregation performed. Second, the optimality condition defines a rest state and, as such, it should be interpreted in *ex post* terms. The firm's decision for tomorrow is determined by what has happened today.

It is possible, of course, to introduce expectations into Marshall's price theory and for some purposes it is indeed necessary to do so (to construct Keynes's *marginal efficiency of capital*, for instance). But in the case at hand it is superfluous to do so. The competitive firm has a simple routine for adapting to a constantly changing environment. It is a price-taker but *not* in the sense of being informed of the market price *before* making its production decision. Rather, it finds out what price its product will fetch only when its output together with the outputs of all its competitors reach the market.

The second generation of Marshallians liked to substitute a fish-market for Marshall's corn-market. Consider for a moment how the process leading to a short-run equilibrium of that market might go. On a given morning, the fishing fleet returns to port. The boats are unloaded and the catch auctioned off to competing middlemen at the local auction house. Each boat owner can now compare the realized market price with the marginal cost incurred. If the difference is positive, he will decide to set the nets one more time next night: if negative, he will work the boat less hard. The process, it is assumed, converges.

Obviously, this process does not require perfect knowledge, much less perfect foresight. More to the point, it does not require large numbers of firms producing perfect substitutes. In fact, the catch of any one boat may consist of a mix of species and boat owners might adapt to realized prices not only by adjusting how hard they work the boat but also by switching fishing grounds to go for a temporarily more profitable mix of species in the catch. The producers need not have identical cost-curves. Marshall's young and old firms differ. And the number of producers and of middlemen need not be particularly large. What matters is that the individual producer is not able to disentangle the effect of his own action on market price in an environment where everyone else is constantly adapting so that his 'fitness landscape' never stays fixed.

The familiar diagram showing the equilibrium of the firm under perfect competition is *not* in Marshall. It is due to A.C. Pigou.[7] This diagram, I believe, came to play a big role in changing the common interpretation of what 'competition' means in analytical economics. It can be seen as depicting *ex post* the rest state of Marshall's representative firm when his market is in short-run equilibrium. The quantity is then the quantity that the firm *has* produced and the price is the price that *was* received. But the interpretation that became the generally accepted one sees the diagram (or the corresponding algebra) *ex ante*. By that interpretation, the firm is *'facing a horizontal demand schedule'* and choosing the optimal output, given the known parametric price.

The conditions for perfect competition to obtain had been discussed for a long time, but it was 'the meticulous discussion' in Frank Knight's 1921 *Risk, Uncertainty and Profit*, says Stigler ([1957] 1965: 256), 'that did most to drive home to economists generally the austere nature of the rigorously defined concept and so prepared the way for the widespread reaction against it in the 1930s'. The conditions included requirements on the knowledge and cognitive competence of agents that added up to 'substantive rationality', but Knight had set his analysis in the context of an isolated society in a stationary state which made this more reasonable than it is in the continuous-time models of our own day. Knight also required divisibility of goods, costless mobility of resources and, of course, a large number of agents trading perfect substitutes. In the fullness of time, the requirement became Auman's continuum of traders. If these were the requirements for perfectly elastic demand schedules, the profession stood ready to accept downward sloping ones.[8]

Yet, imperfect competition theory never took hold, at least not as microfoundations for macro. Instead, optimization by agents all of whom 'take prices as given' was to become standard. There were some casualties as a result. Heterogeneity of both agents and goods was slighted. More significantly, increasing returns would not fit into competitive general equilibrium (GE) theory. The evidence of increasing returns are all around us – every volume discount ever encountered testifies to it – but our analytical apparatus demands convexity so diminishing returns it has to be.

The Austrians

It is time to bring the Austrians onto the stage. Ironically, they played a crucial role in bringing about the great transformation of neoclassical theory which their intellectual descendants were totally to reject.

One must start with Menger and his principled opposition to classical real value theory. Value derived solely from the utility that consumers attached to final goods. To Menger, the classics were wrong and Marshall muddled in his 'two blades of the scissors' compromise. It is appropriate to call Marshall a *neo*classical since he retained and renewed the classical tradition. Menger was *anti*-classical.

Menger's revolt against real cost theory and his insistence that if value was determined by 'a pair of scissors', then both blades were made of utility, created a durable but creative conceptual tension for all his intellectual descendants.

- It meant first of all that cost was opportunity cost as seen by the decision-maker. Cost, therefore, was fundamentally *subjective*.
- Since the value of goods was ultimately determined by marginal utility in consumption, the value of higher order goods had to be found by *Zurechnung* (imputation).
- Production has to come before consumption in time; all aspects of the economic process are necessarily *time spanning*; capital theory is at the core of all production theory.

- The valuation of inputs through *Zurechnung* must be based on *expected* values to consumers. In Austrian economics, attention to expectations cannot be avoided or postponed as a complication to be introduced later.

In Mengerian economics, all activities are time-spanning. There is always a temporal gap between action and utility-relevant outcome. Equilibrium, therefore, is necessarily intertemporal and has to be defined in terms of the realization of expectations. In the terminology of the Swedish school, equilibrium obtains when *ex post* outcomes equal *ex ante* anticipations. So we have a third equilibrium concept: whereas all the q^s of a Marshallian model are to be interpreted as realized, and those of Walrasian models as planned or notional, an explicit Austrian model would have to keep track of both.

The Austrian influence was instrumental in making choice-theory the heart and core of modern economics. The Mengerians insisted on deriving explanations of 'human action' (in Mises's phrase) from the means–ends distinction. Choice of want-satisfaction under the pressure of scarcity was the definition of the economic problem that Lionel Robbins took from Wicksteed and the Austrians in his influential *An Essay on Nature and Significance of Economic Science* (1932).[9] In Britain, this meant a revolt against Marshall and his entire conception of the field of economics. In fact, it acted as a small drop of intellectual poison that in the end was to *kill* the Marshallian tradition and was to take us from Marshall's 'ordinary business of life' to a concern with every type of activity which draws on scarce resources and thus eventually to Gary Becker's theories of optimal child-rearing, church attendance, drug addiction, and suicide.

The transition was *so innocent*. John Hicks and R.D.G. Allen were *protégés* of Robbins in a department dominated by the recently arrived Hayek.[10] From an Austrian–LSE standpoint, their motives were of the purest: to reformulate demand theory so as to rid it of cardinal measurability and interpersonal welfare comparisons. So, they reinvented Slutsky and, in the process, disposed of the problems of handling complements and substitutes in which Austrian theory had been bogged down for decades. No wonder that Hayek approved! Hicks's equally famous 'Suggestion for Simplifying the Theory of Money' from the following year (1935) should also be seen in the same Austrian-influenced context. Mises (1912) had taught that money did not yield utility; one could not, therefore, derive the demand for money in the same way as one did the demand for other goods. Thus, Hicks solved another problem that had emerged in the Austrian tradition when he showed how money could be brought into the choice-theoretical fold – and handled with constrained optimization.

Hicks became a *bête noir* to Austrians much later. But at the time, no one saw where this was headed. The realization dawned only gradually that choice theory, formalized as constrained optimization, dispensed with the market process and trapped you into perfect foresight equilibria.[11]

Yet, as Hicks much later said: 'taking step after step along a road which seemed pre-ordained as soon as one had taken the first step' (1977: Preface) took him to the *atemporal* general equilibrium construction of *Value and Capital* (Part I). He then introduced *dated* commodities. At this point, of course, he was staring intertemporal general equilibrium squarely in the face – and recoiled. Hicks wanted a theory with which one could analyze economic history and, of course, perfect foresight economics was not it. Others were later happily to take this kind of choice theory to its logical conclusions (which included dumping history in favor of teleology). But Hicks had a retreat prepared. Even before beginning work on *Value and Capital*, he had read Myrdal and had learned the temporary equilibrium method through personal acquaintance with Erik Lindahl.

The Swedes and sequence analysis

Marshall's equilibrium is defined by the constancy of realized magnitudes, Walras's by the consistency of optimal plans. Hayek's 1928 article on '*Intertemporales Gleichgewicht*' made explicit what the Austrian concept of equilibrium had to be, namely, expectations fulfilled by realizations. This association of 'equilibrium' with perfect foresight raised philosophical issues that had not been attached to older notions of 'a balance of forces', etc., and which proved productive of theoretical ideas of a type that has not been congenial to the later Austrian School.[12]

On a somewhat more pedestrian level, the Austrian equilibrium concept posed the problem of how to provide a reasonably disciplined way of analyzing the movement of the system when the equilibrium condition was not fulfilled. At this time, everyone regarded it as obvious that it was fulfilled rarely at best. The analysis of the market-clearing disequilibrum processes, where each state of the economy grew out of the preceding one, became characteristic of the Swedish School. It required the careful specification of *ex ante* plans, based basically on short-term expectations, to be compared at the end of each period with *ex post* outcomes. The terminology was introduced by Gunnar Myrdal in his 1927 dissertation, 'The problem of Price formation in a Changing World'.

Among the Swedes, Lindahl (1939) seems in many respects surprisingly modern even today. He generally proceeded by first analyzing the perfect foresight case and did not regard this just as a formality: 'People often do know what is going on.' He would then follow this up by considering various kinds of imperfect foresight and what the consequences of expectational errors would be, assuming in both cases that markets cleared in each period.

The approach of the Swedes differed in subtle ways from that of Keynes. In Lindahl's (and Hicks's) temporary equilibrium method, short-term expectations determined the Walrasian market-clearing prices in each period. Keynes, on the other hand, had long-term investment expectations determine a

Marshallian short-run equilibrium in each period. This short-run Marshallian equilibrium could be subject to effective demand failures, in which case it would have no possible Walrasian counterpart. In addition to that, Keynes considered 'it was safe to omit express reference to short-term expectations' (1936: 51) and in effect equated short-term outcomes with the corresponding expectations.[13]

Erik Lundberg pushed the Swedish approach the furthest. The difference-equation models of his celebrated doctoral dissertation (1937) had considerable influence in the Anglo-American literature through the works of Lloyd Metzler and Paul Samuelson. Already in his earliest writings (1930), Lundberg had, however, revealed considerable skepticism about the usefulness of equilibrium analysis outside purely static theory. He also came to distrust the extrapolation of non-linear models for more than a couple of 'periods' into the future.[14] In the policy-oriented work in macroeconomics that dominated most of his later career, intertemporal equilibrium almost completely fades out of the picture. Instead of 'deep parameters' of tastes and technology fixing a time-path to which the economy must gravitate, path-dependence in private sector expectations and in government policy tends to govern.

By moving thus far from determinate equilibrium analysis, the Swedish school gradually lost the very considerable international influence that it once had enjoyed. The macroeconomics of multiple equilibria of recent years might occasion a reappraisal of this older Swedish brand of theory. Theories where economic crises of one sort or another are explained as *unexpected* jumps from one perfect foresight path to another are not obviously preferable to Lundberg's approach.

Conception creep

Military men talk of 'mission creep' when, in the course of an operation, its goals gradually expand and become increasingly ambitious. Something of the sort has happened to neoclassical economics. As in the case of mission creep, afterwards no one in particular can be found on whom to place the entire responsibility for 'conception creep'.

The first thing to note is that early neoclassical economics had no built-in formal controls that could have prevented the process. Technical limitations prevented the founding fathers (and succeeding generations) from modeling adaptive dynamics explicitly. Formally, one dealt only with the (presumed) point attractors, the properties of which are the same as the optimality conditions of modern models. This makes the two opposed theoretical conceptions more or less indistinguishable in those aspects which have been formalized. Nothing in the formal models, therefore, rang the alarm bells signaling 'Contradiction!' when the interpretation of the statics changed. Thus, the mathematization of economic theory was no obstacle to a complete revolution in how the theory is generally understood but rather facilitated it in so far as economists increasingly identified the theory with the formal model.

Second, there is a significant overlap where the understanding really is the same. The early neoclassicals would recognize that the repetition of similar conditions would quickly teach agents, for example, to maximize the utility of consumption in a relatively small, local part of the commodity space. In situations with which people have gained familiarity, trial-and-error adaptation is pointless. In such cases, therefore, it makes better sense to think of the optimality conditions as characterizing *how people make decisions*.

This switch in interpretation from seeing the (local) optimality conditions as defining the attractor of some sketchily described or entirely unspecified adjustment process to thinking instead of constrained optimization as the way in which economic subjects make choices is, I believe, *the* crucial step in the great transformation. From there, paraphrasing John Hicks, it is a matter of 'taking step after step', each one of them following *almost* with logical inevitability, once this particular one had been taken.

The train of logic is now on its way to the intertemporal general equilibrium model whose properties were summarized at the beginning of this chapter. If observed behavior is to be interpreted in terms of constrained optimization, one must assume that agents know their opportunity set. If this is true for all, the system is always in equilibrium. It is tempting to 'generalize' the theory by expanding the commodity space. Such generalization comes cheaply – for the most part simply at the intellectual expense of keeping track of more subscripts. Intertemporal decisions are most conveniently handled by optimizing over infinite time, since terminal conditions for finite time models are usually an embarrassment. In similar fashion, it is convenient to work with continuous time models in which the 'static state' of the founding fathers holds at every point in time. These extensions into infinite dimensional spaces force the theorist to introduce truly fantastic assumptions about what people are able to know, to forecast and to calculate. But 'as if' mysticism has come to be regarded as a sufficient methodological defense for every variant of these constructions.[15]

The Austrian position

It is possible, of course, to step off the train to modernity at various junctions, as did Hicks, Lindahl and Myrdal, for example. Keynes and other Marshallians never got on. The Austrians are seen by impatient present-day passengers, speeding along in all comfort, as a tribe of unruly Indians, riding alongside, yelling and hollering and firing away at the train with outmoded bows and arrows.

The Austrians, as I have emphasized above, were instrumental in making choice-theory the core of modern economics. When they woke up to the implications of the formalization of choice as constrained optimization, however, they realized that they had to part company. They did so by stressing the *subjectivity* of choice. Already in the 1930s, the subjectivist position was fully elaborated in opportunity cost-theory and became the basis for a quite fundamental critique of the standard theory of cost and the welfare economics based on it (Buchanan 1969; Buchanan and Thirlby 1973). Later on, Ludwig Lachmann reworked Austrian capital theory on subjectivist lines. The Austrians also reacted in another, albeit related way, namely, in opposing the mathematization of economic theory. This, in my estimation, has been a mistake. The objection should be that the modern economics of optimization and equilibrium has come to rely on the *wrong kind* of mathematics.

All that pertains to the 'Austrian schism', that is, to their decision to part company with the modern mainstream. But there is also the question of what happened to the positive Austrian contributions that were once so influential when Austrian economics was still very much part of the mainstream. In the early 1930s, the capital theory of Böhm-Bawerk was still without question the dominant one while the Mises–Hayek business cycle theory was the new frontier of the field. What happened to them?

The Austrian business cycle theory has not, in my opinion, stood up well. The reason, put very briefly, is that most inflations have not been associated with over-investment and that not all over-investment episodes have been associated with inflation. In the Austrian theory inflation and over-investment are inseparably linked, but finding cases that clearly fit the theory is not easy. The reason is that outside money inflations cause disintermediation and tend to kill the markets that finance long-term investments (Latin American cases) while inside money (credit) inflations may produce asset-price inflation and over(mal)investment without necessarily causing CPI inflation (Japan). But the Austrian literature has, as far as I know, ignored the distinction between these two cases.

The fate of Böhm-Bawerkian capital theory is a bit more complicated. It is obvious enough that Irving Fisher's interest theory, explicitly derived from intertemporal preferences and production possibilities, naturally fits into modern theory in a way that the Austrian theory certainly did not. Yet, the total disappearance of the Böhm-Bawerkian conception is more difficult to understand, for Fisher's intertemporal production possibilities do not really yield a clear conception of *capital*. Perhaps, the trouble has been that the corresponding Austrian production possibilities are *not convex*? Böhm-Bawerk's theory, derived from Adam Smith's theory of the division of labor, transposed into a temporally sequential context. Increasing roundaboutness means increasing division of labor. This means that, just as in Smith, Böhm-Bawerk's production theory exhibits *increasing returns*. But increasing returns will not fit into intertemporal competitive general equilibrium theory. Irving Fisher's intertemporal choice structure which has convexity and continuity in every dimension is so much more convenient and is in effect the prototype for Arrow-Debreu. So Böhm-Bawerk's production theory has shared the fate of Smith's. Good company in oblivion, whatever solace that may give!

Notes

1 Knut Wicksell and Gustav Cassel both started out as mathematicians, not as Menger, Böhm-Bawerk and Wieser did as lawyers. The attitude towards the use of mathematics inherited from the founding fathers of these two traditions was quite different.

2 We return to this issue below.

3 Note that, having started from optimal choices of quantity at parametric prices, Walras had precluded himself from providing a 'natural' account of a market process leading to his equilibrium. He had to assume a prohibition of 'false trading' and a *tâtonnement* in 'fictitious' *bons* taking place in effect in fictitious time. If all agents are successfully optimizing simultaneously, the system cannot but be in equilibrium, so no consistent account of some 'equilibrating process' can be given.

4 To a modern audience one need perhaps to point out that for the collective adaptive process to work, the market must actually exist as an institution with given rules governing the interactions of traders. 'Missing markets' will provide no interaction process determining a price shared by all.

5 It is quite remarkable that Marshall achieved such a very useful 'engine of analysis' in this way for he really had no empirical justification for the assumption that prices generally adjust far, far faster than rates of output.

6 A number of other writers have in turn been puzzled over the fact that Keynes made no use of Joan Robinson's theory of imperfect competition, a theory that must naturally have been quite familiar to him. Snowdon and Vane (1999: 46) go so far as to term it 'one of the great puzzles in the history of economic thought. Why did Keynes show such little interest in the imperfect competition revolution taking place on his own doorstep in Cambridge?' The answer, I believe, is that, like Marshall, he did *not* think of a competitive market as one in which all agents faced horizontal *ex ante* demand or supply schedules.

7 Marshall's biographer, Peter Groenewegen, told me that Marshall disapproved of several Pigovian extensions of Marshallian doctrine but felt constrained not to criticize the successor to his chair. The diagram of the competitive firm may well have been one of the objects of his disapproval.

8 Perfect or imperfect competition – both models are static, and assume the firm has all the information beforehand to calculate its optimum. Relaxing all the stringent conditions for the perfectly elastic demand curve may allow a measure of realism to creep into some dimensions of the model. But it makes the information assumptions even worse. Knowing your entire demand curve in an environment where an unknown number of competitors are maneuvering against you is a formidable problem. Keynes, as a Marshallian, used to conceiving of competition as a *process*, would have no use for *either* perfect *or* imperfect competition theory.

9 Cf. the very fine paper by O'Brien (1990).

10 Cf. Kresge (1994: 11): 'With Hayek in London, Lionel Robbins had set forth on a grand design: to establish a unified tradition in economic theory and abolish all separate "schools".' The story is told more fully in O'Brien (1990).

11 Cf. e.g. Shackle (1972).

12   In a different guise, the issue was already part of the Austrian tradition. Before World War I, Schumpeter had posed the problem as change vs equilibrium. Economic development, he explained, meant breaking out of the determinism of the Walrasian circular flow. For his generation, it was a matter of reasserting 'free will' against the legacy of Comtean positivism. Among the prominent members of the post-war generation, Oscar Morgenstern was the one most preoccupied with perfect foresight and determinism. His reflections on problems of strategic interaction among small numbers of agents led to his famous 'Holmes vs Moriarty' riddle and eventually to his collaboration with John von Neumann on the theory of games. The problem of Sherlock Holmes's optimal strategy is, of course, undecideable. Later in life, Morgenstern was Kurt Gödel's best friend. Their generation saw the problem differently from Schumpeter's. Wieser's work on the *Zurechnung* problem, i.e., the intertemporal problem of attributing future expected revenues as remuneration to current factors of production, posed the question of whether a solution would always exist (Punzo 1984). Karl Schlesinger was the first to realize the significance of the question and caused Abraham Wald to work out the first GE existence proof.

13   In his debate with Ohlin, therefore, he did not quite grasp what the Swedes were driving at with their *ex ante–ex post* terminology.

14   His 1937 book also consisted mostly of painstaking period-by-period analysis of numerical examples, rather than analytical differential equation results.

15   Moreover, once you know how people make decisions, why not apply it in areas not previously considered to lie within the economist's bailiwick? That way lies the 'economic imperialism' of the Gary Becker school.

References

Blaug, M. (1990) 'Comment on O'Brien', in Caldwell, B.J. (ed.) *Carl Menger and his Legacy in Economics*, Durham, NC: Duke University Press.

Buchanan, J. (1969) *Cost and Choice: An Inquiry in Economic Theory*, Chicago: Markham Publ. Co.

Buchanan, J. and Thirlby, G.F. (eds) (1973) *L.S.E. Essays on Cost*, London: Weidenfeld and Nicolson.

Hayek, F.A. (1928) 'Das intertemporale gleichgewichts-system der preise und die bewegungen des geldwertes', *Weltwirtschaftliches Archiv*, 28: 33–76.

Hicks, J.R. (1935) 'A suggestion for simplifying the theory of money', *Economica*, N.S. 2: 1–19.

—— (1939) *Value and Capital*, Oxford: Oxford University Press.

—— (1977) *Economic Perspectives: Further Essays on Money and Growth*, Oxford: Oxford University Press.

Hicks, J.R. and Allen, R.D.G. (1934) 'A reconsideration of the theory of value: parts I and II', *Economica*, N.S. 1: 52–76, 196–219.

Keynes, J.M. (1926) *The End of Laissez-Faire*, London: L. & V. Woolf.

—— (1936) *The General Theory of Employment, Interest and Money*, London: Macmillan.

Knight, F.H. (1921, edn 1964) *Risk, Uncertainty and Profit*, New York: Augustus M. Kelley.

Kresge, S. (1994) 'Introduction', in Kresge, S. and Wenar, L. (eds) *Hayek on Hayek*, London: Routledge.

Leijonhufvud, A. (1998) 'Mr. Keynes and the moderns', in Pasinetti, L. and Schefold, B. (eds) *The Impact of Keynes on Economics in the 20th Century*, Cheltenham: Edward Elgar.

Lindahl, E. (1939) *Studies in the Theory of Money and Capital*, New York: Farrar & Rinehart.

Lundberg, E. (1930, edn 1993) 'Om begreppet ekonomisk jämvikt och dess tillämpning', *Ekonomisk Tidskrift*, 32: 133–60; trans. 'On the concept of economic equilibrium', in E. Lundberg, *Studies in Economic Instability and Change*, edited by R.G. Henriksson, Stockholm: SNS Förlag, pp. 13–47.

—— (1937) *Studies in the Theory of Economic Expansion*, London: P.S. King & Son.

Mises, L. von (1912, edn 1980) *The Theory of Money and Credit*, Indianapolis: Liberty Classics.

Myrdal, G. (1927) 'Prisbildningsproblemet och föränderligheten', ('The Problem of Price Formation in a Changing World'), doctoral dissertation, University of Uppsala.

—— (1939) *Monetary Equilibrium*, Glasgow: William Hodge & Co.

O'Brien, D.P. (1990) 'Lionel Robbins and the Austrian connection', in Caldwell, B.J. (ed.) *Carl Menger and his Legacy in Economics*, Durham, NC: Duke University Press.

Punzo, L. (1984) *Essays on Formalism and Empiricism in Economics: Origins, Theory, Methods*, Siena: Institute of Economics.

Robbins, L. (1932) *An Essay on the Nature and Significance of Economic Science*, London: Macmillan.

Shackle, G.L.S. (1972) *Epistemics and Economics*, Cambridge: Cambridge University Press.

Snowdon, B. and Vane, H.R. (1999) *Conversations with Leading Economists*, Cheltenham: Edward Elgar.

Stigler, G. (1957) 'Perfect competition, historically contemplated', *Journal of Political Economy*, LXV; reprinted in Stigler, G. (ed.) (1965) *Essays in the History of Economics*, Chicago: University of Chicago Press.

2 Swedish influences, Austrian advances

The contributions of the Swedish and Austrian Schools to market process theory

Christopher J. Coyne and Peter J. Boettke

Introduction

Market process theory has its origins in the attempt to gain a richer understanding of how the invisible hand operates in coordinating the vast array of economic exchanges that occur on a daily basis. This is in stark contrast to general equilibrium theory, which seeks a price vector that allows all markets to simultaneously clear. As Ludwig von Mises (1978: 36) wrote: 'What distinguishes the Austrian School and will lend it immortal fame is precisely the fact that it created a theory of economic action and not of economic equilibrium.' General equilibrium theory explains the achievement of the desired efficiency in terms of strict behavioral assumptions placed upon economic participants. In contrast, the former methodology focuses on the institutional structure that creates a unique incentive-based framework that in turn influences the behavior of actors. This behavior includes the dissemination of information which then directly influences the decisions and actions of agents in coordinating their activities and hence in improving the overall efficiency of the economic system. The Austrian School was certainly not the only one to focus attention on the market process rather than the equilibrium state. The Swedish School of economics made significant contributions to the development of a theory of the economic process as well. The Swedish and Austrian Schools, while surely not the only contributors to market process theory, have made distinct contributions to the development of this methodology. These contributions have established market process theory as a distinct and robust explanation of economic activity.[1]

On 27 January 1941, Ludwig von Mises wrote a brief letter to F.A. Hayek. At the end of the letter, he commented on the American Economic Association meetings in New Orleans that he had just attended. In Mises's opinion, the most important theoretical paper at the conference was presented by Arthur Marget on Swedish period analysis, which Mises viewed as a new name for the Austrian step-by-step analysis. Both methodologies offered a distinct alternative to the standard method of static equilibrium analysis.[2]

In this chapter, we will examine the history and evolution of the Austrian step-by-step analysis and the Swedish period analysis. In doing so, we will highlight the similarities between the two methodologies, as well as the clear distinctions. It is our contention that, while both methodologies are similar in their foundation and opposition to static general equilibrium analysis, the Austrians' market process analytical framework is far more comprehensive.

The next section traces the historical evolution of the Austrian step-by-step analysis. The following section focuses on the development of the Swedish period analysis. In both of these discussions the connections between the development of the two methodologies will be highlighted. Then the work of the modern Austrians and their role in further developing the Austrian theory of the market process are examined. The final section summarizes and concludes.

Austrian step-by-step analysis

Before providing a historical overview of the development of market process theory and, more specifically, the step-by-step analysis of the Austrian School, we will first clarify what this methodology entails. Market process theories focus on the adjustments of the market economy to changing circumstances. Step-by-step analysis emphasizes the continually changing parameters of the dynamic economy over time and the subsequent impact on the movement of the economy toward equilibrium. This is in contrast to static general equilibrium models which frame economic analysis in terms of a state of general long-run equilibrium. Ludwig von Mises characterized this methodology when discussing his book, *The Theory of Money and Credit*:

> On all its pages I used the 'step-by-step' method which is allegedly being rediscovered today [1940] as 'period analysis' or 'process analysis'. It is the only permissible method, which renders superfluous the argument between short-run and long-run economics. It also makes the distinction between statics and dynamics an idle question . . .
>   The step-by step analysis must consider the lapse of time. In such an analysis the time lag between cause and effect becomes a multitude of time differences between single successive consequences.
>
> (Mises 1978: 57–9)

This analytical methodology offers a unique alternative to static analysis since it allows the economist to study the cause and effect of economic happenings as they work their way through the economy.[3] We now turn to a discussion of the development of the Austrian method of market process analysis in the historical context of the inter-war period.

The beginning of the inter-war period (1919–39) was a time of transition for the Austrian School. Eugen Böhm-Bawerk had died in 1914 and Carl Menger (who died in 1921) had retired from his university professorship. Friedrich von Weiser was the only major pre-war Austrian still teaching after the war. At the same time, a younger generation of economists, namely Ludwig von Mises and Hans Mayer, was ready to carry on the Austrian research program. Mayer assumed Weiser's chair at the University of Vienna upon his retirement. While Mises was never named to a chair, perhaps his greatest intellectual influence on the Austrian School at the time was his bi-weekly *Privatseminar*. As Hayek, one of the participants, recounts (1994: 71–2): 'during the final years of the Austrian School in Austria, it was the center not only for the Austrian School itself but attracted students from all over the world'. The seminar included several participants who later went on to international recognition in their respective fields including Hayek, Gottfried Haberler, Alfred Schütz and Erich Voeglin. Machlup best characterized the conceptual understanding of the Austrian School during this period as: (1) methodological individualism; (2) methodological subjectivism; (3) the importance of tastes and preferences; (4) the importance of the concept of opportunity cost; (5) marginalism; and (6) the time structure of production (Kirzner 1994: x). It is in these foundational tenets that we see the basis of the Austrian notion of the market process. As Kirzner writes:

> In the fullness of time, this would generate an expansion in Machlup's 'Austrian list' so as to incorporate, especially, explicit attention to the importance of (disequilibrium) *process* set in motion by entrepreneurial *discovery* in a world of *open-ended ignorance* and *uncertainty*.
>
> (ibid.: x, italics in original)

This quote shows what was in store for the Austrian School. The foundational tenets of the Austrian program were in place and it was only a matter of time and research before the Austrian analytical framework was fully developed.

If Machlup's list characterized the doctrinal foundations of the Austrian School, it is in the early work of Mayer that we first see the application of the notion of market process analysis. In his 1932 article, 'The Cognitive Value of Functional Theories of Price: Critical and Positive Investigations Concerning the Price Problem', in addition to juxtaposing the market process with general equilibrium analysis, Mayer was the first author who recognized the importance of time in value theory. Further, he was the first to introduce the plans of individual agents into economic theory. Oscar Morgenstern (1935) further developed the foundational contributions of Mayer. In addition to clarifying and extending the role of time in the economic process, Morgenstern also made the connection between the dynamics of the economy and the role of the entrepreneur.

While Machlup, Mayer and Morgenstern clearly understood the importance of the market process in economic analysis, it was Mises and Hayek who later put forward a mature rendering of the Austrian market process analysis. As the quote from Mises at the beginning of this section indicates, he employed the period analysis methodology in his *The Theory of Money and Credit* (1912).[4] In doing so, Mises analyzed the very broad macroeconomic topic of money and general prices. At the time, monetary theory was analyzed at the macro-level of aggregates completely separated from individual choice. Mises, ahead of his time, integrated micro- and macroeconomic theory in developing his analysis of money, the regression theorem and the widespread effects of inflation and its role in the business cycle. This innovative business cycle analysis would become the foundation for Hayek's later work.[5] Mises's *Human Action*, which was released on 14 September 1949, was without a doubt his greatest work. The comprehensive treatise was grounded in the methodology of praxeology that Mises himself had developed. In covering a plethora of topics, Mises skillfully applied and developed the step-by-step methodology to the economics of time, uncertainty, economic calculation, the market economy, the process of price formation, interest, time preference, credit expansion, and the trade cycle as well as many other topics. In this way, Mises expanded on the work of Mayer and Morgenstern in incorporating the dynamic element of the economic process into the Austrian analytical framework.

Hayek was also a key contributor to the development of the Austrian market process methodological framework. In 1931, Hayek accepted a professorship at the London School of Economics and published his *Prices and Production*. This work, in addition to his *Profits, Interest and Investment: And Other Essays on the Theory of Industrial Fluctuations* in 1939, further developed Mises's business cycle theory. In addition to Mises's work, Hayek also drew on Knut Wicksell's theory of the 'cumulative process' of inflation and the continental tradition of multi-sector over-investment in developing his theory of the business cycle (more will be said about the influence of Wicksell in the next section).

In addition to his work on the business cycle, Hayek's 1937 essay, 'Economics and Knowledge' was a critical addition to market process theory.[6] Hayek's major contribution was the development of a new framework for further market process analysis (Boettke and Prychitko 1998). His contention was that equilibrium was achieved when the plans of market participants were coordinated with one another. This coordination is the result of the process of mutual learning by all parties involved. This was in stark contrast to neoclassical price theory where the utility-maximizing behavior of consumers is perfectly coordinated with the profit-maximizing behavior of firms so that an efficient product-mix is achieved. This theme continued in his later essay, 'The Meaning of Competition', where Hayek focused on competition, not as an end state of equilibrium, but rather as an activity which directs the economy on the path toward equilibrium (Hayek 1946). Hayek's framework, further developed by Kirzner, led the Austrian market process theory to focus on the discovery function of the competitive market. Kirzner's contributions will be further discussed below.

While the initial foundations of the Austrian market process theory and step-by-step analysis can be traced to the 1930s, the complete rendering of this methodology was developed by Ludwig von Mises and F.A. Hayek. Both authors incorporated this methodology into their analytical frameworks and applied it to a wide range of macro issues, focusing on the dynamic aspects of the economy which had been generally neglected by the economic profession. Earlier, we noted that Hayek had incorporated the work of Wicksell, a member of the Swedish School, into his development of Mises's business cycle theory. There was clearly some overlap and connection between the step-by-step methodology of the Austrians and the period analysis of the Swedes. We next turn to a deeper consideration of the Swedish methodology.

The contribution of the Swedish School: period analysis

The interest of English-speaking economists in the economic theory developed in Sweden after Wicksell's death peaked with the publication of Bertil Ohlin's (1937a, b) articles in the *Economic Journal*. In these papers, Ohlin first mentioned the existence of a school in Stockholm (i.e., a Swedish School) and also was the first to coin the phrase 'process analysis'. Before considering specific contributions to the Swedish School, it will be beneficial to highlight the underlying tenets of the Swedish period analysis.

The main idea of Swedish period analysis is that the plans of economic agents are the basis of economic behavior. All actions are directed to fulfilling those plans. As time passes and actions are undertaken, plans will be revised as necessary. Further, it is realized that plans will often be interrupted as expected occurrences fail to come to fruition. Expectations play a key role for the Swedes as they represent the crucial connection between past experiences and future plans. Period analysis can be thought of in two distinct but interrelated parts. Initially, the analysis focuses on a single period and more specifically, how *ex ante* plans at the beginning of the period lead to *ex post* results at the end of the period. The second part of the analysis focuses on the connection between the results of the prior period with the *ex ante* formulation of plans in the next period. Ohlin characterizes what he calls process analysis (i.e., period analysis) as:

> [a] combination of *ex-post* and *ex-ante* analysis . . . after a description of actual events during a certain, finished period, and of the differences between these events and the expectations which existed at the beginning of the period, follows an account of those expectations for the future which . . . govern actions during the next period.
>
> (1937a: 127)

The Swedes applied this two-part period analysis in a number of different ways including applications to static or stationary scenarios, intertemporal equilibrium, temporary equilibrium and disequilibrium (Hansson 1991).

A static economic scenario is one in which the factors of the model or situation remain constant. Period analysis can be applied here in the context that the results in period (t−1) lead to plans in the current period (t) that yield the same *ex post* results as in period (t−1). While there is no direct reference to plans in determining equilibrium – plans are assumed to be fulfilled as expected *ex ante* – plans are important in explaining variances around the equilibrium level.

Intertemporal and temporary equilibrium analyses differ in structure but are related in purpose. The former involves a series of periods, each of which differs from the others but where the outcomes of each period are known. The latter is structured so that only one single period is a pre-determined equilibrium while there is no guarantee that subsequent periods will be in equilibrium. The notion of plan is limited in intertemporal analysis since the outcome of future periods is pre-determined. However, it does allow for an analysis of plan coordination since the end result is known. That is, it allows for a consideration of whether plans in fact dovetail or if agents are met with disappointment. Temporary equilibrium allows the analyst to focus on how the plans of agents interact either to keep the economy at or around the initial equilibrium level or how the lack of coordination steers the economy away from its initial equilibrium position.

A situation of disequilibrium is one in which the economic system begins at a position which is different from its equilibrium level. This type of analysis provides the closest approximation to the actual operations of the economy. It allows for the formulation of plans in a situation of uncertainty followed by the process through which the plans either dovetail with those of others or fail to do so. It provides the analyst with insight into the formulation of plans, the actions undertaken given those plans and the subsequent revision as new information is learned.

Writing in the late nineteenth century, Knut Wicksell made several important contributions to the dynamic analysis of the economy. Perhaps his greatest contribution was in the field of monetary theory. He developed the aggregate demand–supply or savings–investment approach to monetary phenomena. Incorporated in this analysis was an explanation of how the value of money influenced individual consumption expenditure and savings, as well as the production decisions of entrepreneurs. Wicksell's monetary theory had a great impact on the founders of the Swedish School.[7] Carl Uhr (1960: 255) argues that while the Swedish School was founded by Lindahl and developed by Myrdal, Ohlin and Lundberg, among others, it was built on the 'heritage of monetary doctrine which came to light in the protracted Wicksell–Davidson polemic over monetary policy norms and related matters'. Axel Leijonhufvud (1981) contends that both the schools of the Swedes and the Austrians are descended from what he refers to as the 'Wicksell connection'. He maintains that both schools built on Wicksell's theme of savings and investment and the implications of a failure of the (real) interest rate, which equates the supply and demand for securities, to equate savings and investment.

In his *Studies in the Theory of Money and Capital* (1939), Erik Lindahl not only recognized the critical role that plans played in the individual actions of economic agents, but attempted to put forward a notion of what a plan involved. Included in his rendering is the 'prognoses of future developments' (Lindahl 1939: 40), ranking and choosing between the alternatives available (ibid.: 42), the realization of the interconnectedness between the present and future actions that are part of the plan, and the realization of a 'degree of definiteness' that allows for the modification of plans as circumstances change (ibid.: 45). Lindahl's notion of plan clearly illustrates that he realized the importance of market process analysis in viewing and studying the economy as a dynamic process that changes over time. Further, he realized that individual agents, in carrying out their plans, deal with general uncertainty in bringing their plans to fruition.

The work of Wicksell and Lindahl was furthered by Eric Lundberg, Gunnar Mydral and Arthur Marget. Lundberg (1937) attempted to consider an economic system during a period of expansion and in doing so focused on the economic process and the impact of the expansion on that process. His analysis assumes that savings, consumption and production all increase at a certain rate and then asks whether, given expansion, this growth will continue in 'some sort of dynamic equilibrium, or whether discrepancies must automatically come into being within the system itself' (Lundberg 1937: 180). Mydral (1939) built on the work of Wicksell and Lindahl in further developing their analysis of monetary equilibrium. He recognized the role of uncertainty and the market process and warned of the danger of starting one's analysis from a stationary state of equilibrium. According to Myrdal, the assumption of a stationary starting point avoids the theoretical problems and fails to solve them. A true theory of monetary phenomena focuses not just on a stationary equilibrium but on how the relevant relationships look under non-stationary conditions (Myrdal 1939: 39–40). Further, he noted the importance of realizing the role of *ex post* and *ex ante* calculations across time periods. Finally, Marget (1942) presented a taxonomy of process theories as well as analytical distinctions regarding time and expectations.[8]

Modern Austrians and the development of market process theory

It is our contention that both the Austrians and Swedes understood the importance of market process theory and accordingly developed an analytical framework which incorporated this understanding. However, while the Swedish School was absorbed into the Keynesian framework, the Austrian research program continued to develop the step-by-step methodology. As a result, we argue that the modern Austrians further developed their market process theory by building on the research paradigm of Mises and Hayek.

While not the focus of his work, Murray Rothbard, following in the footsteps of his mentor Mises, clearly understood the importance of the market process. In his treatise, *Man, Economy and State*, Rothbard employs the analogy of a mechanical rabbit (equilibrium) being chased by a dog (the market process) (1962: 275–6). Due to changing data – values, technology, knowledge, resources, etc. – the economy could never reach a final state of equilibrium but would constantly tend toward it. And, while final equilibrium was the end goal to which the economy strives, it is never attainable, given the dynamic data which characterizes all economic activity.

Ludwig Lachmann built on the market process theory of Mises and Hayek, both in terms of the ever changing information and knowledge that economic actors possess, and also in his work on capital theory. Lachmann emphasized the role of *radical ignorance* in the market process. That is, while agents have knowledge of the past and present, they face, to large extent, uncertainty about the future. There is a connection that can be made here between Erik Lindahl's notion of plan discussed above and Lachmann's work on the notion of plan. Like Lindahl, Lachmann recognized that individual plans would consist of past experiences, expectations about the future, and an element of flexibility to deal with the uncertainty of the future. That is, agents would need to adjust their plans as they discovered new information and knowledge.

In his *Capital and its Structure* (1956), Lachmann, building on the work of Hayek, clearly recognizes the role of the market process in capital markets. For Lachmann, the market processes of exchange and resource allocation reflect the transmission of knowledge which guides resources (capital) to their most economic uses (ibid.: 28–9). The capital market grounded on the market price mechanism serves to allocate scarce capital among competing projects. Additionally, the profit and loss system will minimize the inefficient use of resources and maximize resource use in the most economic manner known to agents.

Israel Kirzner is the modern Austrian most responsible for furthering the Austrian market process theory. Hayek's and Kirzner's writings overlapped in the 1960s and 1970s and, as mentioned above, focused on the emphasis of discovery in competitive markets. Kirzner's insight is that the competitive process provides the incentive of pure profit which compels participants to learn how to use knowledge and production processes to their maximum capacity. In a series of books, *Competition and Entrepreneurship* (1973), *Perception, Opportunity, and Profit* (1979), and *Discovery and the Capitalist Process* (1985), Kirzner rigorously developed the Austrian market process theory, specifically in the context of the role of the entrepreneur.

The basis of Kirzner's analysis is that the market process is driven by the profit and loss mechanism (a point originally made by Mises in 1952). In the dynamic world in which they operate, entrepreneurs confront an array of technologically feasible production projects. Economic calculation provides the means through which the projects are selected and assures that resources are utilized in an economic manner. As a result of profit and loss accounting, errors will quickly be corrected and as a result, waste will be minimized. In this context, entrepreneurial activity is linked to consumer preferences and tastes as well as the endowment of resources and technological possibilities. Profits are realized only in those instances where resources and technological possibilities are arranged in such a manner that consumer wants are satisfied in the most economical fashion. Further, as consumer preferences and tastes continually change over time, the entrepreneur must continue to introduce new products via new combinations of resource and production possibilities to meet the new wants of the consumer. In doing so, if losses are incurred, resources will be reallocated to different and more economic efforts.

A key foundation of Kirzner's market process theory is that the underlying variables, including tastes, technology, resource endowment, and the induced variables of profit and loss accounting are 'demonstrated to be one of a lag but determined order' (Boettke and Prychitko 1998). That is, given the dynamics of the economy, the underlying variables, at any one point in time, are not perfectly aligned. The market discovery process provides the mechanism, through which the induced variables move in the same direction as the underlying variables. Overall, Kirzner's contribution to market process theory provides the missing link to the neoclassical theory. Given the institutional framework of private property and low barriers to entry, the process of entrepreneurship will lead to a pattern of production and exchange which guides the economy toward a state of equilibrium. The missing link that Kirzner provided was an understanding of the disequilibrium foundations of the economy as well as the path from disequilibrium to a state of equilibrium.

Conclusion

Both the Austrian and Swedish Schools realized and made significant contributions to market process theory. As discussed, both were influenced by the earlier work of Knut Wicksell. Further, Mises and Hayek, for the Austrians, and Lindahl, for the Swedes, incorporated their understanding of the dynamic economy into their general analytical framework. The development of market process theory on the part of each school of thought stood in stark contrast to the widely accepted mainstream general equilibrium framework.

However, the influence of the Swedish School, as a distinct school of thought, culminated around 1937–38. Many of the Swedish contributions were absorbed into the Keynesian framework. The modern Austrians, on the other hand, further developed the early market process methodology put forward by Mises and Hayek. The market process and more specifically the step-by-step methodology was at the center of the work of Rothbard, Lachmann and especially Kirzner. Further, the focus on the dynamic market process continues to be a central tenet of the Austrian research paradigm. Both the Swedish and Austrian Schools of thought realized the importance of market process theory as being critical to their research programs. While both originally based their methodological framework on such realizations, it is the modern Austrians who have focused, and continue to focus, on developing their market process analytical framework in response to the failings of the general equilibrium model to yield a realistic analysis of the operations of the market economy.

Acknowledgments

Christopher Coyne is a Research Fellow at the James M. Buchanan Center for Political Economy at George Mason University in Fairfax, Virginia, USA. Peter Boettke is the Deputy Director of the James M. Buchanan Center for Political Economy. The authors acknowledge the financial assistance of the J.M. Kaplan Fund to support their research. The usual caveat applies.

Notes

1   Boettke and Prychitko (1998) provide two volumes of selected readings in the development of market process theory from the classical school to neoclassicalism to modern heterodoxy. The major omission in this collection is a set of selections from the non-Ricardian British economists who argued for a science of catallaxy, e.g., Whatley.
2   Letter from Ludwig von Mises to F.A. Hayek, 27 January 1941. From the Hayek Archives at the Hoover Institution on War, Revolution and Peace, Box #38, Folder 24.
3   In the context of Mises's use of the 'step-by-step' method of analysis, he also developed his theory of the non-neutrality of money. Previous Austrian theorists, such as Böhm-Bawerk, had developed their theory of market economy with the assumption of the neutrality of money. In other words, the theory of the market process they developed was built on the imaginary construction of a direct exchange economy. Mises showed that this theory was incomplete. Mises in 1912, well before Keynes's call for such a theory, had developed a monetary theory of exchange and production, and demonstrated that the older, and mechanical, interpretations of the quantity theory of money were untenable. Mises offered a reinterpretation of the quantity theory of money. Mises's major contribution in *The Theory of Money and Credit* was to demonstrate, through the use of step-by-step analysis, that changes in the purchasing power of money cause prices of different commodities to change unevenly and different times, and thus that it is incorrect to maintain that changes in the quantity of money bring about simultaneous and proportional changes in the price level. This emphasis on the ranged adjustment process (Cantillon effects) as increases in the money supply work their way through an economy via relative price adjustments set the stage for his development of the Austrian theory of the trade cycle as well. We will discuss this contribution more in the text, but it is useful to point out that Mises never accepted the label 'Austrian theory of the trade cycle' and instead was quick to point out the contributions of the British Currency School and those of the Swede Knut

Wicksell that he drew upon in developing a monetary theory of the trade cycle (see Mises 1983).

4   The first edition was published in German in 1912 as *Theorie des Geldes und der Umlaufs-mittel*. The first English translation was in 1934.

5   Mises founded the Institute for Business Cycle Research in 1927 and installed Hayek in the position of director.

6   Many consider this essay to represent Hayek's break with his mentor, Mises. Hayek himself was nervous at showing the paper to Mises (Hayek 1994: 72).

7   The impact of Wicksell's theory of savings and investment on the Swedes can also be seen in Ohlin (1937a, 1937b).

8   John Egger (1985) argues that Marget was in close agreement with the Austrian School of Menger but disagreed with many of his followers. More specifically, Marget rejected the efforts of Menger's followers to use non-monetary general equilibrium constructs to explain the impact of monetary changes on the production process.

References

Boettke, P. and Prychitko, D. (eds) (1994) *The Market Process: Essays in Contemporary Austrian Economics*, Cheltenham: Edward Elgar.

——— (eds) (1998) *Market Process Theories*, vol. I: *Classical and Neoclassical*, vol. II: *Heterodox Approaches*, Cheltenham: Edward Elgar.

Egger, J.B. (1985) 'Monetary economics of Arthur William Marget', doctoral dissertation, New York University.

Hansson, B. (1991) 'The Stockholm School and the development of dynamic method', in Sandelin, B. (ed.) *The History of Swedish Economic Thought*, New York: Routledge.

Hayek, F.A. (1937) 'Economics and Knowledge', reprinted in Hayek, F.A. (ed.) (1948) *Individualism and Economic Order*, Chicago: University of Chicago Press.

——— (1939) *Profits, Interest and Investments: and Other Essays on the Theory of Industrial Fluctuations*, 1975, New York: Augustus Kelley.

——— (1946) 'The meaning of competition', lecture delivered at Princeton University, 20 May; reprinted in Hayek, F.A. (ed.) (1948) *Individualism and Economic Order*, Chicago: University of Chicago Press.

——— (1994) *Hayek on Hayek: An Autobiographical Dialogue*, Kresge, S. and Wenar, L. (eds), Chicago: University of Chicago Press.

Kirzner, I. (1973) *Competition and Entrepreneurship*, Chicago: The University of Chicago Press.

——— (1979) *Perception, Opportunity, and Profit*, Chicago: The University of Chicago Press.

——— (1985) *Discovery and the Capitalist Process*, Chicago: The University of Chicago Press.

——— (ed.) (1994) *Classics in Austrian Economics: A Sampling in the History of a Tradition*, vol. II: *The Interwar Period*, vol. III: *The Age of Mises and Hayek*, London: Pickering and Chatto.

Lachmann, L. (1956) *Capital and its Structure*, London: Bell and Sons Ltd.

Leijonhufvud, A. (1981) 'The Wicksell connection: variations on a theme', in *Information and Coordination: Essays in Macroeconomic Theory*, New York: Oxford University Press; reprinted in Boettke, P.J. and Prychitko, D.L. (eds) (1998) *Market Process Theories*, vol. II: *Heterodox Approaches*, Cheltenham: Edward Elgar.

Lindahl, E. (1939) *Studies in the Theory of Money and Capital*, New York: Farrar & Rinehart, Inc.

Lundberg, E. (1937) 'The construction of model sequences', in *Studies in the Theory of Economic Expansion*, London: P.S. King and Sons; reprinted in Boettke, P.J. and Prychitko, D.L. (eds) (1998) *Market Process Theories*, vol. II: *Heterodox Approaches*, Cheltenham: Edward Elgar.

Marget, A.W. (1942) 'Stream equations and process analysis', in *The Theory of Prices: A Re-Examination of the Central Problems of Monetary Theory* (1966), vol. II, Chap. 7, New York: August M. Kelly; reprinted in Boettke, P.J. and Prychitko, D.L. (eds) (1998) *Market Process Theories*, vol. II: *Heterodox Approaches*, Cheltenham: Edward Elgar.

Mayer, H. (1932) 'Der erkenntniswert der funktionellen priestheorien', trans. 'The cognitive value of functional theories of price', in Kirzner, I. (ed.) (1994) *Classics in Austrian Economics: A Sampling in the History of a Tradition*, vol. II: *The Interwar Period*, London: Pickering and Chatto.

Mises, L. von. (1912; edn 1980) *The Theory of Money and Credit*, Indianapolis: Liberty Press.

—— (1949; edn 1996) *Human Action: A Treatise on Economics*, San Francisco: Fox Wilkes.

—— (1952; edn 1996) 'The economic nature of profit and loss', in *Planning for Freedom*, Pennsylvania: Libertarian Press.

—— (1978) *Notes and Recollections*, Illinois: Libertarian Press.

—— (1983) 'The "Austrian" theory of the trade cycle', in Ebeling, R. (ed.) *The Austrian Theory of the Trade Cycle and Other Essays*, Auburn, AL: The Ludwig von Mises Institute.

Morgenstern, O. (1935) 'The time moment in value theory', reprinted in Kirzner, I. (ed.) (1994) *Classics in Austrian Economics: A Sampling in the History of a Tradition*, vol. II: *The Interwar Period*, London: Pickering and Chatto.

Myrdal, G. (1939) 'The concept of monetary equilibrium', in *Monetary Equilibrium*, New York: Augustus M. Kelly, 1965; reprinted in Boettke, P.J. and Prychitko, D.L. (eds) (1998) *Market Process Theories*, vol. II: *Heterodox Approaches*, Cheltenham: Edward Elgar.

Ohlin, B. (1937a) 'Some notes on the Stockholm theory of savings and investment I', *Economic Journal*, XLVII, March: 53–69; reprinted in Boettke, P.J. and Prychitko, D.L. (eds) (1998) *Market Process Theories*, vol. II: *Heterodox Approaches*, Cheltenham: Edward Elgar.

—— (1937b) 'Some notes on the Stockholm theory of savings and investment II', *Economic Journal*, XLVII, June: 221–40; reprinted in Boettke, P.J. and Prychitko, D.L. (eds) (1998) *Market Process Theories*, vol. II: *Heterodox Approaches*, Cheltenham: Edward Elgar.

Rothbard, M. (1962; edn 1993) *Man, Economy and State*, Auburn, AL: Ludwig von Mises Institute.

Uhr, C. (1960) *Economic Doctrines of Knut Wicksell*, Los Angeles: University of California Press.

Part II
The Stockholm School

3 How did the great Swedish economists consider their role in public debate?

The views of Knut Wicksell, Gustav Cassel, Eli Heckscher, Bertil Ohlin and Gunnar Myrdal

Benny Carlson and Lars Jonung

Introduction

Traditionally, economists have played a prominent role in public debate in Sweden: many are interviewed on radio and television, contributing to the daily press, magazines and books, and functioning as experts for government inquiries and commissions.[1] Economists in Sweden have probably more influence than any other category of social scientist in Swedish public debate. In other countries there is usually a wider gulf between academically active economists and the world of politics and the media.[2]

This has been the case for a long time. A significant number of Swedish economists in the twentieth century have been influential participants in the public exchange of opinions. Some have made the move from policy debate into practical politics. The founders of economics as a scholarly discipline at Swedish universities, most prominently Knut Wicksell, Gustav Cassel and Eli Heckscher, addressed the general public as popular educators and debaters.

In this study, attention will concentrate on five most prominent and mediatuned Swedish professors of economics – Knut Wicksell (1851–1926), Gustav Cassel (1866–1945), Eli Heckscher (1879–1952), Bertil Ohlin (1899–1979) and Gunnar Myrdal (1898–1987) – with a view to ascertaining how they regarded their own and their profession's role in public debate.[3]

These five economists hold a central position in the development of economics in Sweden in the twentieth century, laying the foundations for modern Swedish economics. They represent two generations – the first generation, of Wicksell, Cassel and Heckscher, with a clear set of values but anxious to assert their independence. The second generation, Ohlin and Myrdal, with equally clear values, and critical, at least in Myrdal's case, of the older generation's – i.e. their teachers' – lack of clarity in defining the boundary between scholarship (science) and politics, yet most willing to move from the world of scholarship into public affairs and politics.

The five represent a broad political spectrum. Taking 'liberal' in its European meaning, Cassel was a right-wing liberal with a strong conservative leaning, Heckscher, an ultra-liberal deeply influenced by the great British nineteenth-century economists, and Wicksell, more or less a left-wing liberal. Each held back from direct party-political commitment. Ohlin was a liberal, classifying himself as a 'social liberal' to distinguish him from classical or old liberalism, and Myrdal was a social democrat. Both engaged in party politics; Ohlin as leader of the Liberal Party (1944–67), Myrdal as a Social Democratic Member of Parliament and Cabinet member (1945–47).

The five were deeply engaged in public debate. They produced a copious stream of books and articles addressed to colleagues, politicians and the public at large, gave lectures and participated in debates. One measure of this high ambition to reach the general public is the number of articles in the daily press: Wicksell published about 450 articles, Cassel about 1,500 in *Svenska Dagbladet* alone, Heckscher about 300 articles in *Dagens Nyheter* alone, Ohlin about 2,000 articles, chiefly in *Stockholms-Tidningen* (a large number of them before he moved into party politics), and Myrdal about fifty articles.[4] Between them, the five economists published a round total of 4,300 articles in Swedish daily newspapers, mainly during the first three decades of the twentieth century – an impressive figure. This avalanche of publicity coincided with the period when political economy was establishing itself in Sweden as an academic discipline with a powerful influence on public opinion and politics.[5]

Here we will concentrate on the following questions: How ought economists to deal with the problem of scholarly objectivity and subjective value judgments? Can an economist be scientifically objective and politically committed at the same time? Ought he or she to confine him/herself to scholarly discussions or attempt to play a pedagogical role *vis-à-vis* the general public as well? Ought the economist strive for expertise within a narrow field or for a breadth of approach?

We seek to chart how the five economists themselves answered these questions concerning the role of the economist in public debate. We seek their answers first in their own writings, chiefly their 'mature' works and autobiographical articles or memoirs, and, second, in biographies and other writings concerning them.

Knut Wicksell – a dual nature?

Knut Wicksell is considered Sweden's foremost economic theorist of all time. However, he was not 'merely' an innovator in economic theory, principally monetary theory, public finance and capital theory; he also devoted himself to economic, social and political issues on a broad front. Wicksell stood out as a social critic of rank, questioning established institutions such as marriage, the church, the monarchy and defense. All his life he enjoyed a well-founded reputation as an extravagant radical, always ready to defend and advocate views that were regarded as extreme in public debate.

What is perplexing about Wicksell is how he could simultaneously play these two apparently incompatible roles: on the one hand, the unassuming academic, on the other, the vociferous agitator. There are two different interpretations of the phenomenon. The first, which we can call the Gårdlund–Ohlin line, sees Wicksell as having a dual nature. The second, the Lindahl–Åkerman line, points to Wicksell's passionate commitment to everything he undertook.

Torsten Gårdlund (1956: 371) formulates Wicksell's dual nature in these words: 'Knut Wicksell's character sometimes gives the impression of a strong inner conflict, almost a split personality in fact. He was a wild agitator and an objective scholar at one and the same time.' Bertil Ohlin (1972: 558) muses along the same lines:

> To me it is a riddle that Knut Wicksell, who for most of his life was a fanatical representative of extreme opinions in the social debate, could present a completely different personality in the scholarly context. During the period when I knew him he was the diffident seeker after scientific truth.

In a more detailed discussion of Wicksell's dual nature, Gårdlund (1958: 200) writes:

> In the political sphere he recognized no authority. No institution was sacred; no hallowed law could prevent him applying the test of democracy and utility. To plead tradition in politics was 'obscurantism', to suppress criticism was 'under any conditions an evil'. But as a scientist he submitted himself voluntarily and with remarkable consistency to the traditional demands of the scientific world. His ideal scientist was one who sought the truth sincerely and without prejudice and who presented his findings objectively and modestly.

In the Swedish edition of his Wicksell biography, Gårdlund (1956: 229–30) continues:

> Certainly it could be said that Wicksell strove to conduct the political debate in accordance with the same principles as he applied so strictly to his academic work. For he believed that even in political life, truth should be followed wherever the road might lead, and that even in political debate, truth ought to be supported by proof. However, although at its heart utilitarianism implied an attempt to apply scientific method to politics, in such an orthodox utilitarian as Wicksell there was a manifest limit to this application. He was much more cautious as a scholar than as an ideological politician, and in the

former capacity he imposed a much heavier burden of proof than in the latter.

Erik Lindahl (1953: 304–5) – supported by Johan Åkerman (1956) – preferred to emphasize instead that Wicksell's scholarly and political activities were founded on the same passionate commitment. Lindahl writes:

> Wicksell was both a scholar and a social reformer, the latter on the ideological plane in the capacity of popular orator, debater and author of controversial pamphlets on social policy. One feels that it should have been an abrupt reversal for him to tear himself away from his hyper-theoretical work at the desk in order to make an agitator's speech to a demonstration meeting or to speak from the platform at a young socialists' meeting. But Wicksell performed the one task just as intensely as the other . . . And in his case it is evident that the one activity had as fruitful an effect as the other. [It was] Wicksell's social interest which impelled him to take up economics . . . On the other hand, his social preaching achieved greater cogency through being buttressed by scholarly arguments.

The two interpretations above are not necessarily contradictory. It is partly a matter of where the emphasis is placed: on the unifying commitment or on the dissimilar modes of expression. One explanation of Wicksell's distinction as a dual nature can perhaps be sought in the fact that he had a natural bent for abstract and logical thought – he was the archetype of the deductively-working scholar. 'The abstract intelligence of which he early showed proof must have helped greatly to make him a man of principle and opinion', Gårdlund (1956: 364) contends. In all likelihood, Wicksell's acting in accordance with his nature produced differing effects on his scholarship and his politics, respectively. To argue with uncompromising logic is one thing in an academic discipline where the dominant tradition prizes logic above adherence to reality, but it is something else in a political reality which builds on historical circumstances rather than on logical designs. Wicksell's critics often argued that in his economic policy recommendations he tended to think too straightforwardly, without taking account of the complications entailed in translating ideas into practice.

Wicksell's close friend, Hjalmar Öhrvall, put his finger on the sensitive spot in one of his letters:

> I can understand quite easily that a man can have a definite, contrary idea about a scientific proposition and be willing to defend it against the whole world; but how it can be possible to be as definite on political, strategic or similar questions, I do not understand.

(Gårdlund 1958: 242)

On top of this there was the fact that in his political appearances Wicksell was driven by his urge to provoke scandal.

Wicksell was a radical liberal. He considered that on the whole the market economy would give the best economic outcome but wanted to see changes in the distribution of income and wealth. He cherished a deep sympathy for the social democratic cause and at one time in the 1880s nearly became a member of the party, but he preferred to function as 'a radical taskmaster untrammeled by party ties', according to Gårdlund (1958: 307).[6]

One of Wicksell's clearest manifestos is to be found in his inaugural lecture: 'Ends and Means in Political Economy', in 1904.[7] Here he (Wicksell 1904: 460, 470–3) discusses why it is so difficult to find agreement on anything in economic science. Is it because the problems of political economy are so difficult that we have not found the right way to solve them? Or

> is it perhaps the various scholars' individual sympathies and antipathies, their diverse political ideals, their conception, in a word, of the aim of practical social and economic activity which lends its color even to their treatment of theoretical questions?
>
> (ibid.)

Wicksell goes quickly to the heart of the question:

> That the aim of economic activity must be the greatest possible prosperity of society, individually and collectively, on that point we are all formally agreed; but what is meant here by society? Shall our endeavors embrace all classes, races, linguistic groups, creeds, nations?

Wicksell contends that the answer is yes, and he gives expression to his utilitarian view that 'our aim here on earth is to extend the greatest possible happiness to all'. If economists would only adopt this view, they could also attain unity.

Wicksell believed that modern economics had got past the short-sighted vision of the harmony economists and was no longer the creature of any special interests:

> I have always regarded it as a criterion indicating that modern theoretical economics is on the right road that the scorn for everything that economists stand for, so common among the working class in bygone days, has died away . . . the workers probably sense instinctively that the watchword of economics has again become the unconditional quest for truth.
>
> (ibid.)

It is clear from his writings that Wicksell regarded himself as an educator of the general public on any issue he found of interest to bring to the public. Through his many articles, lectures and comments, he wanted to foster public knowledge of the science of economics or, as he sometimes wrote, of the laws of economics, in particular of Malthus's population theory. He was convinced of his mission as a public educator (*folkbildare*).[8] His view is revealed in a letter to Hjalmar Öhrvall at the Christmas of 1916, shortly after Wicksell had retired from his chair in Lund and returned to Stockholm. Here, he contemplates his future as a professor emeritus:

> Well, it feels a little strange to be 'put aside' but not very, for during the last few years I took little part in university life. H. Hildebrand, an old school-fellow of mine, who retired last summer, says he finds it so peculiar to wake up in the mornings and 'have no obligations'. As for myself, I have always looked on the education of the Swedish people as my chief obligation, and I can certainly go on with that as long as I have the strength.

Here, Wicksell puts his mission in life on paper: 'my foremost duty to educate the Swedish people'.[9]

Wicksell was very outward-looking all his life – he wrote pamphlets, lampoons and articles, and he went out on tours giving – as he said – 'peasant lectures' – and he also held the view that his intuition led him correctly in his communication with the public:

> As for myself, I will say one thing in my favor; that I have a nose for what *can be done*. In other words, I feel that if something is obvious enough to penetrate my simple understanding, it cannot be long before it will conquer the masses – and I have never been wrong about this, although sometimes things have moved a *little* more slowly than I expected.
>
> (Gårdlund 1958: 307)

Gustav Cassel – the voice of reason

In his day – during the 1920s at least – Gustav Cassel was one of the world's most renowned economists, a theoretical innovator as well as a leading expert on current monetary problems. According to Magnusson (1991: 134) his reputation did not rest so much on his role as innovator and theorist. 'His strength lay rather in economic pedagogic, in teaching, and as an indefatigable spokesman on economic themes to the general public and political community.'

For Gustav Cassel, the question of whether the scholar ought to become involved in public debate was easily answered. The scholar represented the clear voice of reason in a world governed by superstition and dilettantism. The task of the scholar of economics was to look at the whole, to elucidate the inexorable economic laws from a standpoint high above the clash of interests and thereby help the public, politicians and businessmen to see beyond their own narrow interests and time-horizons. Out there in the economic and political jungle all kinds of delusions flourished, and it was the task of the scholar to clear up the miserable mess with the shining weapon of rationality.

> [In] my scholarly work I have chiefly been seeking clarity. I have called for rational action in the life of society, with the accent both on a reason which does not allow itself to be tied down by arid dogma or sterile party formulae, and on a robust will that is prepared to act at the right moment. These main aspects of my work have been linked together inasmuch as my efforts to bring clarity to the elements of economic science have become of crucial import-ance to my practical standpoint, and also because my scholarly work has been stimulated by the immense problems with which life has confronted me.

Thus writes Cassel in the preface to his memoirs *I förnuftets tjänst* (In the Service of Reason) (1940: 7). In his final words (1941: 455–6) he returns to this theme:

> It fell to my lot to work in the service of reason. And this is a duty. It requires fidelity all through life . . . To serve reason certainly requires humil-ity in face of the task. But this humility is essentially different from the oblit-eration of one's own personality, when one joins a party or takes refuge in the bombproof shelter of collective programs. He who fights for reason must give himself to the struggle, sticking it out though he finds himself standing alone.

Cassel wrote his memoirs after the crisis of the 1930s and during the Second World War. He thought by then that most of what he had struggled to achieve was reduced to ruins:

> Everything I have fought for now lies in dust and ashes. Scholarly enlighten-ment counts for nothing in an age which feels more comfortable with drivel. Free speech is suppressed and the technical means of reaching listeners are cut off or monopolized. International communications are impeded and mankind is excluded from mutual discussion of its vital affairs . . . Sensible economic management by government is regarded as an obsolete prejudice and huge budgets are run up with nothing on the revenue side. Law is thrust aside by administrative arbitrariness, and democratic essentials are either shattered or diluted to empty formulae. Of the freedom of the individual scarcely more than the name is left, and the value of his personality is set at naught. Wherever one looks, only destruction! Destruction at least of that which I had wished to build.
>
> (Cassel 1941: 456–7)

In Cassel's description of this heap of ruins we discern the foundations of the proud edifice for which he had fought and which bears the characteristic marks of liberal progressive optimism: individualism, free enterprise, free trade, free pricing, policies devoted to the creation of law, order and a stable currency, peace and progress (that is to say, economic growth).

In other words, Cassel saw himself as a scholarly interpreter of economic conditions and relationships which were virtually to be regarded as laws of nature. He summarized the chief tasks of economic science in the introduction to his *Teoretisk socialekonomi* (Theory of Social Economy), (1934) under five points: (1) 'to view society as a whole entity and to try to trace the total nexus of causality within this society' (social economic thinking instead of private); (2) 'to bring real phenomena out into the light of day' (for example, the utilities that in everyday terms are expressed as a sum of money); (3) 'to try to penetrate to the essentials of economic phenomena and situations'; (4) 'to penetrate to the necessary facts of economic life' (for example, the proposition that capital formation is necessary for progress); and (5) 'to give a simplified picture of economic life', in other words, to formulate a theory.[10]

In spite of his lively interest in the issues and realities of the day, Cassel, whose early training was in mathematics, was at heart a logician and he considered that the scientist in economics must certainly make use of deduction and induction by turns, but that the point of departure must be deductive: 'The main thrust of the simplification procedure consists in isolating the essentials from the very start and reproducing them in a logically coherent presentation.' One may think that as a scholar who expresses himself authoritatively on the problems of reality, he exposed himself to a considerable risk here. Suppose his theory has indeed isolated essential relationships and is logically coherent, but is not the only logical model capable of being constructed around a number of essential factors and relationships, what then? The risk is lessened in Cassel's case by his known lively interest in facts, in 'reality'.

At the same time, however, he was aware that his preaching rested not merely on logic but also on value judgments. When other economists and politicians accused him of marketing his political opinions as scholarly conclusions, he admitted without equivocation that his positions rested on certain fundamental value judgments:

> If my theoretical studies have contained any subjective value judgment, then this has amounted at most to a preference for freedom and progress rather than state control of the economy and distribution of such scanty prosperity as may be available for distribution at a given moment. I have wanted to make it clear that this preference is a great common interest of all parties, both in the management of the world economy and in every individual

nation. Such a position may be attacked, but it cannot be denominated as party-politics in the ordinary sense.

(Cassel 1941: 440)

To be slotted into a party-political pigeonhole, in Cassel's eyes, was one of the worst fates imaginable.

Cassel's strong position in public debate rested in large part on his capacity to explain economic issues clearly, simply, and elegantly so that politicians and the public could keep up with him. He himself was very aware of this capacity, and we have testimony as to how hard he actually toiled over texts which apparently flowed with their own momentum. In a letter to Ohlin he declared: 'Economics is in high degree a pedagogical discipline, and an economist must be in close touch with popular psychology in order to know what ought to be said at any particular moment' (see Ohlin 1972: 107).

Eli Heckscher – liberal beacon

Eli Heckscher's work was marked by the tension between scholarship and politics. Rolf Henriksson (1979: 519–20) describes the matter in this way: 'In Heckscher's work as an economist the tension between the political and scholarly sides emerges clearly. In his academic work he never relinquished the politico-ideological starting point, and in his political attitudes the scholarly dimension was always present.'

Heckscher himself was highly conscious of the dilemma:

> For on the one hand he [the scientist or scholar] is a citizen and accordingly has the same duty as others to form a subjective, practical opinion concerning matters which in a democratic society depend on the decisions of all citizens . . . But his practical standpoint must necessarily contain a purely personal value judgment, which is not that of a scholar. On the other hand, however – perhaps even first of all – his duty is that of the scientist or scholar, viz. to present objective truth to the utmost of his ability, regardless of his own sympathies or antipathies. He can – and if he is conscientious must – seek to make clear to his readers and listeners where the boundary lies between the objectively valid and the subjectively evaluated; but even to make it clear to himself is a very difficult task.
>
> (Heckscher 1936: 2)

Heckscher elaborated on this view ten years later:

> In some cases . . . the conclusion has been drawn that scholars ought to keep themselves politically neutral: on this view the representatives of economic

science must not pronounce on what ought to be done but confine themselves to analyzing the actual circumstances of economic life, in other words
analyze what has happened and is happening (and possibly also state what *will*
happen under various conditions) . . . without doubt it is usual for economics
scholars also to make frequent pronouncements about what ought to happen.
This is hardly to be condemned, either, since their theoretical insights and
overall view may be expected to enable them to avoid many mistakes which
otherwise are easily made. Like all citizens they have the right to plead their
case on the problems of society and in their special field more so than others
if they understand the questions better. But the last part of their submission,
amounting to a specification of claim, falls beyond their scope as scholars, at
least as long as they have not clarified for themselves and declared to their
public the unscientific *value-premises* which underlie their recommendations
and advice. Of course it is never easy for economists strongly interested in
the problems of society thus to split their personalities, as it were, into a
scholarly and a civic half.

(Heckscher and Knoellinger 1945: 25–6)

Heckscher's argument concerning the importance of scholars declaring their
value-premises was probably influenced by Gunnar Myrdal's demands in the
same direction.

The only general advice Heckscher was willing to offer those thinking of
studying economics was

that which applies to all honest study: to use your intelligence, to be receptive to all enlightenment but not to take anything for granted beforehand,
whether your own previously formed opinions or statements made by those
who are regarded, or want to be regarded, as authorities, whether in theory
or practice.

(Heckscher and Knoellinger 1945: 16)

Nevertheless Heckscher (1936: 4) considered that an adherence to neoclassical
theory, to concepts of equilibrium and scarcity, and an atomistic approach were a
great help along the road which 'enforced objectivity and respect for given scientific assumptions'. Indeed, he declared outright that economic theory as it evolved
in the 1930s, i.e. the emergence of the theories and economic policy recommendations associated with the Stockholm School and Keynes's *General Theory of
Employment, Interest and Money* (1936), had multiplied the scope for 'cobbling up
theory so as to suit the cobbler's own political or social viewpoint'.

However, for anyone not starting out from the same 'given' (liberal)
premises, it was an obvious step to suspect a subjective/political bottom below
the objective/scientific surface. The economist and conservative politician Gösta

Bagge reproached Heckscher for 'being unwilling to regard liberal politics as politics' but presenting liberal desires as being 'objective' or 'economic'. The economist and left-wing politician Gunnar Myrdal likewise accused Heckscher of promoting liberal policy in the guise of objectivity (Carlson 1995: 21).

Thus, Heckscher stood on liberal ground, and his uncompromising attitude and steadfastness amidst the ideological and political storms blowing in the 1920s, 1930s and 1940s made him, in Ernst Wigforss' (1951: 155) words of reluctant wonderment:

> something of a beacon when navigating the waters of economic policy, inasmuch as he was regarded as a representative of a reasoned and coherent economic ideology whose liberal argumentation the socialist could not by-pass but had to consider and pronounce upon.

In his later years Heckscher came round to the view that 'everything was better in the old days'. By 'in the old days' he meant the liberal era from the middle of the nineteenth century up to the outbreak of the First World War, or what Heckscher called 'nineteenth-century economic order'. Heckscher's stance now was not merely a manifestation of the conservatism which easily comes creeping in with age but a quite reasoned reaction to the horrors visited on the world during the twentieth century – the First World War, the Great Depression, the Second World War – especially if, like him, one regards these horrors as being caused by high-handed politicians and national power-plays and not, as socialists saw the matter, by capitalist rapaciousness and market anarchy.

Like Cassel, Heckscher considered that the economics scholar must begin at the deductive end by abstracting and theorizing, by evolving for himself a view of 'the elements of what is common to all economies'. To avoid the temptation of regarding the economic organization of his own time as a manifestation of ineluctable and universally valid laws he also ought to obtain 'concrete knowledge of the external phenomena of the life of the society, and most especially of its economic life, during different eras'; in other words, he ought to study economic history (Heckscher and Knoellinger 1945: 18–24). Heckscher strove as an economist and economic historian for both breadth and historical depth in the study of economics.

Towards the end of his life Heckscher, like Cassel, felt himself to be standing in a world laid waste; one of his later works is entitled *Ödeläggelsen av 1800-talets hushållning* (The Destruction of Nineteenth-Century Economic Order) (1948). During the 1930s, unlike Cassel, he became less active as a public debater and molder of public opinion – not because he had capitulated to the 'new' currents of economic policy opinion in any way. Rather, he kept a lower profile for two reasons: first, he was concentrating on his research in economic history after obtaining a personal research professorship in economic history in 1929; second, after Hitler's rise to power in Germany, he feared that polemical contributions by a Jewish scholar would spark anti-Semitic reactions.

When the Hitler regime collapsed, Heckscher began to play a leading role again in the economic policy debate as one of the most incisive figures among opponents of the economic planning advocated by Myrdal, Wigforss and other leading social democrats. One of his crucial arguments in the debate was that 'scholars are free because they have access to a free market, they can publish books, they can write in the newspapers, they can make their voices heard generally in national life, because the means of production are free' (see *Röster i Radio* 1945 no. 28: 36). State ownership or direction of the means of production would end up with standardization of opinion and intellectual dictatorship. In this respect, Heckscher followed the same line as Hayek.

Heckscher (1944: 92–3) believed that economists of his own generation had had very limited opportunities to influence economic policy directly: 'As far as I can understand, the only point at which we managed to make any mark was in influencing public opinion.' But the economists of the next generation were deeply involved in party and government machinery. Perhaps they had succeeded in influencing events in certain respects, Heckscher argued, but:

> I believe one may say that independence and influence stand in an inverse relationship to one another; and when influence has now become so great, then scholars more or less inevitably must feel themselves fettered by every possible consideration from which we were free.

Bertil Ohlin – switching roles elegantly

Bertil Ohlin began as a scholar, then wandered back and forth for a time across the boundary between the academic and political worlds, eventually becoming a full-time politician. Ohlin and Cassel are the only two of the five economists who wrote detailed memoirs. He might be expected to have been one of the economists with the most to say about economists' participation in public debate and the art of tightrope-walking between scholarship and politics. In point of fact he did not say much, at least not in his memoirs.[11] As long as the discussion centers on himself as a scholar and a newcomer to politics, it is always 'I' saying and doing this and that; when it turns to him as party leader, the wording changes so that it becomes 'we' saying and doing things.

From the outset, Ohlin was tuned into public debate. He published his ideas from the early days, in *Svensk Handelstidning, Svenska Dagbladet* and elsewhere. As a recently appointed professor at Copenhagen, he declared in an interview with the Danish student journal *Studium*, after his inaugural lecture in 1925, that the 'primary task [of economics] ought to be teaching people to think in economic terms'. Cassel and Heckscher were doing this in Stockholm, said Ohlin, through the medium of *Svenska Dagbladet* and *Dagens Nyheter*. Ohlin himself was writing in both the Danish and the Swedish press at this time. When he returned to Sweden as professor at the Stockholm School of Economics he became an assiduous producer of articles on economic questions. The articles flowed from his pen in the early 1930s in a stream of a swiftness hard to surpass.[12]

Ohlin's transition from scholar to politician seems to have taken place simply and elegantly – and scarcely unexpectedly.[13] It may well have been relatively painless to begin with: Ohlin, as an independent thinker, presented ideas about what a liberal party ought to be doing, whereupon the party approached him with the request that he put his ideas into effect on its behalf. But conflicts must still have arisen sooner or later between the independent thinker and a political party's need for troops and tactics.

Ohlin declares in his memoirs that he counted himself as one of the liberal camp even in his youth. The keystone of his liberal outlook, exactly as with Cassel and Heckscher, was the conviction that an economic system based on individual property rights and competition would give higher growth, and that, in the long run, growth was crucial to the development of prosperity. One of his expressed goals was, just as with Cassel, to 'counteract economic superstition' (Ohlin 1972: 61–2, 184). Gradually, he came into conflict with his teachers, especially with Heckscher. Ohlin argued that a liberal social order was compatible with an 'active' business-cycle policy and – to a certain extent – with economic planning.[14] Heckscher was strongly opposed to such a view.

In his memoirs, Ohlin (1972: 159) discusses very briefly the relationship between scholarship and politics in the course of his references to Myrdal's work *Vetenskap och politik i nationalekonomien* (The Political Element in the Development of Economic Theory):

> It became of importance to Scandinavian economic scholarship through its urging of caution when formulating concepts and asserting objectivity. Of course it is self-evident that an opinion about what ought to be done – that is to say on social policy – is based on subjective value judgments. Caution is advisable here too. What these value judgments are ought to be stated, and naturally terms with a definable content should be used as much as possible. Unfortunately both these requirements are often impossible to fulfil in political work, which I sometimes found embarrassing later on.

Ohlin felt a calling to serve the public, which may perhaps explain why he donned the political mantle instead of continuing to develop as a theoretician, even though theoreticians also serve the public if their ideas can be translated into practical applications or if they can expunge ideas which ought not to be put into practice. 'One problem which I addressed early on', Ohlin (1972: 97) writes, 'was whether one ought to strive primarily to be useful, to perform services for people by one's work. Or ought one to seek to develop oneself. . . ?' He chose the former alternative.

That Ohlin was animated by a desire to serve the public, and that he considered himself a strong enough character not to have to compromise his own (scientifically based) views, is apparent from one of his letters (dated 3 August 1935) to Heckscher:

> For my own part I only want to add that if I ever go into politics more actively, it will be for two reasons. Firstly to try to help to improve the situation of the poorest people in the country, which the Liberal Party ought to be able to do better than the trade union-linked Social Democratic Party. Secondly because our political life needs upright and independent persons, which is what I should try to be.

Gunnar Myrdal – on socialist grounds

Gunnar Myrdal was an economist who held views on most subjects and delighted in sharing them with the world; in this respect he followed in the footsteps of his teacher Gustav Cassel. He expressed his opinion on fiscal and monetary issues, commercial, social or housing policy, population, education or development questions, constitutional issues, etc. In fact, he considered it his duty as a scholar to have opinions about most things. 'As an institutional social scientist I believe in principle that everything can be explored, and also that everything which is important ought to be discussed and explored' (Myrdal 1982: 138).

Myrdal believed that economists could develop their capacity for questioning and searching for truth only by attacking on many fronts, acquiring a wide-ranging knowledge of society and taking part in public debate. Economists who isolated themselves 'in the little model world of their own and their colleagues' risked becoming narrow-minded, uncritical and conservative scholars. In former times economists had begun their active lives as businessmen, mathematicians, historians, philosophers or lawyers.

> Their changing over to economics was regularly caused directly by a strong involvement in the problems of society. Economists almost never started off as economists . . . When economists began life as economists they increased the risk of becoming narrow specialists who never questioned the fundamental value judgments and traditions of their own disciplines.
>
> (Myrdal 1973: 71)

The question of deduction and induction was closely associated with these issues. Myrdal held that it was necessary, on the one hand, to think in abstract terms and to find the essential elements of existence by the deductive route, but, on the other, to keep in close contact with reality, that is, to work inductively.

> The further away a scholarly opinion is from direct observation and the more abstract and 'theoretical' it is, the more defenseless it becomes against insidious opportunist errors of judgment. In economics, model thinking in particular creates scope for systematic biases ... But of course all social studies must nevertheless aim at generalization. It is thus important to be able to think concretely at the same time, as I learnt from Gustav Cassel.
>
> (Myrdal 1982: 265)

Myrdal had a clear party-political profile. He was an active Social Democrat: ideologue, participating in public debate, Member of Parliament and Member of the Cabinet. Thus, he went further than Cassel, who confessed that he had a generally liberal outlook but declined to accommodate himself to any party line.

Myrdal's solution to the scholarship–politics dilemma, as is well known, was for the scholar to work on the basis of explicit value premises. In *Vetenskap och politik i nationalekonomien* he had propounded the view that the scholar should state his value judgments and would then be able to reason objectively, scientifically, logically, rationally. Little by little he came round to the opinion that

> this book's conception of the existence of some solid and 'objective' body of economic theory was mistaken and that value-premises are needed even to establish facts, not merely for drawing political conclusions. The value-premises selected have an influence on how research is approached, in other words on what is studied and what questions are asked, on the focus and conduct of analysis and the conclusions drawn.
>
> (Myrdal 1973: 11, 1982: 265)

Myrdal had written *Vetenskap och politik* (the book was originally published in 1929) as a comment on the earlier economists' 'slipshod and misconceived way of presenting political opinions as scholarly conclusions' (Myrdal 1972: 8). Myrdal expresses his criticism of the older generation without reserve in a letter (dated 26 December 1934) to Heckscher:[15]

> As regards the problem of science and politics I shall confine myself to the following: Here for a generation you have pursued a *liberal* policy in objective guise, that is to say without declaring the moral and political value-premises: 'objective' discussion, in your opinion. When we are writing on policy we say so, and also attempt to state our *value-premises*, and then you talk about fanaticism. You have evidently not understood our critique of

value. You are still stuck in your 'objective' policy, which shuns moral judgments.

In his initial position, nonetheless, Myrdal was inspired by one of these 'slipshod' economists, i.e. by Cassel's endeavors to dispose of utility theory. The efforts made by both Cassel and the Uppsala philosopher Axel Hägerström to avoid 'metaphysical speculation' encouraged Myrdal to start grappling with the problem of science and politics. His final solution to the problem was a pessimistic one as regards the possibility of conducting some kind of value-free, objective research. Value judgments permeate everything. He stubbornly insisted on calling economics by its old name of political economy.

Over and above that of subjective value judgments, party-political activity presents another problem: that is the problem of being forced to adapt oneself to the value judgments of others. Myrdal apparently believed that when he joined the Social Democratic Party it was so open and tolerant that he would never need to adapt himself to any party line. 'With the open-minded character which the party then had, I never had to feel myself subject to the kind of party loyalty which could restrict my freedom of opinion in the slightest degree.' Nevertheless he was aware of the dilemma, which became acute in 1945, if not before, when he became Secretary of Commerce and a cog in the machinery of government:

> When I agreed to become a member of the new entirely Social Democratic government, I remember I was profoundly gripped by the feeling that it must signify a change in the conditions of my work. From having been a wholly independent scholar active in the social and economic field I now became a member of a collective decision-making group.

He went on:

> I had to set a boundary to what I personally thought and even to what I could reveal publicly concerning any possibly divergent opinion I might have. I was strongly sensitive to the limitation on what I could declare openly as my own opinion or divulge about what had preceded government decisions. I had never before needed to observe any such limitation.
>
> (Myrdal 1982: 225, 229)

In his ambition to speak simply to the people, Myrdal did not lag behind his teacher Cassel. Myrdal (1973: 140) considered that two strong traditions from the Age of Enlightenment were being neglected in his own time:

> One of these is that the scholar shall never complicate his exposition more than is strictly necessary to make it as fully clear and penetrating as possible

. . . The second is that no matter how involved the scholar is in his research, he ought to be prepared to devote time to speaking simply and clearly to the general public. This was regarded by earlier generations as the duty of every learned man, and a duty observed particularly by the greatest and most originally creative figures in our field of work. In our branch of learning it has now all too often become a false scholarly ambition to speak only to each other, shutting the public out.

Unlike his colleagues, however, Myrdal did not enjoy writing for the daily newspapers. 'You know my position: I have never written a newspaper article', he wrote (in an undated letter of 1934) to Heckscher. Still, a few articles did appear by him in time as well as many interviews by the media.

Conclusion

The quintet of Wicksell, Cassel, Heckscher, Ohlin and Myrdal represents Sweden's foremost economists. They commanded a wide-ranging repertoire and worked on a great variety of society's problems. For two of them – Heckscher, the economist and historian, and Myrdal, the institutionalist – this breadth of approach was a consequence of their scientific orientation.

Each had a distinct ideological orientation and was at the same time a committed theoretical economist, political ideologue, economic policy expert and debater. Wicksell performed differently in his roles as scholar and political debater – in the one case, unassuming and cautious, in the other, vociferous and bold. He believed that by having adopted a utilitarian position he had found a way of raising scholarship above the clash of value judgments and interests. Cassel admitted that he built on certain liberal values but held that if only economic life were permitted to rest on this foundation, the result would be a growth of prosperity which would benefit the vast majority. On the whole, however, he seems to have regarded himself as the upholder of reason and more or less absolute truth. Of the earlier economists, it was Heckscher who discussed the relationship between scholarly work and politics in greatest detail. He was somewhat pessimistic concerning the scholar's chances of elucidating even for himself where the boundary came between the one and the other, but he believed that the neoclassical theory gave some degree of guidance. Ohlin – thanks to Myrdal perhaps – was conscious of the complications arising from the fact that the scholar is always governed by his value judgments but did rarely let the world know of his possible cogitations over the question. Myrdal did cogitate more, and landed in a relativist position. Value judgments determine most things – choice of problem, method and solution.

The three older economists wanted to stand clear of partisan commitments. They certainly had views about party politics – Wicksell both criticized and commended the Liberal and Social Democratic Parties, and Cassel willingly drew up the guidelines for a 'true' Liberal party and the curtains down for the Social Democrats (one of his books was entitled *Socialism eller framåtskridande* (Socialism or Progress) but, to cite Cassel's favorite expression again, they were reluctant to find themselves 'popped into a particular pigeonhole', because that would curtail their freedom of movement and thus their credibility. The two younger economists do not seem to have let the matter worry them but entered the political fray with gusto. Ohlin gives the impression of having assumed himself to be a strong enough personality not to have to compromise his ideals. Myrdal, on the other hand, expressed distaste for possibly having, as a member of a collective decision-making body, to restrain his personal views.

All five were broad-minded economists, not only in that they addressed a wide set of issues but also by virtue of their endeavors to reach out to the public at large. To speak clearly and simply to the public was in their eyes an imperative duty of the academic economist, and some of them indeed seem to have felt themselves to stand in an intuitive relationship with the 'masses'.

The ideological extremes of Cassel and Myrdal display striking similarities. Both held that a good social scientist ought to strive for breadth of approach; both were clear that they did not stand on ground free from value judgments; both sought realism in preference to 'metaphysical speculation'; both strove for simplicity and clarity; both believed it their duty to speak to the public at large. The point at issue between them consisted of the differences between their value judgments and of Cassel's being more of an 'absolutist' – he considered his value judgments to represent some kind of absolute reason, whereas Myrdal was a 'relativist' who thought it possible to argue in reasonable terms from different value judgments.

Economists in future public debate?

Wicksell, Cassel, Heckscher, Ohlin and Myrdal founded Sweden's tradition of media-tuned economists involved in the current problems of society. Several of today's Swedish economists have followed in their footsteps – often without reflecting very much about how and why this pattern originated. More recently, however, the view held by academic economists, in particular among the younger generations, regarding the economist's role in public debate has shifted away from the ideal which this quintet of earlier scholars endeavored to live up to. A number of tendencies are contributing to this shift, which is found in other countries as well.

There is today an inclination among academic economists either to withdraw from public debate or else to call debating contributions into question by arguing that 'strict' or 'rigorous' scientific proof does not exist for policy recommendations. The 'serious' economist therefore would do best to refrain from expressing himself – in sharp contrast to the relish with which earlier economists hurled themselves into public controversy. Competition for jobs in the increasingly 'technicized' and 'mathematicized' field of economics requires heavy concentration on academic production, that is, on articles accepted by scholarly refereed journals. Professional prestige rests more and more on the number of articles published and on citations.

The training of today's graduate students makes heavy inroads on the time and commitment of professors. Wicksell, Cassel, Heckscher, Ohlin and Myrdal were operating in a different academic environment, far from today's mass production of PhD graduates. In their day, advising and training future doctors of economics was a minute element of a professor's work.[16] Doctoral candidates were expected largely to look after themselves.

A growing group of today's academically active economists, often with an abstruse mathematical specialization, seems to be more isolated from the public debate than earlier generations of economists, while functioning at the same time as trend-setters and role models for young aspiring PhDs and researchers. The researcher who involves herself or himself in burning issues of the day runs the risk of being classified as less earnest and academically ambitious. The next step is to regard polemical articles and debating contributions as demeriting.[17]

If this trend continues, less and less importance will be attached in the future to the duty and social responsibility of participating in public debate and imparting some grasp of economic thought to the public at large. Perhaps we are moving towards a future in which academic economists have abandoned the intensive social commitment which served as a guiding principle for the founding fathers of the subject of economics in Sweden.

Acknowledgments

We would like to thank Anders Björklund, Erik Dahmén, Lars Herlitz, Sven-Erik Larsson, Ingemar Ståhl, Thomas Thorburn, Torbjörn Vallinder and Lars Werin for valuable comments on the Swedish version of this paper. The English version – translated by Geoffrey French – has benefited significantly from the views of Michael D. Bordo, Hans Brems, Bruno Frey, Torsten Gårdlund, David Laidler and Bo Sandelin. We owe a special debt to Hans Brems for his insightful comments. This chapter was originally published in Swedish as 'Hur såg de stora nationalekonomerna på sin roll i samhällsdebatten?' Chapter 4 in L. Jonung (1996).

Notes

1 One confirmation of this is provided by a postal enquiry which was addressed to all Swedish professors of economics in 1989. The aim was to chart their contributions to the daily press, to the journal *Ekonomisk Debatt*, to SOU (*Statens Offentliga Utredningar*

– Swedish Government Reports) and to similar activities. The postal replies disclosed an extensive external activity, according to Jonung (1992: 42). See also Sandelin (2000) on the characteristics of Swedish economists.

2 The word economists refers henceforth to economists employed at universities.

3 We exclude here several prominent economists such as David Davidson and Erik Lindahl because they were not as visible in public debate as Wicksell, Cassel, Heckscher, Ohlin and Myrdal, the quintet considered.

4 *Svenska Dagbladet*, *Dagens Nyheter* and *Stockholms-Tidningen* were daily newspapers with wide circulation, published in Stockholm. Data on the number of articles are from Jonung (1991).

5 See Magnusson (1993) for a discussion of the journalistic activities of Swedish economists during the first three decades of the twentieth century. Similarities and differences between the five economists are discussed, for example, in the Introduction and contributions in Jonung (1991). Sandelin (2000) considers why economists in small countries like Sweden tend to get involved in public policy discussion.

6 According to Erlander (1972: 122), Wicksell was invited to speak at the twenty-fifth anniversary of the Social Democrats in Lund in 1926. Wicksell expressed his appreciation of being the keynote speaker but added: 'I do not belong to the herd. I am a sheep all by myself.'

7 Reprinted in Lindahl (1958).

8 During the controversies surrounding the chair in Lund, the critics of Wicksell opposed his propensity to make his views known to the public. Gårdlund (1956: 244) quotes a comment against Wicksell, based on his 'detrimental activities against his native country as a public educator'.

9 The quote is from Gårdlund (1958: 305). The quote inspired to the title for the recent publication of about eighty previously unpublished manuscripts by Wicksell. See Jonung *et al.* (2001).

10 This introduction is not included in the English edition of 1932.

11 Working with his monumental study of Bertil Ohlin, Sven-Erik Larsson (1998) was unable to find Ohlin discussing in earnest the division of roles between the politician and the scholar. Larsson stated in personal communication with Lars Jonung that this had to do with 'the reticence that Ohlin always displayed with respect to personal problems'. Ohlin, the family man, the professor and the politician, is portrayed in a number of contributions in Findlay *et al.* (2002). This is the best picture of him available in English.

12 An example of Ohlin's enormous productivity: in the years 1932–43 he published on average almost 70 articles a year in *Stockholms-Tidningen* alone. See Carlson *et al.* (2000). Ohlin's newspaper articles have so far not been collected and analysed by scholars. An attempt to convey Ohlin's 'popular message' on the Depression of the 1930s is made in Carlson and Jonung (2002).

13 Professor Thomas Thorburn recalls from his time as a student at the Stockholm School of Economics with Ohlin as his teacher in economics: 'His students were guessing at this time as to whether he would join the Social Democrats or the Liberals, but expected Ohlin to go into politics.'

14 After a debate in Oslo in 1935, Heckscher wrote to Ohlin (in a letter of 21 June 1935) that there was a risk that the 'present powers that be might be able to get you to go along with just about anything' and that Ohlin would not fit in with the Liberal Party but ought to follow Myrdal's example and join the Social Democrats. Ohlin

(3 August 1935) replied very caustically. The relationship between Ohlin and Heckscher was never again what it had once been.

15 Heckscher wondered (in a letter of 18 December 1934) whether Myrdal 'does not at bottom lack the temperament of a scholar and so ought to make his main occupation that of an agitator'. It was precisely in his critique of value judgments that the subjectivism of Myrdal's scholarly work revealed itself. 'Why does *Vetenskap och politik i nationalekonomien* concentrate its fire solely on liberal ideology and not on socialist also?'

16 See Jonung (1991, 1992) for a discussion of the five economists' contribution to the nurturing of new generations of Swedish economists.

17 If these tendencies persist, then the question will be, who is going to ascend to the throne of public debate which academic economists have abdicated of their own accord? Will it be economists associated with banks, brokerage firms and other organizations or will it be representatives of other social sciences than economics?

References

Åkerman, J. (1956) 'Sanningssökare och sanningssägare', *Sydsvenska Dagbladet*, October 16.

Carlson, B. (1995) *The State as a Monster: Gustav Cassel and Eli Heckscher on the Role and Growth of the State*, New York and London: University Press of America.

Carlson, B. and Jonung, L. (2002) 'Ohlin on the Great Depression: the popular message in the daily press', in Findlay, R., Jonung, L. and Lundahl, M. (eds) *Bertil Ohlin: A Centennial Celebration, 1899–1999*, Cambridge, MA: MIT Press.

Carlson, B., Orrje, H. and Wadensjö, E. (2000) *Ohlins artiklar: Register över Bertil Ohlins artiklar i skandinaviska tidningar och tidskrifter 1919–1979*, Stockholm: Institutet för social forskning.

Cassel, G. (1934) *Teoretisk socialekonomi*, Stockholm: Kooperativa förbundets förlag.

—— (1940–41) *I förnuftets tjänst I-II*, Stockholm: Natur och Kultur.

Erlander, T. (1972) *1901–1939*, Stockholm: Tidens Förlag.

Findlay, R., Jonung, L. and Lundahl, M. (eds) (2002) *Bertil Ohlin: A Centennial Celebration, 1899–1999*, Cambridge, MA: MIT Press.

Gårdlund, T. (1956) *Knut Wicksell: Rebell i Det nya riket*, Stockholm: Bonniers.

—— (1958) *The Life of Knut Wicksell*, Stockholm: Almqvist and Wiksell. Reprinted in 1996 by Edward Elgar.

Heckscher, E. (1936) *Det privata näringslivet i tvångshushållningens tid*, Stockholm.

—— (1944) 'Erfarenheter av ekonomi och ekonomisk politik under fyrtio år', *Ekonomen*.

—— (1948) *Ödeläggelsen av 1800-talets hushållning*, Stockholm: Bonniers.

Heckscher, E.L. (1945) *Sveriges mynthistoria – vagledning för myntkabinettets svenska myntsal*, Stockholm: Rasmussan, Nils-Ludvig

Henriksson, R. (1979) 'Eli F Heckscher och svensk nationalekonomi', *Ekonomisk Debatt*, 8.

Jonung, L. (ed.) (1991) *The Stockholm School of Economics Revisited*, Cambridge: Cambridge University Press.

—— (1992) 'Economics the Swedish way 1889–1989', in Engwall, L. (ed.) *Economics in Sweden: An Evaluation of Swedish Research in Economics*, London: Routledge.

—— (ed.) (1996) *Ekonomerna i debatten – gör de någon nytta?*, Otta: Ekerlids Förlag.

Jonung, L., Hedlund-Nyström, T. and Jonung, C. (eds) (2001) *Att uppfostra det svenska folket: Knut Wicksells opublicerade manuskript* (To Educate the Swedish People: Knut Wicksell's Unpublished Manuscripts), Stockholm: SNS.

Keynes, J.M. (1936) *The General Theory of Employment, Interest and Money*, London: Macmillan.

Larsson, S.-E. (1998) *Bertil Ohlin: Ekonom och politiker*, Stockholm: Atlantis.

Lindahl, E. (1953) 'Knut Wicksell 1851–1926', in Schumpeter, J. (ed.) *Stora nationalekonomer*, Stockholm: Natur och Kultur.

—— (ed.) (1958) *Knut Wicksell: Selected Papers on Economic Theory*, London: Allen and Unwin.

Magnusson, L. (1991) 'Gustav Cassel, popularizer and enigmatic Walrasian', in Sandelin, B. (ed.) *The History of Swedish Economic Thought*, London and New York: Routledge.

—— (1993) 'The economist as popularizer: the emergence of Swedish economics 1900–30', in Jonung, L. (ed.) *Swedish Economic Thought: Explorations and Advances*, London and New York: Routledge, pp. 82–108.

Myrdal, G. (1929/1972) *Vetenskap och politik i nationalekonomin*, Stockholm: Rabén and Sjögren.

—— (1973) *I stället för memoarer*, Stockholm: Prisma.

—— (1982) *Hur styrs landet?*, Stockholm: Rabén and Sjögren.

Ohlin, B. (1972) *Ung man blir politiker*, Stockholm: Bonniers.

Röster i Radio (1945) no. 28.

Sandelin, B. (2000) 'The post-1945 development of economics and economists in Sweden', in Coats, A.W. (ed.) *The Development of Economics in Western Europe since 1945*, London and New York: Routledge.

Wicksell, K. (1904) 'Mål och medel i nationalekonomien', *Ekonomisk Tidskrift*, 22(4): 51–66.

Wigforss, E. (1951) *Minnen II*, Stockholm: Tidens förlag.

4 Gunnar Myrdal and the Stockholm School

Lars Magnusson

Introduction

In two famous articles in the *Economic Journal* of 1937 Bertil Ohlin invented the concept of 'The Stockholm School of Economics'. At this time John Maynard Keynes was the economist of the day and Ohlin was keen to present the Stockholm economists as a school who both stood close to and in fact anticipated many of Keynes's ideas. That Keynes also stood in the forefront in the political discussion regarding how the present mass unemployment should be cured triggered Ohlin even more to put his name alongside Keynes; as always Ohlin was more a politician than a scientific economist. There is certainly an important grain of truth in Ohlin's story, of course. As we will see, in policy terms, the Stockholm economists often came to the same conclusions as Keynes. However, at the same time it is certainly a misnomer only to see the 'Stockholm School' as some special kind of Keynesianism. In reality, it was something quite different and built on a quite different doctrinal heritage. Hence, to reduce it as such means in fact that we totally fail to understand what the Stockholm School instead was from a more historical and doctrinal point of view. While doing this I will rely on one of its most important figures, Gunnar Myrdal. Without doubt, he was the first within the school to outline the kind of sequence analysis which really lay at the heart of the Stockholm School.

The concept of 'school'

The concept of 'school' in the history of economic thought is often vaguely and ambiguously applied. In particular, it is seldom made clear whether it is used in the sense of an empirically and historically given intellectual trend (or discourse) or as a mere collection of viewpoints that from the point of view of some late interpreter seems to fit together for some reason.[1] An obvious example of the first would, for example, be the Physiocratic School which certainly can be identified as a group of economic writers sharing a common vocabulary as well as a research programme. As more important examples of historical constructions *ex post* we can mention Marx's creation of a school of Labour Theory of Value – which of course includes a number of writers such Petty and Smith who never identified themselves as 'labour theorists of value', Adam Smith's 'mercantile system' or Keynes's under-consumptionist heresy beginning with Malthus. Hence, when being asked to present some afterthoughts on the 'Stockholm School', one of its alleged founders Erik Lundberg responded:

> The view that the Stockholm School was and is a myth is, surely, generally accepted. As early as 1937, when Ohlin launched the concept in the *Economic Journal*, many of us economists in Stockholm protested at what we felt to be a strange invention. But words dominate thoughts. We came to accept and sparingly use the concept. Even a myth has its real base: the myth may become at least as real as reality itself.
>
> (Lundberg [1974] 1994: 491)

The issue of an independent 'Stockholm School' is further complicated by the fact that even if there existed such a coherent school in the beginning of the 1930s (although its members did not know it themselves), it seems to have disintegrated shortly afterward. As many have pointed out, even if the Stockholm School really existed at some point in time, it was a school with no followers. Hence, from the late 1930s onwards, its founders went in quite different directions. Gunnar Myrdal, for instance, increasingly found inspiration from unorthodox economics, American institutionalism, etc., resulting in his seminal masterpiece *An American Dilemma* and many works after that. For the rest of his life he remained a rather orthodox economist who never really – after the late 1930s – returned to the kind of issues which were discussed in his dissertation of 1927 'Prisbildningsproblemet och föränderligheten' ('The Problem of Price Formation and Change'). Bertil Ohlin, another of the founding fathers of the Stockholm School and the first to coin the phrase in 1937, as we saw, became a famous liberal politician in Sweden. As an economist, he remained faithful to his old subject international trade theory while his macroeconomics after the Second World War gradually was integrated into orthodox Keynesianism. Erik Lundberg, for his part, helped to develop business cycle and macroeconomic stabilisation theory, but his interest from the late 1930s onwards laid mainly in empirical work and not in pure theory. Much of the same can be said of Dag Hammarskjöld and Alf Johansson. Only Erik Lindahl remained faithful to the old ideas when adopting sequential analysis especially to capital theory. He was also one of the very few who remained faithful to the academic curricula, first as a professor in Lund and then in Uppsala.

Hence, the demise of the Stockholm School can to a large extent be seen as a consequence of the disinterest among the school members themselves to develop its theoretical basis and formulate a more definitive position – especially in relation to Keynesian theory. Also other reasons have been suggested, for example, that the school did not publish in English, that its members were not particularly keen in putting their theories to empirical test, that Sweden had too small an academic base at the time, that the members of the school did not care to attract graduate students who would carry on the tradition, etc.[2]

With this ambiguity in mind, I still think it is fruitful to pose the question: what, if anything, was the Stockholm School? I think one can provide two answers to this question: one historical and the other theoretical and analytical.

As a *historical* phenomena the 'Stockholm School' consisted of a rather loose group of young economists who certainly regarded the old guard of Swedish economists such as Gustav Cassel and especially Knut Wicksell as important forefathers. However, at the same time they saw themselves in opposition to some of their colleagues' theoretical fundamentals. Hence, in particular the importance of Wicksell's theory of monetary equilibrium for the young generation of economists, including Myrdal, has always been emphasised – and rightly so. However, the Stockholm economists were ready to draw other conclusions on this basis than Wicksell had done. Moreover, the wish to move away from some of the positions taken by the classical – or the 'old', according to Heckscher – liberalism seems to have been the most pertinent trait in common of these 'young Turks' – a point that I will return to in a moment.

However, it must be pointed out that it is most fruitful to regard the 'Stockholm School' as a generation phenomenon. Hence, the economist at the *Handelshögskolan* in Stockholm, Sven Brisman – who belonged to the older generation – gave this eye-witness account of a stormy meeting taking place in 1930:

> One day about two years ago, a remarkable meeting was held at our political economy discussion club in Stockholm. Here we elder economists had gone for years, basking in our own splendidness, full of an unfeigned mutual admiration, convinced that we had finally found the only True and Correct economic viewpoint. And then came Gunnar Myrdal, who was a young docent at the time, about whom I knew little more than that he had defended a brilliant dissertation. Figuratively speaking, he turned all of us upside down. His presentation was one long glowing sermon from his mouth against everything we had considered most valuable in our economic education. And it was apparent that he had a group of enthusiastic followers among the even younger generation who were indignant at the writing of Cassel, Heckscher and myself. All our old beloved concepts, especially 'maximum welfare', 'efficiency', not to mention 'population optimum' and 'the economic correct distribution of production forces', 'national income', 'price level' and much more – all these were blown away like straw in the wind, until we didn't know if we stood on our heads or on our feet.[3]

After citing from this instructive – but perhaps over-dramatised – eye-witness report, let me return to the main reason which seems to have held this group of 'young Turks' together: their opposition to the old guard on how to cure unemployment and find remedies for the ongoing depression. As in America the old generation of economists tended to blame the Wall Street crash and the beginning of the Great Depression on overspending and a much too loose credit and monetary policy. Hence their answer was to withdraw credit and let the 'real factors' in the economy such as cost-cutting, closing down on surplus capacity, etc., do the job.[4] In the same manner, the only way they saw to combat unemployment was by lowering wages in the business cycle down turn. Most certainly, the young 'Stockholm economists' saw themselves in opposition to such policy recommendations. And it was certainly this opposition which inspired Myrdal in his famous memorandum *Konjunkturer och offentlig hushallning* (1933) which was added to the new Social Democratic Finance Minister's, Ernst Wigforss, budget plan in 1934, launching a new and more offensive and spending-like economic policy, using budget measures to increase total demand. Much of what Ohlin did and said during these years can of course also be seen in the same light. Hence, as we have seen, in his seminal two articles in 1937, Bertil Ohlin emphasised the 'new economic policy' as the cornerstone of 'the Stockholm School'. In Sweden, he argued, a number of economists had anticipated Keynes in arguing for more public spending as a means to combat the depression. Such policy recommendations were, according to Ohlin (1937a, b), at the very core of the Stockholm School.

Hence, according to the old wisdom propagated, for example, by Cassel and Heckscher, the main reason for the present high unemployment was downward wage rigidities caused by – in the main – organised labour. However, according to Myrdal in his 1934 memorandum, wage cuts should not be used generally as a method to combat unemployment as they would lower total demand and thus also total output. This idea, by the way, was worked out more properly in Alf Johansson's (always much too neglected) dissertation of 1934 'Löneutvecklingen och arbetslösheten' ('Wage Development and Unemployment'). Instead, Myrdal recommended public spending and budget deficits as a temporary method to combat the depression – as well as public savings during business cycle upturns. This was certainly also what Keynes said at the same time and it became a cornerstone of the new gospel (but not always the reality, especially in the form of budget cuts) of macroeconomic policy which developed from the 1930s onwards.

The Stockholm School and Keynesianism

Thus, as a historical phenomenon the Stockholm School was a loose confederacy of young economists taught in the tradition of Wicksell and Cassel which shared the same unease with regard to the policy recommendations which 'old orthodoxy' had brought forward in a period of severe economic crisis. But was it also something else? To trace also a common theoretical basis for the Stockholm School is a difficult undertaking which, for example, involves the complicated question of comparing proper 'Keynesianism'[5] – whatever that is – with the Stockholm School. Erik Lundberg, for his part, tended to regard the Stockholm School as part of 'Keynesianism' in the sense that:

1   it shared the view that 'the total effective demand is decisive for total production and employment';
2   that total demand may be either too low or too high;
3   that a freely functioning market economy does not, by its very nature, lead to overall economic balance and full employment of productive resources.[6]

However, at the same time, Lundberg admits that the Stockholm economists were Keynesians 'with a difference'. In relation to Keynes, the Stockholm School was, he argues:

> more orientated towards problems of the business cycle, stabilisation policy and period analysis. This meant, first, a somewhat different method of analysis: instead of primarily seeking a final equilibrium position, one relied on a sequence analysis, i.e. one sought methods of following the course from one period to the next. This sequence analysis should set forth the 'leads and lags' of the business cycle. The question was – the legacy of Wicksell – how the cumulative course of the disequilibrium process was initiated.
>
> (Lundberg [1987] 1994: 493)

Hence, the Stockholm School used sequential analysis following Wicksell to study disequilibrium processes while Keynes still relied on old Marshallian comparative statics. Björn Hansson defines 'sequence analysis' as:

> the notion that a plan epitomises economic behaviour, which means that all economic actions are directed towards fulfilment of plans based on expectations of the future and that the plans will be revised in the light of the actual results.[7]

Furthermore, he suggests that sequence analysis is made up of two separate parts, namely the 'single-period analysis' and the 'continuation analysis'. The first part is thus 'concerned with an analysis of what is going to happen during a single period, showing how *ex ante* plans at the beginning of the period lead to determinate *ex post* results at the end of the period'. The second 'continuation' part 'analyses the effects of the *ex post* results in the current period on the plans for the subsequent period'.[8] Most importantly, sequential analysis in its Swedish version put forward the role of expectations for dynamic economic processes.

However, the Stockholm School put its emphasis on disequilibrium processes. For example, Lars Jonung has pointed out that the Stockholm School approach was noted for its 'disbelief in stable relationships between economic aggregates'. Hence, the Swedes 'were sceptical of constant multipliers, stable propensities to save', etc. The consequence was, still according to Jonung, that

> the analysis of economic processes tended to develop into verbal storytelling where there was no end to the story, i.e. no equilibrium solution to the system, as expectations and thus behaviour and attitudes were subject to continuous revisions and changes as new outcomes and developments were registered.[9]

This, if anything, is certainly not Keynesianism, however we wish to define it. Moreover, as pointed out by Jonung, it is perhaps not so strange that such an 'indeterminate system' could not really have formed the basis of a successful new paradigm of economic theory or served as an alternative to Keynesianism. Hence, the very method of the Stockholm School was to some extent the reason for its disintegration. Most certainly it lost out to the elegance of Keynes's more formally satisfying (but not necessary more realistic) presentation.

In fact, that the Stockholm School had different roots from Keynesianism – and developed differently – has been emphasised by most scholars dealing with the 'school'. Hence, it is mainly emphasised that the Stockholm School was a theoretical tradition building on Wicksell. In particular, Björn Hansson (1982) and Jan Pettersson (the latter who mainly deals with Lindahl's contribution, 1987) have painstakingly tried to follow how the Stockholm School made use of Wicksell's sequence analysis and gradually developed more mature views on *ex ante–ex post* and the role of anticipations. The role of Myrdal in this process I will discuss later. However, alongside Myrdal's dissertation of 1927, Erik Lindahl's early 'The Rate of Interest and the Price Level' from 1929 (but published in 1930) can be seen as a theoretical starting point. Lindahl, says Hansson, by introducing the notion of intertemporal equilibrium, broke with the traditional equilibrium notion. Moreover, sequence analysis was further developed in the works of Lindahl, Hammarskjöld and Myrdal until it reached its high point in Erik Lundberg's disequilibrium sequence analysis used, for example, in his *Studies in the Theory of Economic Expansion* (1937).

Myrdal

Hence, the Stockholm School had its origins in Wicksell and in the attempt to develop a more dynamic analysis of price formation largely based on microeconomic information on the behaviour of consumers, investors, etc. In the

1920s Frank Knight and Irving Fisher had played a major role in putting forward the role of risk and expectations for dynamic analysis. In Sweden, Gunnar Myrdal – as always, a keen observer of anything new and trendy – picked up these ideas and amalgamated them with Wicksellian sequence analysis. This novelty is first set out in Myrdal's dissertation *Prisbildningsproblemet och föränderligheten* (1927). The aim of the dissertation was to 'embody the factor of change in price theory, that is liberate it from the static assumptions'.[10] In this attempt Myrdal took his point of departure from his teacher Gustav Cassel's (static) theory of price. Myrdal attempted to show how prices are formed, profits occur and capital values change due to the anticipations of future changes in market conditions as well from technical change.[11] Hence, his insistence that 'price formation takes place in human minds'.[12] Perhaps the most pertinent exposition of the core contributions of Myrdal's dissertation has once again been put forward by Erik Lundberg. He summarised them in four points:

1   Time contains uncertainty as well as inertia of capital and production structure.
2   For each entrepreneur there is some kind of objective risk as to his expectations of future outcomes.
3   There are personal risks with regard to the enterprise or entrepreneur from the credit supplier's side.
4   The non-neutral evaluation of risks is a central economic problem. Under-evaluation and over-evaluation (optimism and pessimism) and the dispersion of risks and evaluations among investing enterprises will have important effects on the price of risk bearing.[13]

In his dissertation Myrdal mixes more general discussions with concrete 'stylised' illustrations of firm and entrepreneurial behaviour – a typical feature of Swedish economic 'casuistic' writing at the time, one may add. Moreover, by this method of 'subsequent approximation to reality', he tries to demonstrate how anticipation of future prices worked in a concrete manner. To a large extent this mix of different theoretical levels and stylised case-study method is both the strength and weakness of his dissertation. Myrdal, of course, clearly shows the fruitfulness of bringing dynamic change and anticipation into the theory of price formation, and in this sense anticipates by several decades some of the findings of a later 'rational expectation' school. On the other hand, however, his theoretical conclusions were only vaguely put forward and he never really worked them out in any detail. Thus, after making a number of concrete observations, he leaves his readers with a certain ambiguity. This 'unsystematic' treatment was certainly a consequence of Myrdal's personality: eager to introduce new ideas but not always patient enough to work them out in full.

Myrdal returned for the last time to these matters in his 1939 book *Monetary*

Equilibrium which, by and large, of course, was a translation of a paper published in Swedish in *Ekonomisk Tidskirft* in 1931, under the title *Om penningteoretisk jämvikt*, and in an enlarged German version *Der Gleichgewichtsbegriff als Instrument für geldtheorische Analyse*, published in 1933 in a book edited by Hayek. In this book the concepts of '*ex ante*' and '*ex post*' are explicitly used and the analysis here is more coherent and analytical than in the dissertation. However, to some extent, this text has a different focus. It directly takes up the point which Wicksell had worked so hard with – the conditions and consequences of monetary equilibrium. Myrdal shows how *ex ante–ex post* considerations strongly affect the possibility of achieving monetary equilibrium which Wicksell, of course, simply defined as long-run price stability (no inflation). As is well known, Wicksell had presupposed that such price stability could only occur when the rate of interest was equal to the expected rate of return of real capital and when there was equality between invested savings and investments.

In his 1939 book Myrdal shows in particular how varying anticipations of return *ex ante* influence capital values or investments *ex post* but also *ex ante* can determine investment plans. Hence, to the extent that Wicksell's equilibrium was an unstable one – as is well known, Wicksell did not believe that there existed any *natural* tendency which would guarantee that the rate of interest would become equal to the rate of return on real capital but rather predicted 'evil spirals' that would lead away in the other direction – Myrdal's economic world seems to be even more unstable. In his discussion – which to a large extent takes the form of an extended comment on Wicksell – Myrdal criticises Wicksell for his central assumption that monetary equilibrium will also imply a constant price level. On the contrary, according to Myrdal, a situation where the rate of interest is equal to the rate of return on capital can confirm to *any* level of absolute prices. Myrdal emphasises: 'If the equilibrium price relations are fulfilled, any movements of the absolute prices . . . will leave monetary equilibrium undisturbed.'[14] Immediately, however, he finds exceptions to his rule – especially in the case where some prices are sticky – and thus once again leaves the reader bewildered and unsure which conclusions one can really draw from all this: when should the rule be followed and how important are the exceptions?

Conclusion

To conclude this rather sketchy overview of Myrdal as a Stockholm School economist, perhaps at least this can be said. Leaving aside the difficult question of defining a 'school' of economic thought, to some extent at least the Stockholm School was both a historical and a theoretical phenomenon. As a historical phenomenon its basis was the revolt of a younger group of Swedish economists who saw the shortcomings in the older generation's analysis as well as policy recommendations in order to combat the depression and unemployment crisis of the inter-war years. In this context they, independently of Keynes, from Wicksell's dynamic microeconomics – worked out a set of propositions which would form the basis of what since then – rather loosely – has been nicknamed the 'Keynesian revolution'. Second, also in their attempt to build on Wicksell's sequential analyses, they provided some theoretical progress by introducing anticipations and risk along the lines of Knight and Fisher. This also means – and this is important in the present context – that Myrdal picked up his ideas from a radically different tradition of economic thought than, for example, Keynes. As is well known, Keynes was heavily influenced by Marshall while Myrdal's teachers, Wicksell and Cassel, were much more inspired by the Austrian School. After all, as Schumpeter argued, 'the best formulation of the Austrian doctrine was presented later by Wicksell'.[15] Hence, we can, in Myrdal's as well in Lindahl's writings, detect a double influence from Austrians such as Menger, Wieser and Böhm-Bawerk. The first arrived via Wicksell and Cassel – although Böhm-Bawerk's discussion of 'roundabout' methods of production in his capital theory might even have had a direct influence on Myrdal and Lindahl. Second, this influence came through Fisher and Knight. In particular, Böhm-Bawerk's influence on Frank Knight was tremendous and is well recognised. After all, Knight was the translator and first publisher of Menger's *Grundsätze* ('Principles') in English (1950). Hence, it was not at all by chance that Myrdal published one of his most important theoretical papers in one of Hayek's edited works in 1933. Still it is an irony of history that in 1973 they both would share the same Nobel Prize. By this time at least Myrdal was the sworn enemy of Hayek and as the gossip tells, his sharing the prize with Hayek totally spoiled all the fun for him. Still, however, they were perhaps not so different in kind as Myrdal would have preferred them to be. Might we speculate that it was this which made him so furious in 1973?

Notes

1 For a discussion see Lars Magnusson (1994: 13–16).
2 L. Jonung, 'Introduction' to Lars Jonung (1993).
3 Cited from Lars Magnusson, 'The Economist as Popularizer: The Emergence of Swedish Economics 1900–1930', in Lars Jonung (ed.) (1993: 82). Translation by Rolf Henriksson.
4 For a recent proposition, see Michael D. Bordo *et al.* (1997: 35).
5 For example, in his book Peter Clarke (1998) has convincingly shown the great divide between what Keynes actual taught and later 'Keynesianism'.
6 Lundberg ([1987] 1994: 492).
7 Hansson (1982: 17).
8 Hansson (1982: 18).
9 Jonung (1991: 29).
10 Myrdal (1927: 4).
11 For a formal presentation of the subsequent steps in Myrdal's argumentation, see Hansson (1982, Chapter 3).

12   Myrdal (1927: 8).
13   Lundberg (1994: 427).
14   In Lundberg ([1974] 1994: 429).
15   Schumpeter ([1954] 1973: 913).

References

Bordo, M.D., Goldin, C. and White, E.N. (eds) (1997) *The Defining Moment: The Great Depression and the American Economy in the Twentieth Century*, Chicago: University Press of Chicago.

Clarke, P. (1998) *The Keynesian Revolution and its Economic Consequences*, Cheltenham: Edward Elgar.

Hansson, B. (1982) *The Stockholm School and the Development of Dynamic Method*, London: Croom Helm.

Jonung, L. (1991) *The Stockholm School of Economics Revisited*, Cambridge: Cambridge University Press.

—— (1993) *Swedish Economic Thought: Explorations and Advances*, London: Routledge.

Johansson, A. (1934) Löneutvecklingen och Arbetslösheten *Wage Formation and Unemployment*), Bilaga 6 till Arbetslöshetsirtredmingens Betänkanden, Sou: 1934(2). Lindahl, E. (1930) *Penningpolitikens Medel*, Malmö: Forsakringsaktieboldget, English translation in 1939 *Studies in the Theory and Capital, Part II*, London: Allen & Unwin.

Lundberg, E. (1937), *Studies in the Theory of Economic Expansion*, London: PS King & Son.

—— (1974) 'Gunnar Myrdal's contribution to economic theory: a short survey', *Swedish Journal of Economics*, 76: 472–8, reprinted in Lundberg, E. (1994) *Studies in Economic Instability and Change*, Stockholm: SNS, pp. 425–32.

—— (1987) 'Memories of the Stockholm School', *Ekonomisk Debatt*, 15: 280–6, reprinted in Lundberg, E. (1994) *Studies in Economic Instability and Change*, Stockholm: SNS, pp. 491–499.

Magnusson, L. (1994) *Mercantilism: The Shaping of an Economic Language*, London: Routledge.

Menger, C. (1871), *Grundsätze der Volkswirtschaftslehre*, Vienna: Braumüller, English trans., 1950, *Principles of Economics*, Glencoe, IL: The Free Press.

Myrdal, G. (1927) *Prisbildningsproblemet och föränderligheten*, Uppsala: Almqvist & Wiksells Förlag.

—— (1933) Komjhnkturewr och Offentlig Hushållming (Business Cycles and Public Finance), Stockholm.

—— (1939) Monetary Equilibrium, London: W. Hodge & Co, Reprint by Kelley New York, 1965.

—— (1944) *An American Dilemma. The Negro Problem and Modern Democraty*, New York: Harper & Brothers Pub.

Ohlin, B. (1937a) 'Some Notes on the Stockholm Theory of Savings and Investment, Part I,' *Economic Journal*, 47: 221–40.

—— (1937b) 'Some Notes on the Stockholm Theory of Savings and Investment, Part II,' *Economic Journal*, 47: 221–40.

Pettersson, J. (1987) *Erik Lindahl och Stockholmsskolans dynamiska method*, Lund: Dialogus.

Schumpeter, J. (1954) *History of Economic Analysis*, 1973 edn, London: George Allen & Unwin.

Part III
Money and the business cycle

5 Wicksell on technical change, real wages and employment

Mauro Boianovsky and Harald Hagemann

Any fully satisfactory and comprehensive treatment of the problem, once discussed in such a lively manner, of machinery's benefit or harm to workers does not, as far as I know, exist.

(Wicksell 1890: 257)

Introduction

Knut Wicksell's analysis of the influence of technical changes on rents and wages in volume 1 of his *Lectures* ([1901b] 1934: 133–44) has been described as 'the first modern discussion of technical change and distribution' by Paul Samuelson (1965: 354). Wicksell was the first economist to apply the then new marginal productivity theory of distribution to the treatment of the effects of technical change on income shares. His discussion of technical progress was in great part motivated by the new chapter 'On Machinery' in the third edition of David Ricardo's ([1821] 1951) *Principles*, in which Ricardo changed his previous opinion that the introduction of machinery is beneficial to all classes of society, including workers. Ricardo claimed in that chapter that the introduction of machinery could reduce aggregate output, the demand for labour and (although only implicitly) real wages. Wicksell contended that Ricardo was only partly right, since labour-saving technical progress indeed reduces real wages, but cannot lower national income. Wicksell's criticism of Ricardo has been discussed in the literature (see Sylos-Labini 1969: 133–6; Hansson 1983; Coleman 1985; Samuelson 1988, 1989), with an emphasis on Wicksell's claim that the fall in real wages increases the profitability of old labour-intensive technology and leads to the reabsorption of workers displaced by the (partial) introduction of new technology.

We shall argue that, despite Wicksell's full-employment result in the argument of the *Lectures*, his careful interpretation of Ricardo's machinery problem is relevant for his notion of technological unemployment developed later on in the 1920s. Wicksell's insight that technical progress may be accompanied by falling marginal productivity of labour and, therefore, falling real wages was unique in the neoclassical literature of his time, where it was argued that, since the average productivity of labour and aggregate output increase with technical change, real wages must also be higher (see, e.g., Marshall [1890] 1990: 596–7; Walras [1898] 1936: 273; Clark [1899] 1965: 405–6; Carver 1908; Cassel [1918] 1932: 340–1). According to Wicksell ([1923] 1981 and undated manuscript), labour-saving technical change could reduce real wages below their subsistence level or even to zero, turning labour into a free good and causing permanent unemployment. The next section discusses Wicksell's (1890) interpretation of the relation between technical change and real wages in his pre-marginalist days, when he sided with the 'compensation' view that technical progress cannot be harmful to workers. We then discuss how Wicksell used the concept of marginal productivity to put forward a distinction between land-saving, labour-saving and neutral forms of technical change in the printed *Lectures* and in an unpublished lecture delivered in Lund in the spring of 1900. As shown in the next section, Wicksell applied his model of the effects of technical change on real wages to the interpretation of the continuously high rates of unemployment of the 1920s. Finally, a summary is provided.

The compensation view

'Empty Stomachs – and Full Warehouses', published in 1890 in the Norwegian magazine *Samtiden*, was Wicksell's first article in economics (see Gårdlund 1958: 126). It contains a criticism of the theory of over-production and an embryo of Wicksell's approach to the business cycle (see Boianovsky 1995: 391–3). He was particularly critical of the Marxian view which, in Wicksell's interpretation, ascribes both over-production and under-consumption to the replacement of labour power by machinery. The contradiction between higher production made possible by the introduction of machinery, on the one hand, and the reduction in consumption caused by the dismissal of workers and lower wages, on the other, is the main feature of the 'Marxist School', according to Wicksell. Capitalists react to the disappointment of lack of markets and lower profits by increased use of machinery with 'overproduction and underconsumption reciprocally creating each other in a pernicious cycle' (1890: 251–2).[1] Wicksell disputed Marx's analysis on both factual and conceptual grounds, and pointed out that this 'paradox' – that the economic downswing should be seen as the result of the introduction of labour-saving production methods and technical progress in general – has arisen 'simply through an incomplete analysis of the economic phenomena' (ibid.: 255).

Wicksell's rejection of the Marxian discussion of technical change was based on the notion that the long-run effects of labour-saving methods are beneficial to workers through three mechanisms associated with cost reductions caused by technological change. The first and most important one is an increase in the demand for consumption goods brought about either by lower prices or higher profits. If consumers and entrepreneurs increased their saving instead, the demand for capital goods would rise correspondingly. Finally, if consumers reacted to lower prices by increasing leisure and supplying less labour (that is, a negative income-effect), the dismissed workers would take their place in the labour market:

> If the introduction of machinery and improved labour methods makes a certain amount of human labour superfluous, then it follows from that as a simple corollary, after all, that the production cost is also reduced by exactly as much as was previously paid out in wages to the now superfluous workers. The producers now either stuff the entire profit into their pockets or, as should generally be the case, they are forced to share it with the consumers through cheaper prices. In both cases, this profit represents a saving, a retained income, which in one way or another must be employed. If it is used for the consumption of new consumption goods . . . there then arises a new demand for products, and thereby for labour power, which is capable of completely absorbing the unemployed. If the producer and the consumer prefer to capitalize their gain instead of immediately consuming it, the result is exactly the same . . . A third possibility is that consumers would, instead of seeking new uses for their income, content themselves with a smaller income, that is to say, work less themselves. But in this case there would be access to the occupations partly vacated in this manner.
>
> (Wicksell 1890: 255–6)

Wicksell's discussion of the reabsorption mechanisms here is very close to the so-called 'compensation theory' put forward by J.B. Say ([1821] 1971: 87), J.R. McCulloch ([1825] 1965) and others as a reaction to Ricardo's new chapter on machinery (see Gourvitch [1940] 1966: 63–4; Hagemann 1995: 39–40; Woirol 1996: 18). Nevertheless, Wicksell wrote the passage quoted above as a criticism of Marx, not Ricardo, since he put emphasis in the 1890 article on the compensation mechanisms mentioned by Ricardo himself in the rest of his new chapter.[2] Indeed, Wicksell completed his discussion by pointing out that:

> one qualification, already partly pointed out by Ricardo [see *Works*, vol. 1: 393], is that to be effective the new demand must naturally be directed towards necessities (or personal services) where the ratio of human labour to value is *as strong a proportion* as for the articles which have been made cheaper by machines. If this condition remains unmet, then one cannot claim that a complete compensation takes place.
>
> (1890: 256, italics in original)

Wicksell believed that the empirical evidence suggested that such conditions had been met and that the introduction of machinery had been accompanied by higher real wages and employment opportunities (ibid.). The upshot is that:

> besides the occasional frictions and the difficulties involved in changing from one occupation to another, it is consequently impossible to see how the labour-saving methods or these machines could damage the workers, when it is self-evident that in their capacity as consumers they have precisely the same benefit as all other consumers from commodities having become cheaper.
>
> (ibid.: 255)[3]

The relationship between technical progress and the business cycle is, according to Wicksell (1890, sections 9 and 10; see Boianovsky 1995), the opposite of that suggested by the Marxian over-production approach. The pace of technical progress affects aggregate effective demand through its impact on investment in fixed capital, and unemployment is explained by excess saving in the downturn.

Wicksell did not repeat his 1890 'compensation' analysis in the *Lectures*, except in part for a brief discussion of the history of the debates over the apparently conflicting effects of the introduction of machinery on the welfare of workers:

> The most striking feature of machinery is that it replaces human labour, i.e. allows us to produce the same quantity of goods as before with less labour; and consequently, as a rule, more goods with the *same* labour. On the one hand, it may be thought that the greater productivity of labour ought to bring about . . . the payment of higher wages; on the other hand, it is commonly supposed to render a number of labourers superfluous, so that competition among the unemployed would depress wages . . . Opinions on this point have varied in the course of time. Formerly, under the influence of the mercantilist theory, no doubt at all was felt that labour-saving machinery took the bread from the mouths of workers . . . The victory of the physiocratic school produced a sudden change, especially as formulated by J.B. Say, goods must always ultimately exchange against, and therefore constitute a demand for, other goods; an increased productivity of labour should of itself lead to an increased demand for goods hitherto not consumed, or consumed only on a small scale, and therefore for labour to produce them. Hence, machinery would, at most, cause temporary unemployment and inconvenience to certain group of labourers. In the long run it would be beneficial, would lead to increased opportunities for labour, and would rise and not lower wages.
>
> (Wicksell [1901b] 1934: 134–5)[4]

This description of the compensation mechanism fits very well with Wicksell's own interpretation in 1890. The 'Law of Markets' approach to the effects of technical change on employment and real wages became dominant during the theoretical disputes over technological unemployment in the 1930s, especially after the 1931 book by P.H. Douglas and A. Director (see Neisser 1942: section 2; Woirol 1996: Chapter 3). Ricardo's acceptance in his new chapter of the proposition that the introduction of labour-saving methods may be profitable to employers even when it involves a decrease in the size of the product was almost completely passed over as empirically unlikely or theoretically unthinkable by authors from McCulloch ([1825] 1965: Part I, Chapter VII) to Marx ([1905] 1968: 560–1) and Kaldor (1932: 186), among many others. Not by Wicksell, though. He argued that the 'optimistic view' received a setback when Ricardo's new chapter came out, since in this case 'the labourers could not be compensated by an increased demand for other commodities' (Wicksell [1901b] 1934: 135). Wicksell had already mentioned in his 1890 (p. 256) piece that the compensation mechanism would not work:

> if the introduction of particular agricultural machines (for example, hay making machines) made it advantageous for the landowner to turn the fields over to permanent pasture. He would then be employing a smaller number of workers, achieving thereby perhaps a higher net profit, but the gross yield would be decreased.

Wicksell, however, did not dwell on that. In the *Lectures*, nonetheless, Ricardo's machinery problem provided the starting point for Wicksell's own analysis of the impact of labour-saving technical change on real wages and employment, this time based on the theory of marginal productivity instead of an application of Say's Law to the labour market (see Neisser 1942, for a distinction between the 'Law of Markets approach' described above and the 'neoclassical equilibrium approach' based on the analysis of the effects of changes in real wages on the margin of substitution between production factors). As discussed next, Wicksell argued in the *Lectures*, against Ricardo, that labour-saving technical progress cannot bring about a reduction in aggregate output in the long run, but this does not vindicate the 'Law of Markets' view, since real wages fall in the process. As Wicksell put it in a letter of 1924 to J.M. Keynes:

> when [McCulloch] says that the case supposed by Mr Ricardo is 'possible but exceedingly unlikely ever to occur', he turns the argument upside down: in fact Ricardo's *suppositions* are not at all unlikely to occur, but the *conclusions* drawn from them are impossible.
>
> (Jonung 1981: 199)

The machinery problem and real wages

Schumpeter (1954: 943–4) pointed out that the development between 1870 and 1914 of the theory of marginal productivity of labour as a determinant of demand for labour and real wages was a slow process that did not fully show its usefulness in application to particular problems. According to Schumpeter:

> In consequence of this, we find that many labour problems continued to be treated by means of the tools that had served the 'classics'. This holds in particular for the machinery problem. It received plenty of attention but analysis rarely rose above the old arguments pro and con the 'compensation theory'.

Schumpeter's assessment certainly applies to most neoclassical economists of that period, but not to Wicksell, who, immediately after his summing up of the historical development of the debate on the machinery problem, observed that 'the theory of marginal productivity will enable us, I believe, to put it on a firmer foundation, and to substitute something better for this vague, and even in part erroneous, analysis' ([1901b] 1934: 135).[5] The first task, according to Wicksell, was to clarify the meaning of the expression 'productivity of labour' by distinguishing average from marginal productivity. It was in that context that he made the fundamental remark that:

> an increase in the total product as a result of technical changes in the process of production need not by any means lead to an increase – and certainly not a uniform increase – in the marginal productivity of both factors of production [land and labour].
>
> (ibid.)

This remark is followed by a discussion of the several possible cases of change in marginal productivity of land and labour induced by technical changes (ibid.: 135–6), but the treatment is clearer in Wicksell's manuscript lecture notes on technical change, held in the Wicksell archives (Lund University Library). The lectures were delivered in the spring 1900 term.

Wicksell started by pointing out that it is impossible to tell *a priori* which tendency will prevail when technical change increases the average productivity of labour: higher wage caused by an increase in average productivity or lower wage brought about by excess supply in the labour market. He then distinguished between three cases, according to the effect of technical change on the marginal productivity of production factors land and labour: (i) 'a more or less even rise in [average] productivity can take place', so that both the marginal productivity of land and labour are increased, together with real wages and land rent (see Figure

5.1); (ii) 'it can, however, happen that the productivity curve mainly rises on the right, such that the increase in the marginal productivity of labour is greater than the increase in the average productivity', so that wages rise, 'but mainly at the cost of rent', since the marginal productivity of land is reduced when technical change is land-saving (see Figure 5.2); and (iii) 'it can also happen (and this is a very important, though often overlooked case) that the increase takes place on the left side of the productivity curve, whereas the right side is lowered', so that 'the average productivity of labour rises significantly more than the marginal productivity', and rent rises at the cost of wages (see Figure 5.3). In all the figures, the old technique is expressed by alpha and the new one by beta. The third case, corresponding to the introduction of labour-saving machinery in agriculture, is discussed in detail by Wicksell in the *Lectures* ([1901b] 1934: 137–40), while the second case is briefly mentioned (ibid.: 135–6) and the first one is only implicitly discussed (ibid.: 143). One of the striking features of Figures 5.2 and 5.3 is that the curves of marginal (and average) productivity of the old and new technique intersect; that is, the average productivity of labour in one technique never exceeds the average productivity of the other technique for all land/labour ratios. As pointed out by Coleman (1985: 356, 364), this is in marked contrast with modern analysis of technical change in terms of labour (or land) 'augmenting', and lies behind Wicksell's result in his *Lectures* (again in contrast with the usual current approach) that *both* techniques will be used in equilibrium. Coleman's comment that Wicksell did not contemplate the possibility of technical change increasing the average productivity of labour at all labour/land ratios applies only (in part) to the printed *Lectures*, since in the lecture notes he discussed it as

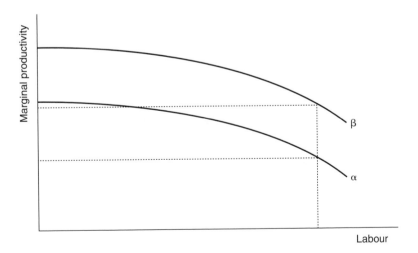

Figure 5.1 Neutral technical change (source: adapted from Wicksell (1900 Lecture notes)).

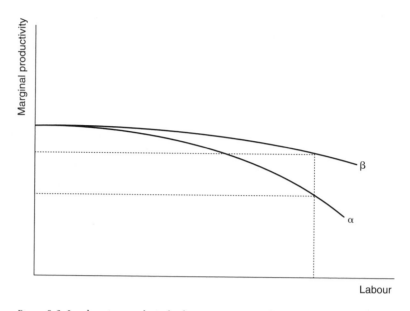

Figure 5.2 Land-saving technical change (source: adapted from Wicksell (1900 Lecture notes)).

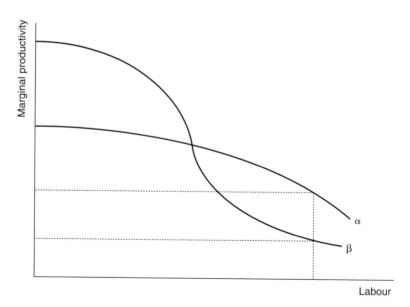

Figure 5.3 Labour-saving technical change (source: adapted from Wicksell (1900 Lecture notes)).

case (i), which may be regarded as 'neutral' technical change in Wicksell's framework. As is clear from Figure 5.1, in that case only the new technique will be used, just as in the modern 'augmenting' approach. This is implicit in Wicksell's ([1901b] 1934: 143) remark that his previous analysis 'does not exclude the possibility that the great majority of inventions and technical improvements may be beneficial in both directions; i.e. may in themselves tend to increase the marginal productivity of both labour and land'.

Wicksell focused on the labour-saving innovation case in the *Lectures* because of his critical interest in Ricardo's claim that the introduction of a competitively viable invention (that reduces average costs of production) may reduce output. Ricardo's analysis of the machinery problem represents, as observed by Wicksell ([1901b] 1934: 137; [1913] 1958: 169), an important apparent objection to the proposition that free competition must result in the maximum possible output, that is, the notion that perfect competition is Pareto optimal:

> But what is of the greatest importance – and what Pareto, with all his learned formulae, has quite forgotten – is to explain the apparent or real contradiction between this proposition and the impressions and opinions of everyday life. No less an economist than Ricardo attempted to show, in the well-known chapter 'On Machinery' added to the third edition of his *Principles*, that the private advantage of a producer might very well be better suited by a *decrease* of his gross product, instead of an increase, and in doing so he appears to have been expressing what experience teaches us . . . Nevertheless, the proposition mentioned is presumably quite correct: Ricardo did not follow the thread of his reasoning to its end.
>
> (Wicksell [1913] 1958: 169–70; italics in the original; see also [1901b] 1934: 196–7)

Wicksell, however, was at pains to stress that Pareto optimality only applies to the maximization of production in free competition, not to maximum utility or satisfaction. As shown elsewhere in the *Lectures* (1901b: 72–83) as criticism of Walras and Pareto, this is only true if the utility functions are the same for all agents and if the final equilibrium is independent of the final quantity of goods possessed, which is the case when all parties are initially equal economically (see also Myint 1948: 104–14). Hence, as illustrated by Wicksell's analysis of the machinery problem, the maximization of output may be associated with a reduction on the distributive share of one of the factors of production (labour in this case). 'This shows the serious error of those who see in free competition a sufficient means for the maximum satisfaction of the needs or desires of all members of society' (Wicksell [1901b] 1934: 141).

The conclusion that, under free competition, a diminution of output cannot result from technical innovation was regarded by Wicksell ([1901b] 1934: 137;

see also [1913] 1958: 168) as 'self-evident', for in that case 'anybody would be able, with the given means of production, to bring about at some point an increase of the product and thereby reap a profit as entrepreneur'. However, the demonstration of the proposition is nothing but self-evident, since it involves the notion that the transition to production with smaller output at the new labour-saving technique cannot be universal, only partial. In order to carry out such a demonstration, Wicksell clearly separated in the *Lectures* the issue of the effects of labour-saving innovation on the distributive shares from the question of the production of the new machines by conversion of circulating capital into fixed capital (that is, a change in the structure of capital, in Wicksellian terms). These two issues were generally mixed together by Ricardo and the classical economists, since they usually assumed that real wages are determined by the wage-fund (circulating capital) in the short run and that machinery substitutes for labour (see Samuelson 1994, on what he calls the 'classical classical fallacy' that fixed capital is prejudicial and circulating capital is favourable to labour). Wicksell discussed changes in capital structure caused by technical change elsewhere in the *Lectures* ([1901b] 1934: 163–4) and later on dealt with the Ricardian wage-fund formulation of the machinery problem ([1923] 1981: 201–3). His detailed treatment of technical change in the *Lectures* ([1901b] 1934: 133–44) was based on an economy with land and labour only, since he was mainly concerned at that stage with the quality of machinery of 'modifying the conditions under which labour and land replace each other at the margin of production', not with the fact that it represents capital. 'In other words, we shall regard machinery as *indirectly* employed (not as saved or "stored up") labour and land' (ibid.: 134). Wicksell assumed, as in the passage quoted above from his 1890 article, that labour-saving machinery is introduced into agriculture and makes pastoral agriculture more profitable than arable farming, so that the value of product (per farm), 'though certainly less, produces a larger net yield, owing to the saving of labour' (ibid.: 137). This is in the spirit of Ricardo's ([1821] 1951: 394; see Samuelson 1989: 50–1) example of horse-labour that replaces man-labour, as pointed out by Wicksell ([1923] 1981: 203).

Wicksell ([1901b] 1934: 136) mentioned the objection that the immediate negative effects of labour-saving innovation on real wages could be compensated for by the expenditure of the increased land rents on consumption of luxury articles, 'so that wages would again rise. But this circumstance is, as will easily be seen, only of secondary importance. It may more or less modify the first probable result but can scarcely reverse it' (see also Samuelson 1988: 278, for a similar result). In order to prevent this secondary complication and simplify the analysis, Wicksell assumed that only one commodity is produced, which is the assumption usually made in his aggregate theory of production and distribution throughout Part II of Volume I of the *Lectures* (see, e.g., p. 103). The introduction of labour-saving machinery is interpreted as a change in the production function of the economy, along the lines of the third case of his lecture notes of 1900. Instead of depicting the old and new marginal productivity curves on the same diagram as in the lecture notes (see Figure 5.3), Wicksell ([1901b] 1934: 139) used two diagrams to illustrate the technical change (see Figure 5.4), but the essential idea that the curves intersect is of course present in figure 5.4. As explained by Wicksell (ibid.), in Figure 5.4. a smaller number of workers are employed on an equal area of land, with a smaller gross product (the total area under the curve at the initial real wage) but a greater 'net profit' (that is, land rent, measured by the upper part of the area under the curve). The equilibrium allocation of land and labour between the two techniques is decided by profit (rent) maximization by landowners, which leads to an allocation so that the marginal productivity of labour and land are the same under both the new and the old technique, as well as real wages and rent (see Figure 5.5). A crucial assumption behind Wicksell's argument is that the introduction of the new technique is gradual, that is, only one or a few farmers/entrepreneurs have access to the new production method, which assures them a temporary extra ('Schumpeterian') profit and stimulates other producers to follow (see Ricardo [1821] 1951: 387, for a similar assumption; cf. Wicksell [1923] 1981: 202). The final equilibrium allocation is explained by the effects of lower real wages (caused by the dismissal of workers from the farms adopting the new technique) on the profitability of the old (labour-intensive) production method.

> The direct consequence [of the introduction of labour-saving machinery] must be that one or more farmers will go over to the more profitable form of production. If all were to follow their example, there would certainly be more or less considerable diminution of the total output (or of its exchange value), *but this does not happen.* For as soon as a number of labourers have been made superfluous by these changes, and wages have accordingly fallen, then, as Ricardo failed to see, the old methods of production . . . will become more profitable; they will develop, using labour more intensively and absorb the surplus of idle labourers. It can be rigorously proved that equilibrium in this case necessarily presupposes a *division* of production between the old and the new methods so that net profits of the entrepreneur will be equally great in both branches of production and the total product, or its exchange value, will reach the maximum physically possible, and will thus finally increase, and not decrease.
>
> (Wicksell [1901b] 1934: 137–8)

Wicksell then shows by means of a numerical example, and by diagrammatic and algebraic analysis that the conditions necessary to maximize profit are the same as those necessary to maximize output, which refutes Ricardo's analysis of technological unemployment (ibid.: 138–40; see also Lederer 1938: 201, for a

(a)

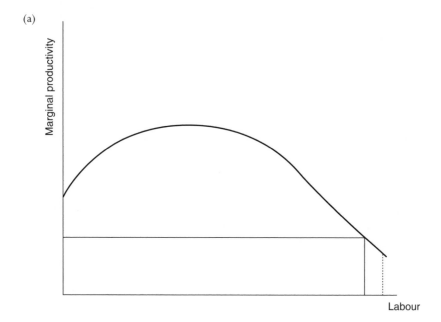

(b)

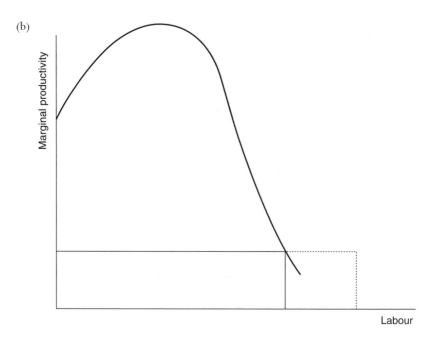

Figure 5.4 (a) Old and (b) new techniques (source: Adapted from Wicksell ([1901a]
1934: 139)).

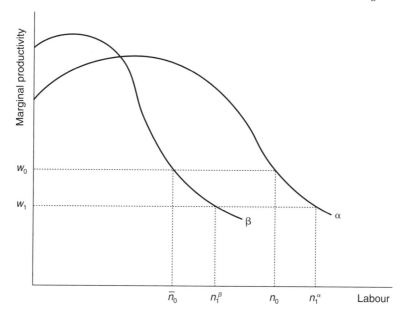

Figure 5.5 Equilibrium allocation between old and new techniques (source: adapted from Hansson (1983, 52) and Coleman (1985: 361)).

discussion of Wicksell's numerical illustration; and Hansson 1983, and Coleman 1985, for a discussion of Wicksell's mathematical and graphical arguments). The numerical example shows that the fall in wages brings about some reabsorption of workers in the farms that adopt the new technique, but that the decisive factor is that the 'old' farms are more favoured by the wage reduction than the 'new' ones, so that they will eventually have the same profit and the inducement to go over to the new technique will disappear. It is only implicit in Wicksell's exercise that the aggregate demand for labour in the new equilibrium will not exceed the number of workers. If there is excess demand for labour, this will not be an equilibrium; instead, real wages will go up (although not as high as their level before technical change) and only the new technique will be adopted. This, however, does not affect Wicksell's original result of maximum output and full employment after the technical change (see Hansson 1983: 53; Coleman 1985: 361).[6]

After all the effects of the labour-saving innovation are accounted for, the economy will settle at a higher aggregate output and the same (full) level of employment, but the absolute and relative shares of workers in national income will be lower. As pointed out by Wicksell ([1901b] 1934: 140), the wage reduction in the new equilibrium follows from the assumption that output is less in the farms cultivated by the new method, that is, the average product of land in the new technique is lower than in the old one. As shown by Coleman (1985: 358–60), this is equivalent to the condition that the (profit-maximizing) average product of labour in the new technique is higher than in the old one, although the marginal product is lower. This means that the elasticity of output with respect to labour (measured by the ratio between the marginal product and the average product of labour) is reduced by the labour-saving innovation (see Kliman 1997: 39). Since that ratio is also equal to the relative share of labour under the assumption of a Cobb-Douglas production function (introduced by Wicksell in his production theory), the effect of technical change on income distribution is readily seen. It is worth noting that the equilibration mechanism put forward by Wicksell does not involve a reversion to old methods of production, but an interruption of the spreading of the new method. It is not, therefore, subject to the criticism (see, e.g., Vivarelli 1995: 38) that such a reversion could not take place because of 'locked in' technologies. Furthermore, the notion (see ibid.: 36) that Wicksell inaugurated the neoclassical view that wage flexibility renders permanent technological unemployment impossible must be examined with care, since (apart from Lederer 1938, and especially Neisser [1932] 1990 and 1942), Wicksell's analysis of labour-saving technical change and of the equilibration mechanism had no impact on the literature on technical change started in the 1930s. Both Hicks ([1932] 1963: 121) and Kaldor (1932: 186) refer to the German edition of Wicksell's *Lectures* in support of their dismissal of Ricardo's claim that output can be reduced by the introduction of machinery, but there is no mention at all of Wicksell's careful discussion of the equilibrating mechanism and its consequences for the determination of real wages. Furthermore, although Wicksell assumed in the *Lectures* a neoclassical production function with continuous substitution between land and labour, this is not necessary for his main result, which is based on the profitability of different techniques at various factor prices ratios. This is clear from Samuelson's (1989: 51–2) 'classical numerical example', where he assumed linear production functions and came to the same conclusion as Wicksell regarding the effects of a labour-saving innovation on the real wage and on the coexistence of the new and old techniques in the new equilibrium with maximum output and full employment. As discussed in the next section, this result also comes out of Wicksell's ([1923] 1981) re-examination of Ricardo's wage-fund model under the assumption of fixed coefficients of production. But in the 1920s Wicksell's main motivation for going back to the machinery problem was no longer purely theoretical.

Capital, population and unemployment

In 1923 Wicksell submitted to the *Economic Journal* a manuscript on 'Ricardo on Machinery and the Present Unemployment' where, instead of reproducing his marginal productivity analysis of the *Lectures*, he attempted to tackle the machinery problem in Ricardo's own terms, that is, by assuming a wage-fund model. The paper was rejected by the then editor J.M. Keynes, on the grounds that 'the time has gone by for a criticism of Ricardo on purely Ricardian lines' (Jonung 1981: 199). It was eventually published with an introduction by Lars Jonung in 1981. Wicksell's 1923 paper on machinery was motivated by the continuous high rate of unemployment in Sweden and elsewhere in the 1920s, which could not be described just as part of a downturn of the business cycle (see Jonung 1981: 195; Boianovsky and Trautwein 2003: section 4). As Wicksell put it in his reply to Keynes in 1924:

> The true refutation of Ricardo's doctrine shows that he was *right* in believing that the introduction of machinery would cause the wages to fall; and indeed this falling of wages would in this case be a necessary condition for the gross product reaching its great amount. In other words the *total* product will increase but the *marginal* product will diminish, and if this latter goes far enough, unemployment will be the unavoidable consequence *unless labour is partly supported from other sources than wages.*
>
> (Jonung 1981: 200; italics in the original)

Despite Wicksell's mention of marginal product in the letter, the argument of his 1923 paper is based on a critical restatement of Ricardo's ([1821] 1951: 388–90) discussion of the introduction of machinery through the conversion of circulating into fixed capital. In his numerical example Ricardo assumed that, before the introduction of the new technique, the capitalist has a capital stock of £20,000, divided into fixed (£7,000) and circulating capital (£13,000). The rate of profit is 10 per cent and consequently the gross product is £15,000, formed by wages (£13,000) and net product (£2,000). In the following (interim) period a new machine is built with half of the workers hitherto used in the production of consumption goods, which involves a corresponding cut in its output. The flow of total output (now formed by consumption and capital goods) in the interim period is thus maintained at its initial level. However, once the transition to the new technique has been made in the next period and the new machine is fully used, the economy reverts to the production of consumption goods only, which remains at the same reduced level of the interim period (£7,500). Hence, only £5,500 can now be allocated to generate demand for labour. As pointed out by Barkai (1986: 601) in his careful description of Ricardo's example, the phasing in of the new technology involves at the same time a reduction in the labour/output ratio and a rise in the capital/output ratio. The sum of the two changes – the reduction in the output of consumption goods in the interim period, and the reduction in the labour coefficient in the last period – reduces the demand for labour from 130 units to 55, under the assumption (made by Wicksell [1923] 1981: 202, and by Barkai 1986: 599) that the initial wage determined by the wage fund is £100. Ricardo stops his numerical exercise at this point, but, according to Wicksell ([1923] 1981), the logic of the wage fund model suggests that the competition among the 75 unemployed men will lower wages and

> as soon as they have diminished by only 1 per cent or even somewhat less, there will be room, i.e. capital enough, for one labourer more in each of those businesses [assuming that there are other 75 capitalists with the same business as the one mentioned by Ricardo], so that the redundancy of labourers will cease.

Although all capitalists benefit by this reduction of wages, the employers in the old-fashioned businesses benefit to a greater extent (say, £100) than the new businesses (£50), so that a point of equilibrium will be reached where no further transition will take place, as in his previous marginal productivity discussion in the *Lectures*. Again, the increase of output in the old-fashioned businesses outweighs the reduction of output in the new businesses, since (under Ricardo's assumption of fixed coefficients and absence of diminishing return), the 75 disengaged men will produce in their new engagements the same amount as before, but the 55 remaining men will (by Ricardo's assumption) produce more than before. Hence, Wicksell's previous result of an increase of aggregate output through a reduction of real wages is replicated by an application of the Ricardian original wage-fund model to labour-saving technical change. He now generalizes the argument for an economy with more than one commodity and some degree of real wage rigidity:

> An important and most remarkable thing is that the fall of wages in this case becomes a necessary condition for the production of the maximum of the aggregate. Of course it may well be the case that the discharged labourers, in order to avoid competition with their comrades, turn to other branches of industry. If so, perhaps all the farmers will adopt the new methods, and the point of equilibrium will then, as it were, be situated not in that particular branch of business, but in some other, but even then our general conclusion remains intact, at any rate so long as the country itself can be regarded as an isolated community.
>
> ([1923] 1981: 203)[7]

In his books Wicksell was, of course, critical of the wage-fund approach to capital theory, since the division of the capital stock between the part used to pay for the wages (circulating capital) and the part accumulated as durable capital goods (fixed capital) should not be seen as given by technology, but as an economic decision determined by the wage level itself (see Wicksell [1893] 1954: 145; Boianovsky 1998: 546–7). In the *Lectures* he introduced the concept of stratification of capital through time, that is, the notion that the capital structure has both a vertical and a horizontal dimension. The former refers to the proportion of primary factors (land and labour) annually invested in the replacement of capital goods of different maturity dates, while the latter describes the length of time for which the various capital goods are invested (see Wicksell [1901b] 1934: Part II, Chapter 2; Uhr 1960: Chapter 5). It was in that context that Wicksell ([1901b] 1934: 164) examined the effects of a technical invention that increases the marginal productivity of capital and renders long-term investment, for a given capital aggregate, more profitable than previously:

> The consequence must necessarily be – as long as no further capital is saved – a diminution in the horizontal-dimension and an increase in the vertical-dimension, so that the quantity of capital used in the course of the year will be reduced; an increased quantity of current labour and land will consequently become available for each year's direct production; and, although this need not necessarily cause their marginal productivity and share in the product to be reduced – since the total product has simultaneously been increased by the technical discovery – yet a reduction may clearly result . . . The great inventions by which industry has from time to time been revolutionized, at first reduced a number of workers to beggary, as experience shows, whilst causing the profits of the capitalists to soar . . . That the 'transformation of circulating into fixed capital', i.e. the changes from short-term to long-term capital investments, may frequently injure labour is beyond doubt. But Ricardo was mistaken in his belief that this consequence was due to the fact that the gross product is simultaneously reduced. This is, as may easily be proved, theoretically inconceivable.

As observed by Gourvitch ([1940] 1966: 117) as a comment to this passage, Wicksell 'was one of the few modern economists writing before 1914 who pointed out the possibility of adverse effects of inventions upon the demand for labour'. It should be pointed out that the reduction in labour demand is caused in this case not by the introduction of labour-saving innovation *per se*, but by the fall in the annual replacement requirements per unit of primary factors invested as the capital structure becomes more vertical, which brings about the possibility of a reduction of the marginal productivity of labour *and* land. In the rest of the quotation Wicksell seems to assume that the 'transformation of circulating into fixed capital' is often associated with the introduction of labour-saving machinery leading to an abrupt fall of real wages, although this is not necessarily the case.[8]

The view that the trend of technical progress was increasingly labour-saving and harmful to workers is noticeable in Wicksell's writings on the topic in the 1920s, in contrast to the *Lectures* ([1901b] 1934: 143). He pointed out ([1924] 1958: 256) that 'most technical innovations, both in agriculture and in industry, tend to be *labour-saving*'. Capital and land are substituted for labour: 'wholly or partly automatic machines, draught animals, or motor engines take the place of the old hand-power'. At the same time, 'capital goods, machines and buildings are made more durable, so that less labour is required for their maintenance or successive renewal'. Hence, Wicksell put together in 1924 the two factors mentioned in the *Lectures*, that is, the substitution of capital (and land) for labour, and the introduction of long-term capital goods with lower replacement requirements. This leads to the 'social paradox' that the efficiency of labour rises significantly because of technical progress, 'whereas the *marginal* productivity of labour and therefore the wage for unskilled work falls very low, perhaps below the subsistence minimum' (ibid.; italics in the original). This scenario is the same discussed in Wicksell's 1923 paper and the policy conclusion is that the fixing of a minimum living wage would only give rise to 'permanent unemployment' and diminish the social product ([1924] 1958: 257; cf. [1923] 1981: 205). In the long-run, of course, real wages below the subsistence minimum would be followed by a reduction in population size through emigration or limitation of births, which would reduce permanently the labour supply and therefore the employment level (see Boianovsky 2001, for Wicksell's views on population). However, as pointed out by Wicksell ([1923] 1981: 205), in the case of a reduction of real wages caused by labour-saving technical change, it is likely that the social output is more than enough to yield a sufficiently high income per capita but at the same time the marginal productivity of labour is below subsistence level. Wicksell's suggested solution to the paradox is to make the difference between the equilibrium wage rate and subsistence by subsidies to workers:

> The only completely rational way to achieve the largest possible production . . . would be to allow all production factors to find their equilibrium positions unhindered, under free competition, however low they may be, but at the same time to discard resolutely the principle that the worker's only source of income is his wages. He, like every other citizen, ought rather to be entitled to a certain share of the earnings of the society's natural resources and capital.
>
> ([1924] 1958: 257)

Wicksell's 1901 criticism of Ricardo has been rejected by Samuelson (1988, 1989, 1994) on the grounds that the introduction of labour-saving machinery is able to bring about a reduction of the social output through its effect on real wages and, therefore, on population and labour supply. Samuelson (1989: 47) claims that, despite the absence of clear textual evidence in the new chapter on machinery, Ricardo assumed that wages are at their subsistence level in long-run classical equilibrium before the introduction of machinery. According to Samuelson (ibid.: 52), Wicksell overlooked the crucial role of the population mechanism in bringing about a reduction of output in Ricardo's machinery problem, so that the employment level falls but there is no unemployment in equilibrium after the introduction of the new machine. However, as should be clear from our discussion above, Wicksell did not neglect the implications for the population size of real wages below subsistence. Already in the *Lectures* ([1901b] 1934: 141, first paragraph), Wicksell considered the possibility that real wages might fall below subsistence and briefly suggested the subsidy plan described above. In the first Swedish edition of the *Lectures*, that paragraph starts with an explicit comment on Ricardo that was later removed from the second and third editions, from which was made the English translation. The remark sounds like an anticipation of Samuelson's criticism: 'One could object that, according to Ricardo's assumption, wages are already at their living minimum and therefore cannot be further reduced; this should then apparently justify his thesis, but actually not' (Wicksell 1901a: 168). Furthermore, Samuelson's (ibid.) conclusion that in Ricardo's new equilibrium with less output, lower population and subsistence wage only the new technique will be used (instead of Wicksell's equilibrium with new and old techniques) is formally the same one obtained by Wicksell ([1923] 1981: 204, italics in the original) under the assumption of a minimum wage:

> If, on the other hand, the original wages were regarded by law as *minimum* wages and were not permitted to be diminished by the employers . . . there would apparently be a general transition on the part of the farmers to the new-fashioned 'labour-saving' methods.

Therefore, contrary to Samuelson (1989), we may say that 'Wicksell was right!'.[9]

Wicksell's conclusion that labour-saving machinery may diminish the marginal productivity and the real wages of labour below subsistence and all the way down to zero is important in order to assess his interpretation of 'permanent' unemployment in the 1920s (for the distinction between normal, cyclical and permanent unemployment in Wicksell, see Boianovsky and Trautwein 2003). In an unpublished, undated and unfinished manuscript on unemployment, probably written in the 1920s, Wicksell referred to the fact that machinery had in some degree replaced labour in all areas of economic activity (the manuscript is translated as an appendix to Boianovsky and Trautwein 2003). 'If you think of all this, you will be no longer surprised by the [present] unemployment, but rather be puzzled that under these conditions human labour – and, in particular, ordinary, simple manual labour – can find a market at all.' Even if there is a demand for part of the labour force, permanent unemployment will eventually bring the short-run market clearing wages down to zero, since labour becomes a free good with zero marginal productivity:

> Assume that a quarter of the existing labour force were sufficient to control the machines and to maintain them, then the other three-quarters would

become redundant and their work would not be of any value; actually all labour would become worthless, since one worker cannot receive more than the other, if both have the same skills.

At first sight, the undated manuscript may look like a recantation of Wicksell's previous analysis of the machinery problem in the *Lectures*, but actually it is a logical corollary of that analysis when the marginal productivity of labour keeps falling until it reaches zero level and the old techniques are no longer used. Indeed, Wicksell refers in the manuscript to the fact that in his 'childhood days' there was a great demand for manual labour in jobs where machines had not been invented yet, that is, the old production methods were still used. Sylos-Labini (1969: 135) realized that, under the assumption that mechanization of production is an uninterrupted process in Wicksell's framework, wages would tend to zero. However, the inference from this is not, contrary to Sylos-Labini's criticism of Wicksell, that the continuance of mechanization is logically incompatible with perfect downward flexibility of real wages, but that the system would converge to a position at zero wages with only part of the labour force absorbed, as suggested by Wicksell in the manuscript. Such a scenario has been discussed by Samuelson (1988: 277–9; 1989: 50–1; 1994: 633) under the assumption of a strong labour-saving technical change.

The notion of labour as a non-scarce production factor with zero price can be found also in Wicksell's published writings. In his well-known review of Cassel ([1918] 1932), Wicksell repeated his thesis that, although free competition tends to maximize aggregate output, it does not generally lead to a distribution of that product consistent with maximum satisfaction. In particular, Wicksell ([1919] 1934: 228) stressed that Cassel's simultaneous equations in general equilibrium 'are no guarantee that any "variable" cannot assume the value nil, even if we are discussing so important a social factor as wages'. This was the first reference in the literature to what would become known later as the 'rule of free goods' (see Neisser [1932] 1990). It should be noted that the undated manuscript is also consistent with Wicksell's general framework in the sense that, despite zero marginal productivity of labour and technological unemployment, output is at its maximum level. This situation is captured by J.S. Mill's ([1848] 1909: 79) famous phrase 'demand for commodities is not demand for labour', of which Wicksell approved: 'We must recognize the truth of Mill's well-known principle that demand for commodities is not the same as demand for labour – unless it results in the accumulation of new capital' (Wicksell [1901b] 1934: 191). In the scenario entertained in the undated manuscript, unemployment can only disappear either through Malthusian elimination of three-quarters of the population or via capital accumulation. As put by Wicksell (ibid.: 164), 'the capitalist saver is . . . fundamentally the friend of labour, though the technical inventor is not infrequently its enemy'. Technological unemployment is, therefore, associated with capital shortage, a thesis that would be further developed by Hans Neisser and other members of the 'Kiel School' in Germany in the late 1920s and early 1930s (see Hagemann 1990).[10]

Conclusion

Our investigation of the development of Wicksell's views on technical change has shown that his notion of technological unemployment is not incompatible with the criticism of Ricardo in the *Lectures* and elsewhere, but a corollary of that criticism. The main conclusion of Wicksell's careful discussion of labour-saving technical change in the *Lectures* and in the 1900 lecture notes is that it tends to reduce the marginal productivity of labour and push the wage rate downwards. This set him apart from most of the contemporary neoclassical literature and represented a change from his 1890 pro-compensation view. Together with Marx, Wicksell was one of the few economists who took seriously Ricardo's attempted demonstration that the introduction of machinery could be harmful to workers. However, Marx's and Wicksell's respective interpretations of how labour-saving technical change affects real wages and employment are, of course, quite different. Wicksell's analysis is based on the notion that, as labour-saving technical progress advances, the labour demand (that is, the marginal productivity) curve tends to become less elastic, which means that a larger reduction of real wages is necessary in order to induce employment to remain at its full level, until eventually (for a given capital stock) the market clearing wage rate reaches zero and the reabsorption of unemployed workers cannot take place; technological unemployment may also come about if real wages become rigid downwards below their subsistence level. Apart from Lederer (1938) and especially Neisser (1942), Wicksell's insight on the effects of labour-saving innovations on wages and employment did not make a strong impact in the literature, since his concept of different forms of technical change differed from the framework developed by Hicks (1932), Robinson (1938) and others in the 1930s.

Acknowledgements

We would like to thank, without implicating, Neil de Marchi, Paul Samuelson and Hans-Michael Trautwein for helpful discussions on an earlier draft. We have also benefited from comments by Gislain Deleplace and other participants at the 2003 meeting of the European Society for the History of Economic Thought. Eric Nicander has kindly helped us with the Wicksell Archives (Lund University Library). This chapter is part of the PROBRAL project on Monetary Stabilization, Capital Flows and Employment funded by CAPES (Brazil) and DAAD (Germany). Mauro Boianovsky gratefully acknowledges a research grant from the Brazilian Research Council (CNPq).

Notes

1 Wicksell's reading of Marx is consistent with interpretations found elsewhere in the literature. See, e.g., Gourvitch ([1940] 1966: 73–9) and Hagemann (1995).

2 One of the difficulties of Ricardo's new chapter is its uncharacteristic vagueness, which has left it open to different interpretations (see Schumpeter 1954: 683).

3 See also Boianovsky and Trautwein (2003) for Wicksell's use of the phrase 'normal unemployment' – consistent with equilibrium in the labour market – to describe unemployment of the frictional kind.

4 See also Gourvitch ([1940] 1966: 20–33, 46–8) on the treatment of the machinery question by the mercantilists, physiocrats and Say.

5 According to Marshall ([1890] 1990: 596–7), 'mechanical progress' is necessarily beneficial to the working classes, since it increases the 'national dividend'. In the same vein, Clark ([1899] 1965: 405) argued that an invention always raises real wages, for 'wages now tend to equal what labor can now produce, and this is more than it could formerly produce'. Like Marshall, Cassel ([1918] 1932: 340) claimed that 'technical progress results in an increase in the total production of society and thus an increase in its total income. From this there results a general increase in the demand for labour.' See also Walras ([1898] 1936: 273) for a similar passage. Walras's comments attracted Wicksell's ([1899] 1999: 179) criticism: 'Concerning the labour question, [Walras] shows no understanding of the drawbacks of labour-saving machines, to which already Ricardo had drawn attention.'

6 Interestingly enough, Marx ([1867] 1938: 390) mentioned that a reduction in the real wage rate caused by the introduction of machinery could encourage capitalists to switch back to labour-intensive methods and interrupt the process of diffusion of the new technology:

> In the older countries, machinery, when employed in some branches of industry, creates such a redundancy of labour in other branches that in these latter the fall of wages below the value of labour-power impedes the use of machinery and . . . renders that use superfluous and often impossible.

Marx, however, did not draw Wicksell's conclusion about the effects of lower wages on the absorption of the dismissed workers.

7 For a discussion of Wicksell's application of his argument about technical change to an open economy, see Herlitz (2002: 491–5).

8 In his 1902 lecture notes on economic crisis, Wicksell suggested that this mechanism could clarify the argument by the classical economists about the upper turning point of the business cycle.

> The classical economists pointed out that crises were preceded by an immobilization of circulating capital, thereby reducing the 'wage fund'. That certainly lacks clarity, like the whole theory of wage funds; but the truth in this argument could perhaps be expressed as follows: productive forces are detracted not only from the production of the usual necessities . . . but from the renewal of the more or less circulating or fixed capital employed in this production, too. In that case, workers cannot be employed before this capital is due to be replaced, etc.
>
> (Boianovsky and Trautwein 2001: 358)

See also Hayek (1941: Appendix II) for a treatment of Ricardo's machinery problem from the perspective of Austrian capital theory. According to Hayek, the transition from one capital structure to another may be incomplete if there is a lengthening of investment periods of some inputs without a compensating shortening of others. This can bring about capital scarcity in the crisis, but of a kind different from the one discussed by Wicksell and the Kiel School in connection with persistent unemployment in the 1920s (see the last paragraph of this section).

9 Wicksell usually assumed an exogenously given labour supply in his general theory of production and distribution, as well as in his treatment of the effects of technical change. As pointed out by Kliman (1997), if labour supply is a positive function of real wages, the equilibrium level of employment will necessarily fall when labour-saving technical change is introduced.

10 Such a notion of technological unemployment can be also found in Dennis Robertson's (1931: 50–1) careful discussion of the marginal productivity theory of real wages.

> The tendency to industrial rationalization is . . . a tendency to install such elaborate and expensive and durable plant, and to devise such a close and intimate co-ordination between it and the labour force required to work it, as to leave as little room as possible for the operation of the Principle of variation . . . A completely rationalized world might turn out to be one in which, if organized so as to obtain their *de facto* economic worth, a certain proportion of workpeople could find employment at a very high wages, while the remainder could hardly find it on any terms at all.

In this scenario, Robertson and Wicksell assumed implicitly John Cairnes's theory of non-competing groups in the labour market (see also Boianovsky and Trautwein 2003).

References

Barkai, H. (1986) 'Ricardo's volte-face on machinery', *Journal of Political Economy*, 94: 595–613.

Boianovsky, M. (1995) 'Wicksell's business cycle', *European Journal of the History of Economic Thought*, 2: 375–411.

—— (1998) 'Wicksell, Knut, as an interpreter of the classical economists', in Kurz, H. and Salvadori, N. (eds) *The Elgar Companion to Classical Economics*, vol. 2, Cheltenham: Edward Elgar, pp. 545–51.

—— (2001) 'Economists as demographers: Wicksell and Pareto on population', in Erreygers, G. (ed.) *Economics and Interdisciplinary Exchange*, London: Routledge.

Boianovsky, M. and Trautwein, H.-M. (2001) 'Wicksell's lecture notes on economic crises (1902/05)', *Structural Change and Economic Dynamics*, 12: 343–66.

—— (2003) 'Wicksell, Cassel and the idea of involuntary unemployment', *History of Political Economy*, 34: 385–436.

Carver, T.N. (1908) 'Machinery and labour', *Quarterly Journal of Economics*, 22: 210–32.

Cassel, G. (1918, edn 1932) *The Theory of Social Economy*, 5th edn, trans. S. Barron, New York: Harcourt, Brace.

Clark, J.B. (1899, edn 1965) *The Distribution of Wealth*, New York: A.M. Kelley.

Coleman, W. (1985) 'Wicksell on technical change and real wages', *History of Political Economy*, 17: 355–66.

Gårdlund, T. (1958) *The Life of Knut Wicksell*, Stockholm: Almquist & Wiksell.

Gourvitch, A. (1940, edn 1966) *Survey of Economic Theory on Technological Change and Employment*, New York: A.M. Kelley.

Hagemann, H. (1990) 'Introduction', in Neisser, H. ([1932] 1990) 'The wage rate and employment in market equilibrium', *Structural Change and Economic Dynamics*, 1: 141–63.

—— (1995) 'Technological unemployment', in Arestis, P. and Marshall, M. (eds) *The Political Economy of Full Employment*, Aldershot: Edward Elgar.

Hansson, B. (1983) 'Wicksell's critique of Ricardo's chapter "On Machinery"', *Journal of Economic Studies*, 10: 49–55.

Hayek, F. (1941) *The Pure Theory of Capital*, London: Routledge & Kegan Paul.

Herlitz, L. (2002) 'Wheat and wood: Wicksell, Heckscher, and the theory of foreign trade, 1896–1920', *History of Political Economy*, 34: 479–98.

Hicks, J. (1932) *The Theory of Wages*, London: Macmillan.

Jonung, L. (1981) 'Ricardo on machinery and the present unemployment: an unpublished manuscript by Knut Wicksell', *Economic Journal*, 91: 195–205.

Kaldor, N. (1932) 'A case against technical progress?', *Economica*, Old Series, 12: 180–96.

Kliman, A. (1997) 'Technological disemployment in the neoclassical model', *Review of Political* Economy, 9: 37–49.

Lederer, E. (1938) *Technical Progress and Unemployment*, Geneva: International Labour Office.

Lindahl, E. (ed.) (1958) *Knut Wicksell: Selected Papers on Economic Theory*, London: Allen and Unwin.

McCulloch (1825, edn 1965) *Principles of Political Economy*, New York: A.M. Kelley.

Marshall, A. (1890, edn 1990) *Principles of Economics*, London: Macmillan.

Marx, K. ([1867] 1938) *Capital*, vol. 1, London: Allen & Unwin.

—— ([1905] 1968) *Theories of Surplus Value*, Part II, Moscow: Progress.

Mill, J.S. ([1848–1873] 1909), *The Principles of Political Economy*, London: Macmillan.

Myint, H. (1948) *Theories of Welfare Economics*, London: LSE.

Neisser, H. ([1932] 1990) 'The wage rate and employment in market equilibrium', *Structural Change and Economic Dynamics*, 1: 141–63.

—— (1942) '"Permanent" technological unemployment', *American Economic Review*, 32: 50–71.

Ricardo, D. ([1817–1821] 1951) *On the Principles of Political Economy and Taxation*, vol. I of *The Works and Correspondence of David Ricardo*, ed. by P. Sraffa, Cambridge: Cambridge University Press.

Robertson, D.H. (1931) 'Wage-grumbles', in *Economic Fragments*, London: P.S. King & Son, pp. 42–57.

Robinson, J. (1938) 'The classification of inventions', *Review of Economic Studies*, 5: 139–42.

Samuelson, P.A. (1965) 'A theory of induced innovation along Kennedy–Weizsäcker lines', *Review of Economics and Statistics*, 47: 343–56.

—— (1988) 'Mathematical vindication of Ricardo on machinery', *Journal of Political Economy*, 96: 274–82.

—— (1989) 'Ricardo was right!', *Scandinavian Journal of Economics*, 91, 47–62.

—— (1994) 'The classical classical fallacy', *Journal of Economic Literature*, 32: 620–39.

Say, J.-B. ([1821] 1971) *A Treatise on Political Economy*, New York: A.M. Kelley.

Schumpeter, J.A. (1954) *History of Economic Analysis*, New York: Oxford University Press.

Sylos-Labini, P. (1969) *Oligopoly and Technical Progress*, Cambridge, MA: Harvard University Press.

Uhr, C.G. (1960) *Economic Doctrines of Knut Wicksell*, Berkeley, CA: University of California Press.

Vivarelli, M. (1995) *The Economics of Technology and Employment*, Aldershot: Edward Elgar.

Walras, L. ([1898] 1936) *Etudes d'économie politique appliquée*, Lausanne: F. Rouge.

Wicksell, K. (1890) 'Tomme maver – og fulde magasiner' [Empty stomachs – and full warehouses]', *Samtiden*, 1: 245–57, 293–304.

—— ([1893] 1954) *Value, Capital and Rest*, London: Allen & Unwin

—— ([1899] 1999) 'Léon Walras, *Études d'Économie Politique Appliquée*', in Sandelin, B. (ed.) *Knut Wicksell: Selected Essays in Economics*, vol. II, Chapter 27, London: Routledge.

—— (1900) 'Lecture notes on technical change', unpublished manuscript, Wicksell Archives, Lund.

—— (1901a) *Förelasningar i Nationalekonomi*, vol. 1, Lund: Gleerups.

—— ([1901] 1934) *Lectures on Political Economy*, vol. 1, trans. E. Classen, 3rd edn, London: George Routledge and Sons.

—— ([1913] 1958) 'Vilfredo Pareto's *Manuel d'Économie Politique*', in Lindahl, E. (ed.) 1958, London: Allen and Unwin, pp. 159–75.

—— ([1919] 1934) 'Professor Cassel's system of economics', trans. S. Adler, in *Lectures on Political Economy*, vol. I, pp. 219–73.

—— ([1923] 1981) 'Ricardo on machinery and the present unemployment', in Jonung, L. (ed.) *Economic Journal*, 91: 195–205.

—— ([1924] 1958), 'Protection and free trade', in Lindahl, E. (ed.) 1958, London: Allen and Unwin, pp. 250–66.

—— (Undated) 'Arbetslöshet – ett kåseri' ['Unemployment – a commentary'], unpublished manuscript, Wicksell Archives, Lund.

Woirol, G. (1996) *The Technological Unemployment and Structural Unemployment Debates*, London: Greenwood Press.

6 The loose link

Hayek, Lindahl and Myrdal on money

Hans-Michael Trautwein

Introduction

When Friedrich August von Hayek and Gunnar Myrdal were jointly awarded the Nobel Prize in Economics in 1974, both of them must have had mixed feelings about their respective co-laureate. Not only did the views of Hayek and Myrdal conflict in almost every respect of political economy, they could also look back on a peculiar personal relationship that had started at an early stage in their careers.

In 1931, when Hayek prepared his German edition of various non-German contributions to monetary theory (Hayek 1933), he asked Erik Lindahl to join the project with a paper on the ends and means of monetary policy (Shehadi 1991: 382). Lindahl, who had great difficulties in meeting deadlines with his slow and careful way of writing, declined and referred Hayek to Myrdal who had written a long essay in Swedish on the reinterpretation of Wicksell's concept of monetary equilibrium (Myrdal 1931). Even though Myrdal had, in that essay, criticized Lindahl rather harshly for his interpretation of Wicksell, Lindahl did not seem to bear him a grudge. In the German version commissioned by Hayek, Myrdal certainly toned down his criticism of Lindahl. But he did not change his basic line of argument, and Hayek never came to like Myrdal's contribution, because it contained many outright attacks on the theoretical tenets and policy conclusions that Hayek had earned a name for.

Even so, Hayek included Myrdal's article in the omnibus volume – be it as a matter of personal integrity or simply due to time pressure. In this way, he helped greatly to make Myrdal famous outside Sweden. In later years, Hayek seems to have turned nastier. He refused to allow Myrdal to give a lecture at the London School of Economics and, together with Lionel Robbins, he made life difficult for younger members of the LSE economics department – such as John Hicks, Nicholas Kaldor, George Shackle and Brinley Thomas – who had started to show a greater interest in the economics of what was later labelled the Stockholm School.[1]

Why should we rake up these old animosities again? A possible answer is that they tell us something about the fundamental issues of macroeconomic theory that were at stake in the early 1930s. There are, at least, two issues that make the confrontation of the ideas of Hayek, Lindahl and Myrdal particularly interesting. The first and foremost is the role of money in the business cycle. The second is the role and design of stabilization policy. This chapter takes a closer look (mainly) at the first issue.

Hayek developed his theory of the business cycle in the late 1920s and early 1930s. At about the same time, Erik Lindahl and Gunnar Myrdal began to work on their contributions to modern monetary macroeconomics. Both Hayek and the Swedes had a common background in the monetary theory of Knut Wicksell. They used Wicksell's analytical framework to explain fluctuations in prices, production and employment, whereas Wicksell himself had not considered his monetary theory to provide an explanation of the business cycle phenomenon.[2]

In his *Interest and Prices* (1898), Wicksell wanted to derive a theory of secular changes in the price level from a reformulation of the quantity theory of money that would hold even in the extreme case of a pure credit economy – that is, an economy in which banks could extend loans without *a priori* binding reserve constraints. Wicksell found the key to this reformulation in gaps between the market rate of interest and the 'natural rate', the rate of return to real investment. Whenever those two interest rates diverged (thereby violating Wicksell's first condition for monetary equilibrium), cumulative processes of inflation (or deflation) would be started by accommodating changes in the credit supply and corresponding changes in the demands for goods and labour. The interest rate mechanism thus helped to integrate monetary theory with (relative) price theory by modelling a direct link between the markets for money and goods through the demand for capital and the supply of credit. This was an analytical property that attracted Hayek, Lindahl and Myrdal and induced them to extend Wicksell's theory of cumulative changes in the price level to theories of changes in output and employment.

The 'Wicksell connection' of Hayek and the Swedes is obvious from the references in most of their relevant works. More recently, it has been pointed out by Leijonhufvud (1981) in his account of where modern macroeconomics lost its Wicksell connection (between Keynes's *Treatise* and *General Theory*); and it has been scrutinized by Laidler (1991, and 1999: Part I) and others. In this chapter, the focus is set more specifically on the role of monetary institutions in the theories of Hayek, Lindahl and Myrdal. In particular, it is discussed in which ways these post-Wicksellians made use of Wicksell's benchmark assumption of a pure credit economy.[3] The discussion starts, in the next section, with a review of Hayek's position. Despite Myrdal's original criticisms of Lindahl, the arguments of the two Swedes are, in this context, highly complementary so that it makes more sense to combine them in one section. The final section summarizes the main contrasts between Hayek and the Swedes.

Hayek

The real effects of credit expansions were a notorious matter of dispute in the 1920s and 1930s, and Hayek was one of the most rigorous and prominent exponents of the pessimists' view. He argued that increases in the volume of credit that are not supported by a rise in voluntary saving may nevertheless induce changes in the structures of prices and production in the short run. The additional lending of the banks redistributes purchasing power towards investment in more roundabout processes of production. In this way, a rise in the level of productivity may be generated by way of forced saving. However, according to Hayek, such non-neutralities of money must sooner or later be 'corrected' by economic crises.

Money, equilibrium and the cycle

Hayek's writings on the credit economy are part of his early research programme in which he attempted to arrive at an endogenous explanation of trade cycles that would be compatible with general equilibrium theory. In his long paper *Intertemporal Equilibrium* (1928) and in his habilitation thesis *Monetary Theory and the Trade Cycle* (1929), Hayek stressed that this could be achieved only by taking account of the fundamental non-neutrality of money. Changes in the volume of money imply one-sided changes in the demand for goods that disturb the intertemporal equilibrium position of the price system. The elasticity of the credit supply in modern banking systems tends to amplify the industrial fluctuations which result from such disturbances, because it helps to create disproportionalities in the capital structure. This is, in a nutshell, Hayek's monetary theory of the trade cycle, in which 'monetary causes . . . start the cyclical fluctuations' and 'successive changes in the real structure of production . . . constitute those fluctuations' ([1929] 1933: 17). In his writings of the late 1920s, Hayek stressed the monetary aspects of his business cycle theory, whereas in *Prices and Production*, his famous LSE lectures of 1931, he set the focus on the transmission of the monetary impulses through the structure of production.

Without referring to Wicksell, Hayek ([1928] 1984: 102) regarded the pure credit economy concepts of Hawtrey (1919) and Hahn (1920) as appropriate benchmark models for his theory. Yet, in the 1928 article he did not want to make use of the concept of a pure credit economy because he considered it to be an unnecessarily extreme construction. In his view, *all* conceivable monetary systems were sufficiently elastic in their supply of credit to produce the critical effects ([1928] 1984: 103). In the 1929 monograph he stated this as a matter of fact, as opposed to the hypothetical benchmark of a barter economy used in the 'static' general equilibrium theory of the 'Lausanne School', i.e. the Walrasian tradition:

Elasticity in the credit supply of an economic system is not only universally demanded but also . . . an undeniable fact . . . An economic system with an elastic currency must, in many instances, react to external influences quite differently from an economy in which economic forces impinge on goods in their full force – without any intermediary . . .

Once, owing to the disturbing influence of money, even a single price has been fixed at a different level from that which it would have formed in a barter economy, a shift in the whole structure of production is inevitable; and this shift, so long as we make use of static theory and the methods proper to it, can only be explained as an exclusive consequence of the peculiar influence of money. The immediate consequence of an adjustment of the volume of money to the 'requirements' of industry is the failure of the 'interest brake' to operate as promptly as it would in an economy operating without credit. This means, however, that new adjustments are undertaken on a larger scale than can be completed; a boom is thus made possible, with the inevitably recurring 'crisis'.

([1929] 1933: 178–9)

Banking and forced saving

Even though Wicksell (1898: Chapter 6) discussed the credit supply in banking *systems*, his model of the pure credit economy had only one bank, the 'ideal bank' – and it was not always clear how far this was to be considered a profit-maximizing firm or a central institution with a political interest in keeping the price level stable. Hayek (1929), on the other hand, observed that the high elasticity of the credit supply is a natural outcome of competition among commercial banks. His notion of a modern credit economy was thus explicitly based on a system with many banks. These differences notwithstanding, Hayek ([1929] 1933: Chapter IV) followed Wicksell in emphasizing that, in modern banking systems, the money supply is essentially demand-determined and that adjustments of bank lending rates generally tend to lag behind changes in profit expectations of real investors. Taken together, these aspects of the monetary system help to create an environment in which a credit expansion is easily generated.

Competing with each other, banks will not (immediately) react with higher interest rate charges once loan demand rises. Instead, they will increase their supply of loans and corresponding deposits to boost their balance sheets. This implies a certain variability in the reserve ratio. The banks' liquid reserves 'are by no means exclusively composed of cash – and are not even of a constant magnitude, unrelated to the size of the profits which they make possible' (ibid.: 172). A large fraction of the additional loans is transferred in payments to other banks that cannot distinguish these reserve inflows from deposits that accrue from 'real savings'. Hence the other banks will regard these inflows as excess reserves that they can use for making loans, and in their view the reserve ratio need not even change. Singular impulses of additional lending may in this way be easily transmitted throughout the whole banking system, leading to multiple growth in the volume of money.

Even though the banks tend to relax the finance constraints of firms, Hayek (1929, 1931) insisted that any such credit expansion must sooner or later be reversed by the effects of binding resource constraints. He argued that all changes in the structure of production that are generated in this manner are unsustainable because they go against consumer preferences. The redirection of resources to investments in more roundabout processes of production will lead to a scarcity of consumption goods that are produced in less roundabout processes. The concomitant excess demands will translate into forced saving, since the prices of those goods will rise. However, in Hayek's view, the forced saving is not just a redistribution of purchasing power, but precisely the mechanism that leads to the reversion of the credit expansion. The excess demands for consumption goods will sooner or later make themselves felt to the extent that the new investments in more roundabout processes of production will become unprofitable, despite their higher productivity. No matter how elastic the credit supply, prices and production will tend to return to their original structures that correspond to the intertemporal preferences of the consumers, i.e. the volume of voluntary saving. The longer and larger the credit expansion, the more this equilibrium tendency will have to work its way through the destruction of capital and a concomitant rise in unemployment (1929: Chapter V, and 1931: lecture III).

Pure credit and the Ricardo effect

In a later, more general exposition of this hypothesis as the so-called 'Ricardo effect', Hayek (1942) finally took recourse to the concept of a pure credit economy. He used it as a thought experiment, to support his claim that a credit boom inevitably leads to a decline in the profitability of more roundabout processes of production, because it results (if preferences are unchanged) in an increasing shortage of consumption goods:

> The assumption that the supply of credit at a given rate of interest is perfectly elastic is not only unrealistic but, when we contemplate its implications, perfectly fantastic; and it makes the analysis rather complicated. But, as it brings us face to face with a fundamental theoretical problem, this is well worth undertaking. It raises in its purest form the question of the relationship between the monetary and the real factors affecting the relative profitability of different methods of production.
>
> (1942: 140–1)

In order to get his story about the unsustainability of credit booms going, Hayek had to assume that additional loans always find their way into projects that are feasible (*ex ante*) precisely because they lead to more roundabout processes of production. In this context, it remains unclear why the lowering of real wages that follows from excess demands for consumption goods should bring about a reswitching to the original production techniques. Hayek's core argument, the decline in the *relative* profitability of more capital-intensive processes of production, does not bite. As long as those 'more roundabout' investments are deemed profitable in absolute terms (or rather: compared with the 'given rate of interest'), there is no obvious limit to such investments – not in a pure credit economy. Moreover, those investments tend to eliminate excess demands for consumption goods by raising the level of productivity. One might, of course, argue along Schumpeterian lines that credit booms have a tendency to produce temporary excess supplies and frustrated profit expectations. However, that would be a far cry from Hayek's story, since there is no tendency in such cyclical growth processes to restore the neutrality of money in the long run.

In other words, taking recourse to the 'Ricardo effect' in combination with the assumption of a perfectly elastic credit supply did not get Hayek around the fundamental critique that he had met a decade earlier, when the publication of *Prices and Production* (1931) drew international attention to his theory of the trade cycle.[4] The main target of criticism was Hayek's assertion that economic crises must be regarded as an inevitable cure of the system, as processes of re-equilibration of the price system that should not be disturbed by political interventions (1931: 99 and lecture IV).

Not a general theory

In the context of this chapter it should be noted that Hayek failed to provide a general explanation of the trade cycle phenomenon simply because his construction of the upper turning point in the cycle does not sit well together with his own assumptions about the monetary system. In a first attempt, Hayek ([1929], 1933: 175–6) explained the downturn with a reduction in the elasticity of credit: 'For this it is quite enough that the banks should cease to extend the volume of credit' – due to increased cash requirements in circulation or to a rise in the discount rate that is set by the central bank. However, this recourse to 'stylized facts' is unsatisfactory, because the reserve restrictions are not explained by the theory. They are *ad hoc* considered to be variable in the upswing, but fixed in the downturn. Later, Hayek argued that the banks' lending rates are determined by the default risks that must rise with the increase in the debt–equity ratios during the credit boom (1942: 138ff., 1969: 282ff.). That argument appears to contradict Hayek's earlier 'consideration that, in the upward phase of the cycle, the risks of borrowing are less; and therefore a smaller cash reserve may suffice to provide the same degree of security' ([1929] 1933: 173). When Hayek (1942) attempted to show, on the other hand, that – due to the 'Ricardo effect' – the reversal in the structure of production must take place even if the supply of credit is perfectly elastic, he failed – as indicated above.[5]

Apart from the upper turning point, Hayek's approach has its problems even in other aspects. A *monetary* theory of the trade cycle should also explain the behaviour of monetary variables in the crisis. Hayek, however, completely ignored the possibility that the capital invested in the abandoned projects remains physically intact, is sold and – by its depreciation – made profitable for other firms. In that case, the economy would not return to its original structure of prices and production. Moreover, Hayek went too far in criticizing Wicksell for his propagation of the price level as a key variable for monetary theory and monetary policy. According to Hayek, all concepts of a general price level conceal destabilizing shifts in the structure of production and help to induce political distortions of the price system ([1928] 1984: 95ff. 1929: Chapter III, 1931: 26ff.). However, in combination with the belief that crises must be left to run their course, the rejection of price level concepts made Hayek ignore the cumulative effects of a debt deflation, as described by Fisher (1933). In a deflationary environment the elasticity of the banks' credit supply is of utmost importance for the level of real activity, at which the economy settles in a (sort of) new equilibrium position, a resting point, before the next cycle starts. Price-level considerations play a significant role for the profit (and loss) expectations of bank managers, and their willingness to lend. In many cases, the survival of the banks may hinge upon the existence and action of a lender of last resort. Hayek, like Mises, was highly critical of such 'easy money' policy in a crisis ([1931] 1935: 125). It is not hard to understand why Hayek's trade cycle theory quickly became unpopular in the years of the Great Depression.

Lindahl and Myrdal

Lindahl and Myrdal had two things in common with Hayek: they based their analysis of monetary equilibrium and macroeconomic disequilibrium on Wicksellian concepts of intertemporal pricing; and they rejected price level stability as a sufficient condition for monetary equilibrium. But they differed from Hayek in almost every other respect.

Lindahl on pure credit and monetary policy

In 1930 Erik Lindahl published a book on 'the means of monetary policy' (*Penningpolitikens medel*), conceived as a companion volume to his earlier book on 'the targets of monetary policy' (*Penningpolitikens mål*). A translation of the 1930 book was later included – as Part two, under the title 'The Rate of Interest and the

Price Level' – in Lindahl's famous *Studies in the Theory of Money and Capital* (1939). The book did not contain much discussion of the techniques in the conduct of monetary policy. More fundamentally, Lindahl re-examined Wicksell's theory in terms of its policy conclusions, i.e. he focused on the scope of monetary policy with regard to interest rates and the price level. Like Hayek, Lindahl aimed at transforming static equilibrium theory into a dynamic theory of intertemporal price relations, though not in the confines of business cycle theory.[6] He started his introduction to the analysis of 'the pricing problem' with the 'simple case' of a pure credit economy in which lending and transfers of payments are centralized and full interest is paid on all deposits. 'These assumptions will greatly facilitate our exposition . . . our results would not be substantially influenced, if more realistic assumptions were used instead' (1939: 140). Unlike Hayek (1929), for whom the competition among commercial banks played a crucial role in generating a credit expansion, Lindahl deliberately designed his model of the pure credit economy like Wicksell's, in the sense that it only had one bank.

Contrary to Wicksell, however, Lindahl argued that the quantity theory of money does not apply to the pure credit economy, but that 'the essential aspects of the pricing problem *can* be treated in complete abstraction from the special problems with the quantity of money' (1930: 235). Cash holding and real balance effects, commercial banking, the gold standard and international relations may all be factors that need to be considered when the analysis is applied to more realistic conditions. But, in Lindahl's view, they do not essentially affect dynamic price theory.[7] Thus he replaced the monetary variables on the left-hand side of the Fisherian equation of exchange ($MV = PQ$) with a flow concept of expected aggregate income and saving in nominal terms:

> In explaining the factors determining the changes in the price level, it is convenient to start from the fact that in each period the portion of total nominal income that is not saved is equal to the total quantities of goods and services consumed during the period, multiplied by their prices. This may be expressed in the form:
>
> $$E(1 - s) = PQ$$
>
> where E denotes the total nominal income, s the proportion of this income which is saved, P the price level for consumption goods and Q the quantity of such goods in a certain period.
>
> (1939: 142)

The main point of this exercise was to define income as a derivative of capital values which, in turn, are based on conjectures about the future (ibid.: 143–6).

In this way, Lindahl began to set the focus on *expectations* about *flows* of income and expenditure. That perspective brings out the importance of the money rate of interest and the credit supply in an aggregate setting, especially when there are no definite reserve constraints to determine the supply of loans, and thereby the development of prices and nominal income.

The next step was to analyse the influence of the central bank, through its interest rate policy, on the price level. Here Lindahl distinguished between various cases in which 'the individual anticipations of coming price developments are to a certain extent the causes of the actual developments themselves' (ibid.: 147). The simplest case is perfect foresight. Future shifts in the price level are then taken into account in all contracts, and the central bank cannot but follow a completely passive interest policy (in the sense that it acts as foreseen), if the system is not to break down.

In reality, however, foresight is imperfect. Expectations and outcomes of market transactions differ systematically and revisions of plans depend on observed changes of macroeconomic variables. In this general framework, Lindahl developed a taxonomy of cumulative changes in the price level that vary with the underlying assumptions. Under imperfect foresight, the central bank can influence expectations and outcomes through a range of interest rate instruments that should be complemented by public expenditure policy. In any case, the bank ought to coordinate and stabilize expectations by following a definite norm for the price level (ibid.: 232). This would allow it to exploit a virtuous circle of credibility. Both Lindahl's analysis of cumulative processes under imperfect foresight and his position on norms for monetary policy will be discussed further below. Let us first take a look at Myrdal's contribution.

Myrdal on bank credit and monetary equilibrium

Shortly after Lindahl's book on the means of monetary policy, Gunnar Myrdal published his long essay on the concept of monetary equilibrium (Myrdal 1931), the paper that – in a slightly different version – came to be included in Hayek's collection and finally was translated into English as *Monetary Equilibrium* (1939).[8] The original version combined a thorough immanent critique of Wicksell's concept of monetary equilibrium with a number of critical remarks concerning Lindahl's approach. Concerning the general modelling of the monetary economy, Myrdal nevertheless praised Lindahl who

> by making use of Wicksell's idea of the 'pure credit economy', succeeds in providing a systematic, elegant and in certain respects deepened analysis of the Wicksellian process without even mentioning the quantity theoretical terms of credit volume, quantity of money and velocity.
>
> (1931: 212; author's translation)

This passage in the Swedish version is the only place where Myrdal referred to the concept of the pure credit economy. He did not use it himself, but based his 'central monetary analysis' on the assumption of a 'free currency . . . which itself requires that the banking system be able to satisfy all demands for credit' (Myrdal 1939: 109).

Even though Myrdal did not specify the structure of the banking system that is able to fulfil this condition, he made it clear that bank credit is of central importance in linking monetary theory with price theory. While Lindahl simply asserted that his Wicksell-style model of the pure economy is incompatible with the quantity theory of money, Myrdal explicitly rejected the causation theorem on the grounds that 'the changes in the price level and in the amount of means of payments are both simultaneously dependent upon factors which lie outside the mechanism of payment proper' (ibid.: 15).

In Myrdal's view, intertemporal pricing, as in credit contracts, is precisely such a factor that is not well explained, neither by the quantity theory nor by general equilibrium theory:

> The prices explained in general equilibrium theory refer only to a single moment. It therefore seems impossible to incorporate time contracts, expressed in monetary units, e.g. credit contracts, into the central theory of price formation in a satisfactory way. This impossibility of working credit into the theory of price formation is naturally all the more to be regretted since credit forms the bulk of all means of payment – or, at least, determines the velocity of circulation, if only coins and notes are counted as means of payment.
>
> The problem of credit, therefore had to be excluded from the theory of price formation and was left entirely to monetary theory. But even monetary theory (quantity theory) had no place for a satisfactory discussion of credit; for credit is a causal factor not only for the price *level* but also for price *relations*, which are partly determined by the profitability of business and, therefore, by the supply and demand price for credit. The problem of credit, therefore, requires a monetary theory which is really integrated with the central economic theory, but this the quantity theory was not.
>
> (1939: 16)

Myrdal then went on to explain that the true challenge of the integration of monetary theory with price theory is to explain the phenomenon of the business cycle (ibid.: 17–19). In his view, important steps towards integration could be taken by a thorough analysis of Wicksell's notions of monetary equilibrium and the cumulative process. Myrdal's research programme thus very much resembled that of Hayek, but – like Lindahl – he came to rather different conclusions.[9]

The non-neutrality of money

Both Lindahl and Myrdal firmly rejected Wicksell's concept of a 'natural rate of interest' that would work like an attractor for the market rate of interest in the cumulative process. The main point of critique was the incapability of Wicksell's concept to deal with a world in which inputs and outputs are not homogeneously identical. Lindahl arrived at the conclusion that the 'capital rate of interest', the rate of return to real investment, cannot be independent of the market rate for loans:

> Only under very special assumptions is it possible to conceive of the natural or real rate of interest determined purely by technical considerations, and thus independent of the price system. For this to be true it must be supposed that the productive process consists only in investing units of goods or services of the same type as the final product, the latter increasing with the passage of time alone without the cooperation of other scarce factors . . .
>
> Under more realistic assumptions it is not possible to measure the investment and the product in the same real unit. To compare services invested and the resulting products, they must be expressed in a common unit which presupposes that the price relation is given. Then the real rate of interest does not depend only on technical conditions, but also on the price situation, and cannot be regarded as existing independently of the loan rate of interest.
>
> (Lindahl 1939: 247–8)

Myrdal (1939: 50–1) noted that Wicksell's construction of a natural rate of interest is not necessarily confined to the homogeneity of inputs and outputs. It would also survive if relative prices in the whole price system were fixed. The assumption of a stationary equilibrium would, however, obstruct 'the progressive completion of the theory' in which changes in the rate of interest, and hence changes in the whole intertemporal structure of prices, constitute the impulses for cumulative changes in the price level, the object of analysis. The punchline of the argument was that the concept of physical productivity needs to be replaced by a concept of exchange value productivity.

Myrdal (ibid.: 51–2) argued that, for the determination of the exchange value productivity of capital, one might initially do with an 'abstract unit of account', a pure *numéraire* that could be defined in terms of any concrete commodity. But as soon as one considers that credit contracts are concluded in terms of the accounting unit, this is no longer conceivable. Relative prices of goods are affected by changes in their 'absolute prices' in terms of the monetary unit:

> The accounting unit receives, through credit contracts, a real importance for the exchange relations; for the process of price formation is then influenced

by *changes* in the exchange value of the monetary unit with respect to other commodities . . .

It is impossible to think of relative exchange values which, in their development, are independent of the absolute money units in which credit contracts are concluded.

(ibid.: 52–3)

Myrdal argued that, in a non-stationary economy, the exchange value of money necessarily varies at different rates *vis-à-vis* different commodities. The determination of the capital rate of interest necessarily includes expectations about absolute prices and about the relative price of loans, as an opportunity cost factor, since the expectations define the *ex ante* profitability of (planned) investment. Since Myrdal assumed, somewhat realistically, that changes in relative prices cannot be completely foreseen with certainty, he deemed this 'anticipation factor' in the determination of the capital rate of interest to be all the more important. Credit relations are fixed in terms of money for certain time periods. While time elapses, some expectations will be disappointed and changed, inducing changes in the plans of others (Myrdal 1939: 45–7; Palander 1953: 10–11).

Myrdal (1939: 52) concluded that monetary analysis 'is fundamentally incompatible with . . . the hypothesis of the absence of all monetary transactions'. Wicksell and Hayek had used the barter economy as a fictitious benchmark for their definitions of a 'natural rate of interest', respectively: the rate at which investment equals (nothing but) voluntary saving. Lindahl and Hayek rejected the classical barter benchmark. They did not base their monetary theories on the notion of a long-run real equilibrium that is distinctly determined by 'fundamentals'. Thus they were open to the possibility that the capital rate of interest adjusts to the market rate in the long run rather than vice versa, as in Wicksell or Hayek. In the following, such non-neutralities of money are exemplified by Myrdal's discussion of a contractionary cumulative process and Lindahl's discussion of expansionary processes.

Income mechanisms

Lindahl and Myrdal not only rejected the barter benchmarks of the 'natural rate' and 'real saving' concepts implicit in Wicksell's two first conditions of monetary equilibrium (market rate equals natural rate of interest, and saving equals investment). They were also highly critical of Wicksell's third condition of monetary equilibrium, namely, price level stability (Lindahl 1939: Chapter V and 254–7; Myrdal 1939: Chapter VI). On the one hand, Lindahl and Myrdal referred to David Davidson's critique of Wicksell, according to which changes in productivity must bring about inverse changes in the price level or otherwise start a cumulative process. On the other hand, they pointed out that, if the first two equilibrium conditions (in particular, the capital rate of interest and saving) are appropriately reformulated in monetary terms,[10] price level stability is not a necessary condition of monetary equilibrium, nor does it necessarily indicate the latter.

Myrdal, moreover, stressed that 'in reality there is not a single rate of interest, but a heterogeneous system of credit conditions' (1939: 159). Therefore monetary equilibrium is not uniquely determined by the correspondence of a certain market rate of interest with the rate of return on real investment, but to be understood as an 'indifference field' of various combinations of credit conditions and constellations of expectations.

In his analysis of this 'indifference field of monetary equilibrium', Myrdal (ibid.: 164–9) described 'the inner mechanics of the depressive process' that is started by a tightening of the credit conditions. The contraction follows 'the general schema of the Wicksellian process' as sketched in an earlier chapter (ibid.: 24–6), where it is stressed that cumulative processes are driven by the expectations implicit in the formation of capital values. However, two things are notable about Myrdal's depressive process. One is that the process has a downward limit in the inelasticity of consumer demand that will slow down the fall in prices and hence the decline in the entrepreneurs' anticipated income. The other is that Myrdal, in the early 1930s, developed a simple scenario with an aggregate income mechanism that replaces the traditional Wicksellian interest rate mechanism. Savings decrease in absolute terms along with incomes, and relatively to consumption, and this is what finally restores monetary equilibrium (in the sense of investment equalling saving plus value change – see note 10):

> Thus after a credit contraction the business situation can under certain conditions attain quite a fair stability,. . . so that the relations fulfil even the equilibrium criterion . . . The new equilibrium position would be characterised by the following: A largely unchanged price level for consumption goods; capital values which will be sufficiently lower to correspond to the higher interest rate, or more generally, to the tighter credit conditions; somewhat lower wages, particularly in the capital goods industries; some, perhaps quite considerable, unemployment, especially in the capital goods industries; a production volume restricted generally but particularly in the capital goods industries. . .; saving sufficiently reduced to make free capital disposal correspond to real investment, which . . . is restricted on the whole and has a less roundabout arrangement of production to maintain.
>
> (ibid.: 148)

This sounds quite Hayekian, but note that Myrdal's depressive process was started by an autonomous tightening of the credit supply, and that the economy lands in an underemployment equilibrium – a scenario that is very similar to the core model of Keynes's *General Theory of Money, Interest and Employment* (1936).

On the other side of the 'interest rate gap', some of Lindahl's constructions of cumulative processes look more like Schumpeterian models of cyclical growth, driven by a redistribution of purchasing power through bank credit. In Chapter II of his 1930 book, Lindahl explored a variety of expansionary cumulative processes under imperfect foresight, and how different measures of monetary policy will influence income, saving and consumption.

In one of the cases, he examined the transmission of a reduction in the bank rate of interest under the assumptions of full employment and 'non-rigid investment periods'. He argued that the subsequent credit expansion will trigger a redistributive income mechanism that equilibrates a higher level of investment with saving *ex post*, even though the process starts at full employment (and thus would not seem to have the capacity for a rise in investment). The rise of the price level that follows from the credit expansion reduces the purchasing power of fixed incomes, but tends to raise the incomes of entrepreneurs. The latter have strong incentives to plough their windfall profits from inflation back into further investment, as long as they can expect further rises in their incomes:

> In every case given, the shift in the price level will be sufficiently large to cause such a change in the distribution of incomes that total savings in the community will correspond to the value of real investment, the extent of which is primarily determined by the rate of interest.
>
> (Lindahl 1939: 175)

The increase in 'unintentional saving'[11] that follows from an autonomous lowering of the bank rate of interest could, in principle, bring the economy onto the path to an equilibrium with higher total income in real terms. Lindahl discussed this possibility more explicitly in alternative scenarios with 'unemployed resources available' (1939: 176–83). In his view, it all depends on expectations: If 'individuals in each period expect existing prices to be maintained in the future', the cumulative price rise 'need not continue indefinitely, but comes to an end when the supply of capital [from unplanned saving through consumer price inflation] has been increased until it corresponds to the new [lower] rate of interest' (ibid.: 180–1).

Lindahl was, nevertheless, like Hayek, sceptical of political attempts to exploit the redistributive income mechanism. He was convinced that people would adapt their expectations to their inflation experience, 'that, seeing a price rise continue for a certain time, they think it most likely that prices will go on rising'. In this case, inflation might accelerate to the extent that would become 'necessary to arrest the movement before the amount of capital appropriate to the lower rate of interest has been accumulated' (1930: 182–3). Even though this conclusion looks very similar to Hayek's conviction that credit booms are unsustainable,

Lindahl never suggested that any credit expansion must inevitably result in the destruction of capital.

In Wicksellian terms, Myrdal's contractionary process and Lindahl's expansionary processes could thus be described as cases in which the capital rate of interest would tend to adjust to the market rate, rather than vice versa. In other words, the monetary equilibrium positions of the respective economies are 'indifferent', not only in the Myrdalian sense of no unique market rate of interest corresponding to the equilibrium 'yield of real capital', but also in the sense that cumulative processes could push the economy to a different equilibrium position and would not have a natural tendency of self-reversion, as in Hayek's stories.

Policy norms

Unlike Wicksell, Lindahl and Myrdal did not confine their analysis of monetary policy norms to price level stability. Along the lines of David Davidson's critique of Wicksell, they also discussed 'the rate of interest as an instrument for regulating the price level in inverse proportion to productivity' (Lindahl 1939: Chapter V; see also Myrdal 1939: 129–31, 200–2).

Lindahl clearly favoured nominal income targeting over inflation targeting – to put the two norms in modern terms (see also Fregert 1993; Berg and Jonung 1999). He nevertheless kept his conclusions in the 1930 book in a rather neutral fashion. As in the case of Hayek, one might criticize that, in his advocacy of nominal income targeting, Lindahl ignored the risks of debt deflation. In a long footnote, Lindahl (1939: 255–7) himself emphasized that it is empirically difficult to distinguish between monetary and real causes of deflation. However, in real life – i.e. in his functions as statistical expert and adviser to the Swedish central bank – Lindahl seems to have been aware that deflation was not a practical option for monetary policy, at least not in the near future, or apart from very special post-war conditions (see Jonung 1979: 488–90; Fregert 1993).

Myrdal, on the other hand, was critical of both types of norms as discussed by Lindahl. He demanded, rather hypothetically, that 'one should attempt to achieve the most complete fulfilment possible of the equation $R_2 = W$' (1939: 199), i.e. the reformulated second condition of monetary equilibrium: aggregate cost of production of new investment = free capital disposal (see note 10). This ideal state would have to be 'compatible with the least possible movement of a price index weighted with regard to the stickiness of various prices and their significance for profitability and real investment' (ibid.). It is obvious that this 'norm' was hardly formulated so as to make it an operational rule for monetary policy.

Not a general theory either

Taken at face value, monetary institutions do not seem to play much of a role in the macroeconomics of Lindahl and Myrdal. Their treatment of the banking system is very general, if not simplistic – in the sense that Lindahl seemed to assume that the monetary authorities are in perfect control of the credit supply, and that Myrdal appears to have regarded the banks as mere accommodators of credit demand even when he discussed the non-uniqueness of monetary equilibrium in terms of credit conditions.

This could certainly be considered a weakness in their approaches. However, the Swedes expressly stated that they were not interested in discussing the complications that arise from more realistic assumptions about banks, before they had constructed a general framework to analyse the 'dynamic pricing problem' in monetary terms. In this framework, expectations provided the main link between monetary theory and price theory. For this, Lindahl and Myrdal considered the widespread existence of credit relations as crucial, but not their specific structure in terms of financial intermediation. So it could be argued that the monetary macroeconomics of those two founding fathers of the Stockholm School were general in the sense of not being specific about monetary institutions, but not – therefore – general in the sense of a core model that is both logically consistent and has explanatory power for (nearly) all empirically relevant manifestations of the phenomena in question.

It has also been argued that the monetary economics of the Stockholm School were flawed because the Swedes refused to take account of well-defined concepts of the volume of money and, in particular, of the demand for deposits for the explanation of changes in the price level (see, e.g., Myhrman 1991; Laidler 1998). To put it in Robertsonian terms, Lindahl and Myrdal (among others) are criticized for dealing only with 'money to spend', but not with 'money to hold'. They were concerned only with the credit channel of monetary policy transmission and completely ignored real balance effects that work through the money channel. Yet one might ask why the Swedes should have paid attention to the real balance effects, since the latter would, at the most, reinforce the transmission of impulses through the credit channel rather than working in the other direction (see Trautwein 1998).

The loose link

Towards the end of his *Pure Theory of Capital* (1941), Hayek aptly summarized his view on the role of money:

> [I]n the short run money may prevent real changes from showing their effect, and may even cause real changes for which there is no justification in the underlying real position. In the long run, however, it will always merely

accentuate the change it has at first prevented, or will bring about changes which are the opposite of the impact effects . . .

Money is of course never 'neutral' in the sense of being merely an instrument or servant: it always exercises some positive influence on the course of events . . . [M]oney by its very nature constitutes a kind of *loose joint* in the self-equilibrating apparatus of the price mechanism which is bound to impede its working.

(1941: 407–8, emphasis added)

Money thus plays the role of a loose link in Hayek's attempt to integrate the explanation of business cycles with the general framework of classical price theory. Money may relax the real constraints of (relative) prices and production as they would be directly felt in a barter system (the hypothetical equilibrium reference). This is all the more obvious in modern economies where the relevant sort of 'money' is produced by way of the credit supply in a system of competing commercial banks. But sooner or later the slackness of the finance constraint would become untenable and be reversed in a crisis.

In this chapter it has been argued that Hayek's 'loose link' strategy did not work because he based his attempt to construct a general theory of business cycles on rather specific assumptions about the working of the banking system. Lindahl and Myrdal, on the other hand, were much less restricted to a specific construction of the monetary system. They generated a host of specific scenarios for macroeconomic developments from rather general assumptions about the supply of money and credit. In their view, money is a loose link in the sense that the underlying credit relations are based on certain expectations that could vary a lot and hence give rise to large variety of cumulative processes. One might argue that the Swedes, too, failed to construct a general theory of business cycles, since they did not have a well-defined core model to work with. However, Lindahl and Myrdal never claimed to have come up with a general theory. They considered their reconstructions of Wicksell's concepts of monetary equilibrium and cumulative processes to be nothing but a demonstration of the need to reformulate macroeconomic theory in a way that would allow it to deal with the dynamics of changes in price levels and other macro variables without having to refer to the entirely fictitious and irrelevant construction of a barter equilibrium.

There is another, more uncomfortable message in Lindahl's and Myrdal's variations on interest, expectations and the cumulative process (and in the writings of the Stockholm School in general). They raise the suspicion that a general theory with unique determination of economic variables cannot be constructed at all – if money and credit are taken seriously. Another way of putting the point is to say that we might have to accept that macroeconomics can, at best, provide a general theory of specific cases and sequences, based on a few common methodological principles of dynamic analysis. This is the way that Lindahl and Myrdal (and others in the Stockholm School) tried to go. It is a hard way, and hardly to our tastes – not to speak of technology and endowments.

Notes

1 Thomas (1991: 390) ironically describes the atmosphere at the LSE in the 1930s: 'The ruling powers [Robbins and Hayek] were passionate believers in freedom, and this included freedom to adjust the constraints within which freedom was exercised by the nonfavorites. The main type of adjustment was the postponement of tenure.'

    In the case of Kaldor, Hayek even went as far as seeing to that Kaldor was refused leave of absence to join the Economic Commission for Europe under the direction of Myrdal in 1946 (Shehadi 1991: 383).

2 For Wicksell's analytical separations between price level instability, crises and business cycles, see Boianovsky and Trautwein (2001).

3 For more general surveys of Wicksellian and modern concepts of the pure credit economy, see Hicks (1989: Chapter 12), Trautwein (1997, 2000), and Realfonzo (1998).

4 Some of the sharpest criticisms can be found in Sraffa (1932), and Kaldor (1942). For critical assessments of Hayek's Ricardo effect, see also Laidler (1994), and Hagemann and Trautwein (1998).

5 See also Laidler (1994) and Trautwein (1996).

6 There is no evidence that Lindahl had read Hayek (1929). He only referred to Hayek (1928) in a footnote (1939: 142) where he expressed his sympathy with Hayek's endeavour to construct 'intertemporal price relations' as 'a starting point' for monetary theory that is to 'be found in the general theory of price' (1939: 141).

7 Towards the end of his treatise, Lindahl (1939: 238ff.) discussed 'complications due to the banking system'. The required alterations of the pure credit model are confined to minor technicalities in the design of open market policy.

8 Despite the difference in their publication dates, the Swedish and German versions were written almost simultaneously in late 1931 and early 1932. There are numerous cross-references in both versions. For comparative discussion, see Palander (1953), Steiger (1978: 425) and Hansson (1982: Chapter 6).

9 Myrdal (1939: 32–4) criticized Hayek for ignoring the importance of expectations.

10 In his reformulation of Wicksell's first equilibrium condition, Myrdal (1939: Chapter IV) arrived at a definition in which monetary equilibrium is attained if Q, the difference between the present value of capital (based on anticipated and discounted returns) and its reproduction cost, is zero. Myrdal's Q thus closely resembles Tobin's q, and may have influenced the formulation of the latter. In the English version of his treatise, Myrdal (1939: 84) explicitly emphasized that this first condition is not independent of the second equilibrium condition, which requires that total investment equals total 'free disposal of capital', i.e. saving in monetary terms plus 'value change, defined as anticipated depreciation minus appreciation'.

11 Lindahl (1939: 176) rejected the term 'forced saving', used by Wicksell and Hayek, as inappropriate.

References

Berg, C. and Jonung, L. (1999) 'Pioneering price level targeting: the Swedish experience 1931–1937', *Journal of Monetary Economics*, 43: 525–51.

Boianovsky, M. and Trautwein, H.-M. (2001) 'Wicksell's lecture notes on economic crises (1902/05)', *Structural Change and Economic Dynamics*, 12: 343–66.

Fisher, I. (1933) 'The debt-deflation theory of great depressions', *Econometrica*, 1: 337–59.

Fregert, K. (1993) 'Erik Lindahl's norm for monetary policy', in Jonung L. (ed.) *Swedish Economic Thought: Explorations and Advances*, London: Routledge, pp. 125–42.

Hagemann, H. and Trautwein, H.-M. (1998) 'Cantillon and Ricardo effects: Hayek's contributions to business cycle theory', *European Journal of the History of Economic Thought*, 5: 292–316.

Hahn, L.A. (1920) *Volkswirtschaftliche Theorie des Bankkredits*, Tübingen: J.C.B. Mohr.

Hansson, B. (1982) *The Stockholm School and the Development of Dynamic Method*, London: Croom Helm.

Hawtrey, R. (1919) *Currency and Credit*, London: Longmans, Green.

Hayek, F.A. (1928) 'Das intertemporale Gleichgewichtssystem der Preise und die Bewegungen des geldwertes', *Weltwirtschaftliches Archiv*, 28: 33–76.

—— (1929) *Geldtheorie und Konjunkturtheorie*, Vienna: Julius Springer.

—— (1931) *Prices and Production*, 2nd edn, London: Routledge & Sons.

—— (ed.) (1933) *Beiträge zur Geldtheorie*, Vienna: Julius Springer.

—— (1941) *The Pure Theory of Capital*, Chicago: University of Chicago Press.

—— (1942) 'The Ricardo effect', *Economica*, 9: 127–52.

—— (1969) 'Three elucidations of the Ricardo effect', *Journal of Political Economy*, 77: 274–85.

Hicks, J. (1989) *A Market Theory of Money*, Oxford: Oxford University Press.

Kaldor, N. (1942) 'Professor Kaldor and the concertina effect', *Economica*, 9: 359–82.

Keynes, J.M. (1936) *The General Theory of Employment, Interest and Money*, London: Macmillan.

Laidler, D. (1991) 'The Austrians and the Stockholm School: two failures in the development of modern macroeconomics?', in Jonung, L. (ed.) *The Stockholm School of Economics Revisited*, Cambridge: Cambridge University Press, pp. 295–332.

—— (1994) 'Hayek on neutral money and the cycle', in Colonna, M. and Hagemann, H. (eds) *Money and Business Cycles: The Economics of F.A. Hayek*, vol. I, Aldershot: Edward Elgar, pp. 3–26.

—— (1998) 'The Wicksell connection, the quantity theory and Keynes', in Streissler, E. (ed.) *Knut Wicksell als Ökonom: Studien zur Entwicklung der ökonomischen Theorie XVIII*, Berlin: Duncker & Humbolt, pp. 15–34.

—— (1999) *Fabricating the Keynesian Revolution: Studies of the Inter-war Literature on Money, the Cycle and Unemployment*, Cambridge: Cambridge University Press.

Leijonhufvud, A. (1981) 'The Wicksell connection: variations on a theme', in *Information and Coordination: Essays in Macroeconomic Theory*, New York: Oxford University Press, pp. 131–202.

Lindahl, E. (1930) *Penningpolitikens medel*, Malmö: Förlagsaktiebolaget.

—— (1939) *Studies in the Theory of Money and Capital*, London: Allen & Unwin.

Myhrman, J. (1991) 'The monetary economics of the Stockholm School', in Jonung, L. (ed.) *The Stockholm School of Economics Revisited*, Cambridge: Cambridge University Press, pp. 267–89.

Myrdal, G. (1931) 'Om penningteoretisk jämvikt. En studie över den "normala räntan" i Wicksells penninglära', *Ekonomisk Tidskrift*, 33: 191–302.

—— (1932) 'Der Gleichgewichtsbegriff als Instrument der Geldtheoretischen Analyse', in Hayek, F.A. (ed.) *Beiträge zur Geldtheorie*, Vienna: Julius Springer, pp. 361–487.

—— (1939) *Monetary Equilibrium*, London: William Hodge.

Palander, T. (1953) 'Om "Stockholmskolans" begrepp och metoder. Metodologiska reflexioner kring Myrdals "monetary equilibrium"', *Ekonomisk Tidskrift*, 43: 88–143; trans. (1953) 'On the concepts and methods of the "Stockholm School"', *International Economic Papers*, 3: 5–57.

Realfonzo, R. (1998) *Money and Banking: Theory and Debate (1900–1940)*, Cheltenham: Edward Elgar.

Shehadi, N. (1991) 'The London School of Economics and the Stockholm School in the 1930s', in Jonung, L. (ed.) *The Stockholm School of Economics Revisited*, Cambridge: Cambridge University Press, pp. 377–89.

Sraffa, P. (1932) 'Dr Hayek on money and capital', *Economic Journal*, 42: 42–53.

Steiger, O. (1978) 'Prelude to the theory of a monetary economy: origins and significance of Ohlin's 1933 approach to monetary theory', *History of Political Economy*, 10: 420–56.

Thomas, B. (1991) 'Comment [on Shehadi]', in Jonung, L. (ed.) *The Stockholm School of Economics Revisited*, Cambridge: Cambridge University Press, pp. 389–90.

Trautwein, H.M. (1996) 'Money, equilibrium, and the business cycle: Hayek's Wicksellian dichotomy', *History of Political Economy*, 28(1): 27–55.

—— (1997) 'Wicksell and the Stockholm School on credit and money', in Glombowski, J., Gronert, A. and Plasmeijer, H. (eds) *The Continental History of Economic Thought*, Marburg: Metropolis, pp. 115–53.

—— (1998) 'Comment [on Laidler]', in Streissler, E. (ed.) *Knut Wicksell als Ökonom – Studien zur Entwicklung der ökonomischen Theorie XVIII*, Berlin: Duncker & Humbolt, pp. 35–8.

—— (2000) 'The credit view: old and new', *Journal of Economic Surveys*, 14: 37–71.

Wicksell, K. (1898) *Geldzins und Güterpreise: Eine Untersuchung über die den Tauschwert des Geldes bestimmenden Ursachen*, Jena: Gustav Fischer.

7 Capital and business cycles

When Lundberg meets Hayek and Keynes

Michel Bellet and Abdallah Zouache

Introduction

One of the aims of the conference held in Saint-Etienne was to write the criss-cross story of Austrian and Swedish economics. This chapter goes further because it makes a connection between three research traditions, first, the Austrian tradition represented by Hayek, second, the Swedish school personified by Lundberg and, finally, Keynes's perspective. In other words, Lundberg intervenes as a third actor to make the connection between the Austrian and Keynesian schools of thought.

The connection between Austrian economics and Keynes can easily be made through the well-known debate which had occurred in the 1930s between Hayek and Keynes. The controversy began with Hayek's lengthy critical review of Keynes's *Treatise* in the August 1931 issue of *Economica*. Keynes published a reply in the November issue of *Economica*. The second part of Hayek's review was published in February 1932. On 29 March 1932, Keynes put a stop to the discussion, announcing to Hayek that he would not reply to the second part of the review because he preferred to devote his time to revising his theory, a revision which led in 1936 to the publication of Keynes's *General Theory*. Hayek, who had invested time and energy into preparing his review, was very disappointed by Keynes's reaction (Hayek 1966: 241). Hayek therefore did not comment on Keynes's *General Theory* in an official journal.

What is the relationship between the Hayek–Keynes debate and Swedish economics? The reference to Lundberg's works makes sense of this connection. At first sight, the relationship between Lundberg's contribution and the Hayek–Keynes debate is not obvious as there are no critical reviews or letters between Lundberg and the two other authors. Nevertheless, the association is not so controversial, even if not much highlighted in the economic literature. In particular, the Hayek–Keynes controversy contributed in an important way to Lundberg's dissertation (1937). In his dissertation, the aim of Lundberg is 'to elucidate the possible applicability of such opposite theories as those presented by Keynes and Hayek upon different types of business cycles, existing in reality',

(1937: 255). This goal itself is based on a permanent concern, an attempt to 'construct a synthesis of three monetary theories, those of Wicksell, Hayek and Keynes' (Lundberg 1934: 51).

The aim of the chapter is to display how the Hayek–Keynes controversy influenced Lundberg's thought. In particular, this study shows to what extent Lundberg's business cycle analysis can be viewed as a 'synthesis' of Hayek's and Keynes's conceptions of the business cycle. Thus, it is argued that from the perspective of the history of economic thought, it is important to understand that the debate between Hayek and Keynes was prolonged by a Swedish economist.[1]

The chapter offers the opportunity to illustrate the extraordinarily rich context of the *Years of High Theory*, emphasising the similarities and differences between the authors who are representative of the three main research traditions in the 1930s. In particular, the meeting of Keynes, Hayek and Lundberg is the result of their use of Wicksell's theoretical framework as the basic tool for studying business cycle theory. In our opinion, the key issues at the heart of this intellectual meeting are capital theory and the co-ordination of investment and saving decisions in the business cycle. This chapter is organised as follows. The second section will analyse the debate between Hayek and Keynes from the point of view of the capital theory, on the one hand and the co-ordination between investment and saving, on the other hand. The next section will show to what extent Lundberg's analysis can be understood as a synthesis of Hayek's and Keynes's analysis of these two issues.

Capital and coordination in the Hayek–Keynes debate

This section does not offer a detailed analysis of the Hayek–Keynes debate as it focuses on two interrelated issues which seems to us crucial to an understanding of the controversy. First, we will insist on the theory of capital as a critical point of discord between Hayek and Keynes. Second, we will specify Keynes's and Hayek's conceptions of the co-ordination between investment (I) and saving (S). Hayek and Keynes both realised that savers and investors are different individuals whose decisions and actions are independent of each other so that the co-ordination between investment and saving is not perfect.

The role of the theory of capital in the debate

The issue of the theory of capital is of the utmost importance in order to understand the Hayek–Keynes controversy. Indeed, a great part of Hayek's review is directly derived from his conception of capital. And Keynes admitted the legitimacy of Hayek's criticism with regard to the lack of a satisfactory theory of capital and interest in the *Treatise*; after defending himself by observing that there was no 'satisfactory theory' of capital in 'completed form':

I agree with him that a clear account of the factors determining the natural rate of interest ought to have a place in a completed *Treatise on Money*, and that it is lacking in mine: and I can only plead that I had much to say for which such a theory is not required and that my own ideas about it were still too much in embryo to deserve publication. Later on, I will endeavour to make good this deficiency.

(Keynes 1931: 394–5)[2]

Indeed, Hayek's claim of the lack of a capital theory in the *Treatise* influenced the development of the *General Theory* (Mongiovi 1990). As Mongiovi (1990: 145) reminds it, a table of contents of the *General Theory* dated 1932 includes a Chapter 8 whose title is 'Definitions and Ideas relating to Capital' (Keynes (1973) vol. 29: 63). In the preparation notes for the *General Theory*, there are many references to the Austrian theory of capital (ibid.: 116–20). Nevertheless, it must be noted that Keynes was not at ease with the Austrian theory: 'God knows what the Austrians mean by "period of production". Nothing, in my opinion, (Keynes 1935, *Collected Writings*, 13: 517). At the same time, according to Mongiovi, Chapter 16 and Chapter 17 of the *General Theory* can be interpreted as 'an unsuccessful effort . . . by Keynes to make sense of Austrian capital theory' (1990: 131)[3]

Two conceptions of capital can be distinguished in the Hayek–Keynes debate. First, Keynes's (1930) notion of capital is in accordance with the methodology of the *Treatise* which consists in building a dynamic analysis of the business cycle from a list of fundamental equations. Indeed, the theoretical heart of the *Treatise* (1930) consists of Books III and IV, in which Keynes presented his fundamental equations, linking the price level to the rate of efficiency earnings of the factors of production and the discrepancy between saving and investment. This discrepancy is related to the existence of windfall profits or losses, which Keynes excluded from his definition of income. Profits Q constitute unexpected gains to entrepreneurs, and are the excess of the market value of current output over the earnings of the factors of production (Keynes 1930, 1: 112–13). Q can differ from zero because of the separation of saving and investment decisions. Windfall profits or losses are the difference between investment and saving in the current period, and, together with the interest rate, determine what investment will be in the next period. Consequently, in the *Treatise*, the discrepancy of profits from its nil value (or windfall profits) constitutes the 'mainspring of change' because this gap influences the level of firms' production and factors demand (Keynes 1930, 1: 141). When profits are nil, I = S and the system is in equilibrium, that is to say, in stationary equilibrium because entrepreneurs are not induced to modify the scale of their production and the level of employment (ibid.: 143).

In this framework, the concept of capital brings together a list of items belonging to various categories which are interconnected. According to Keynes, 'the increment of investment in any period is the net increase of the items belonging to the various categories which make up the aggregate of real and loan capital' (ibid.: 117). Thus, Keynes defines investment as the sum of the aggregate of the real capital and the loan capital. The aggregate of real capital includes first the working capital that is the capital goods which are 'in course of preparation by cultivation or manufacture for use or consumption, or in transport, or with merchant, dealers and detailers, or awaiting the rotation of the seasons' (ibid.: 115). Real capital also covers the fixed capital and the liquid capital which yields nothing but is capable of being used or consumed at any time (ibid.: 116). The loan capital includes the 'net balance of claims on money in a country' (ibid.: 117). The essence of capital is not that it is the result of a production process but that it represents a 'material wealth existing at any time' (ibid.: 115). Consequently, in Keynes's framework, the variations of investment first of all imply variations of incomes rather than variations in the production of capital goods.[4]

Second, Hayek's critique (1931a, b, 1932b) is in great part the consequence of his conception of capital. According to Hayek, business cycle analysis does not have to stop the investigation at the static study of a level of production. It must investigate the temporal production process that examines the insertion of these quantities in the economic system. In line with the Austrian tradition, Hayek (1931c) conceives production as a temporal process. The process takes place in different stages of production, from the primary factors (land and labour) to the consumption goods, with an intermediary passage requiring more or less accumulation in production goods. This production process is represented by the once-famous Hayekian triangles (Hayek 1931c: 38–40). Thus, Hayek considers to be different the two goods that concern two different stages of production.

Now, according to Hayek, Keynes's book totally ignored the Austrian foundations of Wicksell's theory (Hayek 1931a: 279). Hayek maintained that Keynes did not explain the origin of profits. To this was linked the confusion in the definition of investment.

With regard to profits, Hayek agrees with Keynes (1930) to consider them as the mainspring of change in the economic system. But he disagrees with the idea according to which only aggregate profits lead to a change in production. Hayek suggests distinguishing two elements. On the one hand, profit is not only a monetary phenomenon but a real one which even exists in a barter economy (Hayek 1931a: 273). One the other hand, profit is a microeconomic concept which has to be explained from the study of relative supply and demands for goods (ibid.). Profits cannot be defined at the level of entrepreneurs as a whole. They do not correspond to the differences between receipts and expenditures in the same period. Then, product and employment fluctuations occur independently of the existence of a global profit.

According to Hayek (1931a), Keynes's false conception of profits come from his unclear understanding of investment. In Hayek's view, profits (and losses) made at the different stages of production must be considered:

In such a case, profits and losses are originally not the effect of a discrepancy between the receipts for consumption goods and the expenditure on the factors of production, and therefore they are not explained by Mr. Keynes' analysis. Or, rather, there are no total profits in Mr. Keynes' sense in this case, and yet there occur those very effects which he regards as only conceivable as the consequence of the emergence of net total profits or losses. The explanation of this is that while the definition of profits which I have quoted before serves very well when it is applied to individual profits, it becomes misleading when it is applied to entrepreneurs as a whole.

(Hayek 1931a: 275)

The obscurity of Keynes's analysis of investment arose from a misunderstanding of a correct theory of capital (ibid.: 276). The relative movements of intermediary goods in the different stages of production are integrated into Keynes's notion of aggregate capital. But the possibility of fluctuations between these stages is ignored (ibid.: 274). In a horizontal analysis of the production process, a lack in a stage of production is not directly balanced by an excess in another stage. Losses in intermediary goods stages are not offset by profits in consumption goods stages. Thus, Hayek's criticisms are based upon the idea that Keynes's definition of investment as a global variable neglected the variations of investment in the different stages of production. Moreover, investment process is not a static process but an intertemporal one, unlike Keynes's conception:

an explanation of the causes which make investment more or less attractive should form the basis of any analysis of investment. *Such an explanation can, however, only be reached by a close analysis of the factors determining the relative prices of capital goods in the different successive stages of production* – for the difference between these prices is the only source of interest. But this is excluded from the outset if only *total* profits are made the aim of the investigation. Mr. Keynes' aggregates conceal the most fundamental mechanisms of change.

(Hayek 1931a: 277)

To these alternative conceptions of capital correspond two analyses of the business cycle.

Co-ordination and the business cycle in the Hayek–Keynes debate

The debate reveals two alternative conceptions of the co-ordination between saving and investment which lead to two analyses of business cycles. In Hayek's theory, business cycles come from the introduction of *exogenous* shocks or institutional mechanisms – money and credit – which upset the balance between investment and saving. In Keynes's framework, business cycles are the *endogenous* result of the working of the financial sphere. It must be noted that the financial sphere does not only correspond to the bank system, as in Hayek's theory (1931c), since it also includes the 'financial circulation' that is

> the business of holding and exchanging existing titles to wealth (other than exchanges resulting from the specialisation of industry), including stock exchange and money market transactions, speculation and the process of conveying current savings and profits into the hands of entrepreneurs.
>
> (Keynes 1930, 1: 217)

According to Hayek (1931a), Keynes's conception of capital has misleading consequences on the analysis of business cycles. Indeed, in neglecting the foundations of productive activities, Keynes (1930) made a mistake in his analysis of the co-ordination between saving and investment. Hayek fundamentally criticised Keynes for having done away with the relative price between consumption and investment goods. As a consequence, Keynes forgot to establish the conditions under which investment and consumption vary inversely in the short run. If the economy is in a situation of full employment, the resources needed to increase the production of consumption goods come from the investment sector (Hayek 1931a: 286). Thus, it is not possible to build a business cycle analysis without considering the signals that govern saving and investment decisions.

Hayek's review (1931a, b, 1932a) is based on the definition of saving as a delayed consumption. Saving today means a desire to consume tomorrow. Savers willingly release resources to finance investment. The roundabout production process matches with the temporal utility delay due to saving. Thus, an increase in saving corresponds to higher future consumption and, consequently needs an increase in the investment of production goods.

From this Austrian foundation, Hayek (1931c) proposed an analysis of business cycles based on the notion of intertemporal equilibrium (Hayek 1928). First of all, this concept determined the conditions of a perfect co-ordination of individual decisions and actions. The discrepancy from intertemporal equilibrium resulted then in co-ordination failures which led to cyclical fluctuations.

Intertemporal equilibrium is the benchmark of business cycle theory (Hayek 1933: 28–9, 42–4, 95–6), a norm from which we can understand Hayek's analysis of co-ordination failures. Along intertemporal equilibrium, the structure of production is in equilibrium. Firms produce in order to satisfy the demand of consumption goods so that balance between supply and demand is verified in the sector of production goods as well as in the sector of consumption goods. Consequently, entrepreneurs' investment decisions correspond to households' saving intentions. At the intertemporal equilibrium, individual decisions, especially those of savers and investors, are perfectly co-ordinated. In this ideal situation, money is referred to as 'neutral' because it does not interfere with the co-ordination of decisions between buyers and sellers so that relative prices are formed 'as if they were influenced only by the "real" factors which are taken into account in equilibrium economics' (Hayek 1931c: 130).

There is a co-ordination failure when the integration of money in the form of credit breaks the conditions of intertemporal equilibrium, that is, when it modifies the balance between saving and investment. Adaptation of firms to this new situation disrupts the equilibrium of the structure of production so that the economy diverges from its intertemporal equilibrium path. Credit has the effect of artificially lengthening the structure of production and interfering with the regulating function of relative prices (Hayek 1931c: 85–90). Thus, a co-ordination failure cannot take place without the intervention of an exogenous institution, the bank system which perturbs the perfect co-ordination of saving and investment decisions. It is well known that the main difficulty of Hayek's analysis is that it does not explain the origin of these monetary exogenous shocks.

Keynes's business cycle analysis is derived from the Wicksellian equilibrium. 'This condition of equilibrium comes to the same thing as (1) the equality of savings and the value of investment, and (2) the equality of the "market rate" and the "natural rate" of interest' (Keynes 1930, 1: 142). The business cycle is the consequence of the discrepancy between investment and saving. When savings exceeds investment, firms suffer losses, prices decrease, and the economy enters a recession. Inversely, when investment is higher than saving, firms make profits and the economy enters a boom period. At the macroeconomic equilibrium, both the value and the cost of current investment must be equal to the amount of current savings. Aggregate profits are zero. The purchasing power of money and the price level of aggregate output will both correspond to the money rate of efficiency earnings of the factors of production (ibid.: 141). The conditions for the equilibrium of the purchasing power of money require that the banking system should so regulate its rate of lending that the value of investment is equal to savings (ibid.: 137). If the banking system regulates the amount which it lends to entrepreneurs in such a way that the market rate of interest is equal to the natural rate, the value of investment is then equal to the amount of savings, aggregate profits are zero, and the purchasing power of money is stable. If they make positive profits, entrepreneurs will be willing and at the same time influenced by the abundance of the bank credit at their disposal, and the average rate of remuneration which they offer to the factors of production will increase (ibid.: 141). Otherwise, when the bank credit at their disposal is scarce, prices decrease, entrepreneurs make negative profits and remunerations diminish.

Thus, it seems possible to conclude that Keynes's (1930) and Hayek's (1931c) analysis are similar in so far as fluctuations are in both cases the result of changes in the amount of credit lended to entrepreneurs. But this conclusion would be wrong because, in Keynes's conception, fluctuations can appear independently of the actions of monetary authorities in so far as the financial sphere is not reduced to the banks. Changes due to financial factors either modify the supply of money available for industrial circulation or the attractiveness of new investment and of saving, *without an exogenous action from of the banks.*

Indeed, in the *Treatise*, Keynes developed a theory of the interest rate explaining why a co-ordination failure could occur. This theory deviated from Hayek's in that it considered how asset prices can affect the flows of saving and investment (Keynes 1931: 390–1). In his early writings, Hayek (1931c) assimilated these flows with the supply and demand for loanable funds respectively. In contrast, Keynes argued that saving does not automatically constitute a supply of loanable funds:

> I could never have expected, if it had not been for more than one experience
> to the contrary, that a competent economist could read my *Treatise* carefully
> and leave it with the idea that it was *my view* that the difference between
> saving and investment could be exactly measured by changes in the quantity of
> money, whether it be in the inactive circulation or the active circulation
> or the total circulation, corrected or uncorrected for changes in the velocity
> of circulation or the volume of output or the number of times intermediate
> products change hands.
>
> (Keynes 1931: 390)

Keynes (1930) differentiated between the decision to save current resources instead of consuming them and the decision to loan saving to investors. In contrast to Hayek, Keynes realised that households have the choice between a variety of financial assets to determine the form in which savings must command future consumption. Supply and demand of loanable funds are not independent but are influenced by the transactions of other financial markets. For this reason, Keynes argued that, independently of the actions of the monetary authorities, financial markets transmit disturbances which are caused by shifting speculative behaviour. The equilibrating mechanism of the interest rate cannot play the role of co-ordinating saving and investment decisions. Therefore, the disequilibrium between investment and saving may well persist for a while even when the quantity of money in circulation does not change:

> In my view, saving and investment (as I define them) can get out of gear
> without any change on the part of the banking system from 'neutrality' as
> defined by Dr. Hayek, merely as a result of the public changing their rate of
> saving or the entrepreneurs changing their rate of investment, there being no
> automatic mechanism in the economic system (as Dr. Hayek's view would
> imply there must be) to keep the two rates equal, provided that the effective
> quantity of money is unchanged.
>
> (Keynes 1931: 393)

Lundberg's contribution to the debate

Lundberg's analysis has a strong theoretical ambition, as it philosophises a synthesis between Keynes's (1930) and Hayek's (1931c, 1933, 1934) approaches. But, before examining his views about the theory of capital and the co-ordination I/S, we have to recall that his programme is built on a specific methodology which is in line with the Stockholm School: the use of the sequence method.[5] In fact, the whole of Lundberg's work consists of the introduction of temporal lags and the cumulative process to reject the hypothesis of simultaneous interdependence and to lay the foundations for the future sequence method. This already is different from Myrdal and Lindahl's previous questioning, still focusing on the question of prices and the definition of monetary equilibrium. To put it another way, the revival of the Wicksellian connection, which is a common feature with Hayek and Keynes, lies in the Wicksell of the cumulative process as analytical principle, the pioneer of the analysis of sequence. To Lundberg, this analysis is at the forefront of the problem of method.

This initial intuition evolves very quickly towards a complete research programme at the heart of which the relationship to business cycle theory becomes pivotal. In fact, describing in 1934 his two years spent at American universities, Lundberg very clearly indicates the subject for his new work, which will lead him to his 1937 dissertation. The question of method thus becomes intimately connected with a specific subject, the study of the business cycle. From the set of possible economic inter-relations, it is important to identify which equilibrium relationships should be broken to facilitate a sequence analysis. Lundberg examines Wicksell's approaches from the point of view of the general 'technique' of cumulative process (1937: 58), to explain the expansion or contraction process, the 'credit cycle theories' (particularly the Keynes of the *Treatise on Money*). He reaches the conclusion that if a choice of a sequence (unit of period) does not include the variations in investment and saving in fixed capital,[6] it will be seriously flawed when it is transposed into the explanation of business cycles. The methodological concern remains unbroken until the presentation of the most famous typical sequences in Chapter IX and its appendix on cycles. In short, the whole of the 1937 work is organised around this comparison (which is not itself an identity) between the constitution of the sequence method and business cycle theories. And well after the key 1930s period, it is this method which, for Lundberg, brings together the fundamental instability of the economy and the permanence of cycles even during a period of growth. If Lundberg has a specific concern for the sequence method, his Wicksellian roots lead him to be influenced by the Hayek–Keynes debate, notably on two main points, the theory of capital and the conception of I/S co-ordination.

The theory of capital

We have seen that Keynes (1930) did not refer to a specific theory of capital. In contrast to Hayek, he conceives capital as a global variable. There is no strict complementarity between production goods and consumption goods and fluctuations can be explained without the mechanism of forced savings. Lundberg's position on the theory of capital is flexible. He needs it but expands it in several temporal relations (and connected types of expectations).[7] Compared to Keynes, Lundberg reintroduces a modified capital theory, missing in the *Treatise*. Compared to Hayek, Lundberg refuses to assess an investment decision in relation to a simultaneous calculation on the performance of the total capital, and he diversifies the time lags into the structure of production. Theses time lags are defined by a discrepancy between costs and income generating for a period unit. His propositions can be interpreted as an original contribution to the Hayek–Keynes controversy about capital, with regard to three points: (1) the definition of capital; (2) the relationship between the equilibrium method and the theory of capital and the re-introduction of the role of the quantity of capital; and (3) the new notions of 'types of investment and capital'.

First, Lundberg takes up the question of the Austrian theory of capital started by Böhm-Bawerk, but from a very different point of view in comparison with the numerous previous debates. In fact, Lundberg does not directly hark back to Böhm-Bawerk's definition of a natural interest rate. This definition is based on the marginal productivity of the total quantity of capital (the marginal productivity of time): as we know, this provoked some probing examinations from the outset, which continued in the 1920s and 1930s. Without returning here to the common ground behind the controversy concerning the average period of production, and the divergence between the critiquing authors (Knight, Fisher, etc.), we need simply to comment on the major participation of the Swedish movement. The young writers of the Stockholm School (especially Lindahl and Myrdal) propose a definition of the interest rate as the present value of a future flow of income. This enables the circumvention of the difficulties and hesitations concerning the definition, presented by Wicksell, of the natural rate to qualify the situation of monetary equilibrium. So advancing the notion of future revenue helps to divert the analysis towards expectations and how they are formed. Lundberg records[8] and approves of the new expectation-based definition, but what really interests him is different.

Second, in accordance with his method, Lundberg contests the relevance of the notion of equilibrium to study capital and business cycles. Taking the capital variable into account in economic change implies a clean break with the hypothesis of simultaneous determination. The formation of capital (investment) requires time and cannot be automatically associated with the total quantity of capital to generate revenue. It is impossible to place these two aspects of capital (new capital and total capital) on the same temporal level. In the Austrian-Wicksellian theory of capital, the 'natural' interest rate (no matter how defined) is calculated in relation to total capital, and, at equilibrium, this rate must be equal to the monetary rate on new capital. This brings us back to the problem of the equilibrium method mentioned above. If a field exists where application of this method is particularly inappropriate, it is the valuing of capital (and especially fixed capital), on account of noticeable temporal differential. A capital theory is especially inconsistent with the equilibrium method and commands sequence method. Many business cycle theories legitimately take into account the role of capital formation: this is especially the case with Hayek, who applies Böhm-Bawerk's capital theory to the study of business cycles. But these theories suffer from the same weakness, that is, the reference to equilibrium (even if it is disrupted over a period), between capital supply and demand. Lundberg has therefore to cast doubt as well on the equilibrium method with regards to the total quantity of capital, by rejecting the simultaneous adaptation between the decisions of the producers on new capital (investment) and their effects on total capital. Taking place between the two is a process, which constantly shifts the emphasis of the initial conditions of this adaptation. To Lundberg:

> The development is thus traced from period to period. The investments are determined by the consumption expenditures and the quantity of capital during the preceding period, and they will during the period under consideration determine current income, the increase in the quantity of capital, and so on. No mutual and simultaneous adaptation between the variables of the system finds expression in this analysis.
>
> (1937: 46)

Lundberg refers the Wicksellian theory of capital to the role of quantity of capital. He explicitly mentions the Austrian and Wicksellian theory of capital, but in a very specific meaning. Lundberg mentions that Wicksell did not explore the influence of the dependence of the marginal productivity of capital on its total quantity on the nature of the cumulative process (ibid.: 56, also 177, n. 2).

> The conclusion of Wicksell's theory, that the cumulative process will go as long as the real rate exceeds the nominal rate of interest, has to be advanced further by also studying the influence upon the sequence from changes in the nominal rate of interest. The need for such a study follows from our conclusion that the real, or natural, rate of interest is not a given quantity allowing us to simplify the problem to an examination of the difference between the real and nominal rates. When we can show how changes in the nominal rate of interest will influence development, these changes will *ipso facto* also influence the real rate of interest.
>
> (ibid.: 217)

Wicksell takes the real rate of interest as given because he mainly examines the consequences of a discrepancy between the real and monetary interest rates. In fact, the marginal productivity of capital depends on the total quantity of capital. For instance the formation of capital (investment) modifies this productivity (natural interest rate), which will decrease. During the cumulative process, the conditions regarding supply and demand for fixed capital and therefore the real rate of interest change. 'Here, then, Wicksell's capital theory entered the analysis, taking into account the supply impact of investments on production capacity, productivity and structure' (Lundberg [1987] 1994: 497). Capital theory is not simply a theory on saving and investment, but also a theory of total capital employed. So, in Lundberg's view, we take advantage of the 'general capital theory' (1937: 56). As we will see below, this second point about capital will be very important to advance a combination of Hayek–Keynes views, when Lundberg (1937, Chapter IX) will propose a multiplier-accelerator sequence or a sequence with an industrial expansion by way of new machines ('rationalisation process').

The third point is crucial. Lundberg does not want to break with the capital theory: 'Nevertheless, the capital theories of Böhm-Bawerk, Wicksell and Åkerman do not lose their importance . . . On the other hand, the above criticism of Hayek's theory does not imply that it cannot explain the business cycle' (ibid.: 32, n. 1). Lundberg advances a more flexible interpretation of the Hayekian theory of production. To Hayek and Lundberg, the production process takes time, and there is a temporal structure of production, i.e. a relationship between production of capital goods and production of consumer goods. But in Lundberg's view, this complementarity is not conditional upon a strict definition of the stages of structure of production, with an automatic adjustment, the forced savings effect. Lundberg, for his part, introduces a new distinction and a new complementarity, with a disaggregation of the notion of capital. He promotes the concept of 'types of investment' or 'types of capital goods'.[9] These types depend on the temporal discrepancy between costs and expected income (and use of the income), with different time-coefficients during the same period. In particular, Lundberg distinguishes between types of investment connected with the capacity of the industry of consumer goods, and types of investment connected to long time capacities of production. The reproduction of the former is very dependent on income (with an accelerator mechanism). The reproduction of the latter is quasi-independent on fluctuations in income and purchasing power, but very sensitive to the rate of interest. The former is connected with short time expectations; the latter with long-term expectations. For instance:

A time of production lasting several unit-periods evidently means that costs paid out for current production are not covered by corresponding receipts from current sales. This type of investment generates income without corresponding claims on receipts, thus giving rise to a net surplus in the total monetary demand for goods and services.

(Lundberg 1937: 168)

Their cumulative processes are different due to the economic variables regulating the link between costs of the investment, generated income from these costs, and receipts for the producers. Dynamics initiated by investment for consumer goods from period to period depend on income, division between consumption and savings, and the volume of the demand for consumer goods. On the contrary, the other dynamics lie on interest rate, savings as demand for capital goods, and the volume of the demand for these goods. So Lundberg identifies the durability of investment[10] and its implied types of complementarity. This disaggregation of the capital structure and the investment role go beyond to the initial Austrian and Wicksellian, but also Keynesian references. Only certain types of investment require the Hayekian complementarity (roundaboutness); other types are compatible with the Keynesian view. The cycle will take various forms depending on these unequal relationships.

These three specifications on capital theory will allow a very specific conciliation between Keynes and Hayek used to interpret the turning point in an expansion process (hence the business cycle).

The conception of *I/S* co-ordination: what kind of synthesis between Hayek and Keynes?

The second criss-crossing between the Hayek–Keynes controversy and Lundberg is the analysis of co-ordination. The 'Wicksell connection', i.e. the co-ordination between saving and investment, is a common point to Keynes's theory in the *Treatise* (1930) and Hayek's early 1930s business cycle theory. On this broader basis, Lundberg claims to reconcile the outwardly contradictory publications by Keynes and Hayek.

Initially Lundberg bases his analysis of business cycles on a Wicksellian hypothesis widely used at that time. It involves accepting the temporal structure of production (roundabout of production), the possibility of gaps between the two interest rates, and the cumulative process. This heritage was previously widely employed by other authors in business cycle explanation. Such is the case with Hayek (in *Prices and Production*), 1931c – throughout the 1933 publications and in 1934, and with Keynes (*Treatise on Money*, 1930). As we have seen in the preceding section, the main point of discord with regard to I/S co-ordination lies in Hayek's insistence on exogenous money supply whereas Keynes prefers to highlight the role of speculation on financial assets.

If Lundberg agrees with the conception of I/S co-ordination, he still examines it with some temporal developments. Thus, his conception about saving depends on process considerations (1937, Chapter VI). Saving can be analysed as a 'rest' between income and consumption expenses, a passive element in the system. So income paid out during one period is not automatically transformed into new income during a succeeding period. Saving represent a kind of 'short circuit' (ibid.: 137) in income-generation. To maintain equilibrium, a different income (investment), with specific motivations, has to be constituted. Keynes put forward this view. But, in Lundberg's view, saving is also a form of demand as active as that for consumption goods, but directed towards capital goods. New saving claim a transfer of demand from consumption to capital goods, and investment is considered a 'passive' factor. This is the classical concept of saving accepted by Hayek.

Lundberg considers that each of these contradictory visions (Keynes vs. Hayek) presents

> a one-sided picture of the process of saving . . . Savings out of income do not generally constitute a direct demand for capital goods; they can only under certain conditions be transformed into such a demand. It is the investigation of these conditions that constitutes the crux of the theory of capital formation, as well of any business cycle theory . . . On the other hand, . . . when Keynes disputes the active influence of savings and identifies them with investment, he excludes the possibility of discriminating between the varying effects upon the determining factors of investment that different forms of savings might have.
>
> (Lundberg 1937: 138)

The Keynesian view omits the influence of saving upon the formation of real capital.[11] The Hayekian view overlooks the circumstances of that influence. According to Lundberg, the connection between saving and formation of real capital is not automatic, but possible. Lundberg gives an example: increased savings primarily tend to a reduction in demand in formation goods, with losses for producers of these goods. But in their active form, they generate gains within capital industries (in the 'classical' view). If

> however, the producers of consumption goods, in attempting to uphold their liquidity, immediately start selling securities up to an amount corresponding to their losses, the whole of the increased savings may be absorbed in financing 'distress sales'.
>
> (ibid.: 143)

So the problem indicates the 'incompleteness of the formulation of the problem' (ibid.). The concepts of saving and investment are irrelevant in a static system.

The connections depend on temporal relations, progressiveness, and certain expected and realised changes in time, temporal embeddedness (especially total capital, connection with types of investment . . .) which lead to irreversibilities:

> The motives for investing and saving must in some way be related to certain expected and realised *changes in time* . . . [These changes] in anticipations must be incorporated in the system of explanation and finally ascribed to the changes in the economic factors on which entrepreneurs base their plans. Among the factors that have to be included in order to explain their investment plans are savings, just as savings are affected by investment by way of income-generation. The change in question necessarily partakes of the nature of a certain fixation in time which renders the processes irreversible . . . New investments cause an increased quantity and a changed structure of capital; savings effect changes in the long-term interest rate and the credit policy; a discrepancy between the two items leads to a change in the quantity of money in circulation, etc. . . . The relationship between savings and investment and therefore the effects of savings can only be exactly determined if placed in a fully defined sequence system.
>
> (ibid.: 143–4)

Finally, passive or active characteristics of savings must be judged from the angle of expected income during a given period, and must be endogenised into a sequence (with changes in total capital and structure of capital).

With this flexible type of complementarities of saving/investment theories, Lundberg then proposes an analysis of the business cycle, which helps in the consideration of the oppositions between Hayek and Keynes described in the second section. The question of total capital is again at the centre of Lundberg's concerns. Back in 1934, Lundberg sought to connect investment movements with the position of capital within the cycle. In his view, Hayek over-emphasises the monetary factors, by introducing through the money element an *ad hoc* exogenous gap in order to explain the schism between the real and monetary rates of interest. In the *Treatise*, Keynes 'gives nearly nothing' (1934: 52) on the causes of the gap between saving and investment. It is the reference to capital stock within the actual evolution of the cycle, which should resolve 'the main question . . . Why is it an increased demand for consumption goods sometimes means a decreased demand (Hayek) and sometimes an increased demand (Keynes, Clark) for capital goods?' (Lundberg 1934: 52). Lundberg replies in his 1937 famous model sequences (Chapter IX). He examines five cases of an economic system in an expansion phase. The third and the fourth are the most important for our subject. In particular, Lundberg deals with the sequences which take into account fixed capital (unlike other model sequences considered in this chapter). He advances a 'synthesis' or a 'combination' between 'Hayek-type' sequence and 'Keynes-type' sequence[12] (1937: 234). To present these two types in a unified framework Lundberg uses a multiplier-accelerator framework, with a process analysis starting from investment (or a Wicksellian discrepancy between interest rates):

$$I \rightarrow C \rightarrow I$$

The cumulative process can lead to a continued expansion, with a multiplier link between the investment (I) and the consumption (C), and an accelerator link between C and I. But the continuation of this process depends on the durability of the investment. As we have seen, Lundberg identifies two types of investment, and so distinguishes two types of sequence, accounting for two types of disruption of the cycle upswing:

1   the Hayek-type sequence, based on types of investment connected to the creation of production goods and long-term capacities of production;
2   the Keynes-type sequence based on types of investment connected with the production of consumption goods and the short-term capacity.

In the first sequence, investments are independent of the increase of the current generated income and the demand for consumption goods.[13] So the expansion cannot be supplied in this way. Compensation occurs with a development of investment due to the conversion of savings. But Lundberg introduces an increase of costs (included interest rate) during the expansion phase, with specific coefficients. This type of investment reacts against long-term costs as interest rate, and decreases. Lundberg interprets the difficulty of compensation by a Hayekian weakness of savings[14] explaining the break:

> An increase in savings will lower the long-term rate of interest to such an extent that the effects upon the volume of new investments will more than compensate the corresponding decrease in the effective demand for consumption good . . . This conclusion, however, depends upon the type of investment considered. [. . . In our case . . .], it may be argued that the turn in the development is caused by *the amount of savings being too small* . . . This conclusion is similar to that arrived at by Hayek when he analyses a process of 'forced savings'.
>
> (Lundberg 1937: 227, 232)

The second type of sequence focuses on an income effect, with a Keynesian turning point explained by the weakness of purchasing power and under-consumption. The investment in consumption goods has to be increased to maintain the cumulative process (expansion). With certain coefficients, a disruption can appear between, on the one hand, the necessity of a certain volume of the demand for disruption goods to develop investment, and, on the other hand, an increase in investment to correspond to this demand. An excess of production (or weakness of purchasing power) occurs.

Lundberg is cautious about the strict separation between the two types of sequence. He stresses the decisive values of different coefficients to establish the relative importance of each type of sequences.[15] Coefficients cannot be fixed. Moreover, Lundberg's framework also includes other sequences and time lags. But the identification and conciliation of Hayek-type and Keynes-type sequences are two important instances of instability. According to Lundberg, Hayek's sequence has occured in 1873, 1890, 1907 and 1925–28 German crisis. A typical example of Kenyes' sequence was the 1929 crisis.

Conclusion

We have seen that the Hayek–Keynes controversy influenced not only the members of the Cambridge circus and of the London School of Economics but also the Swedish School. In particular, this chapter shows that the traditional interpretation of Lundberg's works through Keynesian glasses is mistaken. Indeed, we have demonstrated that Lundberg's business cycle analysis can appear as an attempt to synthesise Hayek's and Keynes's theories. This kind of synthesis is centred on a redefinition of the theory of capital and a particular conception of the co-ordination between investment and saving. It is to be noted that the conclusion of the chapter is in line with Leijonhufvud's (1997) interpretation of the Wicksellian connection in the 1930s.

If Lundberg tried to build a synthesis of Keynes and Hayek, it must be noted that his conception of the business cycle is closer to Keynes than to Hayek. Indeed, Lundberg rejects Hayek's intertemporal co-ordination problem because it is based upon equilibrium method. He does not accept an exogenous causation by monetary factors. If he integrates a forced savings effect, it is not from the point of view of an initial reference to I–S equilibrium, but in connection with a specific sequence based on a specific type of investment and capital. To Lundberg, 'the fundamental reason why such a development cannot go on does not lie in the original deviation from a total equilibrium between savings and investments. Such a deviation is necessary in order to get the expansion' (Lundberg 1937: 232). Nevertheless, with regard to Keynes, Lundberg does not insert the role of the financial factors in his analysis of the I–S co-ordination. His synthesis between Hayek and Keynes could appear as too flexible (with a dual role of savings) and thus reinforce an 'eclecticism' often mentioned (Laidler 1999: 52) in comments on the Swedish School.

Acknowledgements

The first version of this chapter was presented in the workshop held in St-Etienne (France). We thank the participants for their comments. The chapter has particularly benefitted from M. Boianovsky, A. Leisonnufuud, and M. Trautwein comments.

Notes

1 Other Swedish economists have connected Hayek to Keynes, especially Ohlin (1932, § III and IV), regarding business cycle theories. But they do not claim a synthesis between these two authors. Ohlin proposes a typology between the *Kapitalmangel* theories (including those of Hayek and J. Åkerman) and the *Unterkapitalisationstheorie* (of Keynes). Also see J. Åkerman (1933), and recent papers (Hansson 2002; Wadensjö 2002).

2 Hayek asserts that Keynes's reference to Wicksell on the natural rate of interest is ambiguous. Indeed, Wicksell's natural rate is a real rate determined by the relative supply and demand of consumption and production goods. On the other hand, Keynes's natural rate corresponds to the temporary equilibrium of investment and saving and does not have the long-term regulating properties of Hayek's natural rate. Finally, Keynes replies to Hayek that a complete theory of the real interest rate had not been constructed yet (Keynes 1931: 394).

3 As the aim of this section is not to study the impact of Hayek's capital theoretic attack on the *General Theory*, we would refer the reader to Mongiovi (1990: 145–52) for a further analysis on this point.

4 The production of capital goods during any period corresponds to the increment of fixed capital and the increment of working capital. The production of consumption goods during any period is defined as the flow of available output plus the increment of working capital which will emerge as available output.

5 Even if the whole of the Stockholm School focuses on the dynamic method (Hansson 1982; Zappia 2001), Lundberg has a specific position: mistrust of the equilibrium framework, introduction of disequilibrium sequences, insistence on analysing business cycle (Lundberg 1930, 1934; Trautwein 1996; Henriksson 1996). See also:

> The analysis of Wicksell's conceptions of monetary equilibrium is no interest in this connection. The inconsistencies of Wicksell's conceptions have been analysed by Lindahl . . . and Myrdal . . . We are instead interested in his method of combining states of disequilibrium over successive periods.
>
> (Lundberg 1937: 45, n. 1)

6 Lundberg (1937, Chapter III: 60–1) considers that Keynes (1930) does not take fixed capital into account in the *Treatise*.

7 Non-expected profits or losses have a similar role than Keynes' windfall profits or losses.

8 For instance, Knight has in a number of articles expanded the concept of average period of production' (Lundberg 1937: 199, n. 1).

9 See Lundberg (1937: 44, n. 1; and Chapters VIII–IX). Lundberg takes account of many empirical analyses on business cycles based on the role of the investment.

10 See in this book (Chapter 13) Bellet and Durieu on Lachmann's interpretation of Lundberg's distinction.

11 Lundberg mentions savings in the form of the purchase of new securities: 'The internal savings of a business undertaking approach the classical definition of savings when, instead of being paid out to shareholders in the form of dividends, current surplus is used for the acquirement of new capital equipment' (1937: 139).

12 Respectively Lundberg connects his 3rd (and also 8th and 10th) tables with 'Keynes-type' sequence, and his 6th and 7th tables with 'Hayek-type' sequence (Chapter IX).

13 If the period considered is short, amortisations, dividends, interest and expected profits could not be considered income-generating costs.

14 See Berg (1991) for a precise presentation. The author shows that this break is only temporary: after iteration 5 (break), economic expansion takes off with different booms. So Lundberg's interpretation concerning the inadequate increase of savings is not consistent: inter-relations between other variables influence the process at different times.

15 According to Lundberg (1937: 229):

> In no way do we claim, however, to present an exact formula to show at what point an increase of savings indicates conditions favouring an increase of new investments; or *vice versa* where a decrease in savings, and thus an increase of expenditure on consumer's goods, may heighten the inducement to new investment.

References

Åkerman, J. (1933) 'Saving in the depression', in *Economic Essays in Honour of Gustav Cassel*, London: Frank Cass & Co. Ltd, pp. 11–31.

Bellet, M. (2002) 'Is there a cycle theory in the Stockholm School?', *History of Economic Ideas*, XI(1): 69–93.

Berg, C. (1991) 'Lundberg, J.M. Keynes, and the riddles of a general theory', in Jonung, L. (ed.) *The Stockholm School of Economic Revisited*, Cambridge: Cambridge University Press, Part II, Chapter 8, pp. 205–30.

Hansson, B. (1982) *The Stockholm School and the Development of Dynamic Method*, London: Croom Helm.

—— (2002) 'Bertil Ohlin and the Stockholm School: autonomous changes in consumption demands; Ohlin, 1932 to 1934', in Findlay, R., Jonung, L. and Lundahl, M. (eds) *Bertil Ohlin: A Centennial Celebration (1899–1999)*, Cambridge, MA: MIT Press, Chapter 14.

Hayek, F. (1928) 'Intertemporal price equilibrium and movements in the value of money', in McCloughry, R.M. (ed.) *Money, Capital and Fluctuations: Early Essays of F.A. Hayek*, London: Routledge and Kegan Paul, 1984, pp. 71–117.

—— (1931a) 'Reflections on the pure theory of money of Mr. J.M. Keynes', *Economica*, August: 270–95.

—— (1931b) 'A rejoinder to Mr. Keynes', *Economica*, November: 398–403.

—— (1931c) *Prices and Production*, London: Routledge and Sons, 2nd edn, 1935.

—— (1932a) 'Reflections on the pure theory of money of Mr. J.M. Keynes (continued)', *Economica*, February: 22–44.

—— (1932b) 'Money and capital: a reply', *The Economic Journal*, June, 42, 166: 237–49.

—— (1933) *Monetary Theory and the Trade Cycle*, New York: A.M. Kelley.

—— (1934) 'Capital and industrial fluctuations', *Econometrica*, 2(2): 152–67, in *Prices and Production*, 2nd edn, 1935, 134–62.

—— (1966) 'Personal recollections of Keynes and the "Keynesian revolution",' *The Oriental Economist*, 34: 78–80, in Caldwell, B. (ed.) *The Collected Works of F.A. Hayek*. vol. 9, *Contra Keynes and Cambridge*, London: Routledge, 1995, pp. 240–6.

Henriksson, R.G.H. (1996) 'The early contribution of Erik Lundberg: a commentary to his licentiate thesis "On the concept of economic equilibrium (1930)"', *Structural Change and Economic Dynamics*, 7: 348–60.

Jonung, L. (ed.) (1991) *The Stockholm School of Economics Revisited*, Cambridge: Cambridge University Press.

Keynes, J.M. (1930) *A Treatise on Money*, in Moggridge, D. (ed.) *The Collected Writings of John Maynard Keynes*, London: Macmillan, 1973, vols V–VI.

—— (1931) 'The pure theory of money: a reply to Dr. Hayek', *Economica*, November: 385–97.

—— (1973) *The Collected Writings of John Maynard Keynes*, Moggridge, D. (ed.), London: Macmillan.

Laidler, D. (1999) *Fabricating the Keynesian Revolution: Studies of the Inter-war Literature on Money, the Cycle, and Unemployment*, Cambridge: Cambridge University Press.

Leijonhufvud, A. (1997) 'The Wicksellian heritage', *Economic Notes by Banca Monte des Paschi di Siena*, 26(1): 1–10.

Lundberg, E. (1930) 'Begreppet ekonomisk jämvikt och dess Tillämpning', abbreviated version in *Ekonomisk Tidskrift*, 32: 133–60, English trans. 'On the concept of economic equilibrium', in *Structural Change and Economic Dynamics* (1996), 7: 361–90.

—— (1934) 'Report on my studies as a Rockefeller Fellow of Economics', in Lundberg, E. (1994) *Studies in Economic Instability and Change*, Stockholm: SNS Förlag, pp. 48–66.

—— (1937) *Studies in the Theory of Economic Expansion*, London, reprint of Economic Classics, New York: A.M. Kelly (1955).

—— (1960) 'On comprehending Keynes and understanding others', *Ekonomisk Tidskrift*, 62: 195–205, English trans. in Lundberg, E. (1994) *Studies in Economic Instability and Change*, Stockholm: SNS Förlag, pp. 475–84.

—— (1987) 'Memories of the Stockholm School', originally published in *Ekonomisk Debatt*, 15: 280–6, English trans. in Lundberg, E. (1994) *Studies in Economic Instability and Change*, Stockholm: SNS Förlag, pp. 491–9.

—— (1994) *Studies in Economic Instability and Change*, Stockholm: SNS Förlag.

—— (1996), *The Development of Swedish and Keynesian Macroeconomic Theory and its Impact on Economic Policy*, Marelli, E. (ed.), R. Mattioli Foundation, Cambridge: Cambridge University Press.

Mongiovi, G. (1990) 'Keynes, Hayek and Sraffa: on the origins of Chapter 17 of the *General Theory*', *Economie Appliquée*, XLIII, 2: 131–56.

Myrdal, G. (1939) *Monetary Equilibrium*, London: W. Hodge and Company, English modified version of 'Der gleichgewichtsbegriff als instrument der geldtheoretischen analyse', in Hayek, F.A. (ed.) *Beiträge zur Geldtheorie* (1933), Vienna: Julius Springer.

Ohlin, B. (1932) 'Ungelöste probleme der gegenwärtigen krisis', *Weltwirtschaftliches Archiv*, XXXVI: 1–23.

Trautwein, H.-M. (1996) 'Review article about E. Lundberg, "Studies in economic instability and change"', *Structural Change and Economic Dynamics*, 7: 263–71.

Wadensjö, E. (2002) 'Bertil Ohlin and the committee on unemployment, 1927 to 1935', in Findlay, R., Jonung, L. and Lundahl, M. (eds) *Bertil Ohlin: A Centennial Celebration (1899–1999)*, Cambridge, MA: MIT Press, Chapter 15.

Zappia, C. (2001) 'Equilibrium and disequilibrium dynamics in the 1930s', *Journal of the History of Economic Thought*, 23(1): 55–75.

8 Monetary regimes and international co-ordination

What Hayek said and what Wicksell would have said about them

Dominique Torre and Elise Tosi

Introduction

With the aim of providing the most efficient mechanisms able to ensure international monetary co-ordination, modern analysis does not challenge, from both an analytical and historical point of view, the so-called 'corner solutions' corresponding respectively to nominal anchoring systems, monetary unions and flexible exchange rates. These corner solutions delimit a triangular area within which the other (and inefficient) monetary arrangements are located. The rather successful launching of the Euro, the repeatedly reaffirmed propensity of small dependent economies to adopt currency boards or to dollarise and the tendency of the remaining developed nations to defend flexible parities regimes confirm the polarisation of current monetary regimes around the acceptance of these three corner solutions. This rather stable but asymmetric equilibrium between different monetary systems has something unsatisfactory in the sense that it renders complex the transition processes of monetary systems and traps the national economies in definitive options similar to lock-in.

This chapter deals with systems that are neither as co-ordinated as monetary unions, nor as flexible as floating exchange rates regimes, nor finally as 'credible' as dollarised domestic systems. They correspond to the major part of the monetary arrangements of the twentieth century. Among the observers of these systems, Hayek was certainly one of the most frequently referred to, for having repeatedly defended strict adaptations of free market conceptions to international monetary arrangements. Wicksell's opinions are less known, certainly because they were only expressed in circumstances associated with the monetary choices of a rather small country. We will try to reconsider the contrasting positions of Wicksell and Hayek on international monetary relations, not really to confront their respective and well-known positions on market, money and credit but to explore the range of possible solutions for co-ordinating national economies linked by external exchanges and capital movements. Our intuition is that some invariants exist in the different stages of our monetary history that lead to an analysis of modern economic arrangements with (new or old) theoretical approaches which may also be relevant for historical experiences rather distant in the past. Hayekian as well as Wicksellian works may thus on the one hand contribute to complete our understanding of corner solutions by the analysis of mixed monetary co-ordinating schemas. On the other hand, they could provide analytical elements for the comprehension of the relevant way to manage modern monetary relations in a world characterised by the existence of multiple international monetary systems and areas.

The next section recalls Wicksellian positions on gold and inconvertibility, while the following section tries to question the consistency of Hayekian developments contained in *Monetary Nationalism and International Stability* (1937). This book is not usually considered a major contribution but it includes the most developed presentation of the Hayekian position on inconvertible currencies in the 1930s. Hayek and Myrdal are then compared regarding the definition of the adequate form of co-ordination of modern international monetary systems. Finally, a conclusion is provided.

From gold to inconvertibility: Wicksell on monetary systems

There is little originality in being an opponent of gold when the major part of the world shares an international metallic currency but, on the contrary, only decisive reasons can justify the preference for fiat monies when gold operates as a general equivalent for all the domestic units of payment. Wicksell adopted this uncomfortable but inflexible position with an increasing determinacy, as the European economies moved before 1914 towards a system where gold seemed to be a fair companion for prosperity. In the second part of *Interest and Prices*, along with the discussion about the long-term objectives of monetary policy, he considers convertibility not as a way to improve co-ordination among central banks, but rather as a risk of destabilisation of the price level which depends on the international stock of gold and its distribution among nations:

> It is rather to be feared that if gold continues to be produced on the present or on a higher scale, the monetary institutions will be finally compelled to lower their rates of interest to such extent that a rise in price will be unavoidable.
>
> (Wicksell 1898: 193)

A few years later, he develops a more complete version of his monetary views. In the second volume of the *Lectures*, his opinion is far more negative concerning the presumed regulatory properties of gold. After his defence of the advantages of credit economies, he once more deplores the exogenous shocks resulting from the use of metallic standards:

Gold could easily be replaced by credit, both for internal needs and for inter-national payments of any amount, . . . the great and ever-increasing stocks of gold in minted form, accumulated, with so much toil and trouble, are useless and superfluous . . . Even as a safety reserve for unforeseen circumstances, these reserves of gold would be entirely unnecessary.

(Wicksell 1911: 122)

He then considers that the major way to improve the international monetary rela-tions will be reached when gold is abandoned as a means of payment and as a standard of value. In a world where the stabilising properties of precious metals operate as self-fulfilling expectations, gold becomes an *'unpleasant necessity'* (ibid.: 124). Secular movements in prices are not mainly explained by the role of gold (see Jonung 1979a, on this point). Wicksell's opinion is that:

If the gold standard seems to have functioned satisfactorily, . . . it is not because the central banks were obeying the rules of the game, but because they were operating within a situation where the markets were clearly united by the flow of commodities of which gold was only one.

(Jörberg and Kranz 1989: 1061)

The context of World War I and its consequences on the Swedish monetary situ-ation offered a new opportunity for Wicksell to reaffirm his opposition to the gold standard. The *Riksbank* suspended the convertibility on 2 August 1914, in the belief that the war would be of short duration. After a brief episode of return to convertibility in 1916, the gold standard was once more partly removed: the law of February 1916 excluded the possibility of a conversion of gold bullion into notes of the central banks but maintained the right to convert notes into gold. At this time, Sweden was experimenting with a phase of imported inflation, other countries were shipping gold to Sweden and converting it into Swedish money, thus increasing the money supply and the prices in Sweden (Lester 1939). Then, with the risk of a misunderstanding of his own solution to escape from the infla-tionary context, Wicksell 'rejects various plans to return to a gold standard or to stabilise the dollar exchange rate of the Swedish currency' (Jonung 1988: 339). During this period, his position is indeed equidistant from two opposite solu-tions. On the one hand, he reasserts his opposition to a 'neutral' monetary policy which would accommodate the newly increased money amount. On the other hand, he suggests avoiding all confusion between the goal of price stability and the objective of a return to gold.

How is it conceivable to be deflationist in the inter-war period, when one has no illusions about the stabilising properties of a common standard? In such a situ-ation, contemporaneous endogenists would suggest accommodation. In the same way that a regular progression of monetary aggregates is logically required to adopt the quantity theory of money, discretion seems only able to cope with the objective of allowing a better allocation of financial flows when a reverse causality characterises monetary relations. Wicksell's norms of monetary policy seem therefore somewhat strange from our modern theoretical routines. We can however better understand the contextual motives of the Wicksellian position, since the content of the short articles he published in Swedish from 1917 to 1925 has been analysed (Boianovsky 1998); they confirm the real nature of Wicksell's defence of an original version of monetary orthodoxy which is also apparent in his unpublished manuscripts (Jonung 1988). These modern interpretations of Wicksell's position exhibit the place of nominal contracts in the exposition of the Wicksellian rules for economic policy. 'Wicksell's persistent demand for a return to the 1914 price level [in Sweden] was based on the notion that one of the foundations of the institution of economic contracts is the constancy of the value of money' (Boianovsky 1998: 223). He considers the theoretical discussion about the implementation of the deflationary policy in Sweden as a sort of experimental laboratory for his own monetary conceptions. On this occasion, he presents a spectacular collection of innovative arguments for this inter-war period. In several works, he stresses the role of the announcement of monetary policy measures (ibid.: 225–6). Like the new classical and Keynesian economists, he does not suppose any monetary illusion in the workers' perception of prices to justify the efficiency of his monetary policy; he promotes – in keeping with the rational expectations hypothesis – the device of sliding scales of wages. Finally, he proposes carrying out a fall in prices 'in one step', anticipating the modern analyses of monetary reforms (ibid.: 225–6).

This obstinate defence of the advantages of deflation does not contradict his previous theoretical works. His normative injunctions were already the consequence of his descriptions of the cumulative process. In his 1925 article in the *Ekonomisk Tidskrift*, translated into English and published at the end of the Kelley's edition of *Interest and Prices*, he reformulates the previously presented inflationary process as a consequence of a positive discrepancy between the natural and the money rates of interest. He then develops the way by which, in this case, competition between producers is the origin of an inflationary process. This situation motivates a sort of norm for monetary policy which would prevent the repetition of inflationary pressures in a world free from all economic intervention. Wicksell's norm was already present in his former works. In *Interest and Prices*, after his first exposition of the cumulative processes, he suggested a simple way to avoid instability of prices: 'when the price level is rising, the rate of discount should be raised until the movement of prices is halted; when prices are falling, the rate of discount should be lowered until price stability is achieved' (Jonung 1979b: 459). The norm seems to have been successfully applied by the Swedish government and the *Riksbank*, after the suspension of convertibility in 1931.

From an international point of view, an independent application of Wicksell's norm by countries may be unsatisfactory. Even the international level of transactions is subject to the banking system's management capacity. 'The question with which we are faced is whether banks could continually maintain the rate of interest *below the natural rate*, and so drive up prices *higher and higher*' (Haavelmo 1978: 113). An improvement in such a situation would lie in the definition of a motive for the banks to co-operate. This co-operation could concern the relationship between banks and the states, which represent the general interest. It may also be extended to the relations between banks in the same country:

> Co-operation between the banks of a single country for the regulation of the rate of interest is already, of course, a matter of everyday procedure. Co-operation between the banks of different countries could easily take place, at any rate in times of peace, as soon as it was clear what objective was being aimed at.
>
> (Wicksell 1898: 192)

However, in this perspective, the Wicksellian solution desperately suffers from a lack of a rational motive so that banks could be induced to co-operate: as has frequently been noted, Wicksell's description of the trade cycle does not present any explanation of the exact nature of the mechanisms of control.

Wicksell's norm for monetary policy is a direct consequence of his implicit adherence to some 'horizontalist' conceptions. Without any hesitation about the possible influence of market forces in the determination of the money rate, he considers that 'the main cause of instability resides in the inability or failure of the banks to follow [the] rule' (Wicksell 1898: 189). Wicksell's suggestions on 'managed money' (Laidler 1991: 178–9) can thus be considered a sort of synthesis between a *horizontalist* conception of monetary supply and an *institutionalist* apprehension of monetary policies.

The main features of Wicksell's monetary analysis provide the necessary elements for a diagnosis about the causes of macroeconomic co-ordination failures. Central banks and the other financial institutions have the initiative in the triggering of the cycle. As a consequence of the endogeneity of money, they can cause inflation by maintaining their interest rates below their natural level, but can also stabilise the economy through adequate co-operative behaviour yet to be defined. However, despite the originality of his description of the monetary relations – in contrast to the usual quantitative scheme and in opposition to the dominant metallist option – Wicksell does not provide sufficient assumptions to integrate the way in which individual behaviours and the mechanisms of institutions can be articulated, both during the slump and the recovery periods.

More attention should be paid to these Wicksellian developments devoted to the influence of monetary policy on external equilibrium. Far from being direct extensions of the natural rate literature that, when applied to the financial structure of modern corporations, probably over-estimate the influence of the managed rates of interest on the trade cycle in a closed economy, these develop-ments would also involve the consequences of globalisation of financial flows among developed countries. These financial movements leave no room for independent monetary policies inside free exchange areas. They suggest a consideration of the combined interventions of central banks as the normal way to behave for national or supra-national institutions in a world where, accounting for the complexity of the reaction mechanisms, there is no serious possibility of predicting the effect of any particular action.

Hayek on monetary nationalism and inconvertibility

The Great Depression led the United Kingdom, then France and other European countries, to leave convertibility and to conduct independent monetary policies against the crisis. This situation was encouraged by the majority of Cambridge economists and Keynesian points of view began to gain audience within the circles of both macroeconomists and decision-makers. This period was without doubt one of the most difficult to face for an author like Hayek who suggested in the 1931 edition of *Prices and Production* that the remedy for crisis was not to be found in monetary accommodation but in an increase of voluntary saving. When Hayek was invited to deliver lectures at the Institut Universitaire des Hautes Etudes Internationales in Geneva, the challenge was to find some way to match his conceptions of the remedies for depression and the international components of monetary co-ordination. The five studies that are the transcription of his lec-tures discuss alternative international monetary arrangements among which the optimal option selected by Hayek is rather different from what is nowadays inter-preted as the Austrian solution.

The lectures are collected in *Monetary Nationalism and International Stability* (1937) which states the incompatibility between national monetary sovereignty and the requirements of international regulation. Hayek's demonstration rests on the careful examination of three kinds of international monetary settings, namely the purely metallic systems, the mixed currency ones and what he calls 'national systems'. The former is the situation of the United Kingdom for a few decades after the Peel Act. The second could correspond to the inter-war gold exchange standard; from Hayek's point of view it is also the system at work during the clas-sical gold standard in the majority of the world, including the United Kingdom. The latter is another term for the inconvertibility systems adopted since the early 1930s.

The metallic system 'has never existed in its pure form and the type of gold standard which existed until fairly recently was even further removed from this picture than was generally realised' (Hayek 1937: 8). In such a system, stability would be the consequence of a simple mechanism first described by Hume, according to tradition. When a country is affected by a trade deficit, it is subject to an outflow of gold. This movement induces a contraction of the monetary base which in turn involves a narrowing of the available quantity of means of payment. As a result of the quantitative relationship between monetary balances and the level of prices, the country experiences a tendency towards lower prices (deflation) which stimulates exports and tends to adjust the balance of trade. Thus, some natural limits to the extent of circulation which deprive central banks of the faculty to 'accommodate' the needs of the economy, provide a way of coordinating international trade among nations that have not yet attained the same level of development. These stabilising forces constitute such a widely admitted mechanism that even radical opponents to gold such as Keynes (1923) or Aftalion (1948) include an exposition of the 'gold points' principle in their critical analysis of the system. 'In the case of a homogeneous international currency, [international] redistribution[s] of money [are] effected by actual transfers of the corresponding amounts of money from country to country' (Hayek 1937: 17).

In purely metallic systems, only quantitative adjustments are effective:

> With a homogeneous international currency there is apparently no reason why an outflow of money from one area and an inflow into another should necessarily cause a rise in the rate of interest in the first and a fall in the second.
>
> (Hayek 1937: 25)

From Hayek's point of view and in other defences of gold, this property has the advantage of realising a dichotomy between the nominal effects of monetary regulations and the real ones. Price adjustments are not disturbed by the effects of redistribution generated by changing investment conditions. However, the empirical irrelevance of purely metallic systems forbids their use as a reference for a comparison with inconvertible systems characterising inter-war monetary nationalisms.

Viable international monetary systems founded on gold are governed by more complex relationships. 'With the coming of modern banks, a completed change has occurred . . . There has arisen a hierarchy of different kinds of money within each country, the different unit of which could be regarded as equivalent for all relevant purposes' (Hayek 1937: 9). This hierarchy is not only important from an internal perspective, in the sense that it determines different classes of agents according to the type of money they use, it also matters at the level of international monetary regulations. Such mixed monetary systems are submitted to the interaction of several financial institutions, that determine by their centralised structure a hierarchy of money:

> But the concept of centralisation in this connection must not be interpreted too narrowly as referring only to systems crowned by a central bank of the

familiar type, nor even as confined to branch banking systems where each district of a country is served by the branches of the same few banks . . . The forms of centralisation . . . are partly due to less obvious institutional factors . . . the fact that a country has one financial centre where the stock exchange is located.

(Hayek 1937: 10–11)

In general, a central bank constitutes the top of the institutional hierarchy. This position, comforted by the powers of the central bank associated with legal tender of coined metal and stamped money, induces it to behave as an autonomous decision centre for what concerns monetary creation:

Bank deposits could never have assumed their present predominant role among the different media of circulation, . . . the balances held on current account by banks could never have grown to ten times and more of their cash reserves, unless some organ, be it a privileged central bank or be it a number of or all the banks, had been put in a position to create in case of need a sufficient number of additional bank notes to satisfy any desire on the part of the public to convert a considerable part of their balances into hand-to-hand money.

(ibid.: 12)

The banking system and the monetary institutions, as a whole, introduce new complexity in international regulation channels:

Under the mixed system represented by the traditional gold standard, better called 'gold nucleus standard', [international redistribution of money] is brought about partly by an actual transfer of money from country to country, but largely by a contraction of the credit super-structure in the one country and the corresponding expansion in the other.

(ibid.: 17)

After an imbalance in international trade, the immediate consequence is an increase in monetary flows in the country experiencing a commercial surplus and a monetary outflow in the country showing a deficit:

Considering the methods available to the banking system to bring about an expansion or contraction, there is no reason to assume that they can take the money to be extinguished exactly from these persons where it would in the course of time be released if there were no banking system, or that they will place additional money if it came to the country by direct transfer from abroad. There are on the contrary strong grounds for believing that the burden of the change will fall entirely, or to an extent which is in the real situation, on investment activity in both countries.

(ibid.: 26)

Mixed metallic systems thus imply distortions in relative quantities and prices that may have a permanent effect.

The macroeconomic disorders are of the kind of the credit contraction process described in *Prices and Production* and originate in the discrepancy between the bank rate and the natural rate of interest. After the disequilibrium has occurred:

> with a banking structure organised on national lines, that is, under a national reserve system, it is inevitable that it will bring a rise in interest rates, irrespective of whether the underlying real change has affected either the profitability of investment or the rate of savings in such a way as to justify such a change.

(ibid.: 28)

Such a rise in the bank rate induces an increase of capital inflows. These capital movements partly offset the initial outflow of money. Nevertheless,

> the rise of the bank rate in the country losing gold and the decrease of the bank rate in the country receiving gold have nothing to do [in this kind of system] with changes in the supply or demand of capital. It serves temporarily to speed up a process which is already under way.

(ibid.: 30)

In doing so, it has the same effects on domestic activity as when internal matters are the reason for shifts in the bank rate.

> The changes in productive activity are not of a permanent nature . . . It is a disturbance which possesses all the characteristics of a purely monetary disturbance, namely that it is self-reversing in the sense that it induces changes which will have to be reserved because they are not based on any corresponding change in the underlying real facts.

(ibid.: 31)

The result of these arguments combined is that after imbalances, mixed monetary systems generate two kinds of reactions in prices and quantities. The first induced by inflows from abroad modifies the productive structure in a way that does not generally contribute to restoring external stability. The second is more classical for Hayek: as in a closed economy, it results in the transitory effect of a change of a bank rate on the economic structure. The combination of these two effects explains the sub-optimality of mixed systems.

Would Hayek have considered inconvertibility regimes to be undesirable if they did not constitute an apparent exception to the running of international stabilisation mechanisms?

> By monetary nationalism I mean the doctrine that a country's share in the world's supply of money should not be left to be determined by the same principles and the same mechanism as those which determine the relative amounts of money in its different regions or localities.
>
> (ibid.: 7)

The lack of some universally accepted rule of managing monetary policy in inconvertible systems generated a sort of uncertainty about the internal forms of resolution of macroeconomic perturbations after an initial monetary disequilibrium. While internal mechanisms of stabilisation seemed to be left to discretion, external ones exhibit a rather upsetting determinism:

> An actual transfer of money from country to country becomes useless because what is money in the one country is not money in the other. We have to deal with things which possess different degrees of usefulness for different purposes and the quantities of which are fixed independently.
>
> (ibid.: 15)

After an initial shock on external balance, 'the adjustment is brought about, not by change in the number of money units in each country, but by changes in their relative value' (ibid.: 17). The desire to abstract internal monetary corrections from external regulations was the consequence of voluntary choice of national governments and central banks. However, flexible exchange rates are not considered by Hayek as a way to adapt national economies to imperfectly correlated fluctuations of economic activity, but as a proof of the lack of any international monetary feedback that would offset the initial disequilibrium:

> Any differences between merely interlocal and international movements of money which only arise as a consequence of the variability of exchange rates cannot themselves be regarded as a justification for the existence of separate monetary systems. That would be to confuse effect and cause.
>
> (ibid.: 15)

Without any useful money inflows in the country whose money depreciates, the use of bank rate variations becomes the only regulatory device:

> One of the main purpose of the change of discount rate of central banks is to influence the international movements of short term capital . . . but it is by no means evident that it will attract the funds just from where the gold

would tend to flow, and it may well be that it only passes on the necessity of credit contraction to another country.

(ibid.: 61)

The only remaining way for monetary institutions to stabilise is thus the cause of distortions in international prices by its non-neutral effect on international capital circulation. That is the reason why, in 1937, monetary nationalism (e.g. the co-existence of inconvertible monies in a regime of flexible parities) is considered the less desirable system by Hayek.

These views contrast both with the cautious Wicksellian proposals for implementing inconvertibility when other countries were trying to return to gold in the 1920s and with subsequent Hayekian positions then formulated in the 1970s after the dismissal of the Bretton Woods system.

For modern monetary theory, Hayek is nowadays the rather excessive advocate of the competition of monies, the definitive opponent of all kinds of roles for institutions in monetary regulations, the naïve defender of an emerging economic order founded on natural selection. These positions seem as far as possible from the Wicksellian pragmatic approach of inconvertibility but they are no more in harmony with Hayek's 1937 analyses. In a few lines, our goal would be to suggest one possible way of attaining consistency between these Hayekian successive proposals. This restated consistency could delineate the real differences between the logic of Hayek and what Wicksell would have said about modern inconvertible monetary regimes, that is partly suggested by the positions of Myrdal during the initial years of the Bretton Woods system.

Hayek and Myrdal on modern international monetary systems

At the origin of the new Hayekian proposals, there is something like a theoretical result of a modern micro-founded model:

> It would be possible, if it were permitted, to have a variety of essentially different monies. They could represent not merely different quantities of the same metal, but also different abstract units fluctuating in their value relatively to one another.

(Hayek [1976] 1990: 32)

This assertion is neither really justified in the book nor in other Hayek's interventions during the period but it can be justified as a demonstrated proposition of monetary economics. From 1989 to 1993, Kiyotaki and Wright (1989, 1991, 1993) developed different versions of a search-theoretic model in which money can emerge among goods as a fiat money from convergent expectations of economic agents. A few years after these seminal works, all repeatedly referring to the Mengerian tradition, their results were extended to the case of coincidence of multiple means of payment in the same economic area (see Matsuyama *et al.* 1993; Soller Curtis and Waller 2000; Trejos and Wright 1996; Williamson 1999; Zhou 1997). Some of these extensions are involved in the analysis of international monetary arrangements while others deal with the coexistence of different monies in the same national country. Their conclusions have undoubtedly the result of giving some additional weight to the initial Hayekian assumptions.

But the other Hayekian developments are not really confirmed by modern monetary theory and there is probably little chance that they could be established sooner or later as a formal result of microeconomic analysis in a single consistent approach. The thesis can be summarised in a few assertions:

> *There is no obligation to associate state and money.*

> The term 'legal tender' has, . . . come to be surrounded by a penumbra of vague ideas about the supposed necessity for the state to provide money . . . The superstition that it is necessary for government (usually called the 'state' to make it sound better) to declare what is to be money which could not exist without it, probably originated in the naive belief that such a tool as money must have been 'invented' and given to us by some original inventor.
>
> (Hayek 1990: 37)

The theory of free banking, associated with historical experiences as well as with logical developments in 1980 works in monetary analysis, has suggested that an economy may survive without any centralisation of money. However, although the modern independent central banks may only be considered an expression of a sort of delegation of monetary powers to an institution free from inflationary bias, in no way would this lead to the idea that the centralisation of money is an expression of a common acceptance of the monetary unit. In this point of view, as some recent electronic monies experiments suggest, there could casually be some co-existing monies inside a country (or a monetary union) but one single money could be associated with the delegated authority of the state (or the political authority of the union): this kind of money has 'legal tender' and the bank issuing it can behave, in the case of need, as a lender in last resort.

> *There is no interest for agents to associate state and money.*

> The government monopoly for the issue of money was bad enough so long as metallic money predominated. But it became an unrelieved calamity since

paper money (or other token money) which can provide the best and the worst money, came under political control. A money deliberately controlled in supply by an agency whose self-interest forced it to satisfy the wishes of the users might be the best. A money regulated to satisfy the demands of group interest is bound to be the worst possible.

(ibid.: 31)

These hostile Hayekian institutions rather contrast with the benevolent Wicksellian ones. While with an adapted rule, the *Riksbank* and its contemporaneous followers can adapt monetary policy to the final objective of optimising growth, these Hayekian monetary institutions would tend to alter expectations, to manage for government the optimal rate of seigniorage, to generate negative externalities on the economy.

The origin of the failure of gold is in its association with the state.

It is a misunderstanding of what is called Gresham's law to believe that the tendency for bad money to drive out good money makes a government monopoly necessary ... Gresham's law applies only to different kinds of money between which a fixed rate of exchange is enforced by law. If the law makes two kinds of money perfect substitutes for the payment of debts and forces creditors to accept a coin of a smaller content of gold in the place of one with a larger content, debtors will, of course, pay only in the former and find a more profitable use for the substance of the latter.

(ibid.: 42–3)

It is interesting to observe that Hayek's essential references to gold regulation mechanisms are precisely associated with the question of international stability. As in 1937, Hayek always considers free international movements of gold as the more natural way to restore external equilibrium after an initial shock. The only possible intervention of the state would be to define a fixed rate of exchange between two monies, that would limit the natural economic adjustment (ibid.: 113–14).

National currencies [are] not inevitable or desirable.

There is ... little reason why, apart from the effects monopolies made possible by national protection, territories that happen to be under the same government should form distinct national economic areas which would benefit by having a common currency distinct from that of the other areas.

(ibid.: 113–14)

If national currencies have no natural foundations, the same diagnosis will apply to international currencies inside supra-national political unions. The historical failures of the Scandinavian or Latin unions would suggest the next failure of EMU.

Let us try to interpret the 1990 Hayekian position within the logical categories of the contemporaneous debate on optimal international monetary arrangements. The insistence of Hayek on breaking any logical link between money and state is not founded on the same arguments as is the case for the defence of central bank independence by the credibility literature of the 1990s. Hayek refers to the natural emergence and to the social utility of private monies in areas larger than countries. This would be a way of explaining why some forms of dollarisation may be efficient, not because they bring stability but simply because they participate in some common and non-systematically co-ordinated acceptance of the same kind of money outside the original limits of its legal tender area. In the same way, private monies may co-exist with national ones inside independent nations and provide specific services within a shared monetary area. This great diversity of monetary arrangements, due to the fact that trust and confidence are as important in the characterisation of our contemporaneous international monetary system as are the credible commitments of central banks, is enough to deny any exclusivity to what is the usually called 'corner solutions'.

There is little material concerning the immediate extensions of Wicksell's views, applied to post-war monetary arrangement. In his 1956 book, Myrdal offers the retrospective appreciation of gold standards as international monetary systems that were more founded on social connivance than on natural mechanisms: 'gold standard, before 1914 was essentially a sterling standard – tied to gold – managed by the Bank of England, which acted as a sort of trustee for all the members of the gold standard club' (ibid.: 72). The stability of international exchange and monetary regulations before 1914 was linked to the dominant position of Great Britain but less obviously with complex interactions between agents and institutions in the working of co-ordinating mechanisms:

> The gold standard was in the last analysis founded on certain commonly observed and questioned reaction patterns on the part of the institutions and social groups actively involved in the operation of the mechanism – in this case primarily the central bankers – and certain equally unquestioned inhibitions on the part of governments and parliaments.
>
> (ibid.: 73)

This singular conjunction of interests and beliefs led to the fact that the gold standard once removed 'can never be restored. There are irreversible processes in the field of social relations; and social automatisms, when once the spell is broken, can rarely be revived' (ibid.: 73).

Expectations for the definition of common international monetary order can converge on gold, only if each agent believes that the other agents' beliefs are directed in the same way. These conditions were met during the classical gold standard but were no longer met during the 1930s or the 1950s. Without any material support such as gold, the implicit convention formerly associated with the role of metallic reserves has to be converted into more explicit forms of co-operation between nations: 'agreements would not imply the abolition of national monetary and financial policies, which is out of the question, but rather their co-ordination at an intergovernmental level' (ibid.: 74). The creation of the IMF is thus an important stage in this need. Even when the economic context is not favourable, it operates on a 'symbolic basis', as the representation of an explicit contract about monetary regulations. For Myrdal, such regulations are necessary in the context of national economic planning as well as in the case of free markets (ibid.: 76).

Myrdal is rather lucid as regards the weak performances of the Bretton Woods system. According to him, destabilising international capital movements domi-nate and they prevent the setting-up of a real international monetary order (ibid.: 80–1). Like Hayek in the inter-war period, he denies any efficiency to purely national solutions. He did not fear the temptation of flexible parities since the complexity of the Bretton Woods system (which could hardly be considered as a corner solution) does not exclude this possibility, as much as the temptation of inconvertibility and protectionism. Financial perturbations can only be managed by 'collective arrangements giving operational meaning to the interdependence of the various countries' policies' (ibid.: 81). Beyond the Bretton Woods example, other forms of monetary arrangements must rest on some 'international co-operation to stabilise business and employment conditions' (ibid.: 82).

Conclusion

Beyond the localised monetary arrangements that might confirm the relevance of the corner solutions, the current state of the international monetary system is dominated by the existence of some implicit contract (or economic convention) on the use of three international monetary units at the world level. In this context, Hayekian and (extended) Wicksellian options suggest distinguishing dif-ferent ways to realise the co-ordination of external exchanges and capital move-ments. Hayek's analyses would propose creating competition between monies, and this seems to be implicitly applied by private international investors whose supposedly stabilising influence is regularly challenged. The co-operative (and Wicksellian) option seems to be adopted by central banks and monetary authori-ties. The problem is that there is no single way to co-operate or to co-ordinate monetary policy rules that remains nowadays distinct when applied by the main monetary institutions in their own economic areas. The recent debate on monetary rules is thus something like a continued discussion about what Wicksell would have said on modern monetary regimes.

Acknowledgements

This text corresponds to the final version of our contribution to the workshop *Austrian and Swedish Economics: Criss-Cross Stories and Current Perspectives*, held at CREUSET, University of Saint-Etienne, on 22–23 March 2002. The authors thank the workshop participants for their helpful criticisms and suggestions. They are particularly grateful to Axel Leijonhufvud for his comments.

References

Aftalion, A. (1948) *Monnaie, prix et change*, Paris: Librairie du Recueil Sirey.

Boianovsky, M. (1998) 'Wicksell on deflation in the early 1920s', *History of Political Economy*, 30(2): 219–75.

Haavelmo, T. (1978) 'Wicksell on currency theory vs. the banking principle', *Scandinavian Journal of Economics*, 2: 209–15.

Hayek, F.A. (1931) *Prices and Production*, London, Routledge and Sons.

—— ([1937] 1989) *Monetary Nationalism and International Stability*, Fairfield, VA: A.M. Kelley.

—— ([1976] 1990) *Denationalisation of Money: The Argument Refined*, London: The Institute of Economic Affairs.

Jonung, L. (1979a) 'Knut Wicksell and Gustav Cassel on secular movements in prices', *Journal of Money, Credit and Banking*, 11(2), May: 165–81.

—— (1979b) 'Knut Wicksell's norm of price stabilization and Swedish monetary policy in the 1930s', *Journal of Monetary Economics*, 5(4), October: 459–96.

—— (1988) 'Knut Wicksell's unpublished manuscripts: a first glance', *European Economic Review*, 22(263), March: 503–11.

Jörberg, L. and Kranz, O. (1989) 'Economic and social policy in Sweden', in Mathias, P. and Pollard, S. (eds) *The Cambridge Economic History of Europe*, vol. 8, Cambridge: Cambridge University Press, pp. 1048–1105.

Keynes, J.M. (1923) *A Tract on Monetary Reform*, in *The Collected Writings of J.M. Keynes*, vol. IV, Macmillan and Cambridge: Cambridge University Press, 1971.

Kiyotaki, N. and Wright, R. (1989) 'On money as a medium of exchange', *Journal of Political Economy*, 97(4): 927–54.

—— (1991) 'A contribution to the pure theory of money', *Journal of Economic Theory*, 53: 215–35.

—— (1993) 'A search-theoretic approach to monetary economics', *American Economic Review*, 83(1): 63–77.

Laidler, D. (1991) *The Golden Age of the Quantity Theory*, Princeton, NJ: Princeton University Press.

Lester, R. (1939) *Monetary Experiments: Early American and Recent Scandinavian*, Princeton, NJ: Princeton University Press.

Matsuyama, K., Kiyotaki, N. and Matsui, A. (1993) 'Toward a theory of international currency', *Review of Economic Studies*, 60: 283–307.

Myrdal, G. ([1939] 1956) *Monetary Equilibrium*, New York: A.M. Kelley.

Soller Curtis, E. and Waller, C.J. (2000) 'A search-theoretic model of legal and illegal currency', *Journal of Monetary Economics*, 45: 155–84.

Trejos, A. and Wright, R. (1996) 'Search-theoretic models of international currency', *Federal Reserve Bank of St. Louis Review*, 78, March–June: 117–32.

Wicksell, K. ([1898] 1965) *Interest and Prices*, New York: A.M. Kelley.

—— (1911) *Lectures on Political Economy*, New York: A.M. Kelley, vol. 2, 1967.

—— (1925) 'The monetary problem of the Scandinavian countries', *Ekonomisk Tidskrift*; reprinted in (1965) *Interest and Prices*, New York: A.M. Kelley.

Williamson, S.D. (1999) 'Private money', *Journal of Money, Credit and Banking*, 31(3), August, Part 2: 469–91.

Zhou, R. (1997) 'Currency exchange in a random search model', *Review of Economic Studies*, 64: 289–310.

Part IV
Capital theory

9 Austrian production processes and firms

Jean Magnan de Bornier

Introduction

This chapter studies the Austrian theory of production processes in its relationship with the theory of the firm. Austrian economists, as followers of Jean-Baptiste Say, have thought it necessary to develop the theory of entrepreneurship;[1] but this work has remained isolated from – and indeed has been opposed to – the work on capitalistic production as initiated by Böhm-Bawerk's theory. As we will see, Böhm-Bawerk himself did not include firms in the picture he drew of the overall production and capital accumulation mechanism.

It is, however, important to examine the relations between production processes and firms, because although they have not been explicitly addressed, they gave rise to many implicit statements or arguments, which have been, in my opinion, insufficiently questioned.

As will be shown, Wicksell also has a role in this story. He is the only Swedish economist appearing in the present contribution: only my lack of knowledge of the work of other Swedish economists can explain why I have not taken them into account here, but it would certainly be worthwhile to pursue the present study to integrate the work of Lundberg, Lindahl and other Swedish economists.

This chapter is composed of two sections: the first focuses on the Austrian production process and describes some controversies over its meaning and implications; the second section focuses on the firm–process relations, which are explicitly discussed.

The Austrian production process

Let us begin with some general definitions in modern terms, to be followed by references to the debates and evolutions which took place during the twentieth century.

The production process

A production process, or vertical production function, is a relation between a sequence of non-negative dated *originary* (not produced) inputs λ_t and a sequence of non-negative dated final outputs χ_t:

$$(\lambda_0, \lambda_1, \ldots \lambda_T) \rightarrow (\chi_0, \chi_1, \ldots \chi_T)$$

where $\lambda_0 > 0$, $\chi_T > 0$.

The only factors are labour and natural resources (land), as capital is only saved-up factors. Capital 'disappears' from this picture provided that the length of time T is so defined that it starts when the first input is applied and ends when the last possible output appears (more on this later). The conditions $\lambda_0 > 0$ and $\chi_T > 0$ mean that no output can happen before the first input is applied, and that no input need to be applied after the last output has been released.

It is possible to depict four types of processes[2] according to whether inputs and outputs occur in one period or in several periods:

1 *The point-input point-output process* (PIPO) is the kind of process with labour appearing only at the start of the process, and the product appearing in the last period only. The growing of trees that need to be planted is one usual example, along with Wicksell's maturing of wine. This process is written simply as $(\lambda_0 \rightarrow \chi_T)$.

2 *The flow-input point-output process* (FIPO) is the process where labour is more or less continuously applied, and the product appears only once. This kind of process is the one we find in *Prices and Production* but also the one which Böhm-Bawerk had in mind most of the time. This type of process is written as $(\lambda_0, \lambda_1, \ldots \lambda_n) \rightarrow \chi_T$, with $n \leq T$. This kind of process is mainly viewed as a *circulating-capital process*, i.e. without fixed capital; however, it can be shown that fixed capital is compatible with flow-input point-output processes (Magnan de Bornier 1980).

3 *The point-input flow-output process* (PIFO), where labour is applied only once, giving rise to a durable flow of (self-arising) products does not seem to be more than a theoretical possibility and is seldom studied. One example would be the case where at some date men create plantations to grow a forest, and afterwards each year cut some percentage of the trees. This process, if it exists, can be formalized by writing:

$$\lambda_0, \rightarrow (\chi_m, \chi_{m+1}, \ldots \chi_T) \text{ with } m \geq 0.$$

4 *The flow-input flow-output process* (FIFO) is the most general case. Labour as well as product is present at several (maybe all) periods. There is then fixed capital. This process is illustrated by:

$$(\lambda_0, \lambda_1, \ldots \lambda_T) \rightarrow (\chi_m, \chi_{m+1}, \ldots \chi_T)$$

where $T \geq n > 0$ and $0 \leq m < T$.

In this kind of process, it is not possible to link each labour input to a specific product (as in the point-output case), nor to link each product to a specific labour input (as in the point-input case).

Within these general characteristics, it is possible to be more specific, by assigning particular *profiles* to the processes under study.

This method was particularly used by Hicks (1970, 1973). To study the dynamics of an economy, he defined the 'Simple Profile' of production processes;[3] in such a Simple Profile process, there are two multi-week periods, the *construction period* and the *utilization period*. The former is a series of weeks where labour is applied, in equal quantities (a_c), and no product appears yet; the latter is another set of weeks where the labour inputs are all equal to a_u and output is 1.

Duration and roundaboutness

What is roundaboutness?

A recurrent difficulty stems from Böhm-Bawerk's main proposition that more roundabout methods of production are more productive. What is a more roundabout method? This intuitive concept is easy to define in certain cases, and arbitrary or undefined in others. Duration can be evaluated from the point of view of output, or from the point of view of input:

- *Output perspective*. We answer the following question: how long did it take to produce this output? The answer – if it exists – is a *production period*; this measure looks backward. This perspective can be associated with Böhm-Bawerk who mainly developed it (without limiting his work to it).
- *Input perspective*. The question is: for how long will this input be productive? The answer – if it exists – is an *investment period*; this measure looks forward. We can associate this view more closely with Jevons and later Hayek.

In the case of the PIPO process, the duration of production is of course the time elapsing between the beginning and the end; it is measured by T. This is an *absolute period of production*. This concept is a production – as well as an investment – period.

Average durations

When labour or product happen in more than one period, it is less obvious; no absolute period can be calculated. But we can do as Böhm-Bawerk did, and calculate some average duration. If there is only one output (FIPO), which is what Böhm-Bawerk had in mind most of the time, we are led to calculate an average period of production (APP):

$$APP = \frac{\sum_{t=0}^{T}(T-t)\lambda_t}{\sum_{t=0}^{T}\lambda_t}$$

On the other hand, in the point-input flow-output process, it is possible to calculate an average investment period (AIP):

$$AIP = \frac{\sum_{t=0}^{T}t\chi_t}{\sum_{t=0}^{T}\chi_t}$$

The flow-input flow-output processes

In the general FIFO process, no particular date can be defined, either as a starting point or as a final point; the process has a beginning and an end, but these dates have less significance than they have when calculating the AIP and APP respectively. Hence, the calculation of the average process duration (APD) of the process is done without a reference date; it is a difference between two durations:

$$\frac{\sum_{t=0}^{T}t\chi_t}{\sum_{t=0}^{T}\chi_t} - \frac{\sum_{t=0}^{T}t\lambda_t}{\sum_{t=0}^{T}\lambda_t} \quad \text{i.e. } APD = API - APP + T$$

This is the difference between the average waiting for the (future) product and the average waiting for (future) labour costs, starting from period 1 (the beginning of the process); alternatively, it is also the difference between the average age for the product and the average age for labour costs, viewed from the last period. Even if this kind of measure is not very intuitive, it must be understood that the three other measures – the absolute duration, the APP and the AIP – are special cases of the APD.

With the APD we can compare any two production processes and say which is the most roundabout; but this is certainly not what Böhm-Bawerk had in mind, when stating the law of the greater productivity of more roundabout methods.

Discrete or continuous processes

The degree of flexibility within a process requires some comment. We have defined as a set of labour and product coefficients which, at first sight, are fixed coefficients. This means that a process displays inter-temporal complementarities. But this assumption is not warranted, and it is possible to conceive processes within which a degree of substitutability is introduced. Samuelson recently provided a formulation of this approach:

> Here in modern notations is the typical Böhm-Hayek technology of labour–wheat–flour–bread:
> Q now is a function of (labour one period back, labour two periods back, . . ., labour T periods back), or
>
> $$Q_t = Q = f(L_{t-1}, \ldots L_{t-T}), \, T \geq 1;$$
>
> $$\frac{\partial Q}{\partial L_{t-\tau}} \geq 0, \tau = 1, 2, K, T$$
>
> $$\frac{\partial^2 Q}{(\partial L_{t-\tau})^2} < 0, \text{dim. returns with } f \text{ concave}$$

f to be first degree homogeneous: constants returns to scale (Samuelson 2001: 304).

What Samuelson describes by the function $f()$ is not one single process, it is – if I understood him correctly – the whole technology. In this technology, it is possible, by the assumption of differentiability, to switch *continuously* from one process to another. Shall we now speak of *emit*, instead of *time*, to remember Joan Robinson's *leers*? In this case of maximum flexibility, the producer is able to begin production with a certain set of labour coefficients in mind, and during the execution (at time $t + m$), to modify some of the remaining coefficients because some conditions may have changed.

Two points seem worth emphasizing:

1   It is very doubtful whether such a function is a representation of Böhm-Bawerk's production process; in all his examples, Böhm-Bawerk defined a production process by fixed coefficients, and there is never any suggestion that switching from one process to the other can be done otherwise than at the beginning of production.
2   Samuelson's definition has as an immediate consequence the minimizing of the role of time in production; time is here the environment of production, but is no longer a constraint, or much less so.

Controversies about production processes

The concept of time-consuming production processes as proposed by Böhm-Bawerk has been subject to two kinds of attacks:

1   Direct criticisms arising from the concurrent picture of production where capital goods are a factor of the same nature as labour and nature and time has no place.
2   Implicit attacks from inside the Austrian camp, which weakened the concept of production process by the use some authors (mainly Wicksell and Hicks) made of it.

Goods or processes: two alternative concepts

An accurate picture of the overall production mechanism must rely *either on goods or on processes*. These are incompatible approaches. The essence of the process approach is that capital goods need not appear; capital is no longer a factor, and only labour and nature are the true factors of production. For Böhm-Bawerk, focusing on capital goods is at best misleading:

> There would probably never have been any doubt of all this, had it not been for the fact that division of labour and specialization of vocation broke up the unified work of producing consumption goods into a multiplicity of seemingly independent processes of production. That caused economists to forget to keep their eyes upon the process as a whole.
>
> (1921b: 98)

This 'unified work' is for Böhm-Bawerk the reality economists must study. This was indeed one element of the controversy which faced Böhm-Bawerk and John Bates Clark at the beginning of the twentieth century, and later Hayek and Knight in the 1930s,[4] American authors preferring, as we know, to think of capital as a collection of production goods.

One important argument against the Austrian view in this controversy has been the difficulty or impossibility of actually measuring the period of production. The period of production is not directly observable; the beginning and end of a 'process' are not defined, because a purely 'originary' factor is never observable, and also because a production process might well have effects for an indefinite length of time.

Oscar Morgenstern, successor to Hayek in 1931 as Director of the Austrian Institute for Business Cycle Research, is one of the most convincing on this line of reasoning (Morgenstern 1935);[5] he pointed out that production processes might well have a *nearly infinite duration*, because separation over time is not possible (the production of today has been built with very old instruments, e.g. an ancient road built and rebuilt many time, the first production operations being so far in the past that we could not account for them). The description of production as a process over time would then be impossible, but it could be done in a circular model where we describe the tools of production, which need not be infinite.

To Hayek, who in *The Pure Theory of Capital* seems to give a personal reply to his former assistant in Vienna, this point is misleading: it shows a lack of the necessary abstraction implied by theoretical work:

> For purposes of theoretical analysis it is necessary to isolate the connection between individual units of input and individual units of output, and at the same time we have to recognize that in real life production is as a rule continuous . . . It requires a high degree of abstraction to arrive at the idea of separate individual processes which consist of separable and clearly distinguishable inputs and outputs and which will yield a continuous stream of output only if they are continuously repeated in an unchanged manner. But it is only by means of such abstraction that it is possible to isolate the relevant relationships between the different parts of the continuous process.
>
> (Hayek 1941: 68–9)

On this point Hayek was probably right: if the problem of production is to be treated in such concrete terms as Morgenstern did, this level of concreteness should also be applied to the alternative view of capital goods: it would be possible then to question the very categories of goods, and say: 'This hammer is not exactly like the hammer which was produced one year before, hence they are not the same tool', etc. The number of production goods could be nearly infinite, like the length of production, and no analytical approach of production would ever be possible.

In the second half of the twentieth century, however, it became clear that the two views could be seen as alternative descriptions of the mechanisms of production, rather than as irreconcilable theories (Burmeister 1974; Magnan de Bornier 1990). That the two views are roughly equivalent can be shown by the fact that it is easy to switch from a description of production in terms of goods to one in terms of processes, and vice versa.[6]

Measure of average duration and measure of capital

The average periods may be ambiguous, simply because they are weighted averages, and the weights are defined as the percentages of invested labour, in the production period, and as the percentages of accruing product, in the investment period.

Several authors pointed this out, of which the first was Wicksell. He noted that:

> the assumption that the average period of investment [APP in our terms – JMB] is independent of the rate of interest (i.e. of simple interest) only applies, strictly speaking, where several different capital investments relate

> to one and the same future act of consumption (as in Böhm-Bawerk's example) [FIPO, JMB]. In the opposite case, where one (or more) factors of production are invested in a single capital good or durable consumption good, it may easily be seen that the average investment-period will be dependent on the rate of interest, even with simple interest.
>
> (Wicksell [1903] 1967: 184)

This sentence led several authors to consider that the interest rate must be included in the formula of the average production period, either as simple or as compound interest (Gifford 1933; Hicks 1939; Marschak 1934). But Wicksell's point is far from clear, as far as the problem is only one of measure. We can actually compute – as shown before – an average duration when durable goods are present; introducing the interest rate provides another measure (to be defined below), which transforms a *physical* duration measure into a more *economic* one, a new measure in terms of costs and profitability of the process. It may be accurate or not, according to what its use must be.

Actually, Wicksell's point was not to look for a better measure of the period of production: he attempted to provide a theory of the value of capital and of the relationships between production and distribution. These are separate questions. Hayek (1934) has perfectly shown how the two measures (using interest or not) must be used for their respective purposes.

Later in the 1930s Hicks was looking for a measure, but not to address the same problem as did Böhm-Bawerk: his rejection of Böhm-Bawerk's APP derives from the idea that:

> What we want to find is a numerical index to the character of the plan, which can be relied upon to change in a given direction when the rate of interest varies . . .
>
>   It was the search for such an index which led Böhm-Bawerk and his followers to put forward their 'average period of production' or 'average period of investment'.
>
> (Hicks 1939: 217–18)

Hicks adopted the view that interest was to be included in the average period calculation.

However, the reason why Böhm-Bawerk wanted this index is not what is stated here, but a means to illustrate the greater productivity of more roundabout methods of production, of which the interest rate is (to Böhm-Bawerk) a result and not a determinant, and hence he sought nothing more than a consistent measure of roundaboutness.

Let us call APP' the new measure of the average production period[7] using compound interest:

$$APP' = \frac{\sum\limits_{t=0}^{T}(T-t)\lambda_t(1+i)^{T-t}}{\sum\limits_{t=0}^{T}\lambda_t}$$

The success of this new definition probably comes from the fact that it provides an interesting result: the APP' is equal to the capital-output ratio of the economy;[8] it is then a good indicator of capital intensity.

However, introducing the interest rate is not without costs; and one of these is that the ordering of the processes' durations becomes difficult: it is possible that some process A which is 'shorter' than process B when the interest rate is low, becomes 'longer' when it rises. The condition for that is that the T terms $(\lambda_t^A - \lambda_t^B)$ display at least one sign change, and no economic rationale exists to rule this out. With more than one sign change, we can have several reversals.

We can conclude on definitional matters by saying that during the late nineteenth and early twentieth centuries no definite theory was widely accepted concerning the precise role of measuring the average period of production. Wicksell did not explicitly reject Böhm-Bawerk's approach but proposed another view without stating if it was opposed to or independent of Böhm-Bawerk's. Except for Hayek, his readers wrongly – to my belief – concluded that he had proposed a better version than Böhm-Bawerk's, and the Austrian theory of capital was no longer in their hands a theory of elementary technological relations, but became a theory of the profitability of investment, where interest rate determines the overall investment and capital structure. It was natural then to think of capital theory as a microeconomic subject.

Firms–process interrelations

Böhm-Bawerk's neglect of the firm level

When Böhm-Bawerk indicated that the 'division of labour and specialization of vocation broke up the unified work of producing consumption goods into a multiplicity of seemingly independent processes of production', it can be taken, as we previously did, to apply to goods, but obviously it also applies to the separation of the whole process operations into several firms. So firms are not important for him.

However, they do have a role in the theory of capital, especially as Böhm-Bawerk writes about capital formation (1921b, Book II, Chapter V: *The Theory of The Foundaton of Capital*) (1921b, Book II, Chapter V). There his purpose is macroeconomic, as he describes how savings are transformed into investment. Entrepreneurs are an important part of this process:

So far we have discussed the formation of a nation's capital as if that nation were carrying on a unified economy governed by a single will. Of course that is not the case. We therefore still have to show how, under the actual system of diversified and multiple control of our economy, the dispositions which lead to the formation of capital are actually carried.

(ibid.: 111)

After showing how this happens in a socialist economy, Böhm-Bawerk rapidly describes the 'individualistically organized society':

> Here the prime factor in the control over the assignment of the annually accruing productive forces and over the direction given to the national production is the entrepreneur. But he does not exercise this control as his own desires dictate . . . In the last analysis, then, it is not the entrepreneur who determines the direction the national production shall take, but the consumer – the 'public'.
>
> (ibid.: 112)

The role of firms – entrepreneurs – in Böhm-Bawerk's theory is just to execute orders coming from the markets. There is no interaction between firms and production processes.

The process as a firm

Wicksell and later Hicks included firms in their presentation of production processes but it was in a very artificial way: by associating a firm to each process.

While recognizing his 'masterly manner' (ibid.: 2150), Wicksell felt the need to present Böhm-Bawerk's capital, theory in 'a clearer and more comprehensive form (Wicksell [1903] 1967: 151). This led to a formulation of the capitalistic process of production where the greater productivity of roundabout methods is still the main point, but *profit* appears as another result.

In the example of the matured wine,[9] the production and maturation of wine are the production process; it is a 'national' production process since Wicksell assumes a small economy exchanging wine against other commodities. So exchange is present with the rest of the world, and *profitability*, in addition to productivity, can be appraised:

> we will make no definite assumption about the *value* of this capital in terms of money, but we assume that it just suffices for each year's vintage to be stored for a particular period (say four years). In that case, *as a rule*, the 4-year storage period must be the one which is the most profitable from the point of view of the individual wine growers.
>
> (ibid.: 173)

This example, however, is by no means intended to provide a theory of the firm within the production process; its aim is to formulate the link between the interest rate and roundaboutness.[10]

Wicksell's simplified presentation of the phenomenon of roundaboutness thus implies that one firm (or several competing firms) can perform the whole of the production process – which may be correct – and thus that one can identify the production process, in all its aspects, to just one decision maker – and this is a very strong assumption. The last proposition is *not* Wicksell's view, but a view which can be suggested by the reading of Wicksell.

The association of one process with one decision-maker (entrepreneur, firm . . .) was stated more explicitly by Hicks (1939). Part IV of *Value and Capital* is the study of 'The working of the dynamic system', and one element of this study is the 'production plan', which is thus defined: 'the decision which confronts any particular entrepreneur at any date (say on our "first Monday") may be regarded as the establishment of a *production plan*' (ibid.: 193). Three chapters of this Part of the book (XV–XVII) are about the production plan of the firm. Their aim is to provide a criticism of, and a substitute for, the "classical" theory (that of Böhm-Bawerk)' (ibid.: 213).

These chapters on the production plan make a complete assimilation of Böhm-Bawerk's process of production with the time-structure of the firm's production; what was for Wicksell a simplified presentation with an economy producing nothing but wine, has become for Hicks the standard conception of the time-structure of production. That this is a misunderstanding of Böhm-Bawerk's position does not preclude the validity of Hicks' analysis.

When later coming back to the study of the Austrian processes, in *Capital and Time* (1973), Hicks was far from his previous firm–process conception:

> We are now to define a productive process as a scheme by which a flow of inputs is converted into a flow of outputs. A firm, when it is a producing unit, may itself be regarded as the embodiment of such a process; but there are many (perhaps most) actual firms which are combinations of several producing units, each of which may usefully be regarded as embodying a process. It will still be a process, in our sense, if it would be *possible* to carry it on in a single firm. We must be ready, at least, for that degree of sub-division.
>
> (ibid.: 14)

Whatever does this mean, the association of one firm with one process, which was present in 1939, is now abandoned – although Hicks on the same page (note 1) claims his process is the same as in *Value and Capital*!

Obviously, it is at best a simplification to identify the Austrian process with a single firm; it can be a fruitful one if the role of the interest rate in production decisions is studied, but it certainly does not exhaust the question.

The firm within processes

It is easy to argue that the Wicksell–Hicks way of taking account of firms within the Austrian theory is not suitable. Firms must be independent bodies. Even more, their role is to take economic decisions, which processes cannot do. There is then a real need to introduce firms into this analysis, because a theory of decision-making is needed to explain the moving structure of capital. Few authors have attempted to build such a theory. We will describe here the way Hayek took account of firms in *Prices and Production* (1931).

In this book, Hayek gave a description of the production process which is essentially the same as Böhm-Bawerk's, but has been more closely linked with Jevons' famous triangles (which were used also by Wicksell). Like Böhm-Bawerk with his concentric circles, Hayek with the triangles proposes a description of the production process using the year as the time unit.

One central element of the Hayekian theory of business cycle is the money circulating between firms, and between firms and other agents. This implies that firms must be present in the picture:

> in order to trace the relation between actual money payments, or the pro-
> portional quantities of money used in the different stages of production, and
> the movements of goods, we need a definite assumption in regard to the
> division of the total process among different firms, which alone makes an
> exchange of goods against money necessary. For this does not by any means
> necessarily coincide with our division into separate stages of production of
> equal length.
>
> (Hayek 1931: 45–6)

Hayek then makes three alternative assumptions concerning the position of firms within the process:

1   One firm per year (ibid.: 46), or
2   Only one firm for the whole process (ibid.: 62), or
3   One firm can cover two one-year stages (ibid.: 66).

These firms are not monopolies, however, there is a multiplicity of such firms in each case.

The behaviour of the system is indeed dependent on this assumption about the number of firms, as Hayek shows, for instance, that:

> in this case [only one firm for the whole process – JMB] the demand for con-
> sumers' goods, as expressed in money, will be only temporarily reduced,
> while in the case where the process of production was divided between a

number of independent stages of equal length, the reduction of the amount available for the purchase of consumers' goods was a permanent one.

(ibid.: 64)

Although Hayek's position as to the role of firms is not very different from that of Böhm-Bawerk (firms are not really decision-makers, they are just transmitting an impulse that comes from the banking system or the public and has a final impact on the capital structure), the structure of firms within the process has macroeconomic consequences. The system–process–firms interrelations are an important step in this analysis. This ability to intertwine three different analytical levels – system, process and firm – is perhaps why Hayek's business cycle theory seemed so difficult, and why at the same time it seemed a great achievement. But from our point of view, it is obvious that firms must have a greater role in capital theory and especially for a dynamic capital theory.

Conclusion

Wicksell played a very important role in the evolution of Böhm-Bawerk's capital theory, but this role is an ambiguous one. Wicksell's contributions appear mostly as developments of this theory but were seen by some of his readers as corrections or serious modifications. This has weakened in many ways the Austrian theory's positions. The history of how relations between production processes and firms were conceived seems to provide a good example of this proposition.

Acknowledgements

A first draft of this chapter was presented at the International Workshop 'Austrian and Swedish Economics: Criss-cross Stories and Current Perspectives', organised by the CREUSET – Université de Saint-Etienne (France) 22–23 March 2002.

Notes

1 Schumpeter and Kirzner hardly need to be named.
2 Magnan de Bornier (1990: 126).
3 Hicks (1973: 41–2).
4 Böhm-Bawerk (1906, 1907a, 1907b); Clark (1965, 1907) for the first battle, and Hayek (1935, 1936), Knight (1934, 1935, 1946), for the second one.
5 See also Hill (1933).
6 Actually a common view is that the 'circular' model – based on capital goods – is more general than the 'vertical' – or Austrian – one; I have written in this sense (Magnan de Bornier 1984). But this seems incorrect to me now, because the only argument for this is the impossibility of defining truly originary means of production,

the argument of an infinite period of production; and this argument can also be applied to the circular model to show that it must have an infinite number of goods.
7 Of course, the same transformation can be performed on the AIP.
8 See Marschak (1934), Allais (1947), Dorfman (1959b). Clearly, this is true only if capital is measured at historical cost.
9 In the section 'An Alternative Treatment of the Problems of Interest and Distribution' (Wicksell [1903] 1967: 172ff.).
10 'The rate of interest here appears in its simplest form as the marginal productivity of "waiting"' (Wicksell [1903] 1967: 177).

References

Allais, M. (1947). *Economie et Intérêt*, Paris: Imprimerie Nationale.

Baranzini, M. and Scazzieri, R. (eds) (1990) *The Economic Theory of Structure and Change*, Cambridge: Cambridge University Press.

Böhm-Bawerk, E. von (1906) 'Capital vs capital goods', *Quarterly Journal of Economics*, 20: 3–21.

—— (1907a) 'The nature of capital: a rejoinder', *Quarterly Journal of Economics*, 21: 28–47.

—— (1907b) 'A relapse to the productivity theory', *Quarterly Journal of Economics*, 20: 246–82.

—— (1921a) *History and Critique of Interest Theories*, English trans. of the fourth Austrian edn by George D. Huncke and Hans F. Sennholz, 1959, South Holland, IL: Libertarian Press.

—— (1921b) *Positive Theory of Capital*, English trans. of the fourth Austrian ed. by George D. Huncke and Hans F. Sennholz, 1959, South Holland, IL: Libertarian Press.

Burmeister, E. (1974) 'Synthesizing the neo-Austrian and alternative approaches to capital theory: a survey', *Journal of Economic Literature*, 12(2): 413–56.

Clark, J.B. ([1899] 1965) *The Distribution of Wealth*, New York: A.M. Kelley.

—— (1907) 'Concerning the nature of capital', *Quarterly Journal of Economics*, 20: 351–70.

Dorfman, R. (1959a) 'A graphical exposition of Böhm-Bawerk's theory of interest', *Review of Economic Studies*, 26(2): 153–8.

—— (1959b) 'Waiting and the period of production', *Quarterly Journal of Economics*, 73: 351–72.

—— (2001) 'Modernizing Böhm-Bawerk's theory of interest', *Journal of the History of Economic Thought*, 23(1): 37–54.

Gifford, C.H.P. (1933) 'The concept of the length of the period of production', *The Economic Journal*, 43: 611–18.

Hayek, F.A. (1931) *Prices and Production*, London: Routledge and Kegan Paul.

—— (1934) 'On the relationship between investment and output', *The Economic Journal*, 44: 207–31.

—— (1935) 'The maintenance of capital', *Economica*, 2: 241–76.

—— (1936) 'The mythology of capital', *Quarterly Journal of Economics*, 50: 355–83.

—— (1937) 'Economics and Knowledge', *Economica*, 13(4): 33–54.

—— (1941) *The Pure Theory of Capital*, London: Routledge and Kegan Paul.

—— (1945) 'The use of knowledge in society', *American Economic Review*, 35: 519–30.

—— (1967) *Studies in Philosophy, Politics and Economics*, London: Routledge and Kegan Paul.

—— (1978a) *New Studies in Philosophy, Politics and Economics*, London: Routledge and Kegan Paul.

—— (1978b) *New Studies in Philosophy, Politics and Economics*, London: Routledge and Kegan Paul, pp. 179–90.

—— (1980, 1981, 1983) *Droit, Législation et Liberté*, vols 1–3, Paris: PUF.

—— (1988) *The Fatal Conceit: The Errors of Socialism*, London: Routledge and Kegan Paul.

Hicks, J. (1939) *Value and Capital*, Oxford: Clarendon Press.

—— (1965) *Capital and Growth*, Oxford: Clarendon Press.

—— (1970) 'A neo-Austrian growth theory', *The Economic Journal*, 80(318): 257–81.

—— (1973) *Capital and Time*, Oxford: Clarendon Press.

Hill, M. (1933) 'The period of production and industrial fluctuations', *The Economic Journal*, 43: 599–610.

Jevons, W.S. ([1871 1970) *The Theory of Political Economy*, London: Penguin Classics.

Knight, F. (1934) 'Capital, time, and the interest rate', *Economica*, 1: 257–86.

—— (1935) 'Professor Hayek and the theory of investment', *The Economic Journal*, 45: 77–94.

—— (1946) *Encyclopaedia Britannica*, vol. IV, London: Encyclopaedia Britannica, pp. 799–800.

Lowe, A. (1976) *The Path of Economic Growth*, Cambridge: Cambridge University Press.

Magnan de Bornier, J. (1980) *Capital et déséquilibres de la croissance*, Paris: Economica.

—— (1984) *La production jointe*, Paris: Economica.

—— (1990) 'Vertical integration, growth and sequential change', in Baranzini, M. and Scazzieri, R. (eds) *The Economic Theory of Structure and Change*, Cambridge: Cambridge University Press, pp. 122–43.

Marschak, J. (1934) 'A note on the period of production', *The Economic Journal*, 44: 146–51.

Marshall, A. (1890, edn 1920) *Principles of Economics*, London: Macmillan.

Morgenstern, O. (1935) 'Zur theorie der der produktionsperiode', *Zeitschrift für Nationalökonomie*, vol. Vf: 196–208.

Samuelson, P. (2001) 'A modern post-mortem on Böhm's capital theory: its vital normative flaw shared by pre-Sraffian mainstream capital-theory', *Journal of the History of Economic Thought*, 23(3): 301–17.

Wicksell, K. ([1903] 1967) *Lectures on Political Economy*, New York: A.M. Kelley.

—— (1927) 'Mathematische nationalökonomie', *Archiv für Sozialwissenschaft und Sozialpolitik*, 56: 252–81.

10 The 'Wicksell connection' and the Austrian theory of capital

Which connections?

Olivier Jenn-Treyer

Introduction

The title of this chapter refers to an expression by Axel Leijonhufvud that achieved considerable academic success, that of the 'Wicksell connection'. Indeed, in what one would qualify as a canonical text (Leijonhuvfud 1981), he chose a history of macroeconomics that would not simply be that of Keynesianism. Leijonhufvud's contribution is an attempt to clarify 'the relationships between some of the major schools of modern macroeconomics by tracing the development of the theory of the natural interest rate mechanism' (ibid.: 131), that is in fact what Robertson seems to have been the first to qualify as 'loanable funds theory'.[1] Leijonhufvud uses this classification instrument to draw up a typology of the various currents in macroeconomics.[2]

Leaving aside the monetarist branch of his construction, Leijonhufvud is going to be interested in the 'Wicksell connection'. He will eventually launch a vibrant plea in favour of a return to the loanable funds theory and for the abandonment of the liquidity preference theory.[3] His argument consists of two parts: the first consists in defending the idea that the use of the study of income fluctuations in terms of saving-investment[4] is conditioned by the hypothesis that the mechanism of determination of the interest rate is not able to ensure an appropriate co-ordination of saving and investment decisions. The loanable funds theory would thus be equivalent to an interest rate adjustments analysis.

The second, 'more committed', constitutes in fact Leijonhufvud's main 'message'. It aims at proposing the thesis according to which the widespread adoption of Keynesian theory of interest, by refusing any significant role to the natural interest rate, undermines the bases of the Wicksellian macroeconomics by letting the interest rate 'float in the air'. Difficulties of contemporary macroeconomics would then be widely attributable to this 'loss of content' undergone by the concept of interest rate.

Our comment consists essentially here of trying to extend the first part of Leijonhufvud's argumentation. By referring back to Wicksell's work, we shall try to show that the originality of the 'Wicksell connection' is not only monetary, as is commonly believed. Indeed, Wicksell was, in our view, persuaded that his cumulative mechanism could escape certain criticisms only if it was connected to the Austrian theory of capital.[5] In fact, it appears that Wicksell paved the way for Hayek, who will devote himself to the refinement of the embryonic structure of production concept.

In the first section, we shall develop the idea that Wicksell's project can be defined essentially as an attempt to reorganise the quantity theory. This reorganisation is going to be translated into the conceptualisation of a loanable funds theory, in which demand of investment can durably deviate from supply of saving (*ex ante*); or, in other words, in which it is possible to conceive of the existence of a persisting differential between a natural interest rate and a market interest rate. In this phenomenon the famous 'Wicksellian cumulative process' is strictly correlated. In this, the intervention of the forced saving concept is decisive, because it guarantees the accounting equality between *ex post* saving and investment. Wicksell can convincingly be called 'the father of loanable funds theory'. Wicksell's framework then turns out to be the fundamental point of departure for the 'Wicksell connection'.

However, the 'genealogical typology' of Axel Leijonhufvud, clearly constructed on monetary bases, can be extended to the real sphere. We will thus try to show in the second section that the functioning of the loanable funds theory arouses new theoretical questionings, particularly in the field of capital theory.

Indeed, there is a novelty which it is necessary to take into account: the market interest rate will no longer be able to be directly determined by the 'capital market', upon which would be based supply and demand of capital in their physical aspect. Therefore, the 'conventional' approach to capital is unsuitable when describing the functioning of the economy out of equilibrium, as when conceiving of the existence of a durable gap between both interest rates. The limits of the Walrasian treatment of this problem in the 'Théorie Mathématique du Billet de Banque'[6] are completely revealing in this respect.

The development of a loanable funds approach thus requires a reorganisation of the theory of capital itself. We shall see that Wicksell works on this matter in an Austrian tradition. This will allow him to conceptualise 'the absorption' of forced saving without significant changes in natural interest rate. In this case, we shall show that Wicksell anticipates Hayek on the subject. He is indeed completely aware of real effects (on the structure of production) linked to the effects of distributions engendered by a gap between both interest rates. He proposes in *Interest and Prices* (1898) some ways to integrate real effects in his cumulative process. These ways allow an overtaking of usual limits of the cumulative process as a purely monetary phenomenon. Our aim is not, however, to question the 'official' Wicksellian version of the cumulative process (clearly exposed in the *Lectures*), but to show that this should be 'improved' on bases proposed by

Wicksell himself. One of the principal aims of this chapter is to show that, to understand the stakes underlining the constitution of business cycles theories at the end of the 1920s, it is necessary to keep in mind not only discussions on the loanable funds theme, but also other theoretical debates which envelop them, and which concern capital theory.

The formation of loanable funds theory: an attempt at reconstruction

According to Wicksell, his economics is based on a transformation of the quantity theory. The foundations of such a process should be placed in the historic context of the challenging of the dominant monetary theory at the end of the nineteenth century. In this domain, and even in Great Britain, 'banking' is the current of thought that occupies the forefront of the scene. That of 'currency' is mainly weakened by observations on the real movements of interest rates, which question the conclusions of the quantity theory. Indeed, as Bertil Ohlin notes in his Introduction to the English edition of *Interest and Prices*, nobody could get 'round the fact that the rate of interest, as pointed out by Tooke, had on the whole been low during times of falling prices and high during times of rising prices, whereas the Ricardian doctrine seemed to suggest the opposite' (Ohlin 1936: viii). The quasi-general consensus was that means of payment supply could not exceed the 'needs of the market'.[7]

The controversy begins to settle down when authors such as Walras, Jevons or Menger put forward the thesis of quantitativism again. Wicksell, in this general sphere of influence, is, however, going to distance himself. Indeed, he is convinced that the quantity theory requires a major reorganisation for it to be of use as a healthy base for a coherent monetary theory.[8]

Although Wicksell criticises the quantity theory, he will never question its logical validity. Indeed, he regularly repeats that his own contribution is only an extension of the quantity theory and boasts constantly of being the defender, especially against Tooke's ideas. As Patinkin underlines, 'Wicksell is opposed to a mechanistic interpretation of the quantity theory' (1952: 836). Patinkin should have added that this opposition applied only within the framework of a developed economy, where quantity of money can no longer be exactly estimated. Wicksell's contribution is then going to consist in attributing the role of indicator of the general level of prices variations to the differential between the real and the money rate of interest.

The very heart of the 'new monetary theory' proposed by Wicksell is the cumulative process, in which the key role of the Wicksellian system is held by the differential between the natural and the market interest rate. On the real plan, the persisting gap between both rates (which commands the cumulativity of the process) results in the existence of a difference between planned saving (*ex ante*), and investment. Physical identity between saving and investment (*ex post*) is then ensured by the stake contribution of the concept of forced savings. Wicksell is going to encounter difficulties in setting the cumulative process on an indisputable basis. We shall see in our second section that these difficulties are particularly concentrated in the field of capital theory and concern the stability of the natural interest rate.

Quantity theory: 'empty and barren formalism'

Quantity theory is, according to Wicksell, of no use in the real world because it bases itself on too restrictive postulates, in particular that of the invariance of the proportionality between the quantity of metal money and the level of prices. To illustrate this fact, he will call forth the idea of pure credit economy. This will allow him, according to Bertil Ohlin, to 'successfully escape from the tyranny which the concept "quantity of money" has until recently exercised on monetary theory' (1936: xiv).

Wicksell considers as highly unrealistic the hypothesis according to which every individual would tend to preserve a constant level of cash holdings (with regard to income). According to him, it means supposing 'that the velocity of circulation of money is, as it were, a fixed, inflexible magnitude, fluctuating about a constant average level' (Wicksell 1898: 41). He thinks that reality is quite different and that cash balances may vary very considerably. He starts from the axiom that 'the quantity of money, multiplied by the velocity of circulation . . . must always coincide with the total value of the goods and services turned over against money in a given period of time' (Wicksell 1906: 144). Wicksell then shows that 'the whole dispute controversy turns ultimately on this last point: whether the velocity of circulation of money is of autonomous or merely subordinate significance for the currency system' (ibid.: 143–4).

To show that a fixed circulation velocity of money by the quantity theory is a too binding hypothesis with regard to reality, Wicksell begins by wondering

> whether the magnitude of this velocity of circulation can be regarded as determined by *independent factors*; or rather, as is sometimes maintained, it is not merely the *resultant*, given the quantity of goods exchanged and of available money, of the particular level of commodity prices, themselves determined by *quite different* causes.
>
> (1898: 54)

He answers this question within the framework of a monetary economy shown at three stages of complexity.

First, he notices that the quantity theory works very well within the framework of a *pure cash economy* that is, without credit. Indeed, in such a configuration, the level of cash balances aims, according to him, to remain the same. Velocity of money will have a constant value, or, if it is disrupted, will return very quickly to its reference level. The quantity theory thus applies perfectly in this case.

Second, he transplants a system of *simple credit* to this pure cash economy, a system where the credit is made by mutual agreement among the agents, that is, without intermediary. This simple credit, while it does not offer a substitute to metal money, has the power to largely reduce the cash balance and thus to con-siderably accelerate the circulation of money. Although this strategy is 'theoretic-ally' unlimited,[9] in practice, it is not so. Indeed, one cannot expect the majority of individuals to arouse enough confidence to reach credit through the sole use of beggary. Considering the risks generated by the simple credit and thus the required guarantees, realistically it can only be practised by a very restricted circle of agents. From that Wicksell deduces that, in a cash economy with simple credit, the elasticity of circulation velocity is quite low, so that the conclusions of the quantity theory are still globally valid.

Finally, considering an *organised credit economy*, Wicksell shows that the quan-tity theory is no longer relevant. This will lead him to imagine a borderline case, that of the *pure credit economy*. Thanks to the transfer of debts and to the centrali-sation of credit, which characterise a developed banking system and which expresses itself through instruments such as bank notes, cheques, compensation or discount of exchange letters, risks are decreased and credit becomes accessible to the greatest number of people, the money does not remain idle, precaution cash balance can be reduced (possibility of obtaining loans immediately), and the security ratio of banks can decrease.[10] Pushing the system to its extreme, Wick-sell imagines a world based on bank writings devoid of any physical transactions:

> Suppose now that this system, which is known by the name of the *Virement*, *Giro*, or cheque system is developed up to the point where everybody pos-sesses a banking account. Then all payments could be effected by such book-keeping transfers, except possibly those for which small change suffices. It is true that a substantial amount of *capital* would be required to instil confi-dence and to meet unavoidable risks. But whether the banks are branches of one single monetary institution serving the whole country (like the Austrian Post Office Savings Bank), or independent establishments connected by a common clearing house (on the English or American pattern), they would require *no stock of cash*.
>
> (Wicksell 1898: 68)

In such a world, no quantity of money circulates, nor should a cash balance be constituted. 'The Quantity Theory of Money would appear to be deprived of its very foundations' (ibid.: 76). And as the real economy, which is an organised economy of credit, tends to get closer to a pure credit economy,[11] it becomes consequently less and less 'explicable' by the quantity theory. So Wicksell shows, by leaving an economic situation favourable to the quantity theory (the pure cash economy) that this theory becomes useless under the organisation of credit.

Indeed, if he makes the effort to consider an intermediate situation (cash economy with simple credit), it is to show that it is not the credit in itself that makes the quantity ineffective, because in that case it is still globally effective. If it is the organisation of credit that invalidates the quantity of money as determining general levels of prices, it is then necessary to look for a new tool to explain the organisation of credit – that is towards banks. Now, besides the quantity of money, it is by the manipulation of the interest rates that banks can act.

So, the process which leads Wicksell from a pure cash economy to a pure credit economy allows him to show that, in a realistic economic context, the quantity theory 'proves to be nothing more than empty and barren formalism' (ibid.: 54). But it also allows him to indicate that the relevant determining causes of the variations of the general level of prices should be looked for in banks and interest rates.

We now aim to show that the loanable funds theory is precisely a theoretical construction, which stems from the idea of the possibility of a persisting gap between the natural rate of interest (marginal productivity of the capital, or the rate which would equalise saving and investment) and the current interest rate of the monetary market. The persistence of the divergence between both rates is fundamental because it is that which commands the durability of Wicksellian cumulative process. And it is on this durability that the reach and the efficiency of the loanable funds theory depend.

Interest rates, divergence and saving – investment disparity

If the money rate is simply defined as the rate of the loans effectively practised by banks, Wicksell's definition of natural (or real) interest rate is more complex because it developed in two stages. Until *Interest and Prices*, the natural interest rate is 'the rate of interest which would be determined by supply and demand if no use were made of money and all lending were effected in the form of real capital goods' (Wicksell 1898: 102). One finds here the foundations of the quantity theory. But this definition is not satisfactory to Wicksell as it sends him back to his own criticism of the quantity theory and brings up the question of the aptness of this virtual rate in a real world. It is to mitigate these criticisms that Wicksell will reshape his definition in depth in the *Lectures on Political Economy*:

> Beside the somewhat too vague and abstract concept natural rate of interest I have defined the more concrete concept normal rate of interest, i.e. the rate at which the demand for new capital is exactly covered by simultaneous savings.[12]

It is precisely in the appearance of the normal interest rate, really coming 'to double the natural interest rate',[13] that one can see the founding act of the loanable funds theory. Indeed, it is precisely because the normal natural interest rate is defined as the one which would equilibrate demand of investment and supply of saving that it is possible to confront it with the market interest rate, which ensues from the equality between actual investment and actual saving.

Consider with Wicksell as the point of departure of the monetary mechanism, an increase in the real interest rate as a result of more promising perspectives of capital employment, motivated, for example, by technological progress.

Demand of loanable funds, intended to purchase real capital, will then increase on behalf of the entrepreneurs. And, because supply of loanable funds is elasticised in a system of organised credit, banks will satisfy this demand without any change in market interest rate. Demand of real capital is then made on the commodity market. And there, under the hypothesis of full employment, the general level of prices is going to increase, for two concomitant reasons:

- The increased demand on behalf of the entrepreneurs for goods and services intended to enter the production of future goods increases their prices.
- Considering the increase of incomes from which the various providers of goods and services benefit, the prices of consumer goods will increase. This tendency is strengthened by the fact that the previously available factors of production are now intended for future production. Furthermore, the natural rate being higher than the bank rate, saving is discouraged and the demand for consumption goods rises.[14]

Holders of fixed incomes are finally forced to save due to the price rise, which took place first of all in the sector of production goods. This is forced saving, strictly speaking, or more precisely the 'first distribution effect of forced saving'.[15] This effect only profits the entrepreneurs.

Forced saving, which is at once a macroeconomic and purely automatic phenomenon, is thus inescapable and exists *from the very beginning of the process*. It has as a fundamental property the preservation of the identity between *ex post* saving and investment. This mechanism allows an answer to the problem of the existence of bank credit, which allows (temporary) inversion of the causal relation between saving and investment. Indeed, because the demand for investment by the entrepreneurs was satisfied by the banking system without the preliminary constitution of saving, it is absolutely necessary to find 'the missing saving'. And this difference between demand for investment and supply of saving will simply be taken from the holders of fixed incomes by means of 'forced saving'.

On the other hand, because of the potential inverted effect of distribution that it contains, forced savings is significantly going to complicate the theoretical justification of the cumulative process.

Difficulties in justifying the cumulative process

Here one finds a crucial point in Wicksell's analysis rarely addressed by commentators. Indeed, the Wicksellian rising price process is still not cumulative. It will only be the case if the differential of rate persists. Stability of the market rate is not very difficult to conceptualise and Wicksell justifies it by the idea of banking passivity. It is much more difficult when he has to justify the natural rate stability. Indeed, the traditional conception of the natural interest rate considers that the return on capital falls with its degree of use, which corresponds naturally to the idea of decreasing marginal productivity of capital. Here, traditionally, as we shall see later, in the Walrasian analysis, the natural rate should fall to the level of the market rate. Wicksell's dilemma finally is: how to think about the stability of the natural rate without abandoning the principle of a decreasing marginal productivity?

Justifying the stability of the bank rate

This cumulative process of increasing prices is only possible on a first condition, namely the total passivity of banks towards the divergence between the two rates. Wicksell formulates for that purpose the hypothesis of a routine behaviour by banks:

> The banks are always more or less *bound* in their interest policy, and even if this policy presumably could, through common action on the part of the banks which is nowadays becoming more prevalent, move within somewhat elastic limits, yet there predominates in the field of banking, more perhaps than elsewhere, precisely because of the great sums at stake, a procedure built up upon custom and tradition, in a word – routine. It may, indeed, be said that the banks never alter their interest rates unless they are induced to do so by the force of outside circumstances.
>
> (Wicksell 1906: 204)

This assumption, which caused many to say about Wicksellian approach that it was unrealistic, is not as indefensible as it seems at first sight. One could indeed interpret that the routine behaviour of banks is simply a philanthropic disinterest in profit. This would be indeed the case if the banking system were limited to a unique bank.

In fact, Wicksell justifies the invariance of the bank rate because the competition of banks among themselves makes lending and borrowing rates converge. According to Wicksell, as long as the level of bank reserves (the 'outside circumstances') will allow it, the level of bank rate will remain constant.

The invariance of the natural rate does not seem to be justified

On the other hand, Wicksell is unable to deny the existence of a falling trend in the real interest rate:

> *Ceteris paribus*, a lowering of the real rate unconditionally demands new real capital, i.e. increased saving. But this would certainly occur, even if involuntary, owing to the fact that higher prices would compel a restriction of consumption on the part of those people who had fixed money incomes . . . But if . . . the production is unable to absorb unlimited quantities of new capital without a reduction in net yield, then the incipient rise . . . might yet be arrested, unless the banks reduced their rate still further.
>
> (Wicksell 1906: 199)

In fact, Wicksell's strategy consists in evacuating the 'second forced saving distribution effect' (the balancing effect in favour of fixed incomes holders) by minimising it, including it among 'secondary factors of the problem' (ibid.: 200). There nevertheless does not seem to be a valid justification for this choice.[16] Furthermore, it leads him to postulate arbitrarily that a part of the profits of the entrepreneurs escapes the market:

> Suppose that the natural rate is raised to $i + 1$ per cent., while the banks maintain their customary rate of discount i. To whose advantage will this difference accrue? In the first place, of course, it accrues to the entrepreneurs. At the end of the year their product, valued at the normal price level, will amount to $K\left(1 + \dfrac{i+1}{100}\right)$, while the amount that they owe is only $K\left(1 + \dfrac{i}{100}\right)$. They have just obtained a surplus profit of $\dfrac{K}{100}$, and they can realise this profit by exchanging among themselves the corresponding quantity of goods and laying them on one side for the consumption of the coming year; while they offer the rest of their stocks to the capitalists at the normal prices, that is to say, for a total sum of money $K\left(1 + \dfrac{i}{100}\right)$. In the first place, therefore, the level of prices remains unaltered.
>
> (Wicksell 1898: 141–2)

This problematic aspect of the Wicksellian cumulative mechanism was studied by Solis (1983) and de Boyer (1987):

This unchangingness of the structure of the relative prices also appears as the very condition of the cumulative process. Indeed, to engage the process of business extension and rising prices, the above-mentioned distribution effect has to be actual: it is necessary that the presence of money, that the distance between natural and money rate, is a source of profit for the entrepreneurs. The condition is thus that the expenditure of incomes, which are increased following the appearance of this divergence between both rates, does not exhaust the totality of product. Otherwise would appear a disparity between the earnings of work and capital, and not a profit for the entrepreneur. To reach this result, Wicksell is led to make an unacceptable assumption: the entrepreneurs do not present the totality of production to the market; they extract the fraction from it corresponding to their profits, to avoid the price fall.

(de Boyer 1987: 410)

The cumulative mechanism, which Wicksell will present in identical form in the *Lectures*, thus depends on an arbitrary position,[17] without which 'the distance between the two rates cannot exist' (ibid.: 415). We completely subscribe to this analysis. However, in our view, the unacceptable hypothesis is not initially in the Wicksellian cumulative process. In other words, it is the expression of an undue simplification, of which Wicksell wrongly thinks that it 'imposes no essential restrictions on the . . . line of reasoning' (Wicksell 1898: 134). In fact, he is completely aware that certain sectors of his statement could seem 'paradoxical' (ibid.: 154) there. For example,

it might further be asked whether [I am] right in suggesting that it lies in the power of the credit institutions, acting in Cupertino only with the entrepreneurs, to determine the direction of production and consequently the period of investment of capital, without paying any heed to the actual capitalists, the owners of goods.

(ibid.: 155)

In the simplified version of cumulative process, it does not hold (de Boyer 2000: 591). Now, before bringing forth his simplifying hypothesis, in the same Chapter 9 of *Interest and Prices*, Wicksell sketches a more complex version of it. It is based on an Austrian approach to capital, taken from Böhm-Bawerk, and allows a justification of the lack of the entrepreneurs' surplus on the market. It is in this primitive version that we shall be interested in the second section. There, we will attempt to show that the ingredients of a theoretical justification of real interest rate quasi-steadiness are present.

A cumulative process which is not self-maintained

Let us accept for the moment the invariance of the natural interest rate. The process of price increase can then continue. Indeed, from the new general level of prices, entrepreneurs will produce new optimistic forecasts, because the real interest rate is always higher than the money rate; the previously identified sequence is going to be repeated. The process of price increase, according to Wicksell, is thus cumulative. It actually continues as long as the difference between both rates persists. Nevertheless, the process is not *self-maintained* by bullish anticipations of entrepreneurs about the general level of prices. The entrepreneurs are indeed always wrong in anticipating future prices equal to current prices.

So, the increase of the general level of prices is not incorporated by the entrepreneurs into their forecasts of an increase in their profits. However, it turns out finally that this error of forecast has no effect on these profits:

> Entrepreneurs who see their expected additional profits vanishing owing to the rise in prices of raw materials and labour will wholly or partly realise these profits, thanks to the rise – which has already taken place – in the prices of the goods they produce, whereas workmen and landlords whose incomes are apparently increased only to a small extent will derive no benefit because the stocks of the commodities in demand are limited.
>
> (Wicksell 1906: 196)

At this level of the analysis, it thus seems that the cumulativity of the Wicksellian process is really based on the idea of a perpetuation of the gap between the natural and the money rate. Indeed, the entrepreneurs are unable to anticipate the inflation and there is no function of demand for money in the Wicksellian analysis (de Boyer 2000: 587).

So, the cumulative process rests in the first analysis upon the steadiness of the natural interest rate, which *a priori* seems to have no justification. We shall see nevertheless in the second section that one does exist in the Wicksellian framework, which is based on an Austrian approach to capital.

The loanable funds theory: Wicksell in the light of Robertson

To represent the Wicksellian construction, it is convenient to appeal to a contribution from Robertson.[18] In an article of 1934 he produced

> an attempt to bring together (1) his concept of Saving [and his concept of investment], and (2) the attempts which have been made to analyse cyclical fluctuation in terms of a divergence between the 'natural' and the 'market' rates of interest.
>
> (Robertson 1934: 650)

Robertson is going to consider, on the one hand, a demand curve of loanable funds, that is, a 'curve DD' representing the declining marginal productivity of new lendings in industrial uses, in other words, representing 'the rate per atom of time at which industry could employ new lendings at various rates of interest' (ibid.: 651). To it is confronted a supply curve of loanable funds, the 'curve SS' representing 'the rate of new available savings per atom of time' (ibid.) (Figure 10.1).

At the equilibrium, natural rate r_0 is equal to market rate i_0. It is the rate at which 'the new lendings which can be absorbed by industry per atom of time and the new available savings per atom of time are equal' (ibid.). The banking system is only putting the saving of some at the arrangement of the investment of the others.

Let us suppose now that, because of technical progress, the demand of loanable funds moves from DD' to $D_1 D'_1$, establishing a new natural rate in r_1. However, if banks maintain their rate at the level i_0 and grant to entrepreneurs the loans they are seeking, those amounts will be higher than available savings by MM_1, the amount of the newly created banking money. This injection of new money, which only profits the entrepreneurs, produces (by means of the increase of the general level of prices) a distribution effect from the holders of fixed incomes towards the entrepreneurs. This forced saving will add to voluntary saving, so that, on the capital market, real saving will be exactly equal to real investment.

Robertson's discussion continues by examining the causes of cycle reversal, that is elements which should lead to the rebalancing of both rates, or what turns

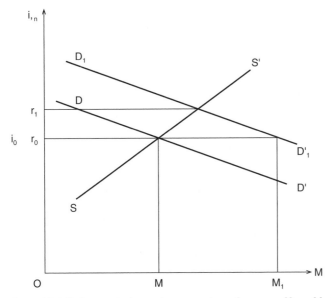

Figure 10.1 Robertson's demand curve and supply curve of loanable funds.

out to be the same, to the equalisation of supply of saving and demand of investment. But we shall put this point aside, because our aim here is simply to isolate the founding principles of the loanable funds theory: that the money rate can deviate durably from its equilibrium value before possible forces of reminder can exercise and effect on one or other of the two rates.

This principle is based on two additional ideas. The first is not, contrary to a widespread opinion, a Keynesian innovation.

It is clearly expressed by Robertson and had already been presented by Wicksell. It consists in saying that

> the amount of saving which the public wish to do in monetary form and the amount of circulating capital which industry requires are determined by entirely separate and independent forces, the one mainly psychological in nature [*thrift*] and the other mainly technical [the marginal productivity of capital].
>
> (Robertson 1922: 106–7)

There is no mechanical link between *ex ante* saving and *ex ante* investment from the moment that there is a possibility of money creation (or of a divergence between the two rates). On the other hand, *ex post*, real saving and real investment are necessarily equal. Here is introduced the concept of forced saving. It is a macroeconomic concept at the outset, asked to equalise saving and investment in a problematic case: when the demand of investment is satisfied by money creation and overtakes the supply of initial saving. Forced saving is a transfer of purchasing power from the consumers (holder of fixed incomes) to the producers (beneficiary of the extra money) by means of an increase in prices.

The second is the idea of a permanent gap between both rates. We saw that even if one accepts the idea of market rate steadiness (the routine of the banking system . . .), there is still the much more delicate problem of the natural interest rate stability. Indeed, before being the rate at which demand of investment and supply of saving become equal, natural rate is the marginal productivity of capital, which, in the standard theory of capital, is meant to represent the equilibrium price between realised saving and investment.

Cumulative process and the Austrian theory of capital

Wicksell, in his reappraisal of the quantity theory, thus seems to be the initiator of what will be called by Robertson the 'loanable funds theory'. But this renewed monetary approach is confronted with internal coherence difficulties, apparently connected to the functioning of the capital market.

The reconstruction of Wicksell's work should thus continue in the field of capital theory. His first task will consist of fixing different places of determination for the natural and market rates of interest: the capital market for the former and the loanable funds market for the latter. Wicksell on this platform is clearly in opposition to Walras.

Nevertheless, Walras had produced with his 'Théorie Mathématique du Billet de Banque' an analysis of the monetary disturbances due to an issue of banknotes. In this analysis, the market and natural rates deviated temporarily one from the other. What is surprising is that Wicksell does not seem to have noticed it, while most probably extracting from it the idea of forced saving for his own use.[19] Be that as it may, Walras's text allows one exactly measure the limits of loanable funds theory within the framework of the standard theory of capital.

This, in our view, is why Wicksell chooses to adopt a Böhm-Bawerkian conception of capital. We shall see that it is in this typically Austrian framework that he proposes a solution to the problem of a long-standing divergence between natural and money rates. This solution seems to anticipate the much more systematic treatment that Hayek will perform on the same problem.

Separation of capital and loanable funds markets

It is the variations of the interest rates that should assume the leading role in the determination of the value of money. All of Wicksell's effort should then focus on the project 'to distend the link' between real rate (the marginal productivity of capital) and money rate. It is then, according to him, impossible to content himself with the Walrasian theory of capital. Indeed, '[Walras] still drags in his disadvantage the rather awkward definition of the capital given by his father' (Wicksell 1899: 830).

As for Walras, he defines capital as 'the part of the social wealth which is lent into money . . . When one says capital, it is about things which were borrowed and will be paid off not in kind but in currency' (Walras [1898] 1992: 283).

The Wicksellian criticism of this approach does not concern the role of intermediation played by money in the operations of capital transfer and factors of production payment. On the contrary, he takes it as a point of departure to argue against the idea of real capital *lending*. In this pattern, the interest rate, of market as well as natural, would be simply the price of capital services. Here saving naturally permanently commands the investment.

The introduction of money into the mechanism of loan in kind is not harmless for Wicksell, in the sense that it does not simply modify the shape of the process, but also its 'very essence' (Wicksell 1898: 135). Indeed, it is money that is lent and borrowed. Real capital is sold and bought in money. The effect of a modification of real capital demand (due to a variation in the marginal productivity of capital) no longer has an influence on the market of loanable funds (that is on the interest rate), but simply on the market of the goods (that is on prices). But, as has been seen previously, in an organised economy of credit, the supply of money fluctuates considerably. Modifications of real capital demand may engender adaptations of the money supply without any variation of interest rates. And investment can, at least ephemerally, command saving.[20]

The Walrasian theory of capital unsuitable for the cumulative process

Wicksell clearly presents the disjunction between capital and loanable funds markets in opposition to the Walrasian framework. Nevertheless, we saw that there was in the *Etudes d'économie politique appliquée* a text in which Walras developed a reflection, which rests on the existence of a divergence between a money interest rate and a natural interest rate (the 'net income rate'). The crucial point is that Walras, in the 'Théorie Mathématique du Billet de Banque', makes use of the forced saving concept, which permits such a divergence.

During their period of issue, the circulation of banknotes makes the money interest rate fall with regard to the income rate. It allows the release of the forced saving process via the increase of production goods prices with regard to consumer goods prices. It is the first distribution effect, in favour of the entrepreneurs and unfavourable to landowners and workers.

The increase of the quantity of capital (and thus the decrease of its marginal productivity) provokes a decline of the rate of net income (the natural interest rate). There is a decline on behalf of the entrepreneurs in the social income *R*. Here is the second distribution effect ensuing from an issue of paper money, allowing a compensatory adjustment in favour of fixed incomes holders.

However, even if there is in Walras a possibility of a decrease in the money rate with regard to the natural rate, this abnormality will very quickly be compensated for by an identical decline in the natural interest rate. One deduces two important results. The first that *there is no possibility of durable forced savings, that is of cumulative process*; the second that *this impossibility lies in the functioning of capital theory*.

There is thus in Walras's system no means to think of the absorption of new saving, forced or not, without an automatic decrease in the real interest rate, as Walras reminds Wicksell in one of his letters:

> I continue to believe that my conception of production equilibrium is not a fiction but an abstraction completely similar to the conceptions of mechanics, and that the price of services, which is determined by the theory of production, should serve for determining the price of capital, by virtue of the net income rate unity principle and of the condition of equality of new capital supply and demand, in the theory of capitalisation.
>
> (Walras 1965, vol. II: 596)

Production process deepening and stability of natural interest rate

Wicksell's main aim is exactly to avoid this realignment between the two rates imposed by Walrasian capital theory. We think that it is precisely for that reason that he judges himself obliged to substitute for it a fundamentally Austrian approach, taken from Böhm-Bawerk. Wicksell thinks, moreover, that it is the only major difference between him and Walras, and he writes to him:

> I possess at this very moment a rather complete collection of your works, now so famous; and their worn-out backs testify that I make a very diligent reading . . . I hope that you will find the time to go through my book [*Über Wert, Kapital und Rente*]. I tried there to exploit on all the points your way of arguing and of putting the equations of prices, much superior to that of Jevons . . . On the other hand, I was not able to completely follow you about production, capitalisation and credit. But it does not hinder, really, it is always your general method to deal with problems which I use myself with the only change to have introduced the new capital and interest conception of Mr Böhm-Bawerk.
>
> (Walras 1965, vol. II: 596)

To define Austrian capital theory is a very thorny problem. We personally chose to consider it only as a theory of production, without a direct link to a subjectivist theory of interest.[21]

The mixture of genres indeed leads to particularly difficult confusions, of which Wicksell was one of the victims:

> Walras and his successors (Pareto, Barone, and others) still continued to hold a theory of interest which contains both formal and material defects and which is seriously incomplete. Walras' formula for interest, as may easily be seen (cf. the preface to the second and subsequent editions of his *Eléments d'économie politique pure*), reduced itself, on the assumption of *stationary* conditions, simply to the equation $F(i) = 0$, in which $F(i)$ is the amount of annual savings conceived as a function of the rate of interest i. In other words, it expresses the truism that, in the stationary state, the inducement to new savings must have ceased . . . The importance of the time-element in production was never properly appreciated by Walras and his school. The idea of a *period* of production or capital-investment does not, as we have said, exist in the Walras–Pareto theory.
>
> (Wicksell 1901: 171)

Wicksell was later to change his opinion regarding the validity of the Walrasian theory of interest under steady state, and he even goes on to insist on the difficulty of the Walrasian theory to describe the future production out of steady state (Wicksell 1919: 226–7). Nevertheless there remains the second part of Wicksellian criticism: the future modifications of the production structure cannot be appreciated in the Walrasian pattern.

Before examining the Wicksellian theory of capital, let us now try to understand why Wicksell preferred the Austrian theory of capital. We have just seen that the main theoretical difficulty of Wicksell was to justify the cumulative process. All of Wicksell's efforts should logically concern the annihilation of the 'second forced saving distribution effect', which depreciates natural interest rate and restores equilibrium, as it occurs in Walras.

We were able to see above that Wicksell was fully aware of the difficulty of getting rid of this effect. He even seemed, upon first analysis, to come to terms with it, before claiming that it could be ignored after all. His justification was, however, not convincing, as it implemented 'an out of market operation to preserve the natural rate during disequilibrium. He introduces there even an accumulation of the surplus which suggests a notion of enrichment based on the accumulation of unsold goods' (Solis 1983: 90). One of the aims of this chapter is to show that Wicksell attempted to produce such a justification, but that he did not, however, use it in the main body of his theory. This justification is based on a Böhm-Bawerkian theory of capital.

Indeed, in *Interest and Prices*, Wicksell dedicates the first part ('The Causes which Determine the Natural Rate of Interest on Capital') of his key Chapter 9 ('Systematic Exposition of the Theory') to try to show how the natural rate can remain at an upper level in spite of an increase of investment. To do so he relies on Böhm-Bawerk's theory. In this chapter, he develops a rather rudimentary representation of the production process which one can doubtless consider an anticipation of Hayek's 'capital structure'. Nevertheless, the driving principle of the capital structure 'deepening' is still not, as in Hayek, a change of relative prices, even if Wicksell was already conscious of it:

> Actually the complications are greater. We have been making the implicit assumption that the relative values of commodities in exchange remain unaltered. But they are, of course, affected by the change in the conditions of production, and they in their turn exert an influence on the conditions of production.
>
> (Wicksell 1898: 132)

The whole Wicksellian construction rests in fact on the distinction between fixed and circulating capital, which are respectively called 'rent-earning goods' and 'capital in the narrow sense'. This differentiation concerns the nature of these two entities. Indeed, earnings of the former are similar to a rent, and only the latter is determined by the level of interest rate.

Thus Wicksell is going to define the 'rent-earning goods' as

> [all the] products of man's labour which have a very high and sometimes unlimited *durability* . . . While by origin, having regard to the manner by which they are obtained, they have the attributes of capital and of other capital goods, they play a part in further production which comes nearest to that played by *land*. I have therefore proposed that they shall be regarded, not as capital goods, but as a kind of 'rent-earning goods', which contribute to output, either with or without the assistance of further labour and land, and earn for their owners a certain rent (analogous to the rent of land).
>
> (ibid.: 126)

What remains of capital goods, that is all goods except labour and land, will then be qualified as 'capital in the narrow sense':

> By capital, in the narrow sense of the word, I mean only tools, machines, improvements in land, etc., of relatively *low* durability (though the dividing line has to be drawn somewhat arbitrarily), furthermore raw materials and semi-manufactured products, and finally stocks of finished consumption goods.
>
> (ibid.: 127)

The distinction between rent-earning goods and capital goods is fundamental. Indeed, their respective earnings are not similar. In fact, 'the new rent-earning goods compete only with the other rent-earning goods of the same type. It gives rise to a rent, and unlike real capital goods, it is not offset by the payment of interest' (ibid.: 127).

Now, what is the peculiarity of rent with regard to interest? Except for the fact that it is served in exchange for the service of a 'long-lasting' good, its supply curve should be vertical. In other words, the price elasticity of this good is nil. If demand for this good increases, it will thus have for only effect to increase its price.

With regard to this last criterion, the assimilation of long-lasting capital goods with land is completely justified in Wicksell's short-term pattern. Indeed, long-lasting goods also require a relatively long time to be produced. The new rent-earning goods will be available on the market only at the end of this long period of production. During this period, the supply of these goods cannot effectively be increased.

This distinction is of the utmost importance since Wicksell's argumentation is based on the fact that 'in a rapidly developing economic system, a considerable part of the available capital is invested for a long term; in other words, it is converted into our rent-earning goods' (ibid.).

The quasi-assimilation of some of the manufactured products with land gives a key role to the rent in the Wicksellian perception of capital. The Böhm-Bawerkian wage fund theory will become, through the model set up by Wicksell, a 'wage and rent fund theory', whose functioning we are now going to examine.

A representation of the capital structure

Wicksell begins by supposing that a first producer pays in advance wages (l_1) and rents (r_1) to produce a machine (of low durability) during the next year. The year after, a second producer will buy this machine and will advance l_2 and r_2 to produce a certain quantity of raw materials, the machine being worn out at the end of this second period. The third year, a third producer will advance l_3 and r_3 to produce a certain quantity of finished goods which will be sold at the end of the year. The capital, in wages and rents, dedicated to this production is thus:

$$(l_1 + l_2 + l_3) + (r_1 + r_2 + r_3) = l + r = k$$

Wicksell deduces from it the average investment periods, t_l for the wages and t_r for the rent:

$$\begin{cases} \dfrac{3l_1 + 2l_2 + l_3}{l} = t_l \\[2em] \dfrac{3r_1 + 2r_2 + r_3}{r} = t_r \end{cases}$$

For the whole of invested capital, we have

$$\frac{3(l_1 + r_1) + 2(l_2 + r_2) + (l_3 + r_3)}{l + r} = \frac{l_{t1} + rt_r}{k} = t \text{ years.}$$

By aggregating every k of every individual industry, one obtains $K = \Sigma k$, the total capital that is the total value of the consumer goods invested at any time in the form of capital. The average period of investment of K is then

$$T = \frac{\Sigma(k.t)}{\Sigma k}$$

The ratio $\dfrac{K}{T}$ thus represents the quantity of capital that becomes free every year from the process of production. It is the 'annual wages-and-rent-fund'. And K (the circulating capital) can be thus defined as the 'aggregate wages-and-rent-fund'.

Wicksell expands the Böhm-Bawerkian 'wage fund theory' because the new approach allows the coupling of the two following parameters: the amount of the 'wage-and-rent-fund' and the average investment period of capital. These two parameters are susceptible to influence each other by means of changes of proportion between wages and rents. It is the object of the following equation, 'approximately true' according to Wicksell, for whom A represents the number of available workers, B the total amount of available land, l and r the average rates of wages and rent per unit of land:

$$(A.l + B.r).T = K$$

As Wicksell points out, this equation simply translates the hypothesis that all factors of production are fully employed. But what is more important here is that '$B.r$ really stands for the sum of all "rent-earning goods" [and not only land], each measured in terms of its own unit of measure (for instance . . . kilometres in the case of railways) and multiplied by the corresponding rent' (Wicksell 1898: 131).

Functioning out of equilibrium

To analyse the capital structure modifications out of equilibrium, Wicksell is going to add a functioning hypothesis, essentially to allow for the fast modification of the current processes of production. These hypotheses concern mainly the entrepreneurs' behaviour. Thus, he adds to the profit maximisation objective as determiner of entrepreneurs' behaviour, an assumption of substitutability of labour and rent-earning goods (including land) as well as a hypothesis of producers' mobility in the choice of the goods which they are going to produce.

Under these hypotheses, if, for example, wages fall (because of an increase of workers), a replacement of the labour factor in the factor rent-earning goods is going to take place. Entrepreneurs now prefer labour-intensive products. And, because the demand of labour increases and that of rent-earning goods decreases, 'economic equilibrium is restored . . .; and all available factors of production will find employment at prices determined by the market situation (ibid.: 132).[22] According to Wicksell, exactly the same principle is going to determine the real interest rate.

Let us resume the Wicksellian process when it is not yet cumulative, that is when the 'first forced saving effect' in favour of the producers takes place after an increase of the natural interest rate. One should now expect, according to Walras, that the restabilising effect would occur, by means of a decrease in the real interest rate. Wicksell's aim is to show that this effect should be strongly eased and postponed.

An increase in the natural interest rate, that is a relative decline in the money rate of interest, is, according to Wicksell, going to increase the demand of production factors. The competition among the entrepreneurs is going to increase wages and rents, because demand increases while supply remains fixed. The real rate is therefore going to fall, as it is only associated with circulating capital, the production of which is now more expensive. Here is the Walrasian 'bow net'! But Wicksell is not affected, because, according to him, 'this effect, which by itself might rapidly depress the rate of interest to a very marked degree, is not decisive' (ibid.: 133). Indeed, the profit of 'fixed capital' is not affected by this fall. In fact, because it is a rent, it will increase.

Profits coming from the production of rent-earning goods (that is stemming from a long process of production) thus exceed profits coming from the production of circulating capital-intensive goods (that is stemming from a short process of production). Entrepreneurs are thus going to privilege the production of rent-earning goods and quickly begin production of those kinds of goods. This is going to lengthen the period of investment. It is going to provoke, during the maturation period of those new rent-earning goods, a decrease in the available consumer goods, that is of the 'wage and rent fund'. The consequence is again a lowering of wages and rents (and thus a rise in the interest rate on circulating capital, that is the natural rate). The unacceptable hypothesis concerning the extraction of a fraction of the production by the entrepreneurs is no longer necessary, because this problematic fraction of the production will only appear on the market later.

The fall of the interest rate on circulating capital, caused by an increase in the natural rate, was thus paid off with the average lengthening of the production processes. The Walrasian re-stabilisation effect is thus strongly weakened with regard to what one would expect, which allows Wicksell to claim 'the practical possibility that in a rapidly progressive society the rate of interest [natural] may be maintained at a relatively high level over a considerable period of time in spite of continual accumulation of capital' (ibid.: 134).

In the end it seems possible to summarise the results of this second section in three points:

1   The cumulativeness of the increasing price process depends on the durability of the disparity between both rates. This gap should be absolutely analytically protected. Now, such a justification is impossible within the framework of the standard marginalist capital theory. It thus seems to be unsuitable as a background to the Wicksellian cumulative process.

2   That is the reason why Wicksell confirms the Böhm-Bawerkian schism in the marginalist framework. He effectively chooses an Austrian capital theory and develops a basic capital structure model, which should be considered as a starting point for more complex future constructions, especially those of Hayek.

3   It is this capital theory which allows him to open new perspectives for an

effective use of the loanable funds theory as an interesting tool to study business cycles.

Conclusion

As a reappraisal of Wicksell's project, our attempt to recount the process of the construction of his system arouses some reflections.

The appearance of loanable funds theory, which implies the possibility of a persisting gap between the money and the natural rates of interest, or between demand of investment and supply of saving, manifestly comes from the Wicksellian revision of the quantity theory, where the quantity of money lost ceases to determine the general level of prices.

Furthermore, it seems interesting to us to complete the 'Wicksell connection' idea by a reflection taking into account the real dimension of economy. Indeed, the 'pre-Keynesian' macroeconomics does not seem to have developed simply from a superimposition of the natural and money rates of interest, it in turn was made possible simply by redoubling the capital market by the new 'loanable funds market', dedicating the interest rate 'as the price of credit'.

The loanable funds framework appears to be otherwise strongly correlated to the questioning of the standard theory of capital. The integration in the analysis of the time factor following another logic than that of the intertemporal allocation of resources (which will later come to strengthen the 'mainstream'), via the Austrian theory of capital, is fundamental to the use of the loanable funds theory to perform a dynamic analysis. The adoption by Wicksell of the Austrian theory of capital, although incomplete, constitutes the starting point of a whole literature in terms of 'sequential analysis', whose main characteristic lies in the consideration of time lags in the propagation of exogenous disturbances within the production structure. This analysis, which emphasises the idea of the production period, is going to give birth to explanations of cycles which at the same time protect the essential idea that, in the long term, saving commands investment. This idea is fundamentally based on a *petitio principii*: the real existence of the natural interest rate.

Allow us here to mention a point of view different from Leijonhufvud's. Kohn (1981, 1986) defends the idea that Leijonhufvud is right to say that 'the acceptance of the General Theory results . . . in the loss of a major component of monetary theory'. However, he adds, 'the loss . . . went far beyond the loanable funds theory to include the whole infrastructure of sequence analysis on which the theory of loanable funds rests' (Kohn 1981: 878).

Indeed, it is known that the Keynesian approach, at least in the *General Theory*, is led in essentially static terms. Kohn is convinced that it is not necessary to look further for the causes of the contemporary problems of macroeconomics, searching for its microeconomic foundations and failing to integrate money. Pushing his reasoning further, he thinks that the solutions to all these problems 'are all there in the pre-General Theory sequence analysis, waiting to be rediscovered' (ibid.).

This pre-Keynesian sequential analysis seems to us to be perfectly represented by Hayek and Robertson. Both will make every effort to produce 'complete' theories of the business cycle, which take into account in particular the mutual influences of the real and monetary spheres. This concern is revealed in their business cycle theory by the central place occupied by the idea of 'capital structure', thus extending the ideas of both Wicksell and Böhm-Bawerk.

Finally, the reflections of Kohn or Leijonhufvud bring forth the following fundamental question: if one rejects the not very stimulating hypothesis of a fashion phenomenon, why did Keynes's theses supplant those which had been developed within the Swedish or Austrian Schools? The answer could be found in the criticisms made on about approach towards loanable funds, notably that of Sraffa, but also in the many attacks that the Austrian conception of capital had to face.

Notes

1 It would seem that 'loanable funds' is mentioned for the first time in Robertson (1936).
2 The following diagram is exactly that of Leijonhufvud (1981: 133) with the exception of 'Z-theory', presented as an improvement to the *Treatise on Money*, and which we do not use here.

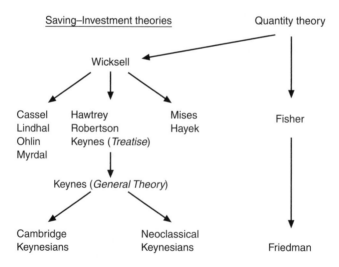

3 The controversy over the interest rate is very prolific and contains numerous ramifications. On the other hand, one can place very exactly the moment and where it began: in 1937 (just after the appearance of the *General Theory*), in volume 47 of the *Economic Journal*. It is Bertil Ohlin who opened the debate: Ohlin (1937a), 'Some Notes on the Stockholm Theory of Savings and Investment', and (1937b),

'Some Notes on the Stockholm Theory of Savings and Investment II'; and Keynes (1937a), 'Alternative Theories of the Rate of Interest'; Ohlin *et al.* (1937), 'Alternative Theories of the Rate of Interest, Three Rejoinders'; Keynes (1937b), 'The "Ex-Ante" Theory of the Rate of Interest'.

4 For a study of the 'saving–investment method', but only in Cambridge, see Bridel (1987).

5 See on this subject also Siven (1997).

6 An exhaustive study has been done by Pascal Bridel (1994), as well as in Bridel (1997); see also Jenn-Treyer (2001).

7 See, for example, Tooke (1844).

8 According to Wicksell:

> It is true that many of the well-known workers on the theory of value, such as Jevons, Walras, and Menger, have entered fairly deeply into questions concerning money. But their treatment of such questions runs, for the most part, in the old ruts. For instance, Walras' exposition consists fundamentally of nothing more than a mathematical version of the quantity theory (. . .); there is no substantial development or extension of the theory itself.
>
> (1898: 18)

9 Wicksell again:

> Were it possible to increase these to an unlimited extent a very large proportion of all the world's business of exchange and lending could actually be paid for *in cash* by sending backwards and forwards (*very* rapidly, it is true) one single ten-mark piece.
>
> (1898: 60)

10 According to Wicksell:

> The greatest the number of the bank's customers, . . . the smaller is the stock of cash which the bank has to maintain in relation to the total extent of its business; and the greater *pro tanto* is the velocity of circulation of money.
>
> (1898: 68)

11 The pure credit economy is, according to Wicksell, only a tendency, a borderline case.

12 Wicksell, introduction to the first Swedish edition of the second volume of the *Lectures*, quoted by Ohlin (1936: xiii).

13 According to Wicksell:

> The rate of interest at which *the demand for loan capital and the supply of savings* exactly agree [the normal rate] and which more or less corresponds to the expected yield on the newly created capital, will then be the normal of natural real rate. It is essentially variable.
>
> (1906: 193)

14 And even if the assumption of full-employment is abandoned, it does not change the general tendency:

It is, of course, not impossible for the rise in prices to be counteracted to a certain extent by an increase in production, for example if previously there had been unemployment, or if higher wages had induced longer working hours . . . But all these are secondary considerations.

(Wicksell 1906: 195)

15 The idea of two opposite distribution effects connected to forced saving is well developed in Bridel (1994).
16 For an examination of the first controversies about cumulative process, see Siven (1998).
17 This is, for example, the position of Patinkin: 'Wicksell admits that "this possibility certainly cannot be entirely rejected", but he makes no further reference to it in the rest of his analysis' (1952: 839n).
18 As, for example, Kohn (1981), Rogers (1989), and Tsiang (1956).
19 It is, for example, the opinion expressed by Hayek (1932: 195).
20 The duration of this phase depends on the 'pureness' of the banking system:

The two rates of interest still reach *ultimate* equality, but only after, and as a result of, a previous movement of prices. Prices constitute, so to speak, a spiral spring which serves to transmit the power between the natural and the money rates of interest; but this spring must first be sufficiently stretched or compressed. In a pure cash economy, the spring is short and rigid; it becomes longer and more elastic in accordance with the stage of development of the system of credit and banking.

(Wicksell 1898: 135–6)

21 On this subject, see Ravix (1999) or Jenn-Treyer (2001), Chapter 1.
22 Here appears the limit of Wicksell analysis, built on the 'implicit assumption that the relative values of commodities in exchange remain unaltered. But they are, of course, affected by the change in the conditions of production, and they in their turn exert an influence on the conditions of production' (Wicksell 1898: 132). This limit should be considered as the starting point of Hayek's work.

References

Bridel, P. (1987) *Cambridge Monetary Thought*, London: Macmillan.
—— (1994) ' "Dépréciation de la monnaie" et épargne forcée, une contribution négligée de Walras à la théorie monétaire des cycles', *Economies et Sociétés*, 20–1: 89–114.
—— (1997) *Money and General Equilibrium Theory*, Cheltenham: Edward Elgar.
de Boyer, J. (1987) 'Théorie de la monnaie et politique monétaire', PhD thesis, Université Paris 1, Panthéon-Sorbonne.
—— (2000) 'La monnaie dans la pensée néo-classique pré-keynésienne', in Béraud, A. and Faccarello, G. (eds) *Nouvelle histoire de la pensée économique*, vol. 2, Paris: La Découverte & Syros, pp. 572–607.
Hawtrey, R.G. ([1937] 1952) *Capital and Employment*, London: Longmans, Green and Co.
Hayek, F.A. (1932) 'A note on the development of the doctrine of forced saving', *Quar-*

terly Journal of Economics, 47: 23–33; in *Profits, Interest and Investment*, London: Routledge & Sons, 1939, Chapter 7.

Jenn-Treyer, O. (2001) 'Théorie des fonds prêtables, épargne forcée et théorie autrichienne du capital: une contribution à l'histoire de la macroéconomie wicksellienne', PhD thesis, Université Paris XII, Val de Marne.

Keynes, J.M. (1936a) *The General Theory of Employment, Interest and Money*, in *The Collected Writings of John Maynard Keynes*, vol. VII, London: Macmillan, 1973.

—— (1936b) *The General Theory and After: Part I: Preparation*, in *The Collected Writings of John Maynard Keynes*, vol. XIII, London: Macmillan, 1973.

—— (1937a) 'Alternative theories of the rate of interest', *The Economic Journal*, 47(186): 241–52.

—— (1937b) 'The "ex-ante" theory of the rate of interest', *The Economic Journal*, 47(188): 663–9.

Kohn, M. (1981) 'A loanable funds theory of unemployment and monetary disequilibrium', *The American Economic Review*, 71(5): 859–79.

—— (1986) 'Monetary analysis, the equilibrium method, and Keynes's "general theory"', *Journal of Political Economy*, 94(6): 1191–224.

Leijonhufvud, A. (1981) 'The Wicksell connection: variations on a theme', in *Information and Coordination*, Oxford: Oxford University Press.

Ohlin, B. (1936) 'Introduction', in K. Wicksell (ed.) *Interest and Prices*, London: Macmillan.

—— (1937a) 'Some notes on the Stockholm theory of savings and investment', *The Economic Journal*, 47(185): 53–69.

—— (1937b) 'Some notes on the Stockholm theory of savings and investment II', *The Economic Journal*, 47(186): 221–40.

Ohlin, B., Robertson, D.H. and Hawtrey, R.G. (1937) 'Alternative theories of the rate of interest, three rejoinders', *The Economic Journal*, 47(187): 423–43.

Patinkin, D. (1952) 'Wicksell's "cumulative process"', *The Economic Journal*, December: 835–47.

Ravix, J.L. (1999) 'Nature et mesure du capital dans la théorie du capital productif de Böhm-Bawerk', *Cahiers d'économie politique*, 35: 37–61.

Robertson, D.H. ([1922] 1948) *Money*, Cambridge: Cambridge University Press.

—— (1934) 'Industrial fluctuation and the natural rate of interest', *Economic Journal*, December, in Robertson, D.H. (ed.) *Essays in Monetary Theory*, London: P.S. King & Son, 1940, pp. 83–91.

—— (1936) 'Some notes on Mr Keynes's general theory of employment', *Quarterly Journal of Economics*, November: 187–8.

Rogers, C. (1989) *Money, Interest and Capital*, Cambridge: Cambridge University Press.

Siven, C.H. (1997) 'Capital theory and equilibrium method in Wicksell's cumulative process', *History of Political Economy*, 29(2): 201–17.

—— (1998) 'Two early Swedish debates about Wicksell's cumulative process', *The European Journal of the History of Economic Thought*, 5: 120–39.

Solis Rosales, R. (1983) *Banque centrale et taux d'intérêt monétaires. Essai sur les théories de Thornton, Wicksell et Hawtrey*, PhD thesis, University of Paris X, Nanterre.

Tooke, T. (1844) *An Inquiry into the Currency Principle*, 2nd edn, London: Longman, Brown, Green & Longmans.

Tsiang, S.C. (1956) 'Liquidity preference and loanable funds theories, multiplier and velocity analysis: a synthesis', *The American Economic Review*, 46(4): 539–64.

Uhr, C.G. (1960) *Economic Doctrines of Knut Wicksell*, Berkeley, CA: University of California Press.

Walras, L. (1898) *Études d'économie politique appliquée (Théorie de la production de la richesse sociale)*, vol. X, des Œuvres economiques complètes d'Auguste et Léon Walras, Paris: Economica, 1942, xxix, 571p.

—— (1965) *Correspondence of Léon Walras and Related Papers*, Jaffé W. (ed.), 3 vols, North Holland: Amsterdam.

Wicksell, K. ([1898] 1936) *Interest and Prices* [*Geldzins und Güterpreise: eine Studie über die den Tauschwert des Geldes bestimmenden Ursachen*], London: Macmillan.

—— (1899) 'Recension of the *Etudes d'Economie politique appliquée*', *Jahrbücher für Nationalökonomie und Statistik*, III, 18: 825–30.

—— ([1901] 1934) *Lectures on Political Economy* [*Föreläsingar i nationalekonomi*], vol. 1, London: Routledge & Kegan.

—— ([1906] 1935) *Lectures on Political Economy* [*Föreläsingar i nationalekonomi*], vol. 2, London: Routledge & Kegan.

—— (1919) 'Professor Cassel's system of economics', published as an appendix to K. Wicksell, *Lectures on Political Economy*, vol. I (English edition of 1934), Fairfield, VA: A.M. Kelley, 1977, pp. 219–57.

11 To what extent is the Austrian theory of capital Austrian?

Böhm-Bawerk and Hicks reconsidered

Sandye Gloria-Palermo and Giulio Palermo

Introduction

Since its birth in the 1870s, the Austrian tradition has always faced the problem of defining itself as a specific and identifiable school of thought, distinct from marginalism and later on from neoclassical economics. The whole story of the Austrian School is marked by internal tensions, ambiguities and misunderstandings that undermine its identity: from the outset, Menger had to emphasise the specificity of his approach in relation to Walrasian marginalism; Böhm-Bawerk, who presented himself as a faithful follower of the Austrian founder, elaborated a theory of capital and interest that Menger considered the biggest error ever committed; in the 1930s, Hayek and Mises clashed on methodological ground, the former firmly rejecting the excess of the apriorist approach and proposing instead some kind of falsificationist perspective; despite his contribution to the theory of economic development, Schumpeter was never considered a genuine Austrian author because of his admiration for the general equilibrium construct of Walras and his non-Hayekian cycle theory;[1] and so on . . .

Today, Austrian economics still does not constitute a unified paradigm and the label conveys some ambiguities. The modern exponents of the Austrian ideas are divided into three streams of thought, more or less compatible: the Misesian apriorists led by Rothbard, the radical subjectivists led by Lachmann and the group led by Kirzner focusing on the theory of entrepreneurship.[2] Things become even more complicated when 'neo' (and not 'modern') Austrians enter the scene. The term neo-Austrian was coined by Hicks in his 1973 book in reference to Böhm-Bawerk's theory of capital and interest, but the modelling approach which develops later on under the impulsion of Faber in particular and referred to as 'neo-Austrian' draws on two other sources of inspiration: the work of Koopmans, applying activity analysis to production theory, and the work of Georgescu-Roegen, applying thermodynamic principles to economic analysis.[3]

Modern Austrians totally ignore the work of this group of authors. The reference to Böhm-Bawerk does not seem to be sufficient to create a synergy between them and moreover, the technicality of this approach clashes with the traditional reluctance of Austrians since Menger to use mathematical tools. Ultimately, modern and neo-Austrians have very little in common and this reciprocal lack of interest is not surprising. What is more surprising however, is the cold reception and lack of enthusiasm with which Hicks's original neo-Austrian theory of capital has been received by the Austrians. The aim of this chapter is to investigate the reasons for such a rejection, by focusing on the nature of the so-called Austrian theory of capital, in his Böhmian and Hicksian version.

Among modern Austrians, Lachmann has been the most open to dialogue, maybe this stems from the fact that both Lachmann and Hicks position themselves directly in the continuity of the research programme initiated by Menger rather than that of Mises and Hayek as Rothbardians and Kirznerians do and that their interpretation of the Austrian founder is very similar. An interesting angle from which to analyse this issue is given by Hicks himself (Hicks 1976: 145) who, very sensitive to the criticism addressed by Lachmann, sees the extent of the dissent between Lachmann and himself to be of a similar nature to the one separating Menger and Böhm-Bawerk. In what follows, we first show that the extent of the dissent between Menger and Böhm-Bawerk resides mainly in the nature of the subjectivist dimension of the theory of capital and interest; in the second section, we focus on Hicks's reappropriation of this theory and, following the polemical exchanges between Hicks and Lachmann, we question the legitimacy of the 'neo-Austrian' label self-arrogated to his theory by the Nobel prize.

'The greatest error'

Böhm-Bawerk is traditionally presented, along with Menger and Wieser, as a member of the Austrian School founder triumvirate. His objective is to pick up again the research programme initiated by Menger and to complete it with his own theory of capital and interest. But, although Böhm-Bawerk presents himself as pursuing a strict continuity of Menger's logic, the latter is more than reluctant to support the Böhmian theory of capital and interest which the author of the *Grundsätze* even describes as 'one of the greatest errors ever committed'.[4] The reasons for this rejection stems from the way in which Böhm-Bawerk deals with the subjectivist dimension.

The nature of capital

Böhm-Bawerk distinguishes between two concepts of capital: social capital and private capital. Social capital, a key concept in his theory of production, brings together all the means of production such as installations, warehouses, machines, tools, stock, raw materials and draught animals. The concept of private capital, at the heart of his theory of interest, refers to capital as a specific source of income and consists of all goods composing social capital and first-order goods not used for consumption.[5] Böhm-Bawerk (1889: 70) lists the content of these two concepts in detail, thereby arriving at a generic classification of goods according to their very nature. At this stage of the analysis, subjectivism is set aside; the role of individual judgement in the characterisation of goods has vanished. Böhm-Bawerk provides a narrow definition of capital goods and in particular, a close definition which is meant to be exhaustive for each category of good. The relationship between items and human needs is no longer the main determinant factor for an object to acquire the character of capital good as in Menger's definition of higher-order goods. An objective dimension has been introduced into the analysis. Menger explicitly and sharply criticises the idea that goods derive their character of capital goods from their intrinsic nature. The author is most eager to define open concepts of goods and capital, whose content is continuously changing according to the conditions of the production process and to the nature of the individual plans having originated that process.

The period of production

In the first book of his *Positive Theory of Capital*, Böhm-Bawerk's aim is to grasp the essence of capital. Like Menger, the author focuses upon essential causes of complex phenomena rather than on their manifestations. For instance, Böhm-Bawerk explains that capital is not the fundamental cause but the symptom of the phenomenon of higher productivity of more roundabout production processes. The introduction of capital into a process is the result of a deliberate choice by economic agents to undertake more and more advantageous (i.e. longer) production processes. The use of capital in a process results from individual judgements. Individual behaviour at the beginning of the causal chain explains the complex phenomenon of capital; it represents the essential cause of its economic existence. However, the introduction of the concept of average period of production leads Böhm-Bawerk away from Menger's essentialism and at the same time away from a dynamic subjectivist perspective.

The concept of a period of production synthesises the principle of higher productivity of more roundabout processes of production which bring together two variables: duration and productivity of processes. It leads the whole capital structure of a process to be represented by one single objective figure. At this level, Streissler (1972) emphasises the one-dimensional nature of Böhm-Bawerk's analysis which definitely contrasts with Menger's subjectivism based upon the infinity of dimensions produced by the human mind. Here, on the contrary, only the technical aspect of production matters, irrespective of any human appraisal. Böhm-Bawerk focuses upon the material point of view of production whereas Menger always maintains a subjectivist foundation of production in his analysis by using a definition of productive activity considered as an economic relation between human needs and means at one's disposal.

The theory of interest

Böhm-Bawerk's theory of interest is torn between two competing directions; the first, which is compatible with Menger's subjectivist foundation, presents interest as a phenomenon of exchange – the expression of individual preference for present goods as compared with future goods. The other, which is the one finally asserted, tends toward the traditional theory of marginal utility, according to which interest is a mere technical consequence of productivity of roundabout production processes.

Book IV of *The Positive Theory* is devoted to the theory of interest. It begins as follows: '*Present goods are as a general rule worth more than future goods of equal quality and quantity.* That sentence is the nub and the kernel of the theory of interest which I have to present' (Böhm-Bawerk 1889: 259). Interest is directly depicted as a phenomenon of exchange, resulting from the difference in evaluation between present and future. The theory of value thus plays a central role here and its scope is widened to future goods. Böhm-Bawerk lays the foundations of the inter-temporal theory of value as Fisher was to develop it. More precisely, interest stems from the fact that production takes time: Böhm-Bawerk described production as an inter-temporal exchange of present production goods with future consumption goods. The entrepreneur is considered as 'a merchant who offers present goods for sale' (ibid.: 337). The ownership of capital goods is equal in value to the holding of a stock of future consumption goods: 'means of production, when compared in value with present goods, are equal in value to a smaller number of units of the consumptible end product than can be produced from those means of production' (ibid.: 300). This difference in value represents interest and its level is determined using the same principle governing all evaluation phenomena. At least, this is the result Böhm-Bawerk plans to reach. However, progressively the author veers towards a different conception of interest which has little to do with the subjective field of exchange. 'We said above that in his subjective circumstances the capitalist as a rule places the same valuation on a sum of present goods as on an equal sum of future goods' (ibid.: 353). In other words, Böhm-Bawerk is explaining here that the former proposition concerning individual preferences for present goods over future commodities, a proposition which was indeed supposed to lay the foundations for the phenomenon of interest, no longer plays any role. The only determinant for interest turns up to consist of the difference in productivity brought about by additional investments. There is no longer any room for subjective factors: 'On which figure is the capitalist to base his valuation? The answer might well be "according to the product that is turned out when that method of production is adopted which is economically the most reasonable"' (ibid.: 353). The only remaining determinant for interest is thus a mere technical element.

It is obvious that Menger could not subscribe to such a result. Ultimately, Böhm-Bawerk views interest as an equilibrium variable flowing from the confrontation between supply and demand for available resources; not only is equilibrium the very reference, but also there is no room for any disruptive force such as uncertainty or error. All subjective criteria have been permanently put aside and interest is mechanically determined according to technical and purely objective criteria.

The subjectivist dimension

Menger's well-known criticism of the Böhmian theory of interest consists of a punctual attack which concerns a definite field of economics. However, the origin of divergences between the two authors is much deeper and all the more painful as Böhm-Bawerk presents himself as a faithful follower of Menger. No doubt the starting point of his developments is Austrian in its very essence, but the results he reached could not be supported by Menger. At the heart of the dispute is the treatment of the subjectivist dimension, the key feature of the Mengerian originality, which Böhm-Bawerk's theory fails to carry on.

Mengerian subjectivism is not limited to the theory of marginal value but is rather involved in the explanation of all economic phenomena, human behaviour being the primary essential cause. The value of goods, but also their character of first- and higher-order goods, as well as the set of prices and the structure of production, are the results of individual actions guided by human needs and desires, knowledge and interpretations of the surrounding reality. It would be misleading to limit Menger's contribution to the theory of subjective value which only represents one of the many manifestations of human behaviour. Menger's originality stems from his systematic subjectivist vision of economic phenomena.

Austrian subjectivism, as Menger introduces it, is much more radical than the marginalist conception: it is not limited to preferences but is rather enlarged to include expectations, costs, the conception of time (Bergsonian), and knowledge perception. Austrian subjectivism considers human choices in terms of a means–ends framework. Individual choice is the result of a two-step process: the adoption of a specific objective and the laying down of a plan of actions intended to best satisfy the objective. This scheme is much more general than the marginalist one in which individual objectives are limited to the maximisation of utility, and individual choice results from the comparison within a closed set of alternatives of all available possibilities. Austrian subjectivism challenges such a mechanical conception of human behaviour, limited to mere calculation.

The kernel of the differences stems from a distinct conception of time: the marginalist *Homo Economicus* makes his decision in a neutral temporal setting; the passage of time leaves his objective and preferences unchanged, his answer is mechanically a function of his tastes and of the quantitative constraints of his environment. Austrians reject this static conception of subjectivism and advocate a dynamic view: the agent makes his decisions within a continuously changing environment; the passage of time is the cause for the evolution of individual perceptions. Decision-making takes into account the creative activity of human mind and becomes a non-deterministic process.

The Mengerian conception of subjectivism comes from many points of dynamic nature: the means–ends framework is at the core of Menger's definition of 'economising'; agents are engaged in a process of information gathering in order to modify and improve their plans of action; information depends on the knowledge agents can acquire about causal connection between their desires and economic goods; the Mengerian agent lives in a world of uncertainty where occurrence of errors is indeed possible; decisions should be based upon expectations agents make about an unknown future, leaving room for their creative abilities.

The 'greatest error' once again?

If we now turn to the relationship between Hicks and the modern Austrians and with Lachmann in particular, the scenario looks very similar: Hicks claims analytical continuity with the work of Menger and Böhm-Bawerk but his self-labelled 'neo-Austrian' theory of capital is rejected by the 'official' modern Austrians. The subjectivist dimension of his theory is once again at the centre of the dispute.

Mister Hicks and the Austrians

The Austrian influence which appears in the work of Hicks might be traced back to his participation in the seminar held by Hayek at the LSE from 1931 to 1935. There is evidence of the Austrian influence as early as 1939, in *Value and Capital*, even though Böhm-Bawerk's theory of capital and interest is considered from a critical point of view rather than a constructive perspective. In *Value and Capital*, indeed, Hicks critically considered and rejected the concept of average period of production and along with it the whole 'Austrian' theory of capital and interest, without contemplating the possibility of taking some of Böhm-Bawerk's insights as a starting point for an alternative theory of interest. In the second volume of his trilogy on capital theory, *Capital and Growth* (1965), the Austrian influence is not explicit and expresses itself only indirectly through the interest in the implications of time for the theory of capital. The problem of the 'traverse' is precisely concerned with the analysis of the transition from one steady state to another. The 1970s were to mark the passage from the status of fellow traveller to that – in his way – of Austrian activist: in a 1970 paper in the *Economic*

Journal, Hicks adapted the Austrian approach to the application for time series and came up with his famous 'neo-Austrian' growth theory; in 1973 appeared the last book of the trilogy on capital theory, *Capital and Time: A Neo-Austrian Theory*, where Hicks again picked up Böhm-Bawerk's insights and deepened the implications of the temporal nature of production processes; the same year, Hicks co-edited the collected papers of a symposium held at Vienna in June 1971 to celebrate the hundredth anniversary of the publication of Carl Menger's *Grundsätze der Volkswirtschaftslehre*; this volume, *Carl Menger and the Austrian School of Economics*, gathered a number of influential contributions that in the 1970s were at the origins of the modern Austrian revival.[6] Still in the 1970s, Hicks published a series of contributions specifying his 'neo-Austrian' approach and more generally his interest with the implications of time in economics (1973b, 1976, 1979a, 1979b).

Despite the fact that in the 1970s the Austrian tradition was just emerging from long decades of neglect and was in a structuring phase, modern Austrians hardly welcomed Hicks's contribution to capital theory. Among the leaders of the modern Austrian revival, Lachmann was the privileged interlocutor. He published a review of *Capital and Growth* (Lachmann 1966), another review of *Capital and Time* (Lachmann 1973), completed a few years later by another paper on Austrian capital theory (Lachmann 1976) and answered Hicks's rejoinder (Hicks 1979a; Lachmann 1979). Ultimately, the diatribe between the two authors is summarised as the following question: can Hicks's theory of capital and growth legitimately be considered a part of the Austrian corpus, does the author of *Capital and Time* deserve the label of Austrian author? From the Austrian side, the answer is unambiguously no. The investigation into the reasons for this snub brings into question the definition of the very essence of the Austrian tradition. As shown below, Lachmann and Hicks propose two different definitions. Following Lachmann's definition, it follows that Hicks's theory of capital is not Austrian and the author suggests an alternative Austrian theory of capital.

The Böhmian point of departure

Hicks describes himself as an 'irregular and defective' Austrian (Hicks 1979: 51) rather than as a 'Particular' Austrian. This position is in line with the kind of methodological eclecticism that the author has often been advocating. As a matter of fact, his set of books on capital theory is a good illustration of this position: as is well known, *Value and Capital, Capital and Growth, Capital and Time*, although not planned as a trilogy, show *a posteriori*, how the same object of analysis – the concept of capital – may be studied from different angles, with different approaches and tools according to the point of view the theorist wants to highlight. More generally, Hicks (1985) insists on the fact that there is no such a thing as *a method*, understood as a class or family of models, like statics or dynamics, which may win the primacy. Rather, the theorist should choose the most appropriate method according to the very nature of the object under examination. In that perspective, Hicks is 'neo-Austrian' only to the extent that his aim is to investigate the consequences of the temporal dimension of the production process.

More precisely, Hicks investigates the consequences of a technological change on the – temporal – structure of production. In order to offer a theory that would accommodate both fixed and circulating capital, he defines the production process as a flow-input and flow-output process and focuses on the investment decision to begin, continue or stop a productive process. Non-viable processes will be truncated and replaced by different techniques. In a steady state, the technique which is chosen remains the same over time; and production processes having a definite length of time, the steady state is also characterised by the fact that there are as many new processes – of the same kind – that are being implemented as there are processes that reach an end and, in a steady growth economy, the number of processes beginning and ending is increasing at a constant rate. In the steady state, however, the time dimension has vanished. Such a representation does not constitute the object of investigation but is only the point of departure for studying the dynamic problem of the traverse. The traverse describes the path from a steady growth equilibrium disturbed by a technological shock – the possibility of implementing a new technique – to the new steady state. It analyses the temporal transformation of the productive structure in terms of the progressive replacement of the old technique by the new one and questions the viability of this transition process.

The description 'neo-Austrian' to this theory thus stems from a general and loose reference to the work of Böhm-Bawerk. This is a 'neo-Austrian' theory simply because, like Böhm-Bawerk's analysis, it investigates the consequences of the fact that production takes time. Apart from this general premise, Hicks's theory takes its distance from Böhm-Bawerk's one:

> there is much of the traditional Böhm-Bawerk construction that must be abandoned. There is no period of production; there is no roundaboutness; . . . These are drastic excisions. If we perform such a surgery, is there anything left? . . .
>
> What we must not abandon are Böhm-Bawerk's (and Menger's) true insights – the things that are strengths to the Austrian approach. Production is a process, a process in time. Though there are degenerate forms . . . the characteristic form of production is a sequence, in which inputs are followed by outputs. Capital is an expression of sequential production. Production has a time structure, so capital has a time-structure.
>
> (Hicks 1973b: 193–4)

Taken at such general level, Lachmann accepts the appellation. 'It is futile to quarrel about labels. A thinker who carries on Böhm-Bawerk's work cannot be gainsaid the predicate "Austrian" if he claims it' (Lachmann 1973: 205). At the same time, however, the Austrian leader notes that the fact that production takes time is not exclusively Austrian and might well refer, with the same legitimacy, to a classical analytical framework. The problem conveyed by the theory of capital and growth proposed by Hicks consists precisely in the fact that one might ask whether it is not more classical and Ricardian than Austrian and 'this is more than a matter of intellectual genealogy' (ibid.: 205).

Lachmann begins by emphasising the problematic aspects of Böhm-Bawerk's theory of capital and interest. Faithful to Menger, he argues that Böhm-Bawerk's theory could not properly be called Austrian for several reasons: first, it is essentially macroeconomic, denying to the level of the individual action the role of primary explanatory element; second, the question raised by this theory is more Ricardian than Mengerian, it consists in justifying the profit and determining its level with the intertemporal structure of production only being a by-product of this investigation; third, this theory is bound to the same failure as the Ricardian theory as soon as the analytical framework is extended to a multicommodity world. In the same way as the conclusions holding in the simple Ricardian corn model could not be generalised to a multicommodity world, Böhm-Bawerk's theory only applies to a situation where there is only one input, labour, and one consumption good. The attempt to generalise the results collides with the impossibility of finding a system of relative prices invariant to changes in the rate of interest. Finally, the reduction of the structure of production to a single number, the period of production, does 'too much violence . . . to the diversity of the world' (Lachmann 1976: 146).

Of course these critiques only partly apply to Hicks's theory because, as emphasised above, Hicks substantially criticised and modified the theory of Böhm-Bawerk with in particular the passage from a stream-input and point-output to a stream-input and stream-output analysis, the abandonment of the fundamental concept of roundaboutness and of the period of production. The criticism that certainly concerns the 'neo-Austrian' approach is the macroeconomic level of the analysis, the fact that individual decision-making is not the first and simplest causal element of an explanation of the dynamic of the production structure. Subjectivism turns out to be the main issue at stake at the origin of the dissent between modern and neo-Austrians.

From the above discussion, it flows that the reference to Böhm-Bawerk can hardly be the criterion put forward to prove the legitimacy of the Austrian description of Hicks's theory for, if too strictly followed, the Böhm-Bawerk reference leads to a complete rejection as the continuation of the greatest error, and if too loosely followed, it leads one to question any specificity at all of the approach. Rather, one might confront directly what the two authors identify with Austrian economics.

What is an Austrian theory?

Contrary to Lachmann, whose aim is to precisely characterise the essence of Austrian economics and to propose a research agenda, Hicks did not spend a lot of time defining the specificity of the tradition whose label he claims to borrow for his own theory of capital and growth. He simply singles out two main doctrines of the Austrian tradition: the insistence on subjectivism or what he calls the 'Supremacy of Demand' or the 'Supremacy of Marginal Utility' (Hicks 1979a: 51), and the insistence on the temporal nature of the production process. As a result of his participation in the intellectual effervescence of the LSE in the 1930s, Hicks focuses on the second doctrine and admits having neglected the first one. What is questionable from an Austrian perspective is that, according to Hicks, these two doctrines are independent from one another. 'There are relations between these two doctrines, but they are separate. It is possible to hold to one without attaching much importance to the other' (ibid.). The fact that production takes time is not exclusively Austrian but to insist on the nature of production as a process of time without a subjectivist foundation is certainly not Austrian in essence. Ultimately, the whole quarrel between Hicks and Lachmann stems from this neglect of the subjectivist dimension. Production takes time, Lachmann certainly agrees, but this is not enough: the aim of the (Austrian) theorist is then to make the structure of production intelligible in terms of human actions and the pursuit of plans. This prerequisite has far-reaching analytical consequences, the most important concerning the role of the concept of equilibrium in the analysis, a point on which the two authors openly clash.

Basically, if one follows the Lachmannian subjectivist research programme, the very concept of equilibrium becomes irrelevant. On the contrary, Hicks remains attached to the reference to equilibrium, even though the author gives a very broad definition to this concept, equilibrium being simply understood as a condition in which norms are unchanging. Here lies the kernel of the discussion between the two authors: according to Hicks, economists cannot dispense with models and equilibrium concepts for any extrapolation stem from some assumed normality; according to Lachmann, economists should accept a reduction in the degree of abstraction of their models and stop making predictions, economics having the task of making phenomena intelligible in terms of human actions.

Lachmann's quite extremist position, close to theoretical nihilism, is the natural consequence of the continuing deepening of the subjectivist dimension of the analysis and in particular of the extension of subjectivism to expectations. The subjective dimension attached to expectations illustrates the fact that a particular economic situation gives rise to different expectations according to the individual. In the same way that Hayek defines knowledge as the subjective interpretation of past experience, expectations represent the result of a necessarily subjective interpretation of the situation. The subjective dimension is, to a certain extent, accentuated by the fact that the expectation is, in a forward-looking perspective, directed towards an 'unknown but not unimaginable future'. In as much as they are a creation of the individual mind, expectations are unpredictable and cannot be formalised. Lachmann thus rejects all kind of adaptive, extrapolative, static or rational expectations, to the extent that the individual would then be reduced to the condition of an automata, leaving no space for the freedom of choice.

In this way, the Misesian category of human action is enriched by an explicit development of the speculative dimension which Mises mentions but does not deepen. The process of forming expectations is then raised to the rank of 'mental act' (Lachmann [1966] 1977: 56); the divergence of expectations is the illustration of an individual's free will when faced with a choice. It represents 'a manifestation of spontaneous action' (Lachmann 1986).

An Austrian theory of capital

According to Lachmann, the problem with the theory of capital and interest developed by Böhm-Bawerk is that it belongs more to a Ricardian research programme than a Mengerian one. The main question Böhm-Bawerk raises is typically a Ricardian question: what justifies the profit and what determines its level? All the remaining theoretical considerations and in particular the intertemporal nature of the structure of production, are just by-products of this inquiry. In order to rectify Böhm-Bawerk' greatest error and pick up again the Mengerian agenda, Lachmann proposes to reverse this logic and to make the capital structure the primary object of analysis:

> Our main task is to lay the foundation for a theory of the capital structure. Our theory, unlike Böhm-Bawerk's, is not devised to serve as a basis for an interest theory. Its purpose is to make the shape, order, and coherence of the capital structure intelligible in terms of human action.
>
> (1976: 147)

A genuine Austrian theory of capital should then be renewed with the subjectivist paradigm, its objective being to understand the process of continuous evolution of the productive structure of a system in terms of the interaction of the individual plans of actions of producers and consumers. As regards the question of cause and magnitude of the rate of return on capital, this is a typical neoclassical question which expresses the allegiance the economist has to formalism, doing his utmost to find an equilibrium figure. To Lachmann, it is meaningless to talk about an *equilibrium* rate of interest and furthermore of a *uniform* rate of interest. Indeed, the basis for an Austrian theory of capital should remain micro and break with any form of aggregation.

Capital is heterogeneous, this is the – Mengerian – point of departure of Lachmann's reconstruction. The intertemporal structure of capital of a system is the outcome of the interaction of the individual plans of investments of the producers who try to best anticipate the future needs and preferences of the consumers. The composition of the structure of capital reflects at any moment in time the complex network of past and present plans of investment, that is, the means–ends frameworks which imply capital goods (Lachmann 1986: 61). The heterogeneity of capital to which Lachmann refers does not concern any physical property of capital goods but rather the variety of uses which it is possible to assign to capital goods according to the knowledge, experience, expectations and imagination of the producers. Beside the concept of – subjective – heterogeneity, Lachmann introduces another property of capital goods, namely, their complementarity. There are technological and economic constraints on the possible modes of combining resources. The entrepreneur chooses under these constraints which combination of capital goods is better in order to satisfy the expected needs of the consumers. It stems from these properties of heterogeneity and complementarity that the relevant unit of analysis, in order to study the capital structure of a system, is neither the notion of a capital good which, taken in isolation, does not give any information about the plan of production which originated its utilisation, nor the notion of aggregate capital which relegates the subjectivist foundation of the analysis backstage, but rather the notion of 'capital combination'. A capital combination is the material manifestation of a plan of production; a good, whatever its intrinsic properties are, obtains the status of capital good insofar as it belongs to a specific capital combination. At the firm level, the complementarity of resources composing the capital combination simply expresses the internal coherence of the investment plans at its origin; the capital theory is rather concerned with the *structural* complementarity of the different combinations of capital between firms, that is, the whole coherence of the different investment plans continuously revised by the producers as their knowledge, experience, expectations and imagination change with time. Each firm, with its specific capital combination, is always in disequilibrium and in the process of revising its plans, contributing in this way to the continuous reshaping of the capital structure of the system.

Conclusion

The above analysis has questioned the legitimacy of the Austrian appellation of the theory of capital inherited from Böhm-Bawerk and developed by Hicks. What might appear at first glance a simple quarrel about labels turns out to be the manifestation of a much deeper rift. What is at stake is the definition of the essence of the Austrian tradition and, in particular, the importance of the subjectivist dimension in the analysis. It is for having neglected this dimension that the theory of capital and interest of Böhm-Bawerk was irremediably rejected by Menger and the neo-Austrian theory of capital and growth of Hicks was ignored by modern Austrians. These theories do not belong to the subjectivist paradigm Austrian economists have been developing since Menger. These theories convey a distinct ontology which is compatible with the logic of equilibrium. Austrian economics, on the contrary, has the task of continuously deepening and extending the subjectivist dimension of the analysis in order to make economic phenomena intelligible in terms of human actions. The most significant consequence of this approach is that it leads – as soon as subjectivism is extended also to expectations – to the progressive abandonment of any reference to equilibrium, with the risk of proposing, as Lachmann did, a nihilist conception of the work of the economist.

Notes

1   See Gloria-Palermo (2001).
2   See Gloria-Palermo (1999).
3   See the general introduction in Faber *et al.* (1999).
4   Reported by Schumpeter (1954: 847, footnote 8) who remembers Menger's assertion: 'Time will come when people will realise that Böhm-Bawerk's theory [of capital and interest] is one of the greatest errors ever committed.'
5   We are here using Menger's famous distinction between first-order goods, that is consumption goods, and higher-order goods, that is capital goods, the rank depending on the place of the goods within the productive process, the more upstream the good is used in the productive process, the higher the order.
6   In particular, Streissler (1972), Jaffé (1976), Dolan (1976), Spadaro (1978).

References

Böhm-Bawerk, E. von (1889) *Positive Theorie des Kapitales*, trans. (1959) *Capital and Interest*, vol. 2: *The Positive Theory of Capital*, South Holland, IL: Libertarian Press.

Dolan, E. (ed.) (1976) *The Foundations of Modern Austrian Economics*, Kansas City: Sheed and Ward, Inc.

Faber, M., Proops, J., Speck, S. and Jost, F. (eds) (1999) *Capital and Time in Ecological Economics: Neo-Austrian Modelling*, London: Edward Elgar.

Gloria-Palermo, S. (1999) *The Evolution of the Austrian Tradition: From Menger to Lachmann*, London: Routledge.

—— (2001) 'Schumpeter and the old Austrian School: interpretations and influences', in Arena, R. and Dangel, C. (eds) *The Contribution of J.A. Schumpeter to Economics*, London: Routledge.

Hicks, J.R. (1939) *Value and Capital*, Oxford: Clarendon Press.

—— (1965) *Capital and Growth*, Oxford: Clarendon Press.

—— (1970) 'A neo-Austrian growth theory', *The Economic Journal*, 318, LXXX: 257–81.

—— (1973a) *Capital and Time: A Neo-Autrian Theory*, Oxford: Clarendon Press.

—— (1973b) 'The Austrian theory of capital and its rebirth in modern economics', in

Hicks, J.R. and Weber, W. (eds) *Carl Menger and the Austrian School of Economics*, Oxford: Clarendon Press.

—— (1976) 'Some questions of time in economics', in Tang, A.M. *et al.* (eds) *Evolution, Welfare and Time in Economics, Festschrift in Honor of Nicholas Georgescu-Roegen*, Lexington, MA: Lexington Book.

—— (1979a) 'Is interest the price of a factor of production' in Rizzo, M.J. (ed.) *Time, Uncertainty, and Disequilibrium*, Lexington, MA: D.C. Heath.

—— (1979b) *Causality in Economics*, Oxford: Basic Blackwell.

—— (1985) *Methods of Dynamic Economics*, Oxford: Clarendon Press.

Jaffé, W. (1976) 'Menger, Jevons and Walras de-homogenized', *Economic Inquiry*, 14(4): 511–24.

Lachmann, L. (1966) 'Sir John Hicks on capital and growth', *South African Journal of Economics*; reprinted in Lachmann, L. (ed.) (1977) *Capital, Expectations, and the Market Process: Essays on the Theory of the Market Economy*, Kansas City: Sheed Andrews and McMeel, Inc.

—— (1973) 'Sir John Hicks as a neo-Austrian', *South African Journal of Economics*, 41, September: 195–207.

—— (1976) 'On Austrian capital theory', in Dolan, E. (ed.) *The Foundations of Modern Austrian Economics*, Kansas City: Sheed and Ward, Inc.

—— (1979) 'Comment: Austrian economics today', in Rizzo, M.J. (ed.) *Time, Uncertainty, and Disequilibrium*, Lexington, MA: D.C. Heath.

—— (1986) *The Market as an Economic Process*, Oxford: Basil Blackwell.

Schumpeter, J.A. (1954) *History of Economic Analysis*, London: George Allen and Unwin Ltd.

Spadaro, L. (ed.) (1978) *New Directions in Austrian Economics*, Kansas City: Sheed Andrews and McMeel, Inc.

Streissler, E. (1972) 'To what extent was the Austrian School marginalist?', *History of Political Economy*, 4(2).

Part V

Expectations and money

12 Hayek and Lindahl on disequilibrium dynamics

Carlo Zappia

Introduction

In reviewing Lindahl's *Studies in the Theory of Money and Capital* in *Economica*, Hayek (1940: 332) expressed his 'intense regret that Professor Lindahl's ideas should not have become more widely accessible when they were first outlined in Swedish some ten years ago'. Significantly, Hayek ignored the fact that the opening essay, entitled 'The Dynamic Approach to Economic Theory', had not previously appeared in print. To Hayek, in fact, the essay that 'will prove to be of the greatest permanent value' was not the one just mentioned but an earlier one, which appeared in Swedish in 1929 and was translated in the 1939 volume as 'The Pricing Problem from the Point of View of Capital Theory'. The reason for Hayek's preference lay in his lasting interest in what Lindahl had attempted in this essay: 'to incorporate capital theory into the general theory of prices'. The 1928 essay 'Intertemporal Price Equilibrium and Movements in the Value of Money' had been Hayek's first work aimed at incorporating the economic phenomena related to time into general equilibrium theory. These two essays by Lindahl and Hayek are usually considered the loci where the notion of intertemporal equilibrium was first introduced and discussed (Milgate 1979).

As for the first essay in Lindahl's volume, Hayek (1940: 333) wrote that it was 'undoubtedly the clearest and most systematic exposition of the modern "period analysis"'. However, Hayek's attitude was quite dismissive, on the grounds that 'not only they [Lindahl's ideas] lost most of the attraction of novelty but even that what might have been a revelation to us now mostly represents a stage through which we ourselves have passed'. Clearly enough, Hayek's implicit reference was to his own 1937 essay 'Economics and Knowledge'. Significantly, Lindahl himself had quoted Hayek's essay in a footnote appended to his 1939 essay. Lindahl (1939b: 38n), in pointing to the impossibility of full consistency of the intertemporal plans of individual agents, wrote that Hayek's 1937 article provided 'a good exposition of this problem that is quite in harmony with the ideas developed in this essay'. It will be shown why Hayek was much less positive than Lindahl about the similarities between their views.

This chapter deals with the contributions of Hayek and Lindahl to the development of a dynamic theory. The two authors first made a point which was innovative in the late 1920s and early 1930s, when reference to stationary conditions was dominant. The point was that equilibrium analysis could be meaningful only if it included the role played by individual agents' expectations about an uncertain future; introducing the notion of intertemporal and temporary equilibrium would serve this purpose. Thus, the two economists discussed how the static approach to exchange could be re-elaborated within a dynamic framework. Granted that their common goal was to improve understanding of the dynamics of economic systems, they came to share the viewpoint that expectations should be consistently introduced in economic theory.

However, though both regarded frustrated expectations as the reason for the practical impossibility of intertemporal equilibrium, Hayek and Lindahl differed about their approaches to the dynamic realm. On the one hand, Lindahl concentrated on the institutional context within which the adjustment process takes place, focusing on the dynamics of the pricing process. He elaborated a sort of disequilibrium dynamics of the economy based on the processes of revision of individual plans, in the tradition of what is known nowadays as the Swedish *ex ante–ex post* analysis. On the other hand, Hayek put forward a generalisation of the concept of equilibrium. This generalisation, that was to be known as 'spontaneous order' (Hayek 1968), was aimed at making equilibrium compatible in principle with non-equilibrated individual actions.[1]

In an influential assessment of the respective roles of Hayek and Lindahl, Currie and Steedman (1989: 97, 1990: 105) argue that the lack of interest in the individual processes of revision of plans is a serious drawback of Hayek's approach if compared with Lindahl's. According to Currie and Steedman, this drawback would make Hayek's 1937 essay much less path-breaking, in a methodological sense, than Lindahl's 1939 essay, mainly because Hayek did not venture into a detailed analysis of the pricing process as Lindahl did. On the contrary, this chapter is intended to show that Hayek's alleged drawback was rooted in his deep conviction that there was an alternative way to pursue the analysis of the process of exchange, a way that Hayek deemed more fruitful than Lindahl's.

Thus, the main point made in this chapter is that, although Lindahl's approach to disequilibrium might appear more remarkable than Hayek's discussion of how order may emerge, Hayek's perspective is based on a useful hint. Namely, that the evolution of the system depends on the relations between agents rather than on agents' attributes. As will be made clearer in what follows, an implication of Hayek's argument, and one which was not dealt with by Lindahl, was that the agents' theories of the workings of the system could not be regarded as given, that is, as if they were held *ex ante*. As a result, for Hayek a sound analysis of disequilibrium adjustment could not be provided until the processes through which knowledge was acquired and communicated were fully understood.[2]

The chapter is organised as follows. The next section deals with the notions of equilibrium which Hayek and Lindahl introduced in order to take time into account. The fact that both authors intended these notions only as preliminaries to move forward to dynamic analysis is stressed. The third section presents Lindahl's view on dynamics. Lindahl's refusal to conceptualise the theory of dynamic movements as a generalisation of static theory is discussed. Then Hayek's views on dynamics are presented. It is argued that Hayek's discussion of how the emergence of order entails the reasons why the revision of individual plans is given less emphasis in his analysis than in Lindahl's. Finally, a conclusion is provided.

Beyond intertemporal equilibrium

Hicks's *Value and Capital* (1939) encapsulates the mainstream approach to dynamics in the post-Walrasian era. Part III of the book, entitled 'The Foundations of Dynamic Economics', introduces the notions of temporary equilibrium and equilibrium over time, 'spot economy', and 'futures economy' in a form which is still referred to today. Hicks's contribution was so far-reaching that his version of the temporary equilibrium approach is considered a textbook reference (see e.g. Grandmont 1987). This chapter does not concentrate on Hicks, however. In fact, although in later writings, and especially in *Capital and Growth* (1965), he came to acknowledge its fundamental shortcomings, Hicks never offered a fully-fledged alternative to temporary equilibrium. Hicks admitted that 'the fundamental weakness of the Temporary Equilibrium method is the assumption, which it is obliged to make, that the market is in equilibrium even in the very short period' and that 'even in a very competitive economy such very short-run equilibration is hard to swallow' (Hicks 1965: 76).[3] But he did not move forward to the proposal of a new framework for dynamic analysis.[4]

Granted that Hicks gave the first systematic assessment of the new equilibrium approach to dynamics, the seminal suggestion for research was to be found in the work of Hayek (1928) and Lindahl (1929, 1930).[5] This was the view of perfect foresight as the new reference point for an accurate analysis of the behaviour of individual agents over time, an analysis intended to replace the stationary model.[6] Hayek and Lindahl's approach changed the equilibrium perspective for good. The Arrow-Debreu model, for instance, is based on the notion of intertemporal equilibrium and has perfect foresight among its rationality requirements for individual agents; the rational expectations programme rests on a stochastic version of the perfect foresight approach; and the literature on learning usually assumes intertemporal equilibrium as the state of the economy to be learned by agents.

Equilibrium is defined by Lindahl as a situation in which 'there exists a *mutual* connection between supply and demand on the one hand and actual prices on the other, and then therefore at existing prices exchange can continue until full satisfaction has been attained'. To put it from the standpoint of expectations, 'in a given period of time people perfectly foresee the price level that will prevail in this period as a result of their action during the period' (Lindahl 1929: 339n). Similarly, Hayek (1928: 76) stated that

> to conclude that an economy can persist in a static condition . . . all that needs to be assumed is that the wants and the means of production existing at every point in time [within the period under consideration] are known to the individual economic subjects at the time at which they frame their economic plan for the period as a whole.

However, both Hayek and Lindahl were very positive not only about the fictitious nature of intertemporal equilibrium, but also about its limited value as an interpretative tool. They contended that intertemporal equilibrium could only be used to characterise an imaginary state of 'rest', namely, one in which all economic forces have already unfolded their implications. Intertemporal equilibrium was intended as the counterpart of stationary equilibrium, in situations in which data were not necessarily constant.

Lindahl was dissatisfied with the perfect foresight assumption from the very beginning. He admitted that the hypothesis that individuals know future prices was equivalent to the assumption that they know in advance the outcomes of their actions, and, therefore, use this knowledge to act (Lindahl 1929: 285). In the last part of his 1929 article, he envisaged the changes in his analysis of capital and interest required by a situation of imperfect foresight, thus implicitly referring, for the first time, to the notion of temporary equilibrium. Later on, Lindahl made extensive use of the temporary equilibrium approach in the 1930 essay on the rate of interest. Lindahl developed this approach to relax the restrictive assumptions that an intertemporal equilibrium requires.[7] But, in the introductory section of his 1939 essay, he maintained: 'The plans of the economic subjects at any given point of time are neither fully consistent with one another nor with the external conditions, and therefore they must be successively revised.' To Lindahl, the problem of inconsistency of individual plans became the main question to be addressed by a dynamic theory, because the alternative view (as Lindahl himself adopted in his 1929 essay) that:

> all plans prevailing at the starting point are based on expectations in conformity with reality, and that they will undergo no change with the lapse of time . . . can be treated in essentially the same manner as the equilibrium of static theory.

> (Lindahl 1939b: 38, 38f.)

As far as Hayek is concerned, in commenting on what is required that individuals know for an intertemporal equilibrium to hold, he argued: 'that this will never be so in reality is obvious' (Hayek 1928: 76). Moreover, in the attempt to clarify the links between the analysis of equilibrium relationships over time and his own theory of the trade cycle, Hayek came to the conclusion that there was a 'very pressing question' inherent in the conceptualisation of the trade cycle. This was the question of 'how the entrepreneurs will react to the expectations of particular price changes'; in other words, Hayek wondered about 'what determines the expectations of entrepreneurs and particularly . . . how such expectations will be affected by any given change of present prices' (1935: 155).[8]

It will be argued that both Hayek and Lindahl strove over a long time for a proper conceptualisation of dynamics, and that their methodological perspectives had much in common. Hayek and Lindahl agreed, albeit on different grounds, that a dynamic analysis would entail both a close examination of the process of revision of plans and an analysis of the causal connections between certain given initial conditions and the subsequent outcomes at a future date. But their respective ways forward differed considerably. Lindahl, who first introduced the notion of temporary equilibrium with the aim of giving an equilibrium representation of the phenomena induced by imperfect foresight, pursued the abandonment of the equilibrium approach as the ultimate goal of his research. Conversely, Hayek neither used the notion of temporary equilibrium nor regarded it as a meaningful tool for dynamic analysis. Rather, he concentrated on the task of generalising his own notion of equilibrium, which he viewed as a more effective starting point for dynamic analysis than temporary equilibrium.

Lindahl on dynamics

Lindahl's 1939b essay 'The Dynamic Approach to Economic Theory' still constitutes one of the most comprehensive demonstrations of the inadequacy of both the intertemporal and the temporary equilibrium approach. From the viewpoint of the requirements of a dynamic method, the essay summarises many themes which defined the so-called Stockholm School of economics. The school included Myrdal, Lindahl, Lundberg, Hammarskjold, Johansson and Ohlin.[9] Having said that, in my opinion, Lindahl is the most important representative of the school, Myrdal's achievements are particularly impressive: his 1927 dissertation is probably the first place where it is contended that dynamic theory is inherently different from static theory, and hence it is not correct to draw on static assumptions to analyse the disequilibrating factors (see Hansson 1991: 178–81). Moreover, Myrdal's *Monetary Equilibrium*, though mostly an attempt at a reconstruction of Wicksell's notion of the normal rate of interest as an equilibrium rate, developed the *ex ante–ex post* method for disequilibrium analysis.[10]

But Lindahl's 1939b essay made the new line of thinking of the school clear.[11]

He stressed the importance of reversing the standard approach which developed dynamics on the basis of a static corpus, that is, he criticised the very approach that he himself had followed in the 1929 essay, and which was systematised by Hicks in *Value and Capital*. Lindahl argued that the static model should be viewed as a particular case within the framework of a general dynamic theory, albeit still to come. As he put it:

> We cannot fully understand the true character of the static simplification, if we do not begin with a broad formulation of the problem. As in mechanics the concept of equilibrium can be defined only on the basis of a theory of forces, so the significance of a reiterating process which . . . is the central concept of the static theory in economics, can be explained only on the basis of a more general theory of economic development.
>
> (Lindahl 1939b: 32)

The issue of plan revision was considered essential by Lindahl. The abandonment of the perfect foresight assumption, in fact, implied that 'though each plan is in principle designed for the entire future, it . . . has immediate relevance only for the period next in time. The actions undertaken in later periods will be determined by new or revised plans' (ibid.: 47). Lindahl's dismissal of the hypothesis of consistency between *ex ante* plans and their *ex post* realisations rested on the view that it was unlikely that individuals with imperfect foresight could completely carry out their plans, even when short periods of time were considered. As a result, the temporary equilibrium approach could not account for the occurrence of unforeseen events over a period. Thus, Lindahl discussed whether it was correct to assume that plans would be revised only at the end of each current period, as required by the temporary model, where supply and demand are made equal for the current period. The Hicksian Monday is a case in point (Hicks 1939: Chapter III). Lindahl argued that, although this assumption could be made in the case of each single agent by means of an analysis of the length of the 'period of registration' of relevant events, taking groups of agents into account rendered that assumption unlikely. This point is particularly relevant when the plans of individuals are not synchronised, that is, when their revision does not take place at the same time.

In discussing the appropriate length of the period over which the assumption of consistency of plans (required by temporary equilibrium) was satisfied, Lindahl (1939b: 55) stated:

> In reality, however, the synchronisation is very incomplete, and the period during which the relevant plans of all members of the group are retained unchanged, must therefore be taken to be fairly short . . . One cannot count upon all these plans being kept wholly unaltered during any long period. The

attempt to realise the plans must quickly reveal that they are more or less incompatible. The actual course of events cannot correspond to all anticipations of the individuals about the behaviour of the others. The result must therefore be a modification of some of the plans.

Furthermore, it emerged from the analysis of the pricing process that 'in an actual dynamic case, there is no necessity for equality of demand and supply' to occur within each period. However, Lindahl (ibid.: 60) also contended that 'the opposite concept of prices as continuously changing under the influence of the demand and supply function is equally not correct'. It is well known that Lindahl opted to frame dynamic theory in the terms of period analysis, which was to become the distinctive trait of the Stockholm School. Here the hypothesis of an instantaneous process of equilibration in each period – as that occurring on the Hicksian Monday – is dropped, thus making possible the manifestation of inconsistencies between *ex ante* plans and their *ex post* realisations in each current period. As a result, the link between static (i.e. equilibrium) and dynamic theory established by instantaneous equilibration in each current period is definitively severed.

Thus, Lindahl's 1939b essay first made clear why even the most sophisticated temporary equilibrium analysis could not account for the 'true' dynamics entailed by the revision of individual plans. Unlike the temporary equilibrium model, which took the various periods as discrete and self-contained representations of the workings of the economy, Lindahl was looking for a linkage between periods. His goal was to devise a causal sequence of events showing how the *ex post* outcomes of the current period could influence the *ex ante* plans for the following one.[12]

The notion of individual planning became the main focus of the dynamic method because it served to deal with the causal elements of dynamic analysis. In particular, Lindahl worked on unfulfilled expectations as the main cause for revision of individual plans; he emphasised that most planned actions depend on the realisation of certain conditions in the future. As a consequence, changes in expectations and the related revision of plans should be considered the normal course of events. Lindahl proceeded to explain how the analysis of the pricing process should be amended to include exchanges at disequilibrium prices. This type of exchange, in fact, was instrumental in bringing to light causal connections. It is during the process of determination of prices, Lindahl maintained, that the expectations of individuals are either fulfilled or revised, and causal chains of events are sparked off.

Accordingly, the dynamics of the system, which Lindahl called 'the theory of economic development', could be explained by means of two basic elements: the mentioned assumptions concerning individual planning and the possible emergence of unexpected exogenous events. The interaction of these two elements does not lead to an equilibrium if individuals are forced to revise their expectations, either by external events or by the realisation of planned actions. Lindahl (1939b: 60–4) made a point about the latter: the revision of plans and expectations can have its origin in the realisation of planned action, because the organisation of exchanges is such that the announcement of prices for exchange and the acts of exchange do not always happen at the same time. Namely, prices announced by dealers at the beginning of a period may be associated with agreements to exchange by other dealers which do not necessarily correspond to those anticipated by the agents who set prices, so that some dealers may be rationed at those prices. This discrepancy between supply and demand would force a change in the announced prices of the subsequent period.

It is worth stressing that, in his attempt to explain the causal link between announcements and acceptances, Lindahl dispensed with the assumption of perfect competition. In order to examine the dynamic connection between cause and effect – that is, the path from *ex ante* anticipations to *ex post* realisations – each agent is thought to be a price-setter. The abandonment of equilibrium dynamics went along with the rejection of tatonnement processes of the Walrasian type.

Lindahl's close investigation of the process of revision of individual plans was his main contribution to the Swedish approach.[13] But Lindahl was unable to build a convincing theory of the price mechanism on these foundations. In fact, while it is true that, in his model, prices are fixed at the beginning of each period so as to induce adjustments of quantities with respect to the *ex ante* plans, Lindahl assumed that prices adjust instantaneously at the conjunction of two consecutive periods; this difficulty leaves unexplained a crucial aspect of the pricing process. This missing link notwithstanding, the outgrowth of Lindahl's analysis is clear: even over a very short period of time, it cannot be taken for granted that a Walrasian process of equilibration (that is, by prices) would occur. Hence, to Lindahl the process of price adjustments brings about an endogenous process of revision of expectations whose explanation requires the analysis of the organisation of exchanges. This is the core of dynamics.

Hayek on dynamics

Hayek's opposition to the temporary equilibrium approach rested on a methodological argument, which he put forward in the preliminary chapters of *The Pure Theory of Capital* (1941). Any attempt to make equilibrium theory more realistic was inevitably incoherent, Hayek argued, for equilibrium analysis could not be conceived as a tool to represent actual economies. Though no explicit reference is given, it is likely that one of Hayek's targets was Lindahl's 1930 essay. A thorough account of the dynamic properties of actual economies would require 'an explanation of the economic process . . . in terms of causation which must necessarily be treated as a chain of historical sequences . . . a unilateral dependence of the succeeding event on the preceding one'; it ensued that 'kind of causal explanation of the process in time is of course the ultimate goal of all economic analysis'. Equilibrium analysis, therefore, was not appropriate to conceptualise the workings of actual economies, since these were characterised by causal connections over time – the current concept of path dependency comes to mind here. Hayek concluded that 'equilibrium analysis is significant only in so far as it is preparatory to this main task' (1941: 17).

These statements amount to a research programme, which seems very much in accordance with Lindahl's perspective in his 1939b essay. But the *Pure Theory of Capital*, though intended as a 'preparatory' step in the direction of a 'causal explanation of the process in time', to be followed by a second volume on dynamics, remained Hayek's last piece of 'pure' economics, and Hayek never carried out a proper causal analysis. This fact seems to substantiate Currie and Steedman's (1990: Chapter 5) claim that it was Lindahl, and the Swedish in general, who actually endorsed Hayek's research call. Admittedly, unlike Lindahl who concentrated on the adjustment process in disequilibrium, Hayek chose to focus on those aspects of his own notion of equilibrium which explained why equilibrium was impossible to use. But Hayek did not praise Lindahl's attempt in his review of Lindahl's volume; this fact suggests that Hayek's direction was different from Lindahl's. It is contended in this section that Hayek's insights into the dynamics of economic systems are to be found in his refinement of the notion of equilibrium.

Hayek's (1937) essay, 'Economics and Knowledge', showed that the proper subject matter of equilibrium theory was the compatibility of individual plans.[14] But the achievement of this compatibility and hence of Hayekian equilibrium, with all its peculiar features, depended on the amount of knowledge that the market mechanism can aggregate and transmit throughout the system. In Hayek's view, economic analysis should address the process of discovery and transmission of knowledge, which traditional equilibrium analysis implicitly neglected. As noted before, Lindahl considered this way of dealing with the expectations of individuals as 'quite in harmony' with his own, while Hayek disagreed.

The peculiarities of Hayek's stance are worth stressing. To be useful, a notion of equilibrium should manage to account for the actions performed by individual agents, who are endowed with specific personal knowledge; these actions end up being compatible with both exogenous events and the actions carried out by other individuals. To Hayek, the various opinions held by individual agents on how the system behaves are first and foremost a consequence of informational differences.

An outgrowth of Hayek's approach that is not usually noticed by commentators needs pointing out. In Hayek's theoretical system, the agents' theories of the economy cannot be regarded as data given *ex ante*; it is also implausible that the adjustment to equilibrium only takes place because of the emergence of exogenous uncertainty. This aspect of Hayek's analysis is crucial in order to understand why his approach is different from Lindahl's. Hayek's insistence on personal, disperse knowledge was not limited to knowledge of objective data. He was also concerned with the ways in which individuals subjectively assess the environment, that is, with the individuals' theories of the working of the economy. The knowledge which Hayek referred to, moreover, becomes available to individuals only through the process of exchange in the market. As a result, the individual processes of expectation formation, as well as the dynamics generated by revision of plans, are not simply individual phenomena. Rather, they relate to the market process as a whole, and, Hayek maintained, should be dealt with as such.

Having Lindahl's framework as a term of comparison, the novelty brought about by Hayek becomes apparent. Hayek's fundamental insight is that, while it is true that trading at disequilibrium prices implies that the plans of agents are not independent of the way the market is organised, the problem of how the revision of expectations unfolds cannot be solved at an individual level, that is, by a closer consideration of the process of individual planning. It is essential to distinguish between the process of revision of expectations and the process of revision of the expectation function of individuals. In the former, which is the facet of dynamic theory Lindahl mostly concentrated on, individuals enter the market equipped with a theory of how the economy works, and then, progressively, upgrade it. In the latter, the interaction with other individuals makes it necessary to incorporate the possibility that certain individuals may find their theories inadequate and therefore drop them in favour of new ones. This second process is more comprehensive in character, and it is in relation to it that Hayek's contribution reveals all its peculiarity and brilliance.[15]

Admittedly, the evolution of Hayek's thought is contradictory on this point. The question whether the process of revision of individual expectation functions can be dealt with at the individual level or not was not explicitly addressed in the 1937 essay. The 1941 volume amounted to an exercise in intertemporal equilibrium analysis and the volume on dynamics never followed. Moreover, in the 1945 essay 'The Use of Knowledge in Society' the question itself seemed downgraded, inasmuch as the co-ordinating properties of the price system were focused on. But this question was so important to Hayek that it explicitly re-emerged in the essays on competition, probably as a consequence of a reconsideration of the methodological base for a subjective approach to economic theory (on which, see Caldwell 2000).

From the essay on competition of 1948 onwards, Hayek argued in favour of a kind of analysis of the formation and revision of expectations by individual agents which focused on the social process of co-ordination through the market, and on the social institutions that this process generates. In his analysis of competition, Hayek wrote:

Competition is essentially a process of the formation of opinion: by spreading information, it creates that unity and coherence of the economic system which we presuppose when we think of it as one market. It *creates* the views people have about what is best and cheapest, and it is because of it that people know at least as much about the possibilities and opportunities as they in fact do. It is thus a process which involves a continuous change in the data and whose significance must therefore be completely missed by any theory which treats these data as constant.

(1948: 106, italics added)

The methodological underpinnings of this argument are relevant. In his methodological essays of the 1940s, notably 'Scientism and the Study of Society' (1942) and 'Individualism: True and False' (1946), Hayek gave a slightly different reason for his interest in the market process as the outcome of the plans of individual agents. In discussing the basis of 'true' individualism, he stated:

human Reason, with capital R, does not exist in the singular, as given or available to any particular person, as the rationalist approach assumes, but must be conceived as an interpersonal process in which anyone's contribution is tested and corrected by others

(Hayek 1946: 15)

And, in commenting on the results of conscious human action, he added: 'The individuals are merely the *foci* in the network of relationships and it is the various attitudes of the individuals towards each other . . . which form the recurrent, recognisable and familiar elements of the structure' (Hayek 1942: 34).

An increasing number of scholars (see, in particular, Birner 1999 and Rizzello 1999) have recently pointed out that there is a close relationship between these methodological statements and Hayek's theory of cognitive psychology (Hayek 1952). Though apparently unrelated to Hayek's work as economist and social philosopher, *The Sensory Order* is relevant to our argument so far, because it analyses through a cognitive framework the individual's perception of the external world. Hayek distinguished between the 'physical order', in which the objects of the external world are interrelated through their physical properties, and the 'sensory order', in which the objects of the external world are classified according to the categories of the human mind. This means that, for example, two phenomena can be classified as different in the sensory order but as identical in the physical order, and the other way round. As a result, the task of theoretical psychology is to explain why 'events, which on the basis of their relations to each other can be arranged in a certain (physical) order [the explanation of which is the task of physical science], manifest a different order in their effects on our senses' (Hayek 1952: 5). Hayek identifies the nervous system as an 'instrument of classification' and the single neurons constituting it as the elementary units whose stimulation originates the process of classification. Hayek (ibid.: 53) was particularly perceptive in arguing that:

> the sensory (or other mental) qualities are not in the same manner originally attached to, or an original attribute of, the individual physiological impulses, but that the whole of these qualities is determined by the system of connections by which the impulses can be transmitted from neuron to neuron; . . . that this system of connections is acquired in the course of the development of the species and the individual by a kind of 'experience' or 'learning'; and that it reproduces therefore at every stage of its development certain relationships existing in the physical environment between the stimuli evoking the impulses.

That is to say that individuals become endowed with an 'apparatus of classification' – namely, 'a theory of how the world works, rather than a picture of it' (ibid.: 130–1) – by means of a process of interaction with the outside world.

Anticipating modern developments in cognitive sciences, *The Sensory Order* portrayed the mind as a network of neurons, which in principle could be analysed by a formal mathematical model, now known as a 'neural network'. It is a fundamental feature of network theory that the evolution of the system depends not so much on the evolution of the elementary units (called nodes), as on that of the links among them. In recent years, moreover, neural network theory has proved applicable to the analysis of social dynamics: the neurons are taken to be individuals, and the connections between them are supposed to be institutions, the competitive market being one of these.[16] Interestingly, a defining property of neural network theory is that the 'aggregate' outcome is much more complex than the one described, for instance, by general equilibrium theory; namely, the outcome of neural network theory could be classified, in Hayekian terms, as a typically 'unintended' result of individual behaviour. To be more specific, in informationally complex environments the informational constraints affect not only the informational sets of individual agents but also the ways in which people act and learn the environment.[17]

Conclusion

This chapter has discussed the respective contributions of Hayek and Lindahl to the development of a dynamic approach. The two authors' starting points were similar. Both Lindahl and Hayek, in fact, focused on how to model the process of revision of expectations, although the former author put emphasis on plans conditioned upon future (unknown) events, while the latter concentrated on plans resting on personal (unshared) knowledge. This notwithstanding, the research programmes suggested by their models are substantially different. On the one hand, Lindahl concentrated on how the dynamic of the economy forces individual agents use to revise their expectations. Lindahl's proposal of a disequilibrium approach is based on the view that agents do not usually exchange at equilibrium prices, so that the dynamic of the economy can be seen as the product of individual adjustments to non-equilibrated aggregate outcomes. However, this process has no effect on individuals, in that they do not learn from past experiences.

Unlike Lindahl, Hayek made much of the idea that agents' behaviour cannot be apprehended if their theories of the system are supposed to be given *ex ante*. Hayek's proposal was not so much to abandon the equilibrium approach, as to generalise it in order to understand how different institutional contexts influence both the actions of individuals *and* their ways of thinking about economic activity. It has been shown that Hayek's prominent interest in the evolution of the institutions favouring exchange, as well as his relative disregard for the individual process of planning, have a common origin in his conceptualisation of competition.

The different attitudes of the two authors towards this issue – namely, that frustrated expectations may lead not only to a revision of individual plans but also to a change in the world-view which generates expectations – help to account for their different dynamic perspectives. As documented in the previous section, Hayek's idea of competition as a matter of relations among individuals, rather than as a matter of the attributes of individuals, explains why he did not follow Lindahl's approach. Hayek's perspective is more effective, it has been argued in this chapter, because it posits a fundamental problem: how the theories of the system held by agents are generated.

Acknowledgements

I am grateful to Salvatore Rizzello and Roberto Romani for their valuable comments. Financial assistance from MURST is gratefully acknowledged.

Notes

1 It hardly needs emphasising that modern general equilibrium theory still fails to provide a convincing analysis of both the disequilibrium behaviour of individual agents and out-of-equilibrium adjustments. Most general equilibrium models loosely assume that the perception of profit opportunities, which is characteristic of disequilibrium situations, would make agents pursue plans leading to equilibrium. But it is not at all clear whether the pursuit of profit opportunities brings about an equilibrium bereft of such opportunities. Both demonstrations achieved on extremely strong assumptions for tatonnement stability (Scarf 1960) and the controversial outcome of non-tatonnement processes, such as the 'Hahn process' (Hahn and Negishi 1962),

leave unanswered the crucial question of how disequilibrium actually takes place when individual plans are frustrated (see, in particular, Fisher 1987).

2 This argument has been presented in Zappia (2001), on which this chapter draws heavily.

3 In relation to the necessity to assume that equilibrium prices remain unchanged throughout the single period, Hicks recognised that 'the artificiality of such construction is only too obvious' (1965: 73).

4 On the evolution of Hicks's thought, see Hamouda (1990).

5 Hicks acknowledged Hayek's influence in his first essay on dynamics 'Equilibrium and the Trade Cycle', published in German in 1933. Hicks supported the translation of Lindahl's essays in English, up to the point of reading the page proofs (see Lindahl's Preface to Lindahl 1939a). Hicks's own recollection of the relationships with Hayek and Lindahl in the 1930s can be found in Hicks (1991).

6 Lindahl (1929: 284–5) postulated 'individuals [who] consider not only the needs of the moment but also those of the future in their economic actions'; hence, he assumed that 'individuals have full knowledge of all future data which they take into consideration in their economic planning'. Hayek (1928: 75) argued that if

> at the time a person decides upon a particular distribution of his given resources among various uses, he also has knowledge of all the conditions under which his individual actions will be taken . . . there will only be one quite particular configuration of these decisions which will correspond to an equilibrium position.

7 Hansson (1982: 67–73) discusses the subtle point that imperfect foresight means, in Lindahl's 1930 analysis, perfect foresight for short periods only. Temporary equilibrium, therefore, would become a method of introducing dynamic problems in a static framework. In Hansson's view, Lindahl was forced to move on to disequilibrium analysis after Myrdal's and Lundberg's critiques on this point. A brief analysis of Myrdal's critique is provided in what follows.

8 It is worth noting that Hayek's 1935 essay from which this passage is taken is mostly a concise restatement of his theory of business cycle apt to emphasise the role of expectations in the starting phase of a cycle. Myrdal's allegation that expectations play no role in Hayek's *Prices and Production* (and in Keynes's *Treatise on Money*) is probably at the origin of Hayek's essay (Myrdal 1939: 32–4). It must be recalled in fact that a previous version of Myrdal's magnus opus, *Monetary Equilibrium*, was published in German in a volume edited by Hayek in 1933.

9 Hansson (1991) indicates the years from 1927 to 1937, from Myrdal's dissertation to Ohlin's 1937 essays in the *Economic Journal* on Keynes's *General Theory*, as the period when a proper school was active. After 1937, Hansson argues, one main circumstance defining the school, that is, the isolation of the Swedes working on dynamics, was no longer present. Both Lindahl's 1939b essay and Myrdal's 1939 volume are viewed by Hansson as products of the first ten years of the school, because their gestation in the mid-1930s is attested by Lindahl (1934) and Myrdal (1933).

10 Myrdal's, and Lindahl's, monetary analysis is not the subject matter of this chapter. The links between the representatives of the Stockholm School and Hayek on monetary issues is the topic of Trautwein's contribution to this volume (Chapter 6).

11 As noted by Magnusson in Chapter 4, Lindahl was probably the single representative of the school who continued working on sequence analysis after the 1930s.

12 Of course, this was Myrdal's point as well:

One possible method is to think of stationary (equilibrium) periods of time with all changes confined to the timeless points dividing the periods from each other. To make the schema more reasonable, the periods are then thought as 'very short'. But in spite of that assumption, this method does not seem workable. The most essential quality of the mutual adjustments to be studied is, that they *take time* and that even the *time order* in which they occur is decisive for the outcome. By concealing the changes within timeless demarcation points within the periods, the dynamic problems are in fact less unsolved.

(Myrdal 1939: 44)

13 Currie and Steedman (1990: 93) praise the fact that 'Lindahl does not have a purely mechanistic conception of the activity of planning. Nor does he suppose that all human actions are necessarily the result of conscious deliberation.'

14 Hayek's refusal to abandon equilibrium theory is also indicated by his opposition to Morgenstern's point that the notion of perfect foresight equilibrium was logically inconsistent. On the relationship between Hayek and Morgenstern on this issue, see Zappia (1999).

15 Currie and Steedman (1990: 97) recognise that the main deficiency in Lindahl's treatment of the impact of events on expectations is 'his failure to acknowledge that there may be changes in the *ways* in which individuals formulate their expectations'. But they do not note that this same deficiency cannot be ascribed to Hayek's analysis, as argued in what follows.

16 For a sample of this literature, see Birner (1996).

17 Hayek was not from the beginning completely aware of the potential of his cognitive theory for the study of society, but, later on, he came to recognise that there could be an analogy between the functioning of the human mind and society as a neural network. For an insightful assessment of Hayek's notion of spontaneous order in the lights of the modern theory of adaptive systems, see Vaughn (1999).

References

Birner, J. (1996). *Mind, Market and Society: Network Structures in the Work of F. A. Hayek*, *CEEL Working Paper 1996–02*, Trento: University of Trento.

—— (1999) 'The surprising place of cognitive psychology in the work of F. A. Hayek', *History of Economic Ideas*, 7: 43–84.

Caldwell, B. (2000) 'The emergence of Hayek's ideas on cultural evolution', *The Review of Austrian Economics*, 13: 5–22.

Currie, M. and Steedman, I. (1989) 'Agonising over equilibrium', *Quaderni di Storia dell'Economia Politica*, 7: 75–99.

—— (1990) *Wrestling with Time*, Ann Arbor, MI: Michigan University Press.

Fisher, F.M. (1987) 'Adjustment processes and stability', in Eatwell, J., Milgate, M. and Newmann, P. (eds) *The New Palgrave. General Equilibrium*, London: Macmillan, pp. 26–8.

Grandmont, J.-M. (1987) 'Introduction', in Grandmont, J.M. (ed.) *Temporary Equilibrium: Selected Readings*, New York: Academic Press.

Hahn, F.H. and Negishi, T. (1962) 'A theorem of non-tatonnement stability', *Econometrica*, 30 (July): 463–9.

Hamouda, O.F. (1990) 'Hicks's changing views on economic dynamics', in Moggridge, D.E. (ed.) *Perspectives in the History of Economic Thought*, Aldershot: Edward Elgar.

Hansson, B.A. (1982) *The Stockholm School and the Development of Dynamic Method*, London: Croom Helm.

—— (1991) 'The Stockholm School and the development of dynamic method', in Jonung, L. (ed.) *The Stockholm School of Economics Revisited*, Cambridge: Cambridge University Press.

Hayek, F.A. (1928) 'Das intertemporal gleichgewichtssystem der preise und die bewegungen des "geldwerts"', *Weltwirtschaftliches Archiv*, 28: 33–76, English trans. as 'Intertemporal price equilibrium and movements in the value of money', in Hayek, F.A. (1984) *Money, Capital and Fluctuations. Early Essays*, ed. R. McCloughry, London: Routledge).

—— (1935) 'Preiserwartungen, monetare störungen und fehlinvestitionen', *Nationalökonomisk Tidsskrift*, 73, English trans. as 'Price expectations, monetary disturbances and malinvestments', in Hayek, F.A. (1939) *Profit, Interest and Investment and Other Essays on the Theory of Industrial Fluctuations*, London: Routledge & Kegan Paul).

—— (1937) 'Economics and knowledge', in Hayek, F.A. (1976) *Individualism and Economic Order*, London: Routledge.

—— (1940) 'Review of Studies on the Theory of Money and Capital', by E. Lindahl, *Economica*, 7(27): 332–3.

—— (1941) *The Pure Theory of Capital*, London: Routledge.

—— (1942) 'Scientism and the study of society', in Hayek, F.A. (1955) *The Counter-Revolution of Science*, Chicago: The Free Press.

—— (1945) 'The use of knowledge in society', in Hayek, F.A. (1976) *Individualism and Economic Order*, London: Routledge, pp. 77–91.

—— (1946) 'Individualism: true and false', in Hayek, F.A. (1976) *Individualism and Economic Order*, London: Routledge, pp. 1–32.

—— (1948) 'The meaning of competition', in Hayek, F.A. (1976) *Individualism and Economic Order*, London: Routledge, pp. 92–106.

—— (1952) *The Sensory Order: An Inquiry into the Foundations of Theoretical Psychology*, London: Routledge.

—— (1968) 'Competition as a discovery procedure', in Hayek, F.A. (1978) *New Studies in Philosophy, Politics, Economics and the History of Ideas*, Chicago: Chicago University Press, pp. 179–90.

—— (1976) *Individualism and Economic Order*, London: Routledge.

Hicks, J.R. (1933) 'Gleichgewitcht und konjunktur', *Zeitschrift für Nationalökonomie*, 4, 441–55, English trans. as 'Equilibrium and the trade cycle', in Hicks, J.R. (1982) *Money, Interest and Wages*, Oxford: Blackwell.

—— (1935) 'A suggestion for simplifying the theory of money', in Hicks, J.R. (1982) *Money, Interest and Wages*, Oxford: Blackwell.

—— (1939) *Value and Capital*, Oxford: Clarendon Press.

—— (1965) *Capital and Growth*, Oxford: Oxford University Press.

—— (1982) *Money, Interest and Wages: Collected Essays in Economic Theory*, vol. II, Oxford: Basil Blackwell.

—— (1991) 'The Swedish influence on value and capital', in Jonung, L. (ed.) *The Stockholm School of Economics Revisited*, Cambridge: Cambridge University Press.

Lindahl, E. (1929) 'Prisbildningsproblemets uppläggning från kapitalteoretisk synpunkt',

Ekonomisk Tidskrift, English trans. 'The place of capital in the theory of price', in Lindahl, E. (1939a) *Studies in the Theory of Money and Capital*, London: George Allen and Unwin.

—— (1930) *Penningpolitikens Medel*, partial English trans. 'The rate of interest and the price level', in Lindahl, E. (1939a) *Studies in the Theory of Money and Capital*, London: George Allen and Unwin.

—— (1934) 'A note on the dynamic pricing problem', Mimeo. Reprinted in Moggridge, D.E. (ed.) *The General Theory and After: A Supplement*, vol. XXIX of *The Collected Writings of John Maynard Keynes*, London: Macmillan.

—— (1939a) *Studies in the Theory of Money and Capital*, London: George Allen and Unwin.

—— (1939b) 'The dynamic approach to economic theory', in Lindahl, E. (1939a) *Studies in the Theory of Money and Capital*, London: George Allen and Unwin.

Milgate, M. (1979) 'On the origin of the notion of intertemporal equilibrium', *Economica*, 46: 1–10.

Myrdal, G. (1933) 'Der gleichgewichtsbegriff als instrument in der geldtheoretischen analyse', in Hayek, F.A. (ed.) *Beiträge zur Geldtheorie*, Vienna: Springer.

—— (1939) *Monetary Equilibrium*, London: William Hodge.

Rizzello, S. (1999) *The Economics of the Mind*, Cheltenham: Edward Elgar.

Scarf, H. (1960) 'Some examples of global instability of the competitive equilibrium', *International Economic Review*, 1: 157–72.

Vaughn, K.I. (1999) 'Hayek's theory of the market order as an instance of the theory of complex, adaptive systems', *Journal des Economistes et des Etudes Humaines*, 9: 241–56.

Zappia, C. (1999) 'The assumption of perfect foresight and Hayek's theory of knowledge', *Revue d'Economie Politique*, 3: 107–31.

—— (2001) 'Equilibrium and disequilibrium dynamics in the 1930s', *Journal of the History of Economic Thought*, 23(1): 55–75.

13 Lundberg and Lachmann on expectations

Michel Bellet and Jacques Durieu

Introduction

Lundberg (1907–87) and Lachmann (1906–90) are two economists who were very concerned with expectations, especially during the 1930s and the 1940s. They sought ways to explicitly integrate expectations into economic reasoning after the early works of Hayek, Myrdal, and Lindahl. Initially, their interest had its roots in common questions focused on business cycle theories and process analysis, in relation to the capital theory and the role of plans from the well-known Austrian-Swedish tradition or the 'Wicksell connection'. In his first published papers (1938, 1939 and 1940), Lachmann often quotes Lundberg, and he attempts to extend the famous Swedish dissertation (1937). But, very quickly, in spite of their initial similarities, the two approaches are going to diverge on the way to analyse expectations. Lachmann wants to return to an Austrian 'subjectivist' philosophy. On the contrary, Lundberg maintains an 'objectivist' way. They assume these two strands of thought until their last works. But Lundberg and Lachmann are also remarkable for their shared experience: from the 1950s, they scarcely arouse any more interest. On one hand, the prevailing macroeconomic Keynesianism blurs the questioning about expectations and makes Lundberg a clumsy precursor to Keynes. On the other hand, the 'subjectivist' analysis seems to lose its way in an indeterminate approach, whereas the microeconomic way develops a rigorous decision theory.

Our aim in this chapter is to understand why Lundberg's and Lachmann's very important and interesting preoccupation about expectations led to a double failure. In the second section, we recall the initial common features which connect the economists: to improve the Wicksellian-Austrian business cycle theory, with in the background some doubts about capital theory and expectation approaches. During this period (1937–40), Lachmann expresses a positive opinion on Lundberg's works. In the third section, we show how they get to the point of treating two different ways regarding expectations. Both underline the role of expectations and refuse to relegate expectations to the category of 'data'.

They also suggest that failures in co-ordination are due to wrong expectations. But they differ on the process of formation and revision of expectations. Lundberg (1930, 1937) refers to a backward causality with objective aggregate references. From 1943, Lachmann claims a mental experience with heterogeneous interpretations and his references to Lundberg become both positive and negative. In the fourth section, we question the potentialities of the two ways. In spite of many works and long careers, Lundberg (1968, 1994,...) and Lachmann (1956, 1986,...) remained on the periphery of the dynamics of economics. It is argued that the two economists fail to prescribe a tractable way to explain the formation and revision of expectations. In a macroeconomic perspective, that difficulty leads to an occultation of expectation framework (or static expectations hypothesis) until Cagan and Friedman's papers (1956). In microeconomic perspective, in spite of Shackle's works upon which Lachmann lavishes praise numerous times, that same difficulty locks the 'subjectivist' interpretation of unknowable future. Finally, a conclusion is provided.

A common initial preoccupation

The initial foundations of Lundberg's and Lachmann's common interest in expectations are focused on two connected points: the extension of the business cycle theory from its Wicksell connection (the cumulative process), and the role of plans (with the process analysis methodology and the modification of the capital theory).

The business cycle, the 'Lundberg effect' and secondary depression

The initial relationship between Lachmann and Lundberg emerged from the context of business cycle analysis. That context is characterised by a theoretical Austrian-Swedish connection and in the same time a more practical interrogation about the diversity of cycles, with a vast bulk of approaches focused on the role of investment. In his first papers, Lachmann shares the same explicative structure as Lundberg and refers very often to him.[1] He claims a 'Lundberg theorem' or 'Lundberg effect' (1938: 49; 1939: 80; 1940: 185). Let us briefly recall the framework of the argument.

Lundberg, in 1937, attempts to create a general corpus to replace the equilibrium-based corpus. He extends the Wicksellian cumulative process notion and, after Myrdal and Lindahl's works, suggests a dynamic approach well fitted to a business cycle analysis. The discrepancy between the real and monetary interest rates, which is at the root of the Austrian-Swedish business cycle view, induces time-lags between the creation of production goods and the production of consumer goods. But Lundberg introduces two main modifications. First, the cycle does not depend on a distortion of a strict and systematic complementarity effect between these two levels of the structure of production, with forced saving. It depends on various irreversibilities that open or shut different routes to price and output variations. So, for Lundberg, a cycle is always unique (Bellet 2003). Second, these different forms of inertia are mainly based on the temporal discrepancy between costs and expected incomes. In particular, investment in fixed capital implies that high costs are connected with uncertain income in the future, with different periods. These types of investment, for instance, have smaller amortisation quotas, and over a short period, profits play a less important role. The greater the temporal dimension of an investment, the smaller the influence of the development of profits and incomes on the volume on investment during the short periods:

> When the investment-decision has reference to a great number of future unit-periods, the expectations of receipts will probably be founded upon the experiences of a number of past unit-period. Changes in receipts during a short time will not considerably modify the long-run expectations underlying the investment decisions It may in certain cases be fair to assume these expectations are wholly *independent* of changes in current receipts during the short period selected in our analysis.
>
> (Lundberg 1937: 230–1)

So, the break in the upward phase of the trade cycle can be explained by a sequence similar to the 'Hayek-type', i.e. by too weak saving. In this case, the break cannot be explained by a failure of the demand for consumption goods or purchasing power. Investment is independent of the development of consumer goods production (current receipts) and the accelerator does not work. At the same time, the increase in active[2] saving will not be large enough to decrease the interest rate (which increases with the boom), and to stimulate new investments. So there is no compensation between, on one hand, a decreasing investment connected with consumption, and, on the other, a rising investment connected with a falling interest rate. Lundberg interprets the break as caused by the amount of saving being too small. That sequence is the opposite of the 'Keynes-type' sequence, where the break is explained by insufficient purchasing power and too rapid increase in saving (type of investment dependent on changes in current receipts).

Lachmann is very interested in Lundberg' s last definition, but in accordance with a partially modified context. He agrees with the idea that the production process takes time, and takes up the hypothesis of the non-reversibility of the investment operation (the time dimension of an investment). As Lachmann says, in the business cycle theories investment is twice stimulated (or depressed): once by the discrepancy between the two interest rates, then by increased consumption (accelerator effect). The hypothesis of cumulative process assumes these two effects are complementary, with compensations. But the cumulative process may not be so flexible. Lachmann goes beyond Lundberg's notion: there are types of investment (durable investments) which are not sensitive to the demand for consumer goods, but only to the interest rate. If costs increase during the upward phase, and if we generalise Lundberg's idea for all other costs, we obtain the 'Lundberg effect'.[3] So increasing costs during the upward phase lead to a fall in the durable types of investment, and a crisis will be unavoidable if the acceleration effect has no compensation. This compensation is more and more difficult and 'the large shadow of secondary depression falls on the field of knowledge' (1938: 56). The 'secondary depression'[4] would not be an adjustment process in the Hayekian sense (primary depression), and would lead to a negative cumulative process on the whole of economy. The crisis of 1929 would come under this type of global depression.[5] In 1940, Lachmann develops again the 'Lundberg effect' (1940: 185–91) and adds a 'Ricardo effect' to present a stronger Austrian doctrine. During the upward phase of the cycle, the Lundberg effect explains the rise in costs, and the fall in demand for durable investments. At the same time, the full capacity of the economy is reached, and real wages fall: the Ricardo effect (now a decrease in the amount of capital per unit of output) occurs and prevents a compensation with a new demand for production goods. This extension does not prevent Lachmann from adopting a cautious opinion about the general relevance of the Austrian theory of industrial fluctuations.[6]

In our view, the main concern for Lachmann in the initial papers on business cycles (1938, 1939, 1940) is to introduce the first concepts of complementarity and the heterogeneous character of capital. The production system is not completely flexible. The temporal structure of production has to be broken down beyond the differentiation of production goods and consumer goods. There is no automatic compensation between different demands for production or consumer goods. So the references to Lundberg and his notion of 'types of capital or investment' are useful. That interpretation of Lundberg's dissertation anticipates the later idea of a type of plan connected to the type of capital and the total desegregation of the notion of capital.

The link with expectations: dynamic and plans

At this stage of the work, the pivotal role of expectations is not studied. Lachmann is very closed to Hayek's position on expectations, and Myrdal was known not to share that position[7] ([1933] 1939). The references to expectations are limited to a general framework: if we admit the non-reversibility of the investment operation, and the conversion of capital into machinery, buildings, 'any failure of events to conform to expectations will upset everything' (1940: 181). The cumulative process implies expectations on prices and profits, especially entrepreneurs' profit expectations induced by the low rate of interest. But expectations are not really analysed. Indeed Lundberg benefits from the Swedish contributions on plan and 'planning' notions. He indicates that expectations 'can, in a way, be said to mark the stepping stone to dynamic analysis' (1937: 175). But as we will see later, his developments on expectations are not very clear. In any case, when Lachmann in his first period quotes Lundberg, it is on business cycle and capital theory (i.e. temporal structure of production). To the structure more finely broken down correspond some connected variables (consumer goods prices, interest rate . . .); to these variables correspond some temporal differences and expectations differences.[8] Expectations are the non-explicit duplicate of the temporal structure of production.

Nevertheless, an assessment of Lundberg's and Lachmann's contributions on expectations reveals much common ground. First, they agree on the role of the future, with doubt and uncertainty in a changing world. The future is radically uncertain. So agents form expectations, but cannot strictly forecast the future: time lags connected with production structure cannot be reduced by an intertemporal calculation. Sequential time is not a logical time, and unexpected changes occur. Foresight is imperfect. Second, 'causal-genetic' (Lachmann) and 'process analysis' (Lundberg) are very closed in their reasoning and causal explanation. In both the cases, this concerns the dispute about the analytical tool of static equilibrium analysis. Dynamic analysis and sequence analysis pave the way to the role of expectations. Third, both authors use the same two notions: expectation and plan. Expectations are the general framework of a vision for the future; plans are based on expectations, and focus on a specific action (production, investment, and consumption).

To explain his future near-obsessive focus on expectations, Lachmann (1978) quotes Rosenstein-Rodan's remark and the Swedish reference.[9] But, even in the 1930s, other reasons can explain this not-yet explicit preoccupation. The question of the theory of capital is difficult especially concerning the business cycle theories. Lundberg (1937) knows the critical views of the Böhm-Bawerk's capital theory (from Clark and Knight, concerning the insurmountable aggregation problem with the notion of 'quantity of capital', and the notion of production time). He does not insist on it,[10] but agrees with a new definition of capital, which was suggested by Myrdal ([1933] 1939): the interest rate as the present value of a future flow of income. This enables the circumvention of the difficulties concerning the definition of the natural rate of interest to qualify the situation of monetary equilibrium. So advancing the notion of future revenue helps to divert the analysis towards anticipations and how they are formed. Lundberg approves of this new expectation-based definition. During his first phase, Lachmann, who is also aware of the arguments, remains very cautious. He does not reach a decision on capital theory.[11] Later, he will adopt a defence of the Austrian capital theory, with another framework connecting subjectivism and expectations (with a revival of Menger's inspiration) and a meaningful revision of economic theory. Finally, the importance of different works (Myrdal [1933] 1936; Keynes 1930, 1936; Shackle 1938; Hicks 1939) on expectations may have convinced Lachmann that the Austrian cycle theory did not take the problem of the expectations sufficiently seriously.

To sum up, during this first period, the link between business cycle explanations, capital theory, and expectations role is very important. Gradually in Lachmann's analysis and his references to Lundberg, this link will loosen in favour of the analysis of expectations. But it will not vanish completely.

The two ways: subjective or objective foundations for expectations?

1943 represents at the same time an explicit revival of the expectation theme and a break concerning the agreement between Lachmann's perspective and Lundberg's works. Clearly, with his paper, Lachmann appears on the field of expectations, which was opened especially by the Swedes. But now Lundberg's contribution seems more limited than Lachmann's. What becomes apparent on reflection is that the two projects are going to be more and more differentiated: a subjective foundation for expectation analysis, and an objective one. We examine here the evolution of the relationship between Lachmann and Lundberg.

An explicit introduction of the expectations

Two papers (1943, 1945) are very representative of the first explicit treatment of the expectations issue in Lachmann's works. With a 1948 article concerning investment, they show an irreversible evolution towards a subjectivist conception of expectations and investment. During this second phase, the business cycle theory stays in the background.

The first paper agrees with Lundberg (1937) on a precise point: a common refusal to relegate expectations to the category of 'data' and an attempt to endogenise it with causal explanation. Here Lachmann is very close to the well-known analysis that Lundberg introduced in 1930. In his first published paper, Lundberg criticises Myrdal's thesis on the temporal order of determination:

> The connecting link, which according to Myrdal is composed of anticipations, has no *direct* causal effect backward in time from the expected future level. Instead, expectations during a given earlier period have to be based entirely and exclusively on the price constellation during this and previous periods.
>
> (Lundberg [1930] 1994: 35)

According to Lundberg, 'this anticipation cannot be the primary factor' (1930: 35). In 1937, the author develops his critical view against Keynes (1936) from the same idea: expectations connect present plans and activities with future actions, but they are not autonomous. 'Total lack of correlation here would mean the complete liquidation of economics as a science' (1937: 175, quoted by Lachmann in 1943: 13). Lundberg comments that these expectations play an important role in cycle theories, especially in Keynes: the Keynesian concept of the marginal efficiency of capital is clearly dependent on expectations, and seems to be an essential part of the investment decision. However, for Lundberg, Keynes, with his 'concrete and eclectic' (1937: 178) attitude vacillates between various treatments: he is led either to underline the very blurred nature of these expectations for business people, with a resulting difficulty in explaining investment; or he contends that the marginal efficiency of capital may be seen as given, by then explaining that the cycle will depend on the variation in this data, according to an exogenous movement of expectations; or again he seems to make capital efficiency depend on endogenous factors, such as the pool of capital goods. In any event, expectations may under no circumstances serve to 'complete' a causal system in an exogenous way. For Lundberg, one of the ways of escaping this contrary exogenousness to a sequence analysis, as he conceives it, is to reinsert the investment determinants within a broader sequence taking into account the rate of economic expansion, in other words, a variable produced earlier by movements in investment and saving. So, expectations would then be linked to the prior state of the economy.

However, Lachmann quickly modulates his agreement with Lundberg on the determinateness of expectations with a disagreement on the type of determinateness. He contests the objective nature of the causal relation, and introduces his major thesis: the relationship between objective economic variables or 'business situations' and expectations depends on the interpretation which the agents give to the former. These interpretations are different among individuals for a single fact or business situation, because a filter in their human mind changes an experience in an individual expectation. These differences become more pronounced in a world in motion since any convergence of individual interpretations is excluded. Social science is prohibited from determinates because of this subjective interpretation. Expectations are intelligible, but not determined. Now, how does social science make expectations intelligible? Lachmann indicates that social science can find behind the expectations a 'mental pattern of relative simplicity that our problem-solving mind can comprehend' (1943: 17).

In the light of that conception, Lachmann (1943, 1945) examines Hicks's concept of 'elasticity of expectations' (1939)[12] and tries to endogenise it. For the Austrian author, the concept is interesting because it postulates a non-uniform reaction to price changes. The introduction of the concept of 'practical range' due to Lange (1944) enables him to link the level and motion of prices with the elasticity of expectations. The practical range represents the set of the *probable*. Prices give an interpretation of the economic situation. The middle of the practical range forms an 'indifference zone' which contains prices judged as 'normal'. As long as price moves within this zone, elasticity of expectations is equal to zero, i.e. expectations are indifferent to such movements. When prices are outside the indifference zone and tend towards the frontiers of the practical range, elasticity of expectations becomes negative. Finally, once the price passes the limits of the practical range, elasticity is large. The vision of a set of probable prices with the perception of economic forces behind it is not confirmed. A new 'diagnosis' of the situation is necessary.

With these extensions, the concept of elasticity of expectations receives an explanation in connection with the role of interpretation of business situations. In this sense, the market process does not endogenously determinate expectations. As a consequence, Lachmann's theory of expectation cannot provide a complete explanation of expectation and cannot be predictive (since the activity of the human mind is neither directly observable nor predictable).

This theory constitutes a break relative to analyses founded on the notion of 'psychological' class. Given a price movement, it is always possible to classify individuals into groups according to the elasticity of their expectations. But, such an analysis is unfounded, for the same individual repeatedly confronted with the same kind of price movement may react with different degrees of sensitivity. And these various degrees of elasticity are based on different individual interpretations of the business situation.

To sum up, Lundberg suggests that expectations depend on objective data that are the result of a previous sequence, whereas Lachmann considers that they depend on subjective interpretation of these data, connected with a mental picture. However, at this stage Lachmann's subjective orientation[13] remains ambiguous. He seeks to explain the formation of a mental picture and shows how an expectation derives from 'the situation as a whole as the expecting individual sees it' (1943: 20) or on 'judgements on the strength of the economic forces believed to have caused' events ([1945] 1994: 129). And prevailing types of expectation exist: for instance, fairly elastic expectations can be prevalent when we are considering interest expectations (different from price expectations). The Austrian-Wicksellian analysis of the crisis is based on this assumption.[14] It is supposed that people are not governed by expectations derived from the belief that long-run forces govern the interest rate on capital market. And Lachmann suggests that 'such a state of expectations may be typical of an economy in the early stages of industrialisation, or of an economy undergoing "rejuvenation" owing to rapid technical progress' (1943: 23). Even if Lachmann specifies that in a changing world it is difficult to identify the prevailing type of expectation, subjective interpretation seems to give way to a more objective view. Moreover, Lachmann does not indicate how the divergent individual expectations of identical events are connected to produce a macroeconomic phenomenon (a cycle phase, for instance). What is the type of inter-subjective co-ordination? Is there learning between them? On this point, Lachmann is silent. For his part, Lundberg (1937: 173) keeps wavering but finally seems to choose an aggregate hypothesis with groups of agents and stable reaction functions to express 'average conditions for these groups'.

A development of a subjectivist interpretation for Lachmann and the extension of a disagreement with Lundberg

With two papers published in 1947 and 1948, Lachmann completes the subjective way to interpret expectations. A more general capital theory with a subjectivist view of investment is connected with the expectation theory. Especially the latter paper (where Lundberg is still referenced) anticipates the very important book *Capital and its Structure* that will open the third phase of Lachmann's reasoning. With his South African writings, Lachmann will reinforce the opposition between subjective and objective foundations for expectation analysis.

Both texts (1947 and 1948) represent a theoretical return to capital theory. Lachmann tries to elaborate a more general capital theory, with microfoundations on agents' plans. The digression of Böhm-Bawerk's aggregative capital theory, with its Ricardian flavour, is closed. The disaggregative conception initiated in the first step is now extended to a new and wider ground. The two basic notions are complementarity and substitution of capital goods. The different means jointly employed to the same end are complementary capital goods; substitution is a change that modifies the combination of factors. But complementarity and substitution are meaningful only in relationships with a plan: 'capital goods are products of the human mind, artefacts, produced in accordance with a plan' ([1947] 1977: 203). All the capital goods employed within the same plan are always complementary, and a substitution of capital goods is necessarily a plan revision. The capital structure is basically a network of plans, in a state of continuous transformation in a changing world. So capital theory, a subjective view on expectations, and process analysis join together. At the same time (1948), this approach is also a theory of investment and its repercussions. The problem of investment lies in complementarity and substitution between new capital goods and old capital goods, and new investments are necessarily connected with changes in *the use of* existing capital. The decision of an agent is going to affect the decisions of others: investments depend on expectations and production plans, but the supply of existing capital resources depends on plans that have to be revised. The theory is presented as the 'missing link between the microeconomic theory of investment and the macro-economic theory of aggregate investment' ([1948] 1994: 133). In these papers, expectation analysis is unequally developed. The elasticity question with ambiguous objective references vanishes,[15] but the new notion of 'inconsistent expectations' emerges. Lachmann argues that the divergence of expectations (with subjective foundations) leads to inconsistent expectations. Lundberg's 'type of *plan* analysis' (ibid.: 136) is a first step towards a clear recognition of this diversity and non-flexibility. Lachmann and the Swedes would discard the equilibrium method to treat the non-uniform expectations issue.[16] At this point, in our opinion, the reference to Lundberg is very extensive and reveals a shift in meaning. The Swedes do not justify process analysis because of a subjective divergence of expectations, but an objective time lag: production takes time and a discrepancy between expectations *ex ante* and results *ex post* occurs. Again, inconsistent expectations hypothesis raises the issue of the basis for a co-ordination between agents and the existence of macro-level phenomena.[17] Lachmann's reply consists in invoking dynamic method and some early references to a knowledge diffusion view (1949: 433–4). But he contests any idea of knowledge or foresight as 'data'.

The book *Capital and its Structure* (1956) synthesises Lachmann's last orientations. Two chapters are presented as crucial: Chapter II on expectations and Chapter IV on the meaning of capital structure. Lundberg is quite absent from these chapters, but mentioned in a note in Chapter III on process analysis and in the final Chapter VII on capital and trade cycle. The framework is the following. First, the subjectivist way is theoretically and historically situated: after the subjectivism of want or preference, a next step is the subjectivism of expectations or interpretation, or subjectivism of active mind (according to Shackle's expression). Second, the disaggregative analysis of capital (heterogeneity in use, with production plans which determine this use) is confirmed. Third, the method of process analysis based on plans is always employed, but the critical view on Lundberg is clear:

> To assume that entrepreneurial conduct in revising plans at the end of successive periods is, in any objective sense, *determined* by past experience and thus *predictable*, would mean falling into a rigid determinism which is quite contrary to everyday experience.
>
> (Lachmann 1956: 14)[18]

Especially in the book, Lachmann adopts the hypothesis of a world of continuous change, where everything moves all the time.

Here we are interested in specifying two points. The first focuses on the range structure of expected variables and on the relation with the spontaneous order of knowledge on the market. Lachmann (1956, Chapter II) considers again how estimation of economic forces influences the formation of the expectations. He develops a new typology based on meaningful and meaningless price movements. The estimated permanent forces are linked with price changes believed to be meaningful, and the estimated random forces with price changes believed to be meaningless. He clearly adopts the hypothesis of a double range: an inner range which corresponds to the 'indifference zone' (1945) and an outer range which is the set of *possible* prices. He connects these ranges with the typology. Thus, within the inner range, price movements will be interpreted as meaningless (inelastic expectations). When the price movements get close to the upper/lower limits of the inner range, each individual expects the market to regulate the prices within this range (i.e. negative elasticity). When the prices pass the limits of the inner range but remain within the outer range, Lachmann adds two supplementary criteria to judge the mean of this kind of price change: the time factor, and the 'statistical position' of the market (i.e. size of stocks). To provoke a revision of expectations and question the notion of normality implied by the initial range, price changes have to stay a long time outside the inner range, and they must not depend on ordinary stock variations. Finally, if price changes pass the limits of the outer range, this movement will be interpreted as clearly meaningful (attributed to permanent forces). In the last cases, individuals receive more negative information than positive: the initial estimation is invalidated, but we do not know the new one.

Thus Lachmann distinguishes four cases, but admits some limitations to his framework. According to him, his 'generalisation' (1945: 29) by range structure reflects the subjectivism of interpretation only in a sufficiently stable world. Indeed, in such an environment, the interpretations of economic forces by agents should be convergent so that the concept of a 'normal price range' emerges at the market level (1956: 30). However, this process of convergence is never explicitly described. Actually, Lachmann attempts to solve the issue by adopting the hypothesis of a spontaneous order of the market.[19] The subjectivism of interpretation is co-ordinated by 'the insight, vigilance, and intelligence of the market' (ibid.: 32). The market process progressively eliminates unsuccessful expectations. The interactions between individuals are performed via knowledge diffusion. Knowledge is information modified by interpretation, and expectations are not independent of each other. But how could knowledge be diffused without a common (even limited) view of what is happening in a changing world? In our opinion, it seems difficult to reconcile the concept of structure of expectations, on the one hand, with the very bold assumption of knowledge never stabilised in a changing world, on the other. Lachmann argues that the process of expectations revision is continuous in this kind of world, because there are many changes, and consequently much information. No pattern for the acquisition of knowledge exists and no individual learning process is definite. With the notion of expectations structure, Lachmann apparently introduces some points of orientation for divergent expectations; with his notion of running knowledge these points vanish because individuals cannot exploit backward experience in new context.

Moreover, we notice that Lachmann's opinion about probabilities is ambiguous. In 1945, following Lange, he defines the practical range as the 'set of prices expected with various degrees of probability' (1945: 123). In 1956, the definition of the practical range contains no reference to probability. In addition, he quotes Shackle on the irrelevance of probabilities to decisions in a world in motion.

The second point focuses on the state of the relationship Lachmann claims with Lundberg in 1956. In spite of some compromises, the unfolding of the subjectivist framework leads to a clear relativisation of Lundberg's contribution. As we have seen, the references do not focus on expectation analysis. They are mainly directed towards process analysis (1956, Chapter III: 39), with a shift in meaning again. Lachmann has no reticence about advancing a common method with Lundberg, but he presents a process analysis of *human mind* which is of course very different from the Swedish perspective. Another reference is to the trade cycle (Chapter VII: 104). Lachmann briefly mentions a more recent paper written by Lundberg (1950), and several common themes criss-cross along this chapter: cycle dissimilarities, eclecticism claim on models, sceptical attitude about the use of statistical magnitudes, a critical view on the notion of autonomous investment[20] or on constant acceleration coefficient, and, finally, a severe assessment of Harrod–Hicks's growth theories. On our interpretation, these common and striking themes do not succeed in hiding from now a different perspective. For instance, when Lachmann criticises constant coefficients, he has in mind the implicit homogeneous capital conception. With the same critical appreciation, Lundberg (1950) refers to his early works on different kinds of investments, but in particular he defends a decomposition of the economy by sectors, i.e. a macro-economic disaggregation ... Moreover, Lundberg in this article says very little on expectations role for business cycles.

The last phase: 'radical subjectivism'

The outcome of the differentiation between the authors on expectations is provided by Lachmann's last book, *The Market as an Economic Process* (1986). This book still contains two references to Lundberg. They concern the history of subjectivism and its relationships with expectation analysis. In his 'concluding remarks' (ibid.: 146), Lachmann returns to the history of political economy. He mentions the issues for 'a relatively short history' (ibid.: 144) of subjectivism with utility and expectation notions. He gives the post-Wicksellians (especially Lundberg) and Keynes credit for the emergence of an expectation theory, but deplores the fact that this theory was absorbed by the Keynesian context. The subjectivist approach, based on divergent expectations hypothesis will be then neglected, except in Shackle's works. Lundberg is presented in another reference (ibid.: 24) as an obstacle to the progress of subjectivism, because his objectivist analysis of expectations uses dependent variables. To sum up, the link with Lundberg is restricted to a historical reference in political economy, and the confrontation ground is very clear: subjectivism vs objectivism. Nothing is new here.

Nevertheless, the content of this last book reveals an extension of the subjectivism of expectations (Lewin 1994). From his famous article about kaleidic society (1976), Lachmann's thinking grows ever closer to Shackle's.[21] The market is regarded as an economic process, driven by the divergence of expectations in a world of unexpected changes (Torr 1986). The central idea is the following: everything is changing all the time and it is impossible to use past experience as 'data' to explain the future. Moreover, the subjectivist hypothesis leads to a diversity of expectations, because different people learn different lessons from the same events. And that diversity grows as far as the number of individuals, or 'knowers', increases. Lachmann thus takes up Shackle's definition of the kaleidic nature of the world of human action, with a cumulative problem involved in the knowledge of knowledge . . . The formation of expectations, i.e. the problem of the significance of knowledge for action, faces a dilemma. If we include the state of knowledge to understand this process:

> we should have to introduce it either as a datum or as a dependent variable. As the state of knowledge is ever changing it is hard to see how we could treat it as a datum: it is never 'given' to us for long. But to treat it as a dependent variable would mean to treat processes of thought as though they were predictable. We know that cannot be done.
>
> (Lachmann 1986: 28)

Empirical generalisations are impossible due to the unknowable quality of the future.[22] The orientative (not determinative) role of past experiences that Lachmann admitted before (1956) is now called into question. The ideas of 'range', of 'structure of expectations', of probabilistic analysis now vanish.[23] In this respect his last book represents a new stage and a systematisation of some previous elements. In his developments on information and knowledge (1956, Chapter 3), Lachmann indicates we cannot speak of a 'decoding of messages' because the code book does not exist. The logic of means and ends in an individual plan allows one to insert new information into the stock of knowledge, and to revise the plan ('subjectivism of interpretation'). But that logic never generates generalisations on the future ('subjectivism of expectations'). Agents are able to form expectations, but these expectations are indeterminate due to uncertainty in the future. This 'radical subjectivism' (1986: X) has recourse to spontaneous (unexpected) order of the market to explain some convergence, but:

> in the first place, revision of plans in the direction of convergence requires a common diagnosis of the present disequilibrium situation. Divergence of interpretation will prevent it. Secondly, convergence requires that agents expect each other to revise their plans in this direction. Divergence of expectations may prevent this . . . We thus see that divergence of interpreta-

tion and divergence of expectations each play an important but distinct part in the market process.

(Lachmann 1986: 57)

Agents deal with a multitude of market processes. A large network of markets represents the macroeconomic view of the economic system. But with the subjectivist methodology, 'no market process has a determinate outcome'; in a kaleidic world all opportunities lie in the future, and Lachmann supposes that the diversity of markets (especially stock markets), in equilibrium or disequilibrium, is fitted to an ongoing world of spontaneous human action. At this stage, it seems to us that the analysis of expectations is stopped.

To summarise the outcome of the confrontation between Lachmann and Lundberg, we can identify two ways that progressively emerge for a unique challenge: taking account of expectations but refusing an exogenous character. Lundberg always refers to a duality between *ex ante* expectations and *ex post* results. The causality between *ex post* results and formation-revision of expectations is strict. Lachmann insists on a duality between *ex ante* expectations and *ex post* interpreted results. There is no causality linking the two terms, but in the best interpretation (1956), some points of orientation. That disruption between the objectivist and subjectivist analyses of expectations leads to a double failure.

Two ways and a double failure on expectations

Both authors encounter difficulties on the same set of questions: the formation, the revision and the co-ordination of expectations. Their interesting ambition to replace trivial expressions like 'state of expectations' or 'psychological laws' but endogenising explanation fails with this unsolved set. Furthermore, the problem lies in a larger context: from the 1950s, the prevailing dynamics of the political economy with a first codification of macroeconomics and microeconomics closes the expectations framework.

A common issue on formation, revision and co-ordination of expectations

Lundberg (1930, 1937) shows how in process analysis the sequence is identified: expectations *ex ante* – plans – results *ex post* in discrepancies with plans. Hence agents revise their expectations in a new sequence . . . There is no perfect foresight because some unexpected changes necessarily arise in a production economy with fixed capital and time lags. Expectations are not 'rational' in this meaning.[24] Formation and revision of expectations are linked to the prior state of the economy. But Lundberg remains very vague about the connection between expectations and economic results. He retains a limited memory taking into account the previous period, which is reminiscent of a hypothesis of adaptive expectations. Lundberg seems very circumspect about looking forward. Agents do not take the (even failed) very prospective view: they restrict themselves to comparing past with present and apply that comparison to the future. The causal determinism is very strict, respecting a past–present sequence. According to Lundberg, the idea of auto-realised expectations is totally inconceivable. Revision of expectations is automatic: Lundberg did not take advantage of Hayek's famous paper on knowledge,[25] and supposes that agents record *ex post* prices. No probabilistic view exists. As we have seen, their reaction functions are determined by institutional characteristics, and are stable by restrictive hypothesis.

Concerning the co-ordination of expectations, we find with some restrictions a general analysis in 1937 (Chapters VII and VIII): economic units are groups (macroeconomic types), economic variables are referred to 'normal' calculation, such as is made by a 'representative firm' (1937: 155). Expectation groups are linked by mechanical reaction to these economic variables.[26] The co-ordination problem is not the outcome of the diversity of expectations, but the outcome of the time lags of the production process. Finally, expectations are the permanently denied and revised duplicate of the types of timing connected to the types of capital and investment. Disequilibrium is the norm. Despite the initial will of Lundberg, the process becomes a process of macro-magnitudes: in Chapter IX on model sequences (1937), expectations do not play a major role, and the later works will not deny this.

The 'Lachmann problem' (Koppl 1998) also derives from the status of expectations in economic analysis. Expectations are formed and revised but never in any deterministic way. From 1943, Lachmann calls for a subjectivist theory of expectations, a position from which he will not deviate. But just as he accepts Shackle's position on the kaleidic society (1976, 1986), his interpretation becomes more and more evanescent. Until 1956, he tries to elaborate a coherent and tractable framework on expectations. Of course, we have noticed some hesitations: for instance, Lachmann mitigates some theoretical considerations (spontaneous order of knowledge on the market), and practical views (role of stocks for instance). But when he allows the hypothesis of a relatively stable economic situation, his apparatus of probabilities (1943–45) or potentialities (1956) ranges represents an interesting test to improve specific microeconomics. On the contrary, when Lachmann supposes that the economic world is continually changing, and when he rejects the use of probability, there are no more orientation points to understand the formation and revision of expectations. And Lachmann takes refuge in Shackle's kaleidic view. Expectations are endogenous, but they are never functionally related to observable facts. The subjectivism of interpretation cannot be predictive, and cannot be confronted with a set of testable propositions. It is only a construct of individual's minds, with an expectational time. No crystallisation along time exists. Expectations are thus not static, adaptive, or rational: they belong to a different field where every interpretation is unique and uncertain concerning the result of the action. If we can accept the idea that Lundberg adopts an adaptive perspective, it is very difficult to see Lachmann as a precursor of the notion of rational expectations (Kantor 1979).[27] The Austrian author hardly judges this concept as 'a contradiction in terms' ([1982] 2002: 275), that 'emasculates expectations'(1986: 147). Whatever people know derives from the past, and they cannot know the future. However, it is difficult to strictly qualify Lachmann's analysis of expectations as nihilism, or a theoretical individualism, because rationalisation and generalisation of *past* sequences are possible (with 'ideal types' and 'institutions' notions). But we are told nothing about the future. The absolute indeterministic analysis leads to a deadlock. As Hoppe (1997)[28] writes on Lachmann, from the recognition of the fact that the future is uncertain, it does not follow that everything is uncertain: the two extremes of perfect ignorance and perfect knowledge are not consistently defensible. That way would lead back to Lachmann's first contention on probability class or range.[29]

More strictly, on our interpretation, in his developments on expectations, Lachmann comes up against the absence of a decision theory. More precisely, Lachmann does not combine his theory of expectations with a decision-making process. The only indication furnished by Lachmann is that the 'best' alternative is selected. For instance, when an entrepreneur has to draw up a plan, the most profitable combination of capital goods is selected from different plans (1956: 3). But Lachmann does not describe the decision-making process which ensures this result, given expectations about the business situation. This deficiency is going to play a major role in what will happen afterwards.

A break with the development of the political economy in the 1950s

Lundberg and Lachmann did not succeed in providing a tractable way to explain the formation, revision and co-ordination of expectations. But that failure cannot completely explain why both economists remained on the periphery of the dynamics of their subject. The context of political economy in the 1950s is not very favourable to the Austrian and Swedish Schools.

Lundberg is faced with the framework of Keynesian macroeconomics (different from Keynes's views) based on the combination of multiplier and accelerator. The first works on the growth theory (Hicks, Harrod, Samuelson) absorbs him, and his contribution is going to be packaged as a rather clumsy forerunner of Keynesian theories. Even if Lundberg (as Lachmann does) criticises a framework focused on the study of the conditions of stable growth, the equilibrium method and references to an equilibrium path prevail. Expectations do not play an important role in macroeconomics, which is mainly a macroeconomics of global quantities. As we have seen, some of Lundberg's developments (1937: Chapter

IX) gave way to this conception, and his objectivist treatment with strict economic causality blurred the specific character of the expectations. In a later work on business cycles and economic policy (1957), Lundberg writes again on expectations. He stresses the public policy of government analysed as a plan in a general conception of expectations. Agents integrate public expectations into their own plans, and the issue of confidence is very important to pursue a public policy. But these remarks do not rest on a new analysis of expectations formation and revision. In 1959, Lundberg keeps wavering about his objectivist hypothesis to take account of the expectations dispersion:[30] however, he considers a sectoral disaggregation and interdependence to solve the issue, and he admits he has 'not produced a clear alternative line of approach' ([1959] 1994: 244) to explain changes in expectations. In macroeconomics, the revival of expectations analysis (and in this way the return to Keynes's and Lundberg's intuitions) will occur with the first discussions against Keynesian policies (Cagan in Friedman, 1956).

Lachmann is exposed to the capital analysis connected with growth theories. Robinson's book *The Accumulation of Capital* is published at the same time as Lachmann's *Capital and its Structure* (1956). The commentaries on the former book will be numerous while those on the latter will be rare. And in Robinson's book, the expectations issue is almost eliminated, as Lachmann noted, by the assumption

> that at every moment entrepreneurs expect the future rate of profit obtainable on investment to continue indefinitely at the level ruling at that moment; that they expect the rate of technical progress . . . to be steady . . . When something occurs which causes a change, we assume that expectations are immediately adjusted, and no further change is expected.
>
> ([1958] 1977: 217, Robinson quoted by Lachmann)

The macroeconomics of global magnitudes prevails.

Moreover, Lachmann is especially confronted by the elaboration of an axiomatic decision theory. Indeed, the question of the axiomatisation of the theory of choice becomes a crucial preoccupation in economics with the book by von Neumann and Morgenstern (1944) and with Savage's book (1954). This confrontation underlines the fact that Lachmann does not propose a decision-making process which is able to explain how an alternative is selected, given expectations.

At the same time, with the works of Savage (1954), the process of maximisation of the expectation of a real-valued function holds the dominant position in decision theory under uncertainty. Precisely, Savage represents uncertainty as a subjective probability distribution on a given set of states of nature which can be seen as business situations. Subjectivity of probability here means that the probability of realisation of state of nature is not objective, i.e. probabilities do not exist inherently in the economic situation. Each agent forms individual beliefs on occurrences of business situations according to individual preferences on the set of acts. Savage imposes restrictions on the preference relations on alternatives that simultaneously permit the representation of each preference relation as the mathematical expectation of a real-valued function on the set of consequences, with respect to a unique probability measure on the set of states of nature, and the *determination* of this unique *additive* probability measure. In other words, Savage establishes conditions on individual preferences which ensure the existence of subjective probabilities jointly with that of an expected utility representation.

As a reaction to these developments in axiomatic decision theory, Lachmann subscribes to a radical subjectivism. Indeed, the denial of the use of probabilities challenges Savage's theory. This position find a justification in a world of perpetual changes where it is impossible to use past experience as 'data' to know the future (even potentially) and, consequently, where individuals are not able to enumerate all the possible contingencies of the business situation. Thus, in our opinion, the prevailing position in economics held after Savage's book by the subjective expected utility theory is crucial for the explanation of the adoption by Lachmann of radical subjectivism. However, given this orientation, the question of a decision theory becomes particularly acute. Indeed, when the theory of expectations denies the use of probabilities, any reference to a process of maximisation of the mathematical expectation of a real-valued function is impossible. So, an alternative decision theory, in the spirit of Shackle's one, is an absolute necessity. From this point of view, it is not surprising that Lachmann, after 1956, often refers to Shackle's works.

Conclusion

In Lundberg's dissertation (1937), Lachmann finds a connection between expectations role, capital theory, process method, and business cycle analysis. More precisely, in this framework he keeps the idea of a disaggregative notion of capital, with complementarity, and the idea of endogenous explanation of expectations. So the formation of expectations becomes a challenge. From this common starting point, we have shown that Lachmann and Lundberg chose two different ways. The former developed a subjectivism of expectations until an auto-destruction. The latter suggested an objectivist explanation with a very simplified hypothesis and rather vague considerations. Despite their failure, Lachmann and Lundberg maintained the rich inheritance of the 1930s on expectations in a very different context, until a revival at the end of the 1950s. Moreover, they left open two interesting intuitions. On the one hand, in Lachmann's connection, the idea of complementarity of capital and expectations is today exploited for an Austrian theory of the firm (for instance, Loasby 1998). On the other hand, in Lundberg's connection, a modern definition of public regulation advocates non-discretionary intervention because of the expectations role (Lundberg 1996).

Notes

1 In our opinion, Lachmann is the only non-Swedish economist who usually refers to Lundberg. Conversely Lundberg never quotes Lachmann, even in his post-World War II papers. For an analysis excluding Lundberg (except a note), see Siven (1991).
2 Lundberg considers the role of savings as active (classical view), and as passive (Keynesian view).
3 'Mr Lundberg has recently pointed out that those types of investment which are most sensitive to changes in the rate of interest are least likely to be affected by changes in demand for consumption goods and vice versa' (1938: 49). 'In referring to this factor we shall speak of the *Lundberg effect*' (1940: 185).
4 Lachmann mentions Röpke (1933) regarding this notion then much under discussion, but other authors (Schumpeter) refer to it.
5 'It is thus not easy to account for the crisis of 1929 by the help of the Austrian theory' (1940: 195).
6 It is to be noted that Lachmann has no hostile position on Keynes's view, and has this additional point in common with Lundberg:

> The Austrian writers are not entitled to object to measures destined to raise consumers' purchasing power. For the difference between the situation to which they are referring when speaking of crisis and the one in which such measures are to be adopted lies exactly in the fact that in the former case there is no lack of effective demand while in the latter case there is such a lack.
>
> (1939: 86)

In the Austrian over-investment theory, 'nothing is said about total output . . . and total employment' (1939: 85). On this question, see Boettke and Sullivan (1998).
7 'Hayek directs his thorough analysis – in accordance with the Austrian tradition – towards an abstract case where among other things anticipations are excluded by assumptions which are fundamental to the whole analysis' ([1933] 1939: 33).
8 According to Lundberg:

> The expectations underlying decisions to invest should certainly be assumed to differ from those which govern the production of consumption goods. But the kind of difference must depend upon the *type of capital goods* considered. The necessary difference as to the term of expectations may take actual expression in a dependence upon different economic factors.
>
> (1937, Chap. II: 44, n. 1)

9 It was Rosenstein-Rodan who in discussing Austrian trade cycle theory with me said: 'Ah yes, but whatever happens in the business cycle is in the first place determined by expectations.' And then he told me of the work that been done in Sweden.

> (1978: 1)

10 See (1937, Chap. II: 30).

11 In conclusion to his 1938 paper, Lachmann writes: 'we have so far studiously refrained from using the terminology of the Austrian theory of the trade cycle. We have avoided all references to the time structure of production' (1938: 55).

12 Lachmann does not note that this notion can be found in the Lundberg's dissertation (1937), with the idea of 'reaction functions'. But, by simplification, Lundberg considers these functions as constant over a period of time (Chapter VIII: 173; Chapter X: 243). This hypothesis is strictly the opposite of Lachmann's proposals.

13 For the first time in Lachmann's papers, Shackle is mentioned ([1945] 1994: 125, n. 6).

14 See Mises (1943) for a different interpretation: the role of credit expansion creates falsified data and illusion.

15 This point enlightens the fact (mentioned below) that Lachmann does not integrate his theory of expectations in a decision-making process.

16 In his critical reply to Mrs Hahn, Lachmann writes:

> Mrs. Hahn thinks we can reach no 'general conclusions' about a situation in which expectations are not uniform. But inconsistent expectations are the very bread and butter of dynamics. It was precisely in order to be able to deal with inconsistent expectations and their consequences that modern economists discard equilibrium analysis in favour of process analysis.
>
> (1949: 433)

17 Again, Lachmann interprets the trade cycle with his investment repercussions theory ([1948] 1994: 143–4). But his analysis is very rapid and even withdraws on an explicit eclecticism.

18 Lachmann especially addresses sequence models from Lundberg's Chapter IX (1937).

19 '*"Market", in the true economic sense, means a process of exchange and allocation reflecting the transmission of knowledge* . . . The theory of expectations neglects the market process at its peril.' (1956: 28–9). Lachmann extends his hypothesis of structure of expectations from a single market (Chapter II) to several markets (Chapter IV). For instance, forward markets play a specific role 'to bring expectations into consistency with each other' (1956: 67–8).

20 These themes can be found very clearly in his 1937 dissertation.

21 Lachmann refers his 1972 book, *Epistemics and Economics*. In the previous works (1945, 1956), we can find several critical remarks on Shackle.

22 The only reference to business cycle excludes the validity of a model of *the* business cycle, and proposes a historical approach of the different explanations (1986: 30–1).

23 We found only one allusion to a 'price range' (1986: 57).

24 'Rational expectation' is an expression used by Lundberg ([1930] 1994: 34; [1984] 1994: 498). In 1930, it implies unfulfilled expectation; in 1984, it means endogenous expectation.

25 The 'knowledge' expression is only once present (1937, Chapter VIII: 190), while Lachmann often quotes Hayek's 1937 paper.

26   Functions expressing the reactions of producers to change in prices, orders, gains and losses, etc., must be assumed as given for our analysis. They are supposed to express average conditions for these groups, average with cancel internal differences between firms and producers. The degree of heterogeneity tends of course to increase with the size of the group.

>
> (1937: 173–4)

27 For a more cautious view, see Garrison (1986).
28 Hoppe (1997) interprets Lachmann's position as a return to his intellectual begin-
    nings as a student of Sombart. For an appreciation roundtable, see Boehm *et al.*
    (2000).
29 This notion is also used by Mises with a specific meaning, as opposed to case probab-
    ility (people know the behaviour of a class of events, but not the behaviour of the sin-
    gular events inside the class).
30 Lundberg stresses

> the high dispersion of yield expectations from the various kinds of investment
> within a firm, as between firms in the same branch of activity and between dif-
> ferent sectors of the economy . . . Behind all the difficulties of comparison lies
> the subjective nature of every estimate of uncertain future costs and revenues
> . . . There is nothing new; economists working on investment problems have
> always known that there were wide ranges of yield expectations . . . I suggest
> that we should, to a greater degree than we usually do, accept this chaos on the
> capital market and, instead of abstracting from it, analyse the causes and effects
> of very high dispersion of expected investment returns.
>
> ([1959] 1994: 235–6)

References

Bellet, M. (2003) 'Is there a Stockholm School cycle theory?', *History of Economic Ideas*,
    XI(1): 69–93.
Boehm, S., Kirzner, I.M., Koppl, R., Lavoie, D., Lewin P. and Torr, C. (2000)
    'Remembrance and appreciation roundable for Professor Ludwig M. Lachmann
    (1906–1990)', *American Journal of Economics and Sociology*, 59, 3: 367–417.
Boettke, P.J. and Sullivan, S.T. (1998) 'Lachmann's policy activism: an Austrian critique
    of Keynesian proclivities', in Koppl, R. and Mongiovi, G. (eds) *Subjectivism and Eco-
    nomic Analysis: Essays in Memory of Ludwig M. Lachmann*, London and New York: Rout-
    ledge.
Cagan, P. (1956) 'The monetary dynamics of hyperinflation', in Friedman, M. (ed.)
    Studies in the Quantity Theory of Money, Chicago: University of Chicago Press, pp.
    25–117.
Garrison, R.W. (1986) 'From Lachmann to Lucas: on institutions, expectations, and
    equilibrating tendencies', in Kirzner, I.M. (ed.) *Subjectivism, Intelligibility, and Economic
    Understanding: Essays in Honor of Ludwig M. Lachmann on his Eightieth Birthday*,
    Houndsmills: Macmillan Press, pp. 87–101.
Hicks, J. (1939) *Value and Capital*, Oxford: Clarendon Press.
Hoppe, H.-H. (1997) 'On certainty and uncertainty, or: how rational can our expecta-
    tions be?', *Review of Austrian Economics*, 10(1): 49–78.
Kantor, B. (1979) 'Rational expectations and economic thought', *Journal of Economic
    Literature*, 17(4): 1422–41.
Keynes, J.M. (1930) 'A treatise on money', in Moggridge, D. (ed.) *The Collected Writings
    of John Maynard Keynes*, London: Macmillan, 1973, vols V–VI.
—— (1936) 'The general theory of employment, interest and money,' in Moggridge, D.
    (ed.) *The Collected Writings of John Maynard Keynes*, London: Macmillan, 1973, vol. VII.

Koppl, R. (1998) 'Lachmann on the subjectivism of active minds', in Koppl, R. and Mongiovi, G. (eds) *Subjectivism and Economic Analysis: Essays in Memory of Ludwig M. Lachmann*, London and New York: Routledge.

Lachmann, L.M. (1938) 'Investment and costs of production', *American Economic Review*, Sept: 469–81, reprinted in Lavoie, D. (ed.) (1994) *Expectations and the Meaning of Institutions*, London and New York: Routledge, pp. 42–56.

—— (1939) 'On crisis and adjustment', *Review of Economics and Statistics*: 62–8, reprinted in Lavoie, D. (ed.) (1994) *Expectations and the Meaning of Institutions*, London and New York: Routledge, pp. 76–87.

—— (1940) 'A reconsideration of the Austrian theory of industrial fluctuations', *Economica*, VII: 179–96, reprinted in *Capital, Expectations, and the Market Process* (1977), Kansas City: Sheed Andrews and McMeel, Inc., pp. 267–87.

—— (1943) 'The role of expectations in economics as a social science', *Economica*, X(37): 12–25, reprinted in *Capital, Expectations, and the Market Process* (1977), Kansas City: Sheed Andrews and McMeel Inc., pp. 65–80.

—— (1945) 'A note on the elasticity of expectations', *Economica*, 12, Nov., reprinted in Lavoie, D. (ed.) (1944) *Expectations and the Meaning of Institutions*, London and New York: Routledge, pp. 124–30.

—— (1947) 'Complementarity and substitution in the theory of capital', *Economica*, 14, May, reprinted in *Capital, Expectations, and the Market Process* (1977), Kansas City: Sheed Andrews and McMeel, Inc., pp. 197–213.

—— (1948) 'Investment repercussions', *Quarterly Journal of Economics* Nov.: 698–713, reprinted in Lavoie, D. (ed.) (1994) *Expectations and the Meaning of Institutions*, London and New York: Routledge, pp. 131–44.

—— (1949) 'Investment repercussions reply', *Quarterly Journal of Economics* 63(3): 432–4.

—— (1954) 'Some notes on economic thought, 1933–1953', *South African Journal of Economics*, 22, reprinted in *Capital, Expectations, and the Market Process* (1977), Kansas City: Sheed Andrews and McMeel, Inc., pp. 133–48.

—— (1956) *Capital and its Structure*, Kansas City: Sheed Andrews and McMeel, Inc.

—— (1958) 'Mrs Robinson on the accumulation of capital', *South African Journal of Economics*, 26, June, reprinted in *Capital, Expectations, and the Market Process* (1977), Kansas City: Sheed Andrews and McMeel, Inc., pp. 214–34.

—— (1976) 'From Mises to Shackle: an essay on Austrian economics and the kaleidic society', reprinted in Lavoie, D. (ed.) (1994) *Expectations and the Meaning of Institutions*, London and New York: Routledge, pp. 229–40.

—— (1978) 'An interview with Ludwig Lachmann', *The Austrian Economic Newsletter*, 1(3).

—— (1982) 'Why expectations matter', *The Investment Analyst Journal*, 20: 9–15, reprinted in Gloria-Palermo, S. (ed.) (2002) *Modern Austrian Economics: Archeology of a Revival*, vol. 1, *A Multi-Directional Revival*, London: Pickering & Chatto.

—— (1986) *The Market as an Economic Process*, Oxford: Basil Blackwell.

Lange, O. (1944) *Price Flexibility and Employment*, Bloomington, IN: Principia Press.

Lewin, P. (1994) 'Knowledge, expectations, and capital: the economics of Ludwig M. Lachmann', in Boettke, P.J. and Rizzo, M.J. (eds) *Advances in Austrian Economics*, vol. 1, Greenwich, CT: JAI Press.

Loasby, B. (1998) 'Ludwig M. Lachmann: subjectivism in economics and the economy', in Koppl, R. and Mongiovi, G. (eds) *Subjectivism and Economic Analysis: Essays in Memory of Ludwig M. Lachmann*, London and New York: Routledge.

Lundberg, E. (1930) 'Om begreppet ekonomisk jämvikt och dess tillämpning', *Ekonomisk Tidskrift*, 32: 133–60; trans. as 'The concept of economic equilibrium', in Lundberg, E. (1994) *Studies in Economic Stability and Change*, Stockholm: SNS Förlag, pp. 13–47.

——— (1937) *Studies in the Theory of Economic Expansion*, Stockholm: Stockholm Economic Studies.

——— (1950) 'Om ekonomiska expansionens stabilitet', *Ekonomisk Tidskrift*, 52: 196–215; trans. in *International Economic Papers* (1958), 8: 45–64.

——— (1957) *Business Cycles and Economic Policy*, London: George Allen & Unwin Ltd.

——— (1959) 'The profitability of investment', *Economic Journal*, 69: 653–77.

——— (1968) *Instability and Economic Growth*, New Haven, CT: Yale University Press.

——— (1994) *Studies in Economic Instability and Change*, Henriksson G.H. (ed.) Stockholm: SNS Förlag.

——— (1996) *The Development of Swedish and Keynesian Macroeconomic Theory and its Impact on Economic Policy*, Raffaele Mattioli Foundation, Cambridge: Cambridge University Press.

Mises, L. von (1943) 'Elastic expectations and the Austrian theory of the trade cycle', *Economica*, X, August: 251–2.

Myrdal, G. (1933) 'Der gleichgewichtsbegriff als instrument der geldtheoretischen analyse', in Hayek, F.A. (ed.) *Beiträge zur Geldtheorie*, Vienna: Julius Springer, trans. from German with some modifications, *Monetary Equilibrium* (1939), London: W. Hodge & Company.

von Neumann, J. and Morgenstern, O. (1944) *Theory of Games and Economic Behavior*, Princeton, NJ: Princeton University Press.

Robinson, J. (1956) *The Accumulation of Capital*, London: Macmillan & Co.

Röpke, W. (1933) 'Die sekundäre Krise und ihre Überwindung', in *Essays in Honour of Gustav Cassel*, London, pp. 553–67.

Shackle, G.L.S. (1938) *Expectations, Investment and Income*, Oxford: Oxford University Press.

——— (1949) *Expectations in Economics*, Cambridge: Cambridge University Press.

Savage, J. (1954) *Foundations of Statistics*, New York: Wiley.

Siven, C.-H. (1991) 'Expectation and plan: the microeconomics of the Stockholm School', in Jonung, L. (ed.) *The Stockholm School of Economics Revisited*, Cambridge: Cambridge University Press, pp. 141–66.

Torr, C. (1986) 'Convergent and divergent expectations', in Kirzner, I.M. (ed.) *Subjectivism, Intelligibility, and Economic Understanding: Essays in Honor of Ludwig M. Lachmann on his Eightieth Birthday*, Houndsmills: Macmillan Press, pp. 295–300.

14 Have the Swedish and the Austrian Schools influenced the French School?

Gilles Jacoud

Introduction

Until the end of the nineteenth century, economic theory relied on a dichotomous analysis, studying real phenomena in a framework without any money or introducing the latter only to show that it merely influences the absolute level of prices with no real effects. The publication of the *General Theory* in 1936 put an end to the hegemony of the dichotomous analysis and granted money a decisive part in economic mechanisms.

Nevertheless, the success of Keynes's major work should not obscure the fact that the renewal of the economic analysis had already begun long before this publication. In the last years of the nineteenth century Knut Wicksell started to call into question the dichotomous reasoning as he analysed the economic phenomena directly in their monetary form.[1] With the continuation of his work by authors such as Bertil Ohlin, Gunnar Myrdal, Erik Lindahl or Erik Lundberg, one could speak of the existence of a *Swedish School*.

The continuation of Wicksell's work is not limited to the Swedish authors. In Austria, Ludwig von Mises takes part in it from 1912 onwards.[2] And especially with the publication of *Prices and Production*[3] in 1931, Friedrich Hayek reinforces the calling into question of the dichotomous analysis and it is then registered as part of the *Austrian School* contribution.

France is not outdone by this movement which leads to a challenge to traditional analysis and to substitute for it the integration of money into the functioning of economic mechanisms. Two authors, Albert Aftalion and Bertrand Nogaro, embarked on new paths which permitted a consideration that the renewal of the economic analysis had also been provided by a *French School*.[4]

As the contribution of the Swedish school may quite easily be related to that of the Austrian School – one should bear in mind that Wicksell attended Eugen Böhm-Bawerk's lectures in Vienna when the latter developed his theory on capital and also conversely, as Mises and Hayek relied on the Swedish economist's work – the possible influence of the Swedish and Austrian authors on the

French School needs to be proved. The aim of this chapter is thus to show how the emblematic authors of the French School may have been influenced by the Swedish or Austrian authors, or, on the contrary, they may have developed an independent analysis. The first part will be devoted to Albert Aftalion's analysis, the second will be devoted to Bertrand Nogaro's.

Albert Aftalion's analysis

Albert Aftalion (1874–1956), Professor of Economics in Lille, then in Paris, is considered as one of the brightest French economists of his generation.[5] After several works – of which a book on the over-production crisis where in 1913 he exposed the mechanism which will become popular under the name of accelerator,[6] he devoted himself to the study of the relations between money circulation, the level of prices and the exchange rate. He published several articles on the evolution of the internal and external values of money[7] before his major work *Monnaie, prix et change*[8] was first published in 1927. These works led him to confront the Swedish economist, Gustav Cassel, and to continue the theory of the Austrian author, Friedrich von Wieser. First, for Cassel, in fact, price variations determine those of the exchange rate, which is contested by Aftalion who observes the opposite relation. Second, according to him, the understanding of the mechanism through which exchange influences prices comes about through the acceptance of Wieser's income theory. But finally Wieser's theory appears to be insufficient in the case of high increases in prices and Aftalion substitutes the taking into account of expectations.

The rejection of the theory of purchasing power parity by Gustav Cassel

Considered as derived from the quantity theory of money, the theory of purchasing power parity is denied by the facts.

From quantity theory of money to the theory of purchasing power parity

The theory of purchasing power parity was expressed for the first time by Cassel in an article in 1916.[9] The formula 'purchasing power parity' appears in a second article by the author in 1918.[10] According to this theory, the exchange rate of a currency compared to another one is determined by the relation of the purchasing power of these two currencies. If prices increase in country number one while they remain unchanged in country number two, the exchange rate will be modified. Imports from country number two to country number one will particularly be favoured whereas exports will be penalized. On the currency exchange market, the fall in country number one currency demand, compared to that of country number two, will decrease its rate.

This theory is perceived as a mere continuation of the money quantity theory. According to the latter, price variations are due to quantity variations of the money in circulation. Therefore, variations in money circulation – as they affect prices, that is to say internal purchasing power of money – have repercussions on the exchange rate. So Cassel considers that since the general level of prices varies proportionally to the quantity of money in circulation in a country, the exchange rate between two countries varies such as the ratio of the quantities of money circulating in each country.[11] This is precisely what Aftalion questions.

A theory denied by facts

In his 1924 article 'La circulation, les changes et les prix',[12] which title foreshadows that of his 1927 book, Aftalion realizes a series of statistical observations which lead him to reject Cassel's theory. Neither the quantity theory nor the theory of purchasing power parity can be validated by the facts during the 1914–21 period. And in 1922–23, the nine countries which are studied are reduced to three types of situation which refute Cassel's theory: stable prices and exchange rate in spite of an increase in money circulation, an increase in prices and exchange rate with no increase in money circulation, a drop in exchange rate and prices with no substantial drop in money stock.

Several studies by Aftalion in 1925 and 1926 bring new arguments against the causality relation upheld by Cassel.[13] He notices that

> logically if one supports quantity theory it implies that one also supports purchasing power parity theory. But facts deny such a hypothesis. And this denial bounces against quantity theory itself. But prices rather, in these recent times, follow the exchange rate.[14]

If one notices some levelling between the variation of the internal value of a currency and the external value of this currency,[15] this is not therefore because internal prices affect the exchange rate. Aftalion explains this as he relies on Wieser's income theory.

Adoption of Wieser's income theory

Going back to Wieser's income theory, Aftalion is able to show why it is the exchange rate which affects prices.

Wieser's income theory

According to Wieser – Aftalion grants him the most remarkable income theory[16] – the value of goods is founded on the importance each individual gives to the last unit he owns. Money value follows this principle with two particularities, however. First of all, the importance given by the individual to the last money unit does not depend on its direct utility, as it has none, but on its indirect utility, that is to say the utility of the goods it allows one to buy. Then, the last money unit of an individual corresponds to the last unit of his income. As the density of needs decreases as they are fulfilled, the higher the income, the lower the value of this last unit. Each individual has therefore an estimation of money based on the amount of his income, and from all the individual estimations one gets the social value of money.

So, the increase in individual incomes leads to a drop in money value. The variation of the general level of prices therefore reveals a variation in money value due to that of incomes. This approach allows Aftalion to explain why variations in exchange rates are not determined by those of the price level but, on the contrary, they affect this level.

Exchange rate effect on prices

Wieser does not take exchange rate into account as a possible source of income increase and he denies a possibly noticeable influence of exchange rate on internal prices. On the contrary, Aftalion explains the increase of prices through the direct action of the exchange rate on incomes. An increase of the exchange rate – considered as the increase of the quantity of national currency exchanged with a foreign currency – in fact increases the income of various agents. Importers who store goods which were paid before the increase make gains as they sell them at their new importation price. Foreign security holders receive gains in national currency when they are paid coupons or securities. The result is the same for the foreigners who, as they live in the country, get their income from abroad. Exporters' income rises automatically. A modification in exchange rate favours moreover export development, and in this way it contributes to an increase in national income. Aftalion even thinks of an income increase due to a flood of foreigners attracted by the attractive cost of living in the wake of a currency value depreciation. All the increases of income influence a movement of increase of internal prices and allow Aftalion to conclude that price variations are due to exchange rate variations.

Nevertheless, this explanation is limited. Thus, Aftalion notices that at the time of the German hyperinflation, the exchange rate action is almost immediate. 'The general increase in prices is so sudden that it can be seen long before incomes increase and before they have consequences on prices'.[17] Aftalion must then go beyond the previous analysis and he has to correct Wieser's theory.

Psychological theory of money and expectations

Aftalion turns Wieser's income theory into a psychological theory of money.[18] As he transfers this theory to the exchange rate, he makes the exchange rate depend upon agents' expectations.

Psychological theory of money

Because he explains price variations through a proportional income variation, Wieser attaches too much importance to quantity variations, whereas Aftalion sees the necessity of attaching importance to quality, psychological factors. According to Aftalion, one cannot estimate money only from the goods one has just bought with the last unit of income:

> Individual estimations do not depend on the satisfaction *from the exchange* of the last money unit of the income, but they do depend on the satisfaction one *expects* to get through it, the satisfaction everybody is *eager to obtain* from the last money unit of his income.[19]

These quality factors which operate in any individual estimation on money depend on each individual's psychology. Money satisfies needs without being exchanged for goods, when it is meant for donation, savings or building up of capital. Therefore, two individuals who are not similarly inclined to spend it or to keep it, will estimate it in a different way.[20] Each individual does not expect the same results from exchange either, and thus, with the same income, two individuals do not spend their money with the same aptitude. But even if these elements influence the price level, it is mainly estimates on the future money value which explain their variation. For instance, when individuals foresee a depreciation in money value, they immediately depreciate the value they give to it and spend it as they consume, leading thus to a price increase.

Thus, the psychological theory of money leads to the determining role of expectations in money internal variation. As he transfers this theory to exchange rate, Aftalion proposes a new exchange rate theory.

Expectations and exchange rate

As he takes expectations into account, Aftalion can therefore explain why an increase of exchange rate may immediately generate a price increase, even before the consecutive mechanisms of an income increase have started. Economic agents, who have learned from past experience, know in fact that a change in the exchange rate will eventually have repercussions on prices. As soon as they notice a decrease in the national currency compared to foreign currencies, they

anticipate the increase of prices and they act on it so that it comes true.[21] Therefore 'any new money depreciation seems to forecast a real internal depreciation.
And the latter then follows the former'.[22] In this way, even before the income
amount has time to increase, 'money value decreases because everybody is convinced it has to decrease'.[23] Expectations become self-fulfilling. 'Price increase,
money depreciation take place directly and immediately, influenced by forecast-
ing.'[24]

The role of expectations is not limited to the internal value variations of
money. In the same way that Aftalion explains the internal value through a psychological theory of money, he also explains its external value and he sets up a
psychological theory of the exchange rate.[25] The utility of each money unit
owned by an individual 'decreases as the number of units increases. The law of
decreasing utility fits here like somewhere else'.[26] What everybody expects from
currency units is not necessarily related to a commercial operation. The demand
of foreign currencies is highly related to speculative behaviours and expectations
precisely play a decisive part in the exchange rate determination.[27]

Eventually, if one agrees with André Marchal that 'Stockholm School economists
were in fact Cassel's students'[28] and that the latter had long been 'the only Swedish
economist read in France',[29] one has to admit the lack of influence of the Swedish
School on one of the most distinguished representatives of the French school.
Aftalion challenges Cassel and he ignores Wicksell among others. But his questioning of the quantity theory of money and his development of money and exchange
rate are an extension of Wieser's theories. The Austrian influence may also be
detectable in other papers where Aftalion relies on Böhm-Bawerk in particular,[30]
but it does not, however, question the originality of the French economist's work.
As Georges-Henri Bousquet notes, 'If Aftalion is thus a disciple of the Austrian
School to a certain extent, it is not in an orthodox way at all.'[31]

Bertrand Nogaro's analysis

Bertrand Nogaro (1880–1950) had his viva in Paris in 1904 and became an economic sciences *agrégé* teacher in 1908. He was a staff officer during the First
World War, then a Deputy from 1924 to 1934 and the National Education
Minister in 1926. He devoted himself to research again from 1935 onwards. He
regretted, according to Jean Marchal, that those different breaks in his university
life had gone against the deepening and the spreading of his work.[32] His early criticism of quantity theory, at a time when the latter was hardly questioned, makes
him, however, an innovative economist whose writings, together with Aftalion's
ones, allow us to speak of a French School.

Nogaro's work – which took place before he had political responsibilities – is
widely devoted to monetary questions. First, he develops a new approach to

monetary phenomena which leads him to contest the quantity theory in order to stand up for the existence of the influence of money on the economic activity. Second, his other writings, from the end of the 1930s onwards, are more diversified. However, he keeps to a method based on facts which leads him to challenge many of his predecessors and contemporaries.

A new approach to monetary phenomena

The viva Nogaro had in 1904 dealt with *Le rôle de la monnaie dans le commerce international et la théorie quantitative*.[33] It contained an argument on the quantity theory which is extended by Nogaro in different articles in 1906[34] and 1908,[35] and especially in his book published in 1924 *La monnaie et les phénomènes monétaires contemporains*.[36] Nogaro shows that facts sometimes catch out the quantity theory and that money action is not limited to the mere level of prices.

Facts against quantity theory

Like Aftalion, Nogaro bases his studies on observation of facts. Some striking periods in money history – such as the rise in prices in the sixteenth century or the fall of the *assignats* during the French Revolution – seem to confirm quantity theory. Such is the case every time prices and money circulation both follow the same movements. But the concomitance of phenomena does not mean that there is a causality relationship. A rise or a fall in prices may be due to non-monetary factors, for instance, due to production variations or to the evolution of competition between firms.

Moreover, the facts observed after the First World War deny the quantity theory. The example of Germany thus brings several denials. In 1921, 'one can see the increase in prices getting ahead of the growth of circulation',[37] whereas according to quantity reasoning, circulation acts on prices. In 1922, compared to a base of 100 in 1919, prices reach the index 18,377, whereas the quantity of money in circulation only reaches the index 2,587, denying in this way the assertion according to which prices and money quantity vary in the same proportions. In 1923, 'between February and April, circulation has nearly doubled and prices have rather fallen',[38] an observation which tends to deny the idea of a variation in the same direction of both money and prices.

This denial by facts allows Nogaro to reject a quantity theory which makes money a mere commodity with a value which varies inversely to its quantity.[39] Through quantity theory, it is the dichotomous analysis which is questioned, an analysis which appears as if exchanges were made without money, then 'as if the exchanges, once over, would cause a demand for money'.[40] Thus Nogaro reiterates his 1906 criticism of an analysis which reasons on an initial exchange of goods within themselves, while such an exchange does not take place, then on 'a demand of instrument of exchange which is done to nobody and which is meant for nobody'.[41]

Nogaro does not stop at a criticism of quantity theory and dichotomous analysis. He also considers that money may influence economic activity.

The influence of money on economic activity

Not only is any price variation not the consequence of a change in the total amount of money in circulation, but any variation of the latter does not always have repercussions on prices. Nogaro analyses the effects of an increase in the amount of money on the commodity demand. If demand increases, following an additional amount of money perceived by people, prices will not automatically increase. Indeed, firms may react to the additional demand and thus increase their production: 'an additional supply echoes an additional demand'.[42] The adjustment is thus done by quantities and not by prices. The additional demand may even generate a decrease in prices if 'the increase of production decreases cost prices because of either a better employment of people, or a better share of the work, or technical improvements or because of production concentration'.[43] The increase in money quantity may thus not generate an equivalent increase in prices, but it may boost economic activity.

Thus Nogaro is very aware that banks putting money into circulation may stimulate supply as well as demand. As they grant credits:

> banks put into circulation some quantity of money which would not circulate without their intervention and therefore they increase the demand of goods. But as they allow firm managers to get equipment, raw materials, staff, they favour production, then goods supply, causing later in this way, a factor of fall in prices.[44]

From then onwards, far from the consequence of price increase, the additional money in circulation 'may give birth to real richness'.[45]

The relevance of the quantity theory is then brought back to a particular situation where the variation in the money stock causes a corresponding variation in the demand without any increase in production.

Nogaro's analysis is more profoundly developed in a book he published in 1945 *La monnaie et les systèmes monétaires*.[46] As he takes into account the monetary dimension of exchange, it leads him to reject Say's law. Indeed, if the building of capital may lead the sale of a product not to offer an outlet to another product, conversely 'a newly created money represents a demand which does not result from a supply of goods'.[47] His criticism of the quantity theory mainly relies on the fact that the latter does not see that the money created is likely to modify the exchange relations between goods:

A new quantity of money introduced in economy is spread over different markets which are unevenly receptive to the action of supply and demand: hence some inevitable changes in exchange relations. Moreover, one part of it goes to the money market where its flood, far from creating an increase, tends to lower the interest rate and hence the costs, while it is favouring the production development. *So it is not only the equilibrium of prices which is put into question, but that of production.*[48]

If the 1945 book deals again with the same arguments as the 1924 book, it is, however, difficult to consider it as the main reference to grasp the originality of Nogaro's analysis. Indeed, between the two dates, economic theory has greatly improved and Nogaro's ideas have, in the meantime, given birth to important developments. The publication in 1931 of *Prices and Production* by Friedrich Hayek and especially the *General Theory* by John Maynard Keynes in 1936, limit its impact, even if the 1945 book develops an analysis which had already been put forward some twenty years before.[49]

Nogaro's analysis – just like that of the Swedish and Austrian Schools – does not want to understand economic phenomena without taking into account their monetary dimension. Nevertheless, Nogaro develops independent research besides these two schools. In his writings on money, the only reference to the Swedish authors is found in a few pages he devotes to the criticism of Cassel's exchange rate theory. Wicksell is neither mentioned in the 1924 book, nor in the re-issue of 1935, and he is only evoked in footnotes in the 1945 book.[50] Admittedly, the Austrian authors do not seem to influence Nogaro either.[51] If he ignores them in the first part of his work, he then tends to dissociate himself from them in his further writings on the method of political economy.

A method based on facts

As he gives priority to facts, Nogaro is led to face the deductive method and to reject the marginalism of Menger and his followers.

The primacy of facts

Nogaro deals with the methodology of the political economy in several books published after his first work on monetary phenomena.[52] As he considers political economy first of all as a science of observation, he wants it to rely on the study of facts.[53] He goes against

> deductive theorists, who, as they rely on the strength of their reasoning, only refer to facts when they think they are going to find a proof of their *a priori* conceptions, and prefer to ignore them in the opposite case.[54]

The typical example of the deductive method is represented by the approach of Menger, who had not only claimed that economic phenomena obeyed general and constant laws, but that it was up to 'economic science to elaborate them, depriving in the meantime economic reality of its concrete forms'.[55] Ludwig von Mises's position is even more contrasted: he denies the observation method is able to elaborate the economic theory, as experiment is not possible in economics, so observation can only rely on past facts and does not allow any valuable conclusion to be claimed without any limitation of time or place.[56] Nogaro denies this point of view as he shows that when an economic phenomenon has been noticed, it can then be represented in a logical frame where time and place circumstances do not influence its determination.

The authors of the Austrian School do not have the monopoly on the deductive method and Nogaro considers the Swede Cassel as 'one of the most remarkable specimens of the deductive spirit'.[57] The latter not only ignores facts but he is accused of 'a real rigging'[58] of figures so that they may suit his conclusions. 'Thus Professor Cassel uses an arbitrary construction'[59] to make the gold production curve coincide with that of prices during the first half of the nineteenth century, while in fact the rising gold production goes together with a fall in prices.

Nogaro also regrets an over-use of the deductive method in different fields. The explanation of cyclic crisis is thus justified, without any reference to observation, through money quantity variations. Nogaro refers to Wicksell and Hayek in particular as they claim they have discovered the reason for economic crisis in interest rate variations.[60] Opposed to the deductive method, Nogaro is led to reject the marginalism of the Austrian School.

The criticism of marginalism

If marginalism appears in the works of Stanley Jevons, Léon Walras and Carl Menger, Nogaro mainly relies on the latter and his followers in his criticism of marginalism.[61] The criticism of the deductive method concerns marginalism, since it relies on this method, even if it is not the only stream to adopt it. And the Austrian School has not only led economic sciences towards abstract reasoning, but it has drifted away from theory to observation:

> The boost given to abstract political economy study by Carl Menger's *Volk-swirtschaftslehre* has not been followed only by his immediate disciples, von Böhm-Bawerk and von Wieser. Those two had then several followers and some of them continue with their teaching at Vienna University . . . Whereas Carl Menger's immediate disciples had tried to conciliate the master's doctrine with observation data, the new marginalists try to complete the theory of marginal utility as they develop it abstractly, without worrying about the proof of the premise of their reasoning.[62]

Nogaro attacks in particular two postulates of marginalism. The first is 'the existence, in the spirit of the economic subject, of a scale of subjective values, and hence the existence of a *scale of utilities*'.[63] He rejects this postulate, as he asserts that there is no strict hierarchy in needs which allows a scale of utilities to be defined. Determining value from the marginal utility equals considering that the value of production factors is determined by that of the produced goods. Nogaro also rejects this second postulate which consists in denying the cost of production.[64] According to him, 'it is the price of capital goods which acts on the supply price of the products, and through repercussion on the demand price, which is often an adhesion price. It is the old theory which is, on this point, right'.[65]

As he refuses to adhere to those basic postulates, Nogaro nevertheless admits some merits of marginalism. It starts in particular from a true observation of the decrease in utility. But Nogaro rejects an explanation of value based on mere marginal utility, far removed from the data on observation which are no longer taken into account by the new marginalism adherents. He regrets that 'in spite of the real talent of some of them, the new marginalists will finally elaborate, with the abstract logic of their reasoning, a scholastic lost in the abstract'.[66]

Conclusion

The renewal of economic analysis at the beginning of the twentieth century, particularly based on the questioning of the dichotomous analysis, is thus studied by French authors who – like their Swedish or Austrian colleagues – try to integrate money into economic mechanisms. If those authors, and Aftalion and Nogaro are among the most striking figures, can be grouped under the name of 'French School', to use Marchal and Lecaillon's phrase,[67] what is this French School position compared to the Swedish and Austrian Schools? First, Aftalion and Nogaro situate themselves in relation to Swedish and Austrian economists of the first generation. Cassel is rejected by the two authors because of his conclusions and his method. As far as the Austrian are concerned, Carl Menger, Eugen von Böhm-Bawerk and Friedrich von Wieser inspire the two French economists in a different way: Aftalion continues some of their works whereas Nogaro is far more critical. On the contrary, Aftalion and Nogaro's writings nearly ignore the work of their Swedish and Austrian contemporaries. Knut Wicksell or Ludwig von Mises are not mentioned at the time when the French authors deal with quantity theory of money. This statement reveals the originality of the French economists who – several years before the publication of *Prices and Production* by Friedrich von Hayek or of the *Treatise* and the *General Theory* by John Maynard Keynes – show the influence of money on economic activity. This relative ignorance of the work of their Swedish and Austrian contemporaries coupled with some misappreciation of their own work by foreign economists explain why Aftalion and Nogaro will be undervalued for a long time.

Notes

1 Even if Wicksell publishes *Über Wert, Kapital und Rente* in 1893 (English translation under the title *Value, Capital and Rent*) and *Finanz-theoretische Untersuchungen* in 1896, it is mainly with *Geldzins und Güterpreise* published in 1898 (English translation in 1936 by Macmillan under the title *Interest and Prices*) that he became famous, theorizing the relation between the monetary rate of interest, the natural interest rate and the general level of prices. His analyses are completed in various articles and in a fourth book, *Vorlesungen über Nationalökonomie* (first published in Swedish into two volumes in 1901 and 1906, then translated into German in 1913 and 1922 then into English in 1934 by Routledge and Kegan under the title *Lectures on Political Economy*).

2 *Theorie des Geldes und der Umlaufmittel*, 1912, Munich and Leipzig: Duncker and Humbolt; English translation in 1934 by Jonathan Cape under the title *The Theory of Money and Credit*.

3 *Preise und Produktion*, English translation by Routledge.

4 In the second part of their *Théorie des flux monétaires* (1967) devoted to the founders of modern monetary analysis, Jean Marchal and Jacques Lecaillon dedicate a whole chapter to this 'French School' (pp. 241–85).

5 See Bousquet *et al.* (1945). See also the papers presented at the *Journée d'études sur Albert Aftalion* organized by the Social and Economic Sciences Faculty of the University of Lille 1, 19 October 2001, published in *Albert Aftalion: Redécouverte d'un économiste français du XXᵉ siècle*, Paris: L'Harmattan, *Cahiers lillois d'économie et de sociologie*, April 2003.

6 *Les crises périodiques de surproduction*, Paris: Rivière, 1913, 2 vols.

7 The main part of his reflection may be found in a series of articles which were published from 1924 to 1926 in the *Revue économique internationale* and in the *Revue d'économie politique*.

8 *Monnaie, prix et change* (1927). A new edition, published in 1940, is reproduced in a two-volume work on *La valeur de la monnaie dans l'économie contemporaine*. The first volume corresponds to *Monnaie, prix et change* whereas the second, entitled *Monnaie et économie dirigée*, is based on what Aftalion observes in France from 1940 onwards. The editions of 1927 and 1948 are used here.

9 'The Present Situation of the Foreign Exchanges', *Economic Journal*, 26, March 1916.

10 'Abnormal Deviations in International Exchanges', *Economic Journal*, 28, December 1918. If this article and that of 1916 led him to credit Cassel with the theory, Joseph Schumpeter notices that other authors had already mentioned the formula ([1954] 1983: 460, vol. 3). Aftalion, who mainly relies on Cassel's writings, admits the elements of this theory 'already lay in those of the classical English school' (Aftalion, 1927, 1948: 428).

11 Cassel 1916: 62.

12 *Revue économique internationale*, 1, February 1924: 256–86.

13 'Les expériences monétaires récentes et la théorie quantitative', *Revue d'économie politique*, 1925, 39, May–June: 657–85; 'Les expériences monétaires récentes et la théorie du revenu', *Revue d'économie politique*, 1925, 39, July–August: 813–29; 'Les expériences monétaires récentes et la théorie psychologique de la monnaie', *Revue d'économie politique*, 1925, 39, September–October: 1009–31; 'Prix, circulation et change en France de 1920 à 1924', *Revue d'économie politique*, 1925, 39, November–December: 1248–56; 'Existe-t-il un niveau normal du change?', *Revue économique internationale*, 1925, 4, December: 423–50; 'Les théories dominantes du change; Etude critique', *Revue d'économie politique*, 1926, 40, May–June: 769–95; 'La

circulation, les changes et les prix: Les expériences de 1924–1925 et leur enseignement', *Revue économique internationale*, 1926, June: 506–36.

14 'Existe-t-il un niveau normal du change?', 1925: 443.

15 This admission of a parity tendency allows Michel Rainelli to show that if Aftalion
refutes the theory of purchasing power parity, on the contrary, he admits the unique
price law (Rainelli 1986).

16 *Monnaie, prix et change*, 1948: 236.

17 *Monnaie, prix et change*, 1927: 197.

18 Introduced in 1925 ('Les expériences monétaires récentes et la théorie psychologique
de la monnaie'), this theory is developed in the second part of *Monnaie, prix et change*.

19 'Les expériences monétaires récentes et la théorie psychologique de la monnaie',
1925: 1019, formulation taken up again in *Monnaie, prix et change*, 1927: 208.

20 Only the tendency to savings is taken into account in Aftalion's first papers on this
subject, whereas in the reprinting of *Monnaie, prix et change*, he differentiates whether
one is inclined to liberal donation, savings or building up of capital. Moreover, he
adds a behaviour of inertia – referred to as 'the fidelity to former estimations in
money unit' – and he increases from three to six the number of quality factors of
money value.

21   Sellers, when foreign exchange rate is increasing for example, immediately raise
their prices. And buyers follow as well, because they have learnt by experience,
and they also tend to depreciate from then onwards the money unit as they
foresee its nearby depreciation.

(*Monnaie, prix et change*, 1948: 273)

22 *Monnaie, prix et change*, 1927: 223.

23 Ibid.

24 *Monnaie, prix et change*, 1948: 280.

25 Presented in 1926 ('Théorie psychologique du change', 1926), this theory is
developed in the third part of *Monnaie, prix et change*.

26 'Théorie psychologique du change', 1926: 948–9.

27 On elements which rely on these expectations, one may refer to Bertrand Blancheton
(1998). See also Cécile Dangel and Michel Rainelli (2000). One can also see two
papers presented at the *Journée d'études sur Albert Aftalion* organized by the Social and
Economic Sciences Faculty of the University of Lille 1, 19 Octobre 2001, published
by L'Harmattan (*Albert Aftalion: Redécouverte d'un économiste français du XXᵉ siècle,
Cahiers lillois d'économie et de sociologie*, April 2003): Cécile Dangel-Hagnauer, 'La
théorie marginaliste de la monnaie et des changes d'Albert Aftalion' (2003); and Flo-
rence Huart and Philippe Rollet, 'Albert Aftalion et les théories du change à long
terme' (2003).

28 'Les principaux courants de la pensée économique suédoise contemporaine', *Revue
d'économie politique*, 1947, 62: 66.

29 Ibid.

30 The Austrian authors' influence may be found in Aftalion's work on the three notions
of productivity, in recurring over-production crisis and in socialism foundations. See,
on this subject, Georges-Henri Bousquet, 'Albert Aftalion et l'école psychologique
autrichienne', in: *L'œuvre scientifique d'Albert Aftalion*, 1945: 67–79.

31 Ibid.: 78.

32 Marchal and Lecaillon, *Théorie*, p. 243.

33 *Le rôle de la monnaie dans le commerce international et la théorie quantitative*, 1904.

34 'Contribution a une théorie réaliste de la monnaie', *Revue d'économie politique*, 1906, 20.

35 'L'expérience bimétalliste du XIXe siècle et la théorie générale de la monnaie', *Revue d'économie politique*, 1908, 22.

36 *La monnaie et les phénomènes monétaires contemporains*, 1924. This book has been translated into English, King's edition, in 1927 under the title *Modern Monetary Systems*.

37 *La monnaie et les phénomènes monétaires contemporains*, 1924: 158.

38 Ibid.

39 On the refusal of money assimilation to a commodity in Nogaro's work, see Jérôme Blanc (2000).

40 *La monnaie et les phénomènes monétaires contemporains*, 1924: 159.

41 'Contribution à une théorie réaliste de la monnaie', 1906.

42 *La monnaie et les phénomènes monétaires contemporains*, 1924: 163.

43 Ibid.

44 Ibid.: 167.

45 Ibid.

46 *La monnaie et les systèmes monétaires*, 1945.

47 Ibid.: 243.

48 Ibid.

49 The slightest innovative side of Nogaro's analysis seems to be already in the Preface to the second publication of the 1924 book, published in 1935.

> The conclusions of this work, apparently exposed twenty years earlier, would have been considered as subversive by many people. Now, as far as the immediate interpretation of facts was concerned, it suited the conceptions of some foreign economists, who had been following the same paths for some time, and also with some notions which began to spread in France.
>
> (*La monnaie et les phénomènes monétaires contemporains*, 1935: 9)

50 In the first footnote (p. 158), Nogaro refers to Wicksell's theories and refers, for their discussion, to Charles Rist's book (*Histoire des doctrines relatives au crédit et à la monnaie depuis John Law jusqu'à nos jours*) and to Louis Baudin's book (*La monnaie et la formation des prix*). In another footnote (p. 198), he quotes Wicksell on the *encaisse désirée* mentioning *Interest and Prices*.

51 Beside the references to Menger (p. 119, p. 198), the 1945 book refers in footnotes to Mises (p. 8, p. 198) and to Hayek (p. 158).

52 *La méthode de l'économie politique*, 1939; *Principes de théorie économique*, 1943; *Cours d'économie politique*, 1943; *Le développement de la pensée économique*, 1944; *La valeur logique des théories économiques*, 1947.

53 On the method recommended by Nogaro, see Anne-Marie Chartier (2000). See also the book by L. Baudin *et al.* (1950).

54 *La valeur logique des théories économiques*, 1947: 37.

55 *La méthode de l'économie politique*, 1950, 195.

56 Ibid.: 197–8. Nogaro here refers to Mises's 1933 book, *Grundprobleme der Nationalökonomie*.

57 *Le développement de la pensée économique*, 1944: 319.

58 *La méthode de l'économie politique*, 1939: 153.

59 Ibid. Nogaro speaks moreover of the 'skilfully rigged graph by Cassel' (*Cours d'économie politique*, 1947, 4th edn, vol. 1: 401) and reveals the argument developed by the Swedish author to avoid the verdict of facts (*La valeur logique des théories économiques*, 1947: 37).

60 *Le développement de la pensée économique*, 1944: 321.

61 Nogaro considers that Jevons and Walras are mainly concerned with setting equations and that they roughly justify their progress (*Le développement de la pensée économique*, 1944: 219). That is why he mainly exposes the contribution of the Austrian School in the chapters he devoted to marginalism in several of his books (in particular, Chapter 10 in *Principes de théorie économique*, on 'Le coût et l'utilité comme fondements de la valeur', Chapter 3 in the second part of *Cours d'économie politique*, on 'Théorie de la valeur', Chapter 6 on 'L'école de Vienne et le marginalisme', in *Le développement de la pensée économique*, and Chapter 8 in *La valeur logique des théories économiques*, on 'La théorie marginaliste de la valeur').

62 *Le développement de la pensée économique*, 1944: 318.

63 Ibid.: 229.

64 On the analysis of the denial of those two postulates, see Henri Guitton, 'Le heurt de la pensée de M. Nogaro avec la pensée marginaliste', in L. Baudin *et al.* (1950: 79–100).

65 *Le développement de la pensée économique*, 1944: 233.

66 Ibid.: 237.

67 (1967: 241–85).

References

Aftalion, A. (1913) *Les crises périodiques de sur production*, Paris: Rivière, 2 vol.

—— (1924) 'La circulation, les changes et les prix: les expériences de 1922–1923 et leur enseignement', *Revue économique internationale*, 1, February: 256–86.

—— (1925a) 'Les expériences monétaires récentes et la théorie quantitative', *Revue d'économie politique*, 39, May–June: 657–85.

—— (1925b) 'Les expériences monétaires récentes et la théorie du revenu', *Revue d'économie politique*, 39, July–August: 813–29.

—— (1925c) 'Les expériences monétaires récentes et la théorie psychologique de la monnaie', *Revue d'économie politique*, 39, September–October: 1009–31.

—— (1925d) 'Prix, circulation et change en France de 1920 à 1924', *Revue d'économie politique*, 39, November–December: 1248–56.

—— (1925e) 'Existe-t-il un niveau normal du change?', *Revue économique internationale*, 4: 423–50.

—— (1926a) 'Les théories dominantes du change: étude critique', *Revue d'économie politique*, 40, May–June: 769–95.

—— (1926b) 'Théorie psychologique du change', *Revue d'économie politique*, 40, July–August: 945–86.

—— (1926c) 'La circulation, les changes et les prix: les expériences de 1924–1925 et leur enseignement', *Revue économique internationale*, June: 506–36.

—— (1927) *Monnaie, prix et change*, Paris: Sirey.

—— (1948) *La valeur de la monnaie dans l'économie contemporaine*, Paris: Sirey, 2 vols.

Baudin, L. *et al.* (1950) *L'œuvre scientifique de Bertrand Nogaro*, Paris: Domat Montchrestien.

Blanc, J. (2000) 'Questions sur la nature de la monnaie: Charles Rist et Bertrand Nogaro, 1904–1951', in Dockès, P. *et al.* (eds) *Les traditions économiques françaises 1848–1939*, Paris: CNRS Editions, pp. 259–70.

Blancheton, B. (1998) 'Albert Aftalion, précurseur de la théorie moderne du change', *Revue d'économie politique*, September–October, 108(5): 711–28.

Bousquet, G.-H. *et al.* (1945) *L'œuvre scientifique d'Albert Aftalion*, Paris: Domat Montchrestien.

Cassel, G. (1916) 'The present situation of the foreign exchanges', *Economic Journal*, 26, March.

—— (1918) 'Abnormal deviations in international exchanges', *Economic Journal*, 28, December.

Chartier, A.-M. (2000) 'Bertrand Nogaro ou la recherche problématique de l'indépendance de l'économiste', in Dockès, P. *et al.* (eds) *Les traditions économiques françaises 1848–1939*, Paris: CNRS Editions, pp. 65–79.

Dangel, C. and Rainelli, M. (2000) 'Albert Aftalion, théoricien de la monnaie et des changes', in Dockès, P. *et al.* (eds) *Les traditions économiques françaises 1848–1939*, Paris: CNRS Editions, pp. 247–58.

Dangel-Hagnauer, C. (2003) 'La théorie marginaliste de la monnaie et des changes d'Albert Aftalion', paper presented at the *Journée d'études sur Albert Aftalion* organised by the Social and Economic Sciences Faculty of the University of Lille 1, 19 October 2001, published in *Albert Aftalion: Redécouverte d'un économiste français du XXe siècle*, Paris: L'Harmattan, *Cahiers lillois d'économie et de sociologie*, April.

Huart, F. and Rollet, P. (2003) 'Albert Aftalion et les théories du change à long terme', paper presented at the *Journée d'études sur Albert Aftalion* organised by the Social and Economic Sciences Faculty of the University of Lille 1, 19 October 2001, published in *Albert Aftalion: Redécouverte d'un économiste français du XXe siècle*, Paris: L'Harmattan, *Cahiers lillois d'économie et de sociologie*, April.

Lecaillon, J. and Marchal, J. (1967) *Théorie des flux monétaires*, Paris: Cujas.

Marchal, A. (1947) 'Les principaux courants de la pensée économique suédoise contemporaine', *Revue d'économie politique*, 62: 65–111.

Nogaro, B. (1904) *Le rôle de la monnaie dans le commerce international et la théorie quantitative*, Paris: M. Giard.

—— (1906) 'Contribution à une théorie réaliste de la monnaie', *Revue d'économie politique*, 20.

—— (1908) 'L'expérience bimétalliste du XIXe siècle et la théorie générale de la monnaie', *Revue d'économie politique*, 22.

—— (1924) *La monnaie et les phénomènes monétaires contemporains*, Paris: M. Giard, English trans. *Modern Monetary System*, London: P.S. King, 1927.

—— (1939) *La méthode de l'économie politique*, Paris: LGDJ.

—— (1943) *Principes de théorie économique*, Paris: LGDJ.

—— (1944) *Le développement de la pensée économique*, Paris: LGDJ.

—— (1945) *La monnaie et les systèmes monétaires*, Paris: LGDJ.

—— (1947a) *Cours d'économie politique*, Paris: Domat Montchrestien, 2 vols.

—— (1947b) *La valeur logique des théories économiques*, Paris: PUF.

Rainelli, M. (1986) 'Loi du prix unique et théorie de la parité des pouvoirs d'achat: un retour à G. Cassel, A. Aftalion et J. Viner', *Revue d'économie politique*, 96(1): 25–38.

Schumpeter, J. (1954) *Histoire de l'analyse économique*, Paris: Gallimard, 1983, 3 vols.

Part VI

Methodology

15 Hayek's and Myrdal's stance on economic planning

Robert Nadeau

Introduction

It is an understatement to say that, if not as economists, at least as social scientists and, more generally speaking, as political thinkers, Hayek and Myrdal did not place themselves on the same side of the fence. It is perhaps in order to ensure an 'ideological equilibrium' that both were granted the *Sveriges Bank Prize in Economics in Commemoration of Alfred Nobel* the very same year (1974). One can of course find convergent views between the two theorists on several theoretical and methodological questions, but it seems indisputable that they took opposite stands on the question of the efficiency and overall legitimacy of state interventionism in the social and economic order. It is precisely this opposition that I wish to discuss here. In what follows, and for want of sufficient space, my aim will not be to assess in full detail each of the two views. I will content myself with comparing and contrasting Hayek's and Myrdal's analyses – which will of course seem highly polarized – to show first of all what exactly makes these two approaches completely different, but also, and maybe more importantly, to delineate in each case, from an epistemological and methodological perspective, what may be seen as analytical strengths, on the one hand, and inhibitory weaknesses, on the other.

In what follows, I will be reviewing both Friedrich Hayek and Gunnar Myrdal on a central and crucial question: the question of state planning and central regulation of the economy, as both a theoretical possibility and a political reality, is perhaps the most important problem that economics, as a theoretical discipline, has to deal with. As we shall see, Hayek and Myrdal again addressed this question from quite different angles. Be that as it may, both of them came to grips with intricate matters related to this problem, and each articulated a system of arguments which may not evidently clash bluntly, but which can nevertheless be reconstructed as two stages of a 'dialectic', i.e. a discussion – or 'conversation' – where, if we are presented with a thesis and an antithesis, we can purportedly still be searching for a synthesis. I will first expose Hayek's contribution to the controversy opposing those who, like himself, favor market economy over any kind of centrally planned economy. Here I will try to articulate what seems to be a purely *theoretical* argument with a very different one, the evolutionary argument, which has to be qualified as an *empirical* one. I will then expose Myrdal's explanation and justification of the working of state intervention and planning in western capitalist countries. We will here and there be in a position to appreciate Myrdal's views as clearly conflicting with Hayek's ideas, even if never explicitly and with documented evidence. From this comparison, philosophers of economics and historians of economic thought will hopefully learn something valuable.

Hayek on socialist economy

Let us first recall that it was in 1920 that Ludwig von Mises launched the controversy that was to be known afterwards under the general heading of the 'Socialist Calculation Debate' (Mises 1920).[1] As was said from then on, although quite inaccurately, Mises tried in that article to show the 'impossibility of socialism'.[2] Formulated this way, Mises's analysis was rather easily rejected in the 1930s because it was the dominant perception that the existing Soviet Union was empirical proof that socialism was not only possible, but that it represented the optimal solution to the economic problem at a time when all western capitalist countries were profoundly despairing of ever coming out of the slump in their completely depressed economy.[3] But what Mises was in fact arguing, not on empirical but on theoretical grounds, was that rational economic calculus is impossible in socialist states as long as there are no market prices to work with in the decision process (especially for rational decisions concerning higher order or capital goods).[4] Hayek accepts Mises's thesis and especially the Misesian approach to the problem: for him the question is first of all theoretical, it deeply concerns economics as a science and it can be solved by way of scientific arguments and reasoning (Hayek's words are '*a priori* reasoning' Hayek 1935c: 90).[5]

I completely agree with Bruce Caldwell (Caldwell 1988a, 1988b: 74–5) that it is precisely within the conceptual and theoretical framework of this particular debate on the possibility of socialist calculation that Hayek definitively breaks with the standard equilibrium approach to the market economy and finds out that the central problem of economics is related to the complex question of social coordination. From the Hayekian standpoint, this problem cannot be solved without articulating a genuine theory about the role and use of knowledge in society.[6] This forms the hard core of what I will call the Hayekian *theoretical* argument. But one can find a very different kind of argument in Hayek, i.e. an evolutionary argument. I will characterize this argument as the Hayekian *empirical* argument. Hayek first exposed the essential elements of this genuine argument systematically in *Law, Legislation and Liberty* (see, especially, Hayek 1973). But in

Hayek's last book (Hayek 1988), socialism is still appraised from this evolutionary standpoint, and as such is considered by Hayek to be *the* major problem not only of economic theory but also, more globally, of western civilization itself. In that book, published four years before the Soviet Union collapsed, Hayek showed himself to be absolutely confident that economic analysis could prove that socialism was not only a social blunder and a political failure, but above all a formidable scientific error. My reading of Hayek's work is that this evolutionary argument has to be linked to the first argument, which is of a more theoretical nature as far as economics is concerned. Indeed, while the evolutionary argument puts forward a completely different conceptual framework tightening the theoretical argument, it first of all displaces the gist of Hayek's claim against socialism. By calling attention to facts concerning the global process of cultural evolution, typically analyzed by Hayek as a struggle or competition between moral traditions where the most efficient social and economic orders will dominate all the others and win the competition, Hayek now grounds on empirical evidence his argument stating the superiority of the competitive economy over the planned economy. This is to say that, when interpreted systematically, Hayek comes through as trying to prove on theoretical *and* empirical grounds that the market economy is evolutionarily superior to any kind of socialist economy (centrally planned economy, market socialism, partially planned market economy). Methodologically speaking, Hayek is very explicit about the scientific nature of this question. This is not to say that Hayek does not equally approach this problem from a philosophical and sociological standpoint, for it is indisputable that by way of careful analysis he also tries to show socialism to be a moral, political and social disaster. But I would like to argue in the following sections that, while the theoretical argument seems quite sound, the empirical argument, which, it must be said clearly, is plainly consistent and compatible with the theoretical argument, seems to be at least partly inconclusive.

The theoretical argument

In a centrally planned socialist economy, where private ownership of the means of production has been abolished (this is the standard definition which both Mises and Hayek use), there is no market for production and capital goods – and if there is no market, then there are no real economic prices, for this kind of price can only be fixed within an exchange-based economy.[7] As a logical consequence of this, it is said that no rational economic decision is possible, for such rational decisions relative to production can only be grounded on the consideration of all available options and all situational constraints, and, with that in hand, on the calculation of opportunity costs. But why the debate here? This view gave rise to an important historical debate because this argument, first articulated by Mises, was criticized and rejected by economists such as Oskar Lange (1936) and Henry

Dickinson (1933), who found that 'market socialism' was a possibility (and a real one, at least for the consumption process) and that it offered an adequate solution to the legitimate problem raised by Mises. Instead of letting markets fix the prices, it was considered that the market process could be *simulated* in order to identify 'accounting' (i.e. book-keeping) prices. This simulation would be done, following Dickinson, using general equilibrium theory (the technical work would simply involve finding an algebraic solution to the problem of a complicated system of simultaneous equations) in order to ensure that, on all markets, supply would equal demand, but also that prices would equal average marginal costs. This gave rise to the 'computation problem'.[8] Robbins (1932) and Hayek (1935c) argued that a precise economic calculus of this kind was in fact infeasible mathematically speaking because it would rapidly prove to be too complex.[9] Then Lange put an end to this controversy by propounding what was to be called the 'competitive solution'. In that approach to the calculation problem, the economist, theoretically simulating the working of the real market by working by trial and error, would progressively, using accounting prices only as first approximations, come to know the effective clearing prices, anticipating in his planning what the right level of economic activity would have to be if supply were in fact to equal demand in each and every market.

For Oskar Lange (Lange and Taylor 1936–37), the socialist calculation problem could be divided into two separate parts, each related to one precise dimension of the market process. Because the market operates to fix prices, then there is a problem with the real nature of prices. Lange clearly thinks that Mises is completely misguided when he holds that market prices are necessary here. But Lange's demonstration seems to Hayek (see Hayek 1982) to be too thin and superficial to be really convincing. Nevertheless, to Lange's mind, because Robbins (1932) and Hayek (1935c) had theoretically presupposed the very possibility of a socialist calculus, if only to target its extreme practical complexity, the only problem left seemed to concern the allocation of rare resources to alternative goals, a problem that the market process was again said by Mises and Hayek to solve optimally. Lange then argued that a 'Central Planning Board' (CPB from now on) would do a better job, as it would proceed by trial and error but would have access to more complete information than any isolated individual capitalist entrepreneur. Lange's argument boils down to the following reasoning:

> The economic problem is a problem of *choice* between alternatives. To solve the problem three data are needed: (1) a preference scale which guides the acts of choice; (2) knowledge of the 'terms on which alternatives are offered'; and (3) knowledge of the amount of resources available. Those three data being given, the problem of choice is soluble.
>
> (Lange 1936: 60)

Hayek does not contest Lange's right to frame the question this way. Hayek does indeed accept that, given data of type 1, 2 and 3, then the 'socialist calculation problem' can be solved because this would mean that there is a rational way to choose between alternative ends. But the problem is not actually solved by Lange, according to Hayek, because there is no argument in Lange's line of reasoning to prove that the needed data themselves can be known to the CPB. The question is exactly the following for Hayek: who has access to that knowledge? If the necessary knowledge to make rational economic choices is radically dispersed between actors on a market, we cannot take for granted that there will exist a mechanism that will put all this dispersed knowledge together as if it could be aggregated in a central super-brain. Even if we supposed that type-1 data were unproblematic because the CPB would eventually fix the scale of preferences itself or would observe what the preferences were on the market, the same cannot be said of type-3 data. Defining the overall quantity of resources needed for the economy to work properly is possible only if one can represent resources objectively by using precise volume numbers of commodities that can be technologically transformed into other commodities. But Hayek stresses that the very notion of 'resource' is tricky: it is a *subjective* notion and not an objective one, as Lange seems to think. A resource is clearly something inside an individual 'plan of action', and resources, forming the 'terms of the alternative' themselves, can only be defined by reference to a precise production function. Resources cannot be seen, as in Lange's analysis, as if they were stable, fixed, identifiable in advance without a production plan, i.e. as objective data which a CPB could add up globally and systematically put on a list as if they were simply physical entities. In fact, if we understand Hayek properly, we have to say that resources are 'intentional' entities.

What is at stake here is the notion of 'data' itself, and Hayek suggests that we should distinguish between two meanings of the word 'data:'

> It can be used legitimately either for the assumption, necessarily made hypothetically by the theorist, that certain facts exist which are not known to him, or for the assumption that particular facts will be known to specified persons and will have certain effects on their actions.
>
> (Hayek 1982: 55)

The first meaning is a thoroughly theoretical one: we always have to assume that certain facts exist, most of the time by hypothesis, in economics as in all other sciences. The 'data' we are talking about therefore refer to objective, albeit hypothetical, matters of fact in the world, with those putative facts explaining other observable ones. But the second meaning is a *practical* one: the data we are talking about in that instance are facts known only to particular individuals and they make up their 'subjective knowledge'. Following Hayek, Lange misses this conceptual difference and confuses the two kinds of data. It may be theoretically possible for a CPB to know or to suppose what the production functions are in a certain state of the national economy and, in this way, determine what the value of commodities is in that economy. Even if Hayek doubts the achievability or 'practicability' of this approach to the calculation problem, one can imagine that with proper means this can surely be done 'in principle' by having a super-computer solving thousands or even millions and billions of simultaneous algebraic equations, as intricate and complex this matter may be 'for the human mind', as Hayek writes. Nevertheless, this hypothetically successful computation does not give the CPB knowledge of any production technique that can be used in the process of transforming resources for the production of economic goods. This 'knowing how' as opposed to 'knowing that', a distinction that Gilbert Ryle made familiar to us, is 'tacit knowledge', a concept that Hayek borrows from Michael Polanyi (Polanyi 1951, 1969).[10] In any market economy, this knowledge is of a very peculiar kind, so that only the particular entrepreneur can be said to have this kind of knowledge, for it concerns the singular situation in which the entrepreneur finds him or herself. This knowledge is not the kind of knowledge that economists as theoreticians or social engineers can have or can formulate and discuss, for it is not conceptual, propositional or discursive knowledge. In the market economy, the entrepreneur possesses a local and situational knowledge which is necessary for the dynamics of the economy and which consequently cannot be dispensed with. It is easy to see that, if this is true, then socialist administrators acting as engineers of the economy and forming the CPB, cannot replace local entrepreneurs; it will simply not work. Entrepreneurs have to draw on, if not master, the precise technological knowledge that the production function requires. But more than that, they have to know the prices of the resources they need if they are to make rational decisions and opt for profitable courses of actions. This kind of knowledge can never be available globally to any state that would be economically directed and governed by a CPB. Hayek's argument, like Mises's argument, is a kind of impossibility theorem.

This is Hayek's epistemological argument, indeed a strong one, and it is a *theoretical* argument. In that context, Hayek uses ideas that, as indicated earlier, he borrows from Michael Polanyi and which I would like now to unfold more carefully. First of all, we have to concede that not all social and economic orders are alike and that there are some which are more robust and efficient than others as far as allocation of rare resources to fill diverse needs are concerned. As Polanyi has argued, more dynamic and efficient types of order are not *monocentric* but *polycentric*: these are strongly decentralized and form almost local orders, based on parameters that are unpredictable long in advance, but able to adequately solve the kind of problems that emerge in a particular situation (conjuncture problems). Such solutions are, for that matter, inevitably uncertain and temporary, and in no way general.

The nature of the problems we face in societies where economic development is based on commerce and industry are such that the more the economic order is decentralized, the more this order is robust and extended. But then these problems can only be solved by local actors acting on an individual perception of what the situation really is. The situational problems perceived by entrepreneurs are not at all theoretical ones and cannot be transposed into a mathematical model as though it were possible to represent them fully in all their parameters. This is precisely why Polanyi talks of 'tacit knowledge' to characterize this kind of situational awareness and rationality. This knowledge is not articulated in propositional formulas, it answers 'how to' questions and not 'why' questions: 'know how' knowledge, in contrast with 'know that' knowledge, is 'personal knowledge', as Polanyi liked to say. For that matter, it is usually transmitted only locally to persons living in analogous situations where, by imitation of what has already been done somewhere else, the know-how can be transposed fruitfully. Tacit knowledge concerns personal skills and takes time to acquire. It boils down to situational problem-solving and practical ways of thinking, perception rules and behavior principles that people living in groups or communities usually share. Tacit knowledge corresponds to rules and principles that people often follow without being aware of them, or even of why they follow them. People are unable to formulate those rules and principles, much less justify them, even if they were able to articulate them on a conscious level – which they are not. People only know whether the way they do things works appropriately or not. They can also know that, in the long run, those rule-governed behaviors normally give the kind of results they are looking for, proving that they are right. No one can predict whether the multiple practical skills out of which the local, and national, economy is emerging will be fruitful, and nobody knows whether people working their way out following those rules will prove to be better adapted to their situation. No one can know in advance for how long this will in fact be the case because it all depends on many contingencies. No one knows in advance what tomorrow will bring, what the needs will be and what the general situation will be.[11] The kind of knowledge each individual uses for his own and his family's purposes during his lifetime cannot be totally stated and stored somewhere. A CPB cannot work like a super-brain where all those personal skills can be collected and preserved as 'data'.[12]

Following Polanyi, Hayek consequently claims that, in order to be as efficient as possible or at least more efficient than any centrally planned economy, a social system taken as a whole has to be modeled as a system that has no proper center of operation:[13] the more numerous the interacting component parts of a dynamic social and economic system, the more cohesive, robust and productive the socio-economic 'spontaneous order' will be. According to this last argument, the quality of a social and economic order, its efficiency and endurance, are a direct function of the amount of reliable knowledge that millions of individuals living together are capable of using in making their own personal decisions. The more rapidly they can exchange information pertaining to what they wish, what they need and what they are ready to pay for, and especially in terms of opportunity costs, the more they can increase their understanding of the situation they and others find themselves in and, for that matter, the more they are able to produce economic *coordination* among themselves. Like Polanyi, Hayek's understanding of the market economy brings him to argue for the primacy of 'tacit knowledge' over speculative knowledge: for Hayek, it is in a sense unimportant to conjecture that individual economic agents and economists have the same 'model of the economy', as in the rational anticipations theoretical framework, because what matters is that agents and theoreticians do not have the same kind of economic knowledge.[14] As far as the efficient working of the economy is concerned, Hayek gives, by a large margin, prime importance to practical knowledge over theoretical knowledge, and priority to personal knowledge over a bookish sort of knowledge. This epistemological argument amounts to saying that, in all social sciences, one has to start from the fact that the building blocks of the structures whose functions we have to explain are human individuals possessing a certain amount of information which will cause them to act as they decide.[15] But this knowledge is not representational for any individual. Rather, it presents itself as skills, acquaintances or other kinds of personal knowledge, that is, as diverse rule-governed practices that individuals master to a certain degree, some being innate but many others being acquired through education or by cultural transmission and imitation. Most of this knowledge, formed by sets of unconsciously acquired rules of perception and action, is said to be 'tacit' because it is usually doomed to remain more or less inarticulate and not be explicitly formulated. This kind of knowledge is incorporated into very different systems of rules of perception and conduct, most of them being negative rules, and cannot be stored in a super-brain or any calculation device or machinery, as complex as it may be. As Hayek insightfully remarks:

> [s]uch spontaneous orders as those of societies, although they will often produce results similar to those which could be produced by a brain, are thus organized on principles different from those which govern the relations between a brain and the organism which it directs. Although the brain may be organized on principles similar to those on which a society is organized, society is not a brain and must not be represented as a sort of super-brain, because in it the acting parts and those between which the relations determining the structure are established are the same, and the ordering task is not deputized to any part in which a model is preformed.
>
> (1967b: 74)

The core of Hayek's theoretical argument against centrally planned economy is therefore that the very nature of the economic knowledge necessary for the market economy to work properly or as efficiently as possible in a particular conjuncture is by nature practical, fragmented, dispersed, local and inaccessible to anyone as a whole.[16] It surely cannot be held by a CPB such as the one socialists are dreaming of. This is why, as Hayek insists, it is absolutely crucial to see the difference 'between an order which is brought about by the direction of a central organ such as the brain, and the formation of an order determined by the regularity of the actions towards each other of the elements of a structure' (1967b: 73).

The empirical argument

What seems to be quite characteristic of Hayek's analysis of spontaneous social and economic order is that, as theoretical as it is from the start, when closely related to the socialist calculation debate, it cannot be completely articulated if we do not state the superiority allegation that is essentially tied to it. One can surely maintain, as John Gray does, that no moral value judgment is really at stake here (Gray 1984: 33–4; 118–25) but it is difficult not to see that Hayek's theoretical analysis serves to support a pre-eminence claim regarding the market economy. Let us try to be razor sharp here.[17] Asserting that competitive economy is and should be considered superior to centrally planned economy is *per se* a normative statement, but has nothing to do with ethics. Hayek overtly denies committing the genetic or naturalistic fallacy. He writes: 'I do not claim that the results of group selection of traditions are necessarily "good" – any more than I claim that other things that have long survived in the course of evolution, such as cockroaches, have moral value' (1988: 27). But this in no way means that Hayek denies *eo ipso* the evolutionary superiority of competitive economy over planned economy. As a matter of fact, Hayek also denies that the extended society was bound to take place in history: he explicitly considers that this economic system 'has not been deliberately invented, but that it has spontaneously grown up long before we had learnt to understand its operation' and he regards it as 'the result of a more or less accidental historical growth' (1941: 215). Nevertheless, Hayek undeniably sees 'the price system as the best one' (ibid.). Time and time again Hayek insists on the superior efficiency of capitalism over socialism. For instance, starting from the bare fact that '[t]he only known mechanism by which the knowledge of all can be utilized [is] the price mechanism' (Hayek 1939: 196), and being perfectly aware of the fact that sometimes the price system is inapplicable and is supplemented, he writes:

> The problem we are discussing is not, however, whether the price system must be supplemented, whether a substitute must be found where in the nature of the case it is inapplicable, but whether it ought to be supplanted where the conditions for its working exist or can be created. The question is whether we can do better than by the spontaneous collaboration secured by

the market, and not whether needed services, which cannot be priced and therefore will not be obtainable on the market, have to be provided in some other way.

(ibid.: 197)

It may be not clear if this argument can be characterized as a kind of 'invisible hand explanation'. It seems to be more akin to the kind of 'extremal' explanations one can find in evolutionary biology where it is considered that the best adapted organisms, i.e. the fittest, have a better survival rate than the others. One has nevertheless to ask whether this Hayekian optimality argument is plainly consistent with the evolutionary standpoint Hayek adopts. I will try to show that it is.

In the socialist calculation debate, we must remember that Hayek was facing opponents who aimed to establish 'that not only was central direction of economic activity practicable' but that it would even be 'superior to a system of competition' (Hayek 1935b: 71). From the start, then, the terms of Hayek's debate with socialist economists, and Mises's as well, were given a methodically comparative orientation. As stated previously, Hayek opposes the kind of order that results from an emergent evolutionary process to that which is 'rationally constructed' by human beings, for example, legislators. On that basis, Hayek's analysis of spontaneous social and economic order serves indeed to counter the arguments of 'constructivistic rationalism' (Hayek 1973: 8–11, 1979: xii) and undeniably includes as one of its essential elements the thesis that market economies are superior, as social orders, to all centrally planned economies. Preferring the term *catallaxy* to refer to competitive economy considered as a rule-based process and favoring the phrase 'rule of law' over *'laissez-faire'* to characterize the underlying mechanism at work in such a process, Hayek claims that this economic system has to be fully considered as a social spontaneous order because it is an evolutionary and unintentional process based on the price mechanism working in an appropriate institutional set-up.[18] Consequently, the resulting social and economic order is never intended as such, nor is it controlled by anyone. However, it can certainly be argued that the consequences of the actions of each and every individual taking part in the process are necessarily accounted for in its aggregate result. This analysis thus gives grounds not only for an argument in favor of free market economy but also, as I shall insist, against the very essence of the welfare state, and especially the Keynesian brand of the welfare state (Hayek 1995).

Basing himself on this discerning analysis of catallaxy, Hayek puts forward the theoretical claim that it manifestly forms a social order that is far superior to any kind of state-governed social and economic order. Hayek speaks here not only of economic superiority in terms of efficiently allocated resources, but also of social and political superiority in terms of the quality of life that such a free market-based economic order renders possible for the large majority of individuals. Hayek always maintained as a core thesis of his economic theory and of his political philosophy that a socialist economy, that is, a social order generated by an interventionist state and governed or regulated by a decision center, could lead to such undesirable results as limits to human rights and liberty – if not to complete serfdom (Hayek 1944, 1988).[19] The error of constructivistic rationalism is to take it for granted that a designed economic order will necessarily be superior to an unplanned one because it will be formed by and based on reason. But, as Hayek points out, reason itself is the product of evolution and should not be seen as capable of planning and directing evolution. More than that, economic planning by itself does not create order if by 'order' we mean, with Hayek,

> a state of affairs in which a multiplicity of elements of various kinds are so related to each other that we may learn from our acquaintance with some spatial or temporal part of the whole to form correct expectations concerning the rest, or at least expectations that have a good chance of being correct.
>
> (Hayek 1973: 36)

Human reason, and especially the individual minds of a small group of people, as inspired, wise, knowledgeable and thoughtful as they may be, cannot by itself achieve an order that is better than the one from which rationality itself progressively emerges. As one of Hayek's commentators has argued, '[O]n the contrary, by disturbing the regularities based on impersonal rules which are the product of evolutionary learning, rationalist social engineering results, if not in chaos, at least in unworkable or unnecessary coercive organizational structures' (Dobuzinskis 1989: 243).

Thus, Hayek's analysis ultimately presents itself as an *empirical* refutation of socialism. It is an overall scientific question: for Hayek

> [t]he notion that, in the last resort, the whole debate is a matter of value judgment and not of facts has prevented professional students of the market order from stressing forcibly enough that socialism cannot possibly do what it promises.
>
> (Hayek 1988: 8)

But the ultimate aim of the debate is not only to debunk the 'fatal conceit' of socialism, but also to support the general argument that a market economy is largely superior as an efficient socioeconomic order to any kind of planned economic order. Catallaxy is held to be pre-eminent because it is more efficient, and it is said to be more efficient because it is alleged that no central political organism can adequately replace or even simulate the market pricing process. Hence, a full-fledged spontaneous social order will always be economically preferable to a full-blown collectivist planned one. This is surely Hayek's understanding of what the whole socialist calculation debate was about (Hayek 1935a, 1940). He avowedly claims, not on moral but on theoretical and empirical grounds, that a resolutely interventionist state is bound to fail as the source of social and economic order: it could not only lead progressively to serfdom, but it could also ultimately cause the collapse of the whole economy. This argument has to be considered not only an integral part of Hayek's analysis but as its boldest claim. It is also probably its most disputable argument. It has indeed been submitted to fierce criticism (for instance: Dupuy 1988, 1992; Dobuzinskis 1989; De Vlieghere 1994; Jossa 1994; Lukes 1997; Steele 1994; Zappia 1999). It would seem, then, that if one adopts Hayek's evolutionary perspective, one cannot prove that a social order based on market processes is obviously the best possible order:

> If anyone assumes an evolutionary point of view, where the individuals have a severely limited knowledge about the environment and their own rules of conduct, there is simply no room for saying that anything similar to optimality exists in Hayek's world.
>
> (Petroni 1995: 119)

Indeed, if social and economic orders are plainly contingent, that is, if they are the unintended and unforeseeable products of evolution in a struggle for the survival of the fittest traditions, then the question of which is the optimal order is empirically undeterminable because we cannot predict which will outlast all others. If this holds, then advocating that market economies and liberal orders as we now know them are, on an absolute scale, the *best social and economic traditions there can be* is an untestable and thus normative claim, and can only be considered as the expression of an ideological preference. But this reconstruction of Hayek's argument misses the methodological point. First of all we should stress that the kind of evolutionary argument Hayek is using is part of what has been called by Gould and Lewontin the 'adaptationist program', but it has nothing to do with what they called the 'Panglossian paradigm'.[20] For as long as we compare, as ideal-types, the centrally planned economy, on one hand, and the competitive economy, on the other, that is, as long as we look at both to find out which has the comparative advantage over the other, and as long as we do not use any kind of absolute scale to compare their respective merits as social and economic systems, we can surely maintain, at least as a bold conjecture, that capitalism is superior in efficiency to socialism. This hypothesis has to be discussed on scientific grounds, considered for its explanatory robustness and its predictive power, if any, and judged at face value: it can surely not be dismissed from the start as logically flawed. From an evolutionary perspective, it could of course prove false: it is ultimately an empirical matter. As a scientific conjecture it is disputable, and refutable, on a conceptual and observational basis. It would clearly be a methodological blunder to reject it as intrinsically inconsistent or as logically incompatible with the socialist calculation theoretical argument. As such, these two Hayekian arguments form, in my view, both sides of one and the same coin.

Myrdal on the welfare state

I now come to Myrdal's views on economic planning, which are radically different from Hayek's ideas. Myrdal is not at all interested in discussing the respective merits of socialism and capitalism abstractly conceived as adversative or antithetical ideal-types. But perhaps can it be said first that Myrdal's main methodological ideas are not a completely different brand from the ones Hayek approves. For instance, the whole idea of sketching explanations in terms of 'principles' instead of 'factual details' (Hayek speaks of 'explanation by the principle' and Myrdal in terms of 'pattern models'), the idea of systematically putting together causal factors working on different levels, the idea of an emerging social and economic order that would be 'unintended' at least from the start if not after – all Myrdal's views – cannot seem strange from an Hayekian point of view. There is also, of course, Myrdal's idea of 'cumulative causality', i.e. of a 'holistic pattern' where causes and effects would interact together to produce observable social and economic situations, because it is akin to cybernetic theory, is not at all incompatible with Hayek's analysis of 'spontaneous order'.[21] Contrary to Hayek, Myrdal may be uninterested in methodological individualism as such but, like Hayek, he thinks that economics as a scientific discipline is about trying to understand the workings of the economy rather than predicting its future states. A 'pattern model' gives, for Myrdal, a kind of understanding that is bound to remain incomplete and indefinitely open to new empirical observations (Wilber and Harrison 1978). On economic methodology at least, Hayek, who aims at 'pattern predictions', and Myrdal, who looks for 'pattern models', seem to be on a par. But as far as economic theory is concerned, their stances seem to be diametrically opposed. This is easy to see if we follow the very detailed analysis of state intervention and planning Myrdal gives in his 1960 book on the welfare state. This is precisely what I propose to do now, if only through a much summarized and very roughly sketched account of Myrdal's analysis.

It should be said from the very beginning that Myrdal maintains quite explicitly in this book that the very notion of a 'planned economy' is a mere tautology 'since the word "economy" by itself implies a disposal of available means towards reaching an end or a goal' (Myrdal 1960: 3). The question is therefore not about planning as a matter of fact but about its historical causes and significance, its institutional workings and its consequences, good or evil, for the national and international economies. State intervention in the economy, which, for Myrdal, is relentlessly contrasted with the 'free economy' by interest groups and political parties, is a social and political reality that economic analysis has to cope with in order to understand and explain it fully. The whole 'free' versus 'planned' economy discussion thus becomes merely ideological, not factual, for Myrdal. This is a first and a very serious discrepancy between the viewpoints of Myrdal and Hayek. What is astonishing for Myrdal is that people in western capitalist countries – or what I will call, following him, 'Western Capitalist Welfare States' (hereafter WCWS) – generally remain unaware of the degree to which the economy they live in is regulated 'and how important national economic planning of a pragmatic, non-comprehensive type has in fact become' (ibid.: 11–12). Even if Myrdal nowhere refers to Hayek himself, one cannot doubt that Myrdal's analysis runs counter Hayek's doctrine. Myrdal writes:

> Anybody who makes a plea for the ideals of a 'free' economy and who then chooses to point out . . . how we are leaving those ideals behind us, and who from there goes on to characterize what we are indulging in as 'creeping socialism' and warns that we might be on the 'road to serfdom', can be sure of a sympathetic audience, particularly if he does not become too specific.
>
> (ibid.: 12)

Consequently, what is very characteristic of Myrdal's perspective is his 'declaration of non-participation' in the debate opposing proponents and defenders of a 'free' economy to the champions of a 'planned' one. This ideological debate is of no interest at all to Myrdal insofar as state intervention and planning are an indisputable fact and have to be understood and explained as such. Referring to his 1960 book, Myrdal writes: 'This book will deal with factual matters: how economic planning has actually developed in the Western world, what it now is, what its effects are for international relations, and what the prospects are for the future' (ibid.: 15).

State coordination of the market process

Myrdal indeed wants to be quite specific about what counts as state intervention and planning. The national economy of almost every western country has 'become increasingly regulated, organized, and coordinated, i.e. "planned", to an extent nobody would have dreamt of a century, or even half a century, ago', writes Myrdal in 1960. This planning process has all happened in a piecemeal and almost offhand way. As paradoxical as it may seem, state planning is the 'unplanned development' (i.e., the 'unintended result', as Hayek would put it) of state intervention (ibid.: 19).

> When in this inquiry I discuss the trend towards planning in the Western countries, I understand by the term 'planning' conscious attempts by the

government of a country – usually with the participation of other collective bodies – to coordinate public policies more rationally in order to reach more fully and rapidly the desirable ends for future development which are determined by the political process as it evolves. As a result of the historical origin of these attempts at planning, and of the institutional and political conditions under which they have operated in these countries, planning becomes pragmatic and piecemeal and never comprehensive and complete. As a rule, planning in these countries has the nature of compromise solutions of pressing practical issues. It has been gradually growing, and will in all probability continue to grow, in scope and in relative importance. A major force propelling this trend towards planning has been, and continues to be, the steady growth of the volume of state intervention requiring coordination.

(ibid.: 23)[22]

Myrdal is of course particularly aware of the fact that the industrial revolution, which is the remote cause of the typical working of our contemporary WCWS, was absolutely not the result of intended state planning aiming at accelerated economic development. Quite to the contrary, it was the result of 'the undirected and dispersed enterprise of individual entrepreneurs seeking to exploit new inventions for their own profit' (ibid.: 20), a crucial lesson classical liberalism has taught us. But because this historical process brought a crisis-ridden world, large-scale regulations and state undertakings had to be resorted to, something which began gathering speed with the second part of nineteenth century and especially during the twentieth century, with the two world wars and the 1929 crisis. It is therefore not surprising at all, following Myrdal, that 'no country today . . . is willing any longer to accept a level of economic activity and employment determined by the automatic repercussions, through the banking system, of changes in its international payments situation', or to put it another way, 'no country is prepared to abstain from interfering in the "free" economy', and 'no country is now in a position to allow monetary matters to remain outside economic policy – or even outside politics' (ibid.: 28).

Myrdal does not doubt that in many ways the unbroken succession of international crises during the first half of the twentieth century '[bears a major responsibility for the steady increase in the volume of state intervention in the economic life of the western countries' (ibid.: 30). But again, what is quite distinctive about Myrdal's analysis is that he identifies this rapidly increasing state intervention as one of the main forces – and maybe *the* main driving force – behind what he refers to as 'the trend towards economic planning'. The visible hand finally takes the place of the invisible one. Of course this has important consequences for the working of the market economy, and here Myrdal's analysis stands in sharp contrast to Hayek's approach. In a sense, to Myrdal, Hayek was fighting for an ideal model of the economy, the liberal economic theory of perfect competition, which had long faded away. But moreover, for Myrdal this classical theory had very strong presuppositions. In particular,

> [t]he society of which this theory was a very idealized rationalization . . . had to remain stubbornly unchanged. It was possible to conceive of such a rigid frame under the atomistic assumption of instantaneous movements of all the elements contained within this frame towards full adjustment.

For Myrdal, therefore, the main thesis of this theory was

> that *if* the economic units are infinitesimally small in relation to the size of the market, and if they do not act together, then no unit can by its own actions have any influence in the market . . . The markets and the prices were, therefore, to the individual, whether he acted as a buyer or a seller, independent variables, a set of objective and given conditions for his behavior. They were as entirely outside his control as the seasons and the weather, to which he had to adjust in order not to perish. Under the assumptions implicit in the model, the price formation in the market performed continuously and smoothly the 'function' of restoring equilibrium after every change of the primary conditions.
>
> (ibid.: 31)

This situation is no longer the case, according to Myrdal. The situation came to change completely precisely because the individual units 'have found the means by which to combine. They have thereby come into a position where they can influence the markets and manipulate the prices' (ibid.: 32). The markets have therefore progressively lost their characteristic of being spontaneous orders where prices present themselves purely as information signals to the individual economic actors: this is to say that '[t]he markets have become consciously "regulated" by the participants' (ibid.). So individual units in fact began long ago to cooperate in order to influence this market process and, 'going even further, to adjust the framework itself according to their own interests' (ibid.). The institutional reality that Myrdal is observing and, to my mind, putting forth against Hayek, is that all markets are manipulated these days. For that matter, many markets are at the present time completely dominated by one or very few sellers or buyers. And this is precisely the situation which compels the state to intervene. As Myrdal points out, '[s]ociety, faced with this illiberal trend, would become disorganized, if it stayed liberal and declined to intervene' (ibid.: 43). Large-scale interventions become absolutely necessary in order 'to prevent the actual disorganization of society, which would result from the organization of the individual markets, if this development were not controlled and coordinated' (ibid.: 33). Contrary to Hayek's approach, for Myrdal, state intervention and planning should not at all be seen as collective actions contradicting individualistic market-based economies. On the contrary, one of the main internal causes of the development towards a progressive increase in state intervention, at least in the economy of western countries, is the gradual breakdown of the competitive markets 'resulting from the technological and organizational developments and the sophistication of people's attitudes in regard to the economic processes in which they were participating as buyers and sellers of services and goods' (ibid.: 43). This is to say that, for Myrdal, state intervention and planning have to be understood as being there 'to suppress the trend to market organization and restore free competition' (ibid.: 43), which was done only with limited success. He insists that '[t]he main and important reaction by the state, however, has been instead to accept the trend, but to take such measures to regulate its course so that the public interest in both order and equity would be protected'. And Myrdal comes to the conclusion that 'thus a powerful but state-controlled infrastructure of collective organizations has come into being, beneath the constitutional frame of the state' (ibid.: 43–4), a reality which he calls 'the organizational State'. For Myrdal, state interference in economic life is in fact 'the inherited liberal ideal of fair play' which has been translated into the demand that wages, prices, incomes, and profits should be settled by various sorts of collective bargaining, with the organizational state providing bargaining conditions by way of legislation and administration and acting as a sort of umpire service so that agreements can be reached. This way 'a balance of strength between the buyers and the sellers in the market' (ibid.: 46) is established. And one can say that in WCWS '[a]ll prices and wages and, in fact, all demand and supply curves, are then in a sense "political"', which is enough to conclude, as Myrdal does, that '[w]e are as far away as possible from the "free market" of liberal economic theory' (ibid.: 46–7).

Planning the welfare state

Even if Myrdal's analysis strongly suggests – contrary to what a number of economists and historians of economic thought often claim, especially in the Austrian tradition – that the liberal epoch was never completely void of state interventions in and state regulations of the markets, he concurs with Hayek that the increasing state intervention and planning that came with the twentieth century 'raise a number of questions concerning constitutional law and administrative and political science' (ibid.: 56). But Myrdal mainly insists again and again that there is a world of difference between the classical liberal state and the modern organizational state. When we say that the rich countries of the western world slowly but surely became democratic 'welfare states', what we mean is that these countries made explicit commitments to the broad goals of economic development, full employment, equality of opportunity for the young, social security, and protected minimum standards as regards not only income, but nutrition, housing, health, and education for people of all regions and social groups.

(ibid.: 62)

Of course and noticeably, the welfare state is not presented by Myrdal as fully achieved but as an ongoing historical process: it is fundamentally true that the welfare state was in no country planned as such, but it is also factually true that for the last century the tasks of simplification, coordination, rationalization and achievement of efficiency of national economies were needed, and precisely this explains the kind of state planning we are now experiencing almost everywhere in the western world. Accordingly, Myrdal writes: 'The historical and causal order has been that acts of intervention in the play of market forces came first, and that planning then became a necessity' (ibid.: 62). In this process of social change, people's attitudes themselves became more and more 'rational', following Myrdal, so that 'a need for a rationalizing coordination of them all was pressed upon the state as the central organ for public will' (ibid.: 63).

It has to be seen that, for Myrdal as for Hayek, the crucial matter with regard to people's social and economic life in our WCWS concerns *coordination*. But instead of considering that almost all coordination problems can optimally be solved by the market process, as Hayek teaches us, for Myrdal:

Coordination leads to planning or, rather, it *is* planning, as this term has come to be understood in the Western world. Coordination of measures of intervention implies a reconsideration of them all from the point of view of how they combine to serve the development goals of the entire national community, as these goals become determined by the political process that provides the basis for power. The need for this coordination arose because the individual acts of intervention, the total volume of which was growing, had not been considered in this way when they were initiated originally.

(ibid.: 63)

Coordination at the state level means, for Myrdal, establishing short-term and long-run forecasts, but also, of course, it means voting policies for commerce, finance, development and social reform in light of these forecasts. Contrary to Hayek's idea of what state planning means in economic matters, for Myrdal it never means trying to shape a rigid and all-embracing plan. It only means that the state now finds itself responsible for influencing decisively – 'directly through its legislation and administration and that of the provincial and municipal authorities, or indirectly through the organizations in the infrastructure that operate under the state's indulgence and sanction' (ibid.: 65) – the conditions under which people can best work and earn their living. For instance, as cities grow, 'town planning' becomes more and more necessary (building activity, mortgage credit policies, ownership and renting regulations, etc.). This is what state intervention is about for Myrdal.

As Myrdal clearly argues, the strongest commitment to economic planning in our WCWS is to try to preserve full employment. Following the Keynesian revolution, economic theory came to place

> the responsibility for economic depressions and unemployment on an imbalance between aggregate demand and supply, opening up a rational way for the state to raise investment and production and to create employment simply by raising its expenditure while keeping down taxation.
>
> (ibid.: 68)

Myrdal presents this determination to preserve full employment as 'the crowning accomplishment of the democratic Welfare State' (ibid.: 69). The immediate consequence of that is that national budgeting came to be viewed as potentially influencing the trade cycle, even though discussion during the 1930s of a planned, counter-cyclical budgetary policy now appears clearly outmoded to economists. Certainly, '[t]he problems of public finance are now inseparably merged with problems of international trade and payments, wages and incomes, money and credit' (ibid.: 71). Nevertheless, state planning is the order of the day and accepted everywhere because, on the one hand, the distribution of taxes has a significant incidence on every western country's national economy, even when this distribution can be judged insufficiently efficient or inequitable, and because, on the other hand, the influence of public finances on the general business situation, be it national or international, is now widely acknowledged.

With what has to be seen clearly as increasing state planning of the market economy, the discussions like the one over the desirability of a social security net have ended (even the liberal Hayek, often seen as profoundly conservative, acknowledged the need for one).[23] But something else must immediately be added: the central tenet of socialist economic theory, i.e. nationalization and public ownership of the means of production, had to be revised and pragmatically put aside, so that nowadays even the social democrats in our WCWS accept that banks, insurance companies, and industries be privately owned. It is true that almost none of these organizations and enterprises are truly 'private' any more, for they are closely regulated by legislative and administrative controls, initiated primarily to safeguard the interests of the depositors, policy – and capital – holders, so that 'nothing much could be attained by their being taken over by the state' (ibid.: 74): 'As a matter of fact, all private enterprises in the advanced Welfare State are already in essential respects publicly controlled or are becoming so – without any nationalization of formal ownership' (ibid.: 77), so that even in the context of a capitalist and market economy, the industrial firm has to be seen as largely 'socialized' (ibid.: 75), i.e., concerned by equity and solidarity within the national community which is ensuring its economic growth and financial wealth. Something like a high degree of harmony of economic interests seems to be attained through cooperation and collective bargaining, a social process completely supervised by state regulation. If Myrdal's analysis can here be said to be in sharp contrast to Hayek's approach of state intervention and planning, it is because, as Myrdal insists, '[t]his gradual accomplishment of interests is not the old liberalistic one, which was supposed to emerge out of the unhampered working of free forces in the market' (ibid.: 79). Contrary to what Smith had in mind, public virtue and the nation's wealth are not the unintended consequences of private vices and individual undertakings: the invisible hand may be at work in the market process, but the coordination which is the social result of this working is itself a 'created harmony' (ibid.: 80), a market-induced coordination visibly based on state intervention and planned regulation. But, of course, this created harmony never was and is still not 'anybody's intention' (ibid.). *Planning was not planned originally*. It evolved progressively and increasingly, and is now overtly aiming to produce a purposive reorganization of the national and international market economy. But the historical process by which it came about was accidental, 'less direct and less purposive', writes Myrdal, 'by an unending sequence of acts of intervention by the state, and many other collective bodies, in the play of market forces' (ibid.). It should be understood that, as Hayek himself attempts to do, Myrdal's analysis, as divergent as it may seem from Hayek's, is also a tentative explanatory argument of economic coordination. However, while Hayek is satisfied with the explanation 'by the principle' of a highly abstract and *theoretical* mechanism, i.e. social and economic spontaneous order coming into existence through the working of the market process, Myrdal is rather concerned with understanding and precisely qualifying the kind of coordination we are in fact *empirically* observing in our national societies:

> In the same way as the 'created harmony' of interests in the Welfare State of the western countries was never planned, and thus never 'created' in the strict sense of having been purposively attained, so the actual large-scale planning, which is today a major explanation of the high degree of harmony that actually exists, has remained largely unprogrammatic.
>
> (ibid.: 82)

For Myrdal, only public policies regulating what goes on in the national economy, not unhampered forces playing freely in the market, can explain this observable coordination.

A methodological appraisal

One might contest the feasibility or merit of comparing Hayek's and Myrdal's stances on economic planning. For instance, one could perhaps hold that it is like comparing apples and oranges. Of course, if it were simply a question of taste, i.e. a question of esthetic, moral or ideological preferences, then an objective comparison would not be viable, at least not on scientific and methodological grounds. But if the comparison can be made from a social-science and especially from a theoretical-economic perspective, the endeavor is not only acceptable but may in fact be extremely valuable. The differences (intellectual but also moral and political) between the two thinkers are of course substantial, but there is no philosophical gap wide enough to prevent us from crossing from one side to the other. As a methodological point, it may be sound to espouse scientific neutrality if we are working as historians of thought or as sociologists of professional communities. But as philosophers of economics, this approach is neither sufficient nor profitable. We must reconstruct theoretical systems of ideas so as to render them as comparable as possible. Once this has been done correctly, we have to commit ourselves and take a stand, exactly as economists themselves end up doing as part of their own work. An appraisal is needed, and that is ultimately what is at stake here.

It should be noted that Hayek gives a precise definition of 'socialism' and of 'capitalism', and consequently of what exactly he is talking about. By 'capitalism' Hayek means 'a competitive society based on free disposal over private property' (1939: 205). On the other hand, Hayek is quick to identify 'socialism' with the idea of 'planning', not only to say that historically speaking socialism was identified from the start with central planning, but, as he writes in 1935, because 'in so far as the main economic problems are concerned, this is still the case today' (1935b: 61). Hayek is well aware of course that 'the method of collectivist ownership and control which is essential for any of these attempts to dissociate the distribution of income from the private ownership of the means of production admits of application in different degrees' (ibid.: 61–2). What is also very clear to him is that '[t]he method of planning in any case can certainly be used for purposes which have nothing to do with the ethical aims of socialism' (ibid.: 62), so that planning can just as well serve quite different if not opposite ends (tyranny and fascism, for instance). Furthermore, and as a central claim, Hayek upholds in a very Weberian fashion that '[o]n the validity of the ultimate ends science has nothing to say' (ibid.). But what for him is absolutely decisive is that, if such a planning method is going to be workable, there has to be a central authority which, in the end, even if the whole process is largely decentralized, has to decide what the principles for the distribution of income will be. Hayek furthermore sees as a *necessary condition* of this planning method that this central authority work as a unique and exclusive mind;[24] perhaps even be 'some single individual' (Hayek 1939: 205), and keep steady and rigorous control over all resources.[25] For Hayek, this is completely intolerable because '[t]here can be no freedom of thought, no freedom of the press, where it is necessary that everything should be governed by a single system of thought' (ibid.: 218). Be that as it may, for Hayek the only question which should concern economists as social *scientists* is the question of whether planning is the best method to obtain the desired social and economic results without provoking at the same time deleterious unintended consequences. To quote him again:

> the fundamental question is whether it is possible under the complex conditions of a large modern society for such a central authority to carry out the implications of any such scale of values with a reasonable degree of accuracy, with a degree of success equaling or approaching the results of competitive capitalism, not whether any particular set of values of this sort is in any way superior to another.
>
> (Hayek 1935b: 62–3)

Hayek considers that the monopolistic tendencies of the market economy 'have in fact been fostered by interventionist measures', for example, 'tariff protection with respect to the formation of cartels' (ibid.: 81–2).[26] In contrast, Myrdal sees our WCWS as closely regulated, and points out that 'free enterprise [is moving] within a frame set by a fine-spun system of controls, which are all ultimately under the authority of the democratic state' (Myrdal 1960: 84). Policy structures in such fields as international commerce and exchange, taxation, labor legislation, social security, education, health, defense were implemented everywhere and can be said to be, economically and socially, 'a conspicuous success' (ibid.: 86). Myrdal is of course presenting the welfare state's capitalist economy and he is not at all discussing the practicability of a centrally planned or socialist economy. On the other hand, Hayek was for his part interested in discussing not only market socialism *à la* Lange, Dickinson and Dobb, but also planning within the framework of capitalism (see, in particular, Hayek 1939). He does not do so systematically because it is not his first concern. Nonetheless, Hayek does not have tender words for what we now call the 'mixed economy' and, contrary to Myrdal, he is very critical of those who 'hope to "rationalize" the so-called chaos of free competition' (Hayek 1935c: 101). I must further emphasize that Hayek in fact distinguishes between two concepts of 'plan'. First, following Hayek, a plan is to be defined as

> a system of general rules, equally applicable to all people and intended to be permanent (even if subject to revision with the growth of knowledge), which provides an institutional framework within which the decisions as to what to do and how to earn a living are left to the individuals.
>
> (Hayek 1939: 194)

And Hayek is clear about the fact that 'this task of creating a rational framework of law has by no means been carried through consistently by the early liberals' (ibid.: 195). But this is precisely not the kind of plan Hayek intends to be discussing in the socialist calculation debate: the notion of a 'plan' occurs here in a second and much narrower sense, and for that matter Hayek would have preferred to use in this context the French term '*économie dirigée*'. In the context of the socialist calculation debate, planning refers to the economic process by which 'the central authority undertakes to decide the concrete use of the available resources' and in which 'the views and the information of the central authority govern the selection of the needs that are to be satisfied and the methods of their satisfaction' (ibid.: 196).

Pushing the comparison with Myrdal a little further, I must relate that Hayek blatantly proclaims that '[t]he world of today is just interventionist chaos' (Hayek 1935b: 67). This is not to say that for Myrdal state intervention and planning should be radically extended throughout our western democracies. In fact, Myrdal is very critical of such a political view. Indeed, in his 1960 book, he writes:

> I view as short-sighted those would-be reformers, both in the United States and in other Western countries, who, in their urge to improve society, place an almost exclusive trust in continual extension of state regulations, thereby presenting their fellow-citizens with a sort of 'etatistic liberalism'.
>
> (1960: 97)

Myrdal even grants that the welfare state has its failings, just as Hayek grants that there are limits to the market economy.[27] Yet Myrdal is not at all ready to admit that the failings of democracy in the welfare state, or in Russia, for that matter, can be caused by too much planning. In fact, one of Myrdal's central ideas is that the kind of state intervention and planning that was and still is going on in our WCWS has very little to do with Soviet-style planning. Referring to Russia, Myrdal writes:

> The planning which was clamped down after the revolution on that autocratic, poor, and backward country by a totalitarian and monolithic dictatorship is of a totally different nature from the compromise coordination of public policies which has gradually developed in the rich Western countries through a social process in which political democratization, the strengthening of provincial and local self-government, and the growth of an infrastructure of voluntary organizations have been essential elements.
>
> (ibid.: 105)

Contrary to the historical process of state intervention and planning in the western states, the Soviet way of building up an infrastructure implied 'the rule of a single, strongly disciplined political party, stretching out its close direction to every village and every workshop' (ibid.: 132). This is surely the kind of planning that Hayek, and Mises before him, were targeting and radically criticizing, and they were doing it as though, in a sense, all planned economies were alike. But for Myrdal this supposition is unwarranted, and Hayek's criticism leaves open the legitimate question of the nature of state intervention and planning in capitalist countries, its historical causes and its economic and social observable consequences, regardless of their desirability.

Myrdal is perfectly aware that the WCWS has a tendency to run into inflation. He writes: 'To accept an inflationary development without resistance would inevitably have undesirable results for the distribution of real incomes and wealth and for the direction of investment and production' (ibid.: 112). Nor does he consider state intervention to suppress or moderate inflation, and to restore a balance between aggregate demand and supply without a contraction of economic activity, to be problem-free: 'The spreading out of such direct state intervention into detailed regimentation results in all sorts of uneconomic misallocation of production and investment' – the very same argument that is made again and again by Hayek. Myrdal even adds:

> It endangers the standards of morality in business and in the government departments responsible for the controls. The political and economic brains in the governments and political parties, who should be engaged by the major problems of the national economy, become preoccupied with this petty tinkering. Their planning efforts become wasted in a rearguard fight against the price consequences of an inflationary pressure which they have not had the will and strength to prevent.
>
> (ibid.: 113)

Myrdal also acknowledges pretty clearly the unquestionable fact that under prevailing conditions and within the present institutional infrastructure in most WCWS, we are far from having found the solution to the problem of maintaining stable prices with full employment.

Another characteristic of Myrdal's analysis of economic planning is what he has to say about a third form of state intervention and planning, namely the one that defines the situation in the third world. Myrdal starts from the sociological fact that

> Economists now generally endorse the opinion that the underdeveloped countries need much more planning and state intervention if, under very much more difficult conditions than the now-developed countries ever faced, they are to have any chance of engendering economic development.
>
> (ibid.: 14)

But what predominantly characterizes Myrdal's analysis of state intervention and planning as compared to Hayek's is Myrdal's distinction between what he calls 'the three orbits' where this process of state intervention and planning has taken place. If WCWS constitute the first orbit and the Soviet Union the second one, developing countries constitute a third and distinctive orbit. Because '[g]reat poverty is a paramount fact in the underdeveloped countries' (ibid.: 121), Myrdal argues that those countries are to be studied as forming a very special case. Writes Myrdal:

> Indeed . . . it is unlikely that they will develop much, or at all, if the state does not from the outset take a much bigger responsibility for engendering development than was taken by the state during the industrial revolution in the Western countries.
>
> (ibid.: 121)

For him there is absolutely no hope that in developing countries industrialization will come about as 'the outcome of a cumulative process of spontaneous growth nourished by the enterprise of individual profit-seekers, exploiting new techniques to their own advantage' (ibid.). The very fact that those countries must apply planning from the initial stage of underdevelopment makes this process very different from the one that historically occurred in the western countries. In developing countries, the planning process is akin to Soviet planning, the significant difference being the great poverty level of third world countries.

This is to say that instead of 'pragmatic' and 'piecemeal' planning, the Soviet style of intervention in the national economy is a form of 'programmatic', 'comprehensive' and 'complete' planning. But in developing countries, planning is very different, and in a sense it is not even really a *directing* of economic activity. As Myrdal points out, 'None of these countries is even approaching the level of planning and overall economic state control which is common in all the Western countries' (ibid.: 123). But even when it is akin to the Soviet style of planning, the planning that goes on in the third world is different because most of these countries do not accept totalitarianism. They aspire to becoming and being democratic and welfare states, not authoritarian or dictatorial and monolithic states. Following Myrdal, this political aim sets quite narrow limits to the possibility of importing the Soviet style of state planning into these countries, where, in particular, private ownership and management of production and trade are maintained. As he writes, '[t]he offspring of this crossing is a breed of planning which is as different from the planning which has materialized in the Western countries as it is from the Soviet planning' (ibid.: 127). What is mostly characteristic of this kind of state planning is that the developing countries attempt 'to apply planning in advance of development' (ibid.), in order to create and put in place the very conditions of economic development. These conditions are intimately related to the building up of 'organs for self-government, and for collective cooperation and bargaining' (ibid.: 133) – the 'heart of the problem' for Myrdal. Whereas in the WCWS those organs have historically appeared slowly and spontaneously, growing up 'as a result of technological and psychological changes in the gradual development and then, in their turn, [adding] to all the other forces which were driving the state to intervention, coordination, and planning' (ibid.: 134–5), Myrdal insists that '[t]he fundamentally different problem facing the state in underdeveloped countries is that it will have to plan to build up such institutions' (ibid.: 134).

Conclusion

It is now time to conclude. We have seen, albeit in a cursory manner, how different are Hayek's views on socialism characterized as a centrally planned economy, on the one hand, and Myrdal's observations of state intervention and planning in the capitalist countries, on the other. We have, of course, found points of comparison, if not of convergence. But this does not mean that we have found a way to choose between these two approaches in order to exclude one and praise the other. Economics does not feature crucial experiments that could help us in such a matter. Consequently, I will only add two further remarks in concluding this exercise in comparison and contrast.

Something must first be said about the ideological aspect *versus* the scientific nature of what has been characterized by Hayek as '*the* economic problem'. While Hayek seems to me to be quite convincing in his purely *theoretical* argument, he is not and cannot be as conclusive in his *empirical* argument. Myrdal, for his part, is very conclusive in his *empirical* analysis but does not at all address the *theoretical* arguments that tend to show, following Hayek, that the market economy is, *ceteris paribus*, the most efficient way of allocating rare resources to alternative social and economic ends. To go even further, I must say that the empirical data on which Myrdal grounds his moral and political option cannot serve to answer either of Hayek's economic questions, neither the theoretical nor the empirical one.

It is furthermore worth stressing that while Myrdal, quite consistently with his general views on the unavoidable interrelation of empirical research and normative claims in all social sciences and especially in economics (see Myrdal 1953, 1958, 1969), admits that the question of state intervention and planning of national and international economies is ultimately grounded in ideological and moral commitments, Hayek explicitly takes for granted that, contrary to Myrdal's explicit starting point, this economic problem is *exclusively* for economic theory and empirical research to unravel. For Hayek, this problem is for economic science to resolve, not for moral and political philosophy to decide. I suppose that, in sharp contrast to both Hayek's and Myrdal's stance on economic planning, I could argue that an optimal viewpoint on this question would require methodically rearticulating a full-fledged economic argument based on an extensive methodological investigation.

Finally, it must be said that from the standpoint of the history of economic thought and the philosophy of economics, the debate on market socialism, on the one hand, and the discussion on the role of state intervention and planning in the welfare state, on the other, are both important and significant events. In a sense, these two *economic disputes* pertain to one and the same economic debate. As such, this debate, which has certainly not ended yet, may be seen as strongly demarcating the Austrian economic *and* the Swedish research traditions from the standard neo-classical paradigm. But I must emphasize that the philosophical fight and scientific brawl on state economic intervention and planning between the Austrian and Swedish economists, seen as participants in distinct research programs, never really took place.[28] It is a pity that there was actually no theoretical clash between Hayek and Myrdal, because we could have learnt a great deal more about such matters. But since we have been experiencing an Austrian revival for the past twenty years or so, I might suppose that the time has come for this intellectual scrimmage to be launched more systematically.

Acknowledgments

Financial support granted by the Social Sciences and Humanities Research Council of Canada and also by the Fonds Québécois de Recherche sur la Société et la Culture is hereby gratefully acknowledged. I also greatly benefited from discussions held during the International Workshop on 'Austrian and Swedish Economics: Criss-Cross Stories and Current Perspectives' (CREUSET, University of Saint-Etienne, 22–23 March 2002). Many thanks are accordingly due to participants at this meeting.

Notes

1 But Günther Chaloupek notes that '[a]mong socialist writers Otto Neurath was the first to take up the question of economic accounting in a socialist economy, in 1919' (Chaloupek 1990: 662). He refers to O. Neurath (1919) *Wesen und Weg der Sozialisierung*, Munich.

2 Hayek clearly rejects this wording of the problem: 'Mises had occasionally used the somewhat loose statement that socialism was impossible, while what he meant was that socialism made rational calculation impossible' (1935b: 76). For his part, and for reasons which should become clear further on, Hayek talks about the 'impracticability of socialism' (ibid.: 69 and *passim*).

3 For instance, following the publication of *The Road to Serfdom*, Keynes wrote a letter to his friend Hayek in which he showed himself clearly to believe that 'the extreme planners can claim their technique to be more efficient' (cited in Christiansen 1993: 51). Keynes even adds: 'I should say that what we want is not no planning, or less planning, indeed I should say that we almost certainly want more' (ibid.: 52).

4 Bruce Caldwell correctly insists on the fact, most crucial for Hayek, that in Lange's model 'there exists a free market for both consumer goods and labor, but (because of public ownership of the means of production) no market for non-labor productive resources like capital' (Caldwell 1997: 1862). This has bewildering consequences, cunningly identified by Hayek (Hayek 1940, section VIII: 132–5).

5 Bruno Jossa (1994) argues that we cannot find in Hayek's writings a *logical* argument which would prove the inefficiency of a market socialist system where the state-owned enterprises would be administered following a completely decentralized model and where they would compete for resources, material, human *and capital as well*. But Hayek has stressed convincingly that the practicability of such a system is very doubtful.

6 According to Hayek:

> economics has come nearer than any other social science to an answer to that central question of all social sciences: How can the combination of fragments of knowledge existing in different minds bring about results which, if they were to be brought about deliberately, would require a knowledge on the part of the directing mind which no single person can possess?
>
> (1937 [1948]: 54; see also 1945)

7 Most, but not all, of the socialist models that Hayek analyzes also retain two crucial traits: 'freedom of choice in consumption and continued freedom of the choice of occupation' (Hayek 1935b: 63).

8 Don Lavoie (1981, 1985) thinks that we should only speak here of a 'calculation' and not of a 'computation' problem. For Hayek, Pareto established once and for all that the use of a system of simultaneous equations to explain what determines the prices on a market would never give the means for a 'numerical calculation of prices' (Hayek 1940: 117). See also the following note.

9 Hayek makes this point most clearly in 'Scientism and Social Sciences'. Speaking of the Walrasian and Paretian systems of equations to represent the relation between the prices of the multifarious types of commodities of any economic system, he writes: 'but without knowledge of the numerical values of all the constants which occur in it and which we never do know, this does not enable us to predict the precise results which any particular change will have' (Hayek 1979: 75). In a note, Hayek refers to Pareto:

> Pareto himself has clearly seen this. After stating the nature of the factors determining the prices in his system of equations, he adds [*Manuel d'économie politique*, 2nd edn (1927): 233–4]: 'It may be mentioned here that this determination has by no means the purpose of arriving at a numerical calculation of prices. Let us make the most favorable assumptions for such a calculation; let us assume that we have triumphed over all the difficulties of finding the data of the problem and that we know the *ophélimités* of all the different commodities for each individual, and all the conditions of production of all the commodities, etc. This is already an absurd hypothesis to make. Yet it is not sufficient to make the solution of the problem possible. We have seen that in the case of 100 persons and 700 commodities there will be 70,699 conditions (actually a great number of circumstances which we have so far neglected will still increase that number); we shall, therefore, have to solve a system of 70,699 equations. This exceeds practically

the power of algebraic analysis, and this is even more true if one contemplates the fabulous number of equations which one obtains for a population of forty million and several thousand commodities. In this case the roles would be changed: it would be not mathematics which would assist political economy, but political economy which would assist mathematics. In other words, if one really could know all these equations, the only means to solve them which is available to human powers is to observe the practical solution given by the market.

(ibid.: 75, n. 8)

If only to prove the importance Hayek gives to this point, we can note that the very same Paretian argument is also used elsewhere by Hayek (see 1939: 197–8, n. 13; 1940: 117–18; 1945: 90, n. 1).

10 See Hayek (1968 [1978]: 38). See also (1967d: 44).

11 This argument has to my mind something to do with Popper's own logical argument developed in the preface of *Poverty of Historicism* (1976) where he proves that it is impossible to know in advance, i.e. today for instance, what will only be known tomorrow. Future knowledge is unforeseeable and unpredictable as such.

12 More on that topic in Nadeau (1998).

13 It may not always be clear enough everywhere in his writings (to my mind it is most of the time), but I take Hayek's stance concerning socialism and capitalism to be thoroughly comparative: it is only when compared to centrally planned economy that competitive or market based economy is said to be 'the most efficient'. To make sense, and especially when put in an evolutionary perspective, this question has to be formulated in relative terms and never discussed with reference to an absolute scale, for none is available.

14 On the epistemological difference between those two kinds of knowledge, see Nadeau (2001).

15 This corresponds to what Hayek calls 'constitutive ideas' as compared to 'speculative' ones (see Hayek, *Scientism and Social Sciences* (1942–44), now part of Hayek 1952).

16 This crucial fact has already been fully recognized by almost all Hayek's critics and commentators. Indeed, connecting this Hayekian argument with the evolutionary one to which I will turn in the next section, Carlo Zappia offers this clever incidental remark:

in examining how competitive systems could deal with personal knowledge, Hayek realized that even competitive prices could not completely aggregate the knowledge dispersed throughout the system. His appreciation of the market order then shifted from the precise notion of equilibrium – which no longer implies Pareto-optimality, or informational efficiency – to the more qualitative construct of spontaneous order – by means of which other conditions for market efficiency could be better pointed out.

(Zappia 1999: 120–1)

17 Maurice Lagueux's very careful reading of Hayek is a bit different. Lagueux insists that one will not find in Hayek's evolutionary approach to economics any form of teleological view:

[Hayek] ne pouvait pas recourir et il n'a pas vraiment recouru aux critères de l'adaptation et de la survie pour établir qu'une structure comme le marché *est* effectivement apte à favoriser efficacement le bon fonctionnement de la société. Si une telle structure pouvait, à ses yeux, résulter de l'évolution spontanée des sociétés, on ne pouvait en conclure que toute évolution devait forcément déboucher sur une structure de ce type. Il serait donc tout aussi injuste de voir en Hayek une sorte d'apologète inconditionnel du *statu quo* qui justifierait le présent du seul fait qu'il serait le fruit d'une longue évolution ou même d'une longue tradition. Le marché, selon Hayek, ressemble bien plutôt à une structure fragile qui ne s'est réalisée qu'imparfaitement dans l'histoire concrète et que les essais et erreurs de l'humanité ont risqué de détruire tout autant qu'ils sont parvenus à la mettre en place.

(Lagueux 1988: 96)

But as far as moral or political justification is concerned, he adds as a critical remark that 'la dimension anti-téléologique de la sélection ne peut intervenir de façon décisive au moment où entre en jeu le choix des institutions' so that '[l]a seule qualité de *spontanéité* ne véhicule aucunement en tant que telle quoi que ce soit qui puisse fonder un jugement de valeur portant sur l'"ordre social" ou sur la "justice"' (ibid.: 102).

18 As it is usually understood, *'laissez-faire'* is for Hayek a 'misleading and vague term' (Hayek 1941: 219) and he prefers to differentiate the liberal or market-based economy from the planned economy by reference to the 'Rule of Law'.

19 Certainly Hayek never wrote that socialism would unavoidably provoke serfdom (he disputed this point to Samuelson who saw an 'inevitability thesis' in Hayek's argument: on this see Caldwell (1997: 1868, n. 7) and he never claimed that competitive economies would certainly and necessarily replace planned economies in the course of history.

20 Gould and Lewontin (1979) distinguish three forms of 'adaptation':

What physiologists call 'adaptation': the phenotypic plasticity that permits organisms to mold their form to prevailing circumstances during ontogeny . . . Physiological adaptations are not heritable, though the capacity to develop them presumably is . . . Secondly, we have a 'heritable' form of non-Darwinian adaptation in humans (and, in rudimentary ways, in a few other advanced social species): cultural adaptation (with heritability imposed by learning). Much confused thinking in human sociobiology arises from a failure to distinguish this mode from Darwinian adaptation based on genetic variation . . . Finally, we have adaptation arising from the conventional Darwinian mechanism of selection upon genetic variation.

(Gould and Lewontin 1979: 264)

The second kind of evolutionary adaptation by way of cultural selection is obviously what Hayek is talking about.

21 The technical concept of the dynamics of a cumulative causality is presented in (Myrdal 1944, appendix 3: 1065–70). For a discussion, see Radzicki (1988) and also Adair (1990, especially pp. 66–7).

22 It may be interesting to note that 'piecemeal' is the phrase which Popper resorts to in *The Poverty of Historicism* (Popper 1976) to qualify the kind of social engineering made possible by the scientific knowledge incorporated in social sciences and especially in economics. Popper always thought his positions to be very near Hayek's positions. I am really not so sure about that. For a detailed study of Hayek's and Popper's differ-

ent, if not opposite, views on 'piecemeal social and economic engineering', see Nadeau (1986).

23 But Hayek does not consider himself as a conservative (see 'Why I am not A Conservative', Appendix to Hayek 1960).

24 According to Hayek:

> the planner must not only translate the vague and general 'ends' that command popular approval into a concrete and detailed scale of value [. . . and] make people believe that the particular detailed code of values which he imposes is the right one. He is forced to create that singleness of purpose which – apart from national crises like war – is absent in a free society.
>
> (1939: 206)

25 Hayek recurrently insists that the planned society will not be guided by 'impersonal social forces' and that it will have to be 'made subject to the control of a directing mind – that is, of course, in the last analysis, the mind of an individual' (Hayek 1939: 198). This is perhaps the ultimate paradox of collectivism: *one will decide for all*. By comparison, the apparent paradox of Hayek's 'true' individualism could be said to be that society is viewed as the unintended aggregate result and cohesive order of *all* individual economic agents interacting spontaneously together: *all will contribute to create a whole order*.

26 As Gregory Christiansen remarks, in the United States where it is usually considered that one can find the paradigm case of a free market or competitive economy:

> [t]housands of present-day government activities . . . are in conflict with the Rule of Law: farm price-support programs, timber subsidies, state water allocations, diverse tariffs and quotas for thousand of imported items, tax deduction for interest paid on home mortgages, rent control, community-development grants, legislation giving labor unions exclusive representation rights *vis-à-vis* workers, and government grants of monopoly privilege to certain producers such as cable-television companies and the U.S. Postal Service.
>
> (1993: 52)

27 Hayek indeed recognizes the possibility of market failures or, which is about the same, he does not deny 'that some amount of central planning . . . will always be necessary'. He adds:

> There are unquestionably fields, like the fight against contagious diseases, where the price mechanism is not applicable, either because some services cannot be priced, or because a clear object desired by an overwhelming majority can only be achieved if a small dissenting minority is coerced.
>
> (1939: 196–7)

28 As remarked by Bruce Caldwell, '[s]ince the events of 1989, the Soviet central planning model has largely been abandoned by academic advocates of socialism, and a renewed interest in market socialism has taken its place' (1997: 1857). The new proponents of market socialism (reviewed and discussed in ibid.: 1875–86) insist particularly on what could be called 'the Hayekian question', i.e. how planned and competitive economies compare as to the efficient use of knowledge in the economic process (for interesting critical discussions, see also Jossa 1994, and Zappia 1999).

References

Adair, P. (1990) 'Myrdal et l'institutionnalisme: du rejet à l'adhésion', in Dostaler, G., Éthier, D. and Lepage, L. (eds) *Gunnar Myrdal et son œuvre*, Montréal: Les Presses de l'Université de Montréal: 59–70.

Boettke, P.J. (1995a) 'Hayek's the road to serfdom revisited: government failure in the argument against socialism', *Eastern Economic Journal*, 21(1): 7–26.

—— (1995b) 'Why are there no Austrian socialists? Ideology, science and the Austrian School', *Journal of the History of Economic Thought*, 17: 35–56.

—— (1998) 'Economic calculation: the Austrian contribution to political economy', *Advances in Austrian Economics*, 5: 135–51.

—— (2000) 'Introduction: 'towards a history of the theory of socialist planning', *Socialism and the Market: The Socialist Calculation Debate Revisited*, 9 vols, London: Routledge.

Caldwell, B.J. (1988a) 'Hayek's transformation', *History of Political Economy*, 20(4): 513–41.

—— (1988b) 'La méthodologie de Hayek: description, évaluation et interrogations', in Dostaler, G. and Ethier, D. (eds) *Friedrich Hayek: philosophie, économie et politique*, Montréal: ACFAS (Politique et Economie).

—— (1997) 'Hayek and socialism', *Journal of Economic Literature*, 35: 1856–90.

Chaloupek, G.K. (1990) 'The Austrian debate on economic calculation in a socialist economy', *History of Political Economy*, 24(4): 659–75.

Christiansen, G.B. (1993) 'What Keynes really said to Hayek about planning', *Challenge*, July–August: 50–3.

Cottrell, A. and Cockshott, W.P. (1993) 'Calculation, complexity and planning: the socialist calculation debate once again', *Review of Political Economy*, 5(1): 73–112.

Cubeddu, R. and Vannucci, A. (1993) 'Economic planning and the Austrian School', *Revue Européenne des Sciences Sociales*, 31(96): 85–131.

De Vlieghere, M. (1994) 'A reappraisal of Friedrich A. Hayek's cultural evolutionism', *Economics and Philosophy*, 10: 285–304.

Dickinson, H. (1933) 'Price formation in a socialist community', *Economic Journal*, 43: 237–50.

—— (1939) *Economics of Socialism*, Oxford: Oxford University Press.

Dobuzinskis, L. (1989) 'The complexities of spontaneous order', *Critical Review*, 3(2): 241–66.

Donzelli, F. (1993) 'The influence of the socialist calculation debate on Hayek's view of general equilibrium theory', *Revue Européenne des Sciences Sociales*, 31(96): 47–84.

Dostaler, G. (1999) 'Hayek et sa reconstruction du libéralisme', *Cahiers de recherche sociologique*, 32: 119–41.

Dupuy, J.P. (1988) 'L'individu libéral, cet inconnu: d'Adam Smith à Friedrich Hayek', in Auduard, C., Dupuy, J.P. and Sève, R. (eds) *Individu et Justice sociale: Autour de John Rawls*, Paris: Editions du Seuil, pp. 73–125.

—— (1992) 'Friedrich Hayek, ou la justice noyée dans la complexité sociale', *Le Sacrifice et l'envie: Le libéralisme aux prises avec la justice sociale*, Paris: Calmann-Lévy, pp. 241–92.

Gould, S.J. and Lewontin, R.C. (1979) 'The spandrels of San Marco and the Panglossian paradigm: a critique of the adaptionist program', *Proceedings of the Royal Society of London*, B 205: 581–98.

Gray, J. (1984) *Hayek on Liberty*, Oxford: Basil Blackwell.

Hayek, F.A. (ed.) (1935a) *Collectivist Economic Planning: Critical Studies on the Possibilities of Socialism*, London: George Routledge & Sons; reprinted (1975) New York: Augustus M. Kelley.

—— (1935b) 'The nature and history of the problem', introduction to Hayek, F.A. (ed.) *Collectivist Economic Planning*, London: George Routledge & Sons, pp. 1–20; reprinted in Hayek, F.A. (1948) *Individualism and Economic Order*, Chicago: University of Chicago Press, pp. 119–47.

—— (1935c) 'The present state of the debate', in Hayek, F.A. (ed.) *Collectivist Economic Planning*, London: George Routledge & Sons, pp. 201–43; reprinted in Hayek, F.A. (1948) *Individualism and Economic Order*, Chicago: University of Chicago Press, pp. 148–80.

—— (1937) 'Economics and knowledge', *Economica*, n.s., 4(13): 33–54; reprinted in Hayek, F.A. (1948) *Individualism and Economic Order*, Chicago: University of Chicago Press, pp. 33–56.

—— (1939) 'Freedom and the economic system', reprinted in Hayek, F.A. (1997) *The Collected Works of F.A. Hayek*, vol. 10, Caldwell, B.J. (ed.), Chicago: University of Chicago Press, pp. 189–220.

—— (1940) 'Socialist calculation: the competitive solution', *Economica*, n.s., 7(26): 125–49; reprinted in Hayek, F.A. (1997) *The Collected Works of F.A. Hayek*, vol. 10, Caldwell, B.J. (ed.), Chicago: University of Chicago Press, pp. 117–40.

—— (1941) 'Planning, science, and freedom', *Nature*, 143, November 15: 580–4; reprinted in Hayek, F.A. (1997) *The Collected Works of F.A. Hayek*, vol. 10, Caldwell, B.J. (ed.), Chicago: University of Chicago Press, pp. 213–20.

—— (1944) *The Road to Serfdom*, London: George Routledge & Sons; Chicago: University of Chicago Press.

—— (1945) 'The use of knowledge in society', *American Economic Review*, 35: 519; reprinted in Hayek, F.A. (1948) *Individualism and Economic Order*, Chicago: University of Chicago Press, pp. 77–91.

—— (1948) *Individualism and Economic Order*, Chicago: University of Chicago Press.

—— (1952) *The Counter-Revolution of Science: Studies on the Abuse of Reason*, Glencoe, IL: the Free Press.

—— (1960) *The Constitution of Liberty*, London: Routledge.

—— (1963) 'Kinds of order in society', *New Individualist Review*, 3(2): 3–12; reprinted in Templeton, K.S. (ed.) (1979) *The Politicization of Society*, Indianapolis, IN: Liberty Press.

—— (1964) 'The theory of complex phenomena', in Bunge, M. (ed.) *The Critical Approach to Science and Philosophy: In Honour of Karl R. Popper*, Glencoe, IL: The Free Press.

—— (1967a) *Studies in Philosophy, Politics and Economics*, London: Routledge & Kegan Paul.

—— (1967b) 'Notes on the evolution of systems of rules of conduct (the interplay between rules of individual conduct and the social order of actions)', in Hayek, F.A. *Studies in Philosophy, Politics and Economics*, London: Routledge & Kegan Paul, pp. 66–81.

—— (1967c) 'The results of human action but not of human design', in Hayek, F.A. *Studies in Philosophy, Politics and Economics*, London: Routledge & Kegan Paul, pp. 96–105.

—— (1967d) 'Rules, perception and intelligibility', in Hayek, F.A. *Studies in Philosophy, Politics and Economics*, London: Routledge & Kegan Paul, pp. 43–65.

—— (1968) 'The primacy of the abstract', reprinted in Hayek, F.A. (1978) *New Studies in Philosophy, Politics, Economics and the History of Ideas*, London: Routledge, pp. 35–49.

—— (1973, 1976, 1979) *Law, Legislation and Liberty: A New Statement of the Liberal Principles of Justice and Political Economy*, 3 vols, London: Routledge & Kegan Paul; Chicago: University of Chicago Press.

—— (1975) *Die Irrtümer des Konstruktivismus und die Grundlagen legitimer Kritik gesellschaftslicher Gebilde*, Tübingen: Mohr, Walter Eucken Institut, vol. 51.

—— (1978a) *New Studies in Philosophy, Politics, Economics and the History of Ideas*, London: Routledge.

—— (1978b) 'Competition as a discovery procedure', in Hayek, F.A. (1978) *New Studies in Philosophy, Politics, Economics and the History of Ideas*, London: Routledge, pp. 179–90.

—— (1982) 'Two pages of fiction: the impossibility of socialist calculation', *Economic Affairs*, April; reprinted in Hayek, F.A. (1984) *The Essence of Hayek*, Stanford, CA: Hoover Institution Press, pp. 53–61.

—— (1984) *The Essence of Hayek*, edited by C. Nishiyama and K.R. Leube, Stanford, CA: Hoover Institution Press.

—— (1988) *The Fatal Conceit: The Errors of Socialism*, in *The Collected Works of F.A. Hayek*, vol. 1, Bartley, W.W. (ed.) Chicago: The University of Chicago Press.

—— (1995) *Contra Keynes and Cambridge: Essays, Correspondence*, in *The Collected Works of F.A. Hayek*, vol. 9, Caldwell, B.J. (ed.) Chicago: The University of Chicago Press.

—— (1997) *Socialism and War: Essays, Documents, Reviews*, in *The Collected Works of F.A. Hayek*, vol. 10, Caldwell, B.J. (ed.) Chicago: The University of Chicago Press.

Jossa, B. (1994) 'Hayek and market socialism', in Colonna, M., Hagemann, H. and Hamouda, O.F. (eds) *Capitalism, Socialism and Knowledge: The Economics of F.A. Hayek*, vol. II, Aldershot: Edward Elgar, pp. 76–93.

Lagueux, M. (1988) '"Ordre spontané" et darwinisme méthodologique chez Hayek', in Dostaler, G. and Éthier, D. (eds) *Friedrich Hayek: Philosophie, économie et politique*, Montréal: ACFAS, pp. 87–103.

Lange, O. (1936) 'On the economic theory of socialism', *Review of Economic Studies*, 4: 53–71.

Lange, O.R. and Taylor, F. (1936–37) 'On the economic theory of socialism', *Review of Economic Studies*, 4: 53–71; 5: 123–42; re-edited as a book, Lippincott, B.E. (ed.) (1938) Minneapolis: The University of Minnesota Press.

Lavoie, D. (1981) 'Mises, the calculation debate, and market socialism', *Wirtschaftspolitische Blätter*, 28(4): 58–65.

—— (1985) *Rivalry and Central Planning: The Socialist Calculation Debate Reconsidered*, Cambridge: Cambridge University Press.

Lukes, S. (1997) 'Social justice: the Hayekian challenge', *Critical Review*, 11(1): 65–80.

Mises, L. von (1920) 'Die wirtschaftsrechnung im sozialistischen gemeinwesen', *Archiv für Sozialwissenschaft und Sozialpolitik* 47: 86–121; trans. S. Adler, in Hayek, F.A. (ed.)

(1935) 'Economic calculation in the socialist commonwealth', *Collectivist Economic Planning*, London: George Routledge & Sons, pp. 87–130.

—— ([1922] 1981) *Socialism: An Economic and Sociological Analysis*, Indianapolis, IN: Liberty Press.

Myrdal, G. (1944) *An American Dilemma: The Negro Problem and Modern Democracy*, New York and London: Harper & Row.

—— (1953) *The Political Element in the Development of Economic Theory*, London: Routledge & Kegan Paul.

—— (1958) *Value in Social Theory: A Selection of Essays on Methodology*, London: Routledge & Kegan Paul.

—— (1960) *Beyond the Welfare State: Economic Planning and its International Implications*, Yale University School of Law, Storr Lectures on Jurisprudence given in 1958, New Haven, CT, and London: Yale University Press.

—— (1969) *Objectivity in Social Research*, New York: Pantheon Books.

Nadeau, R. (1986) 'Popper, Hayek et la question du scientisme', *Manuscrito*, 9(2): 125–56.

—— (1998) 'Spontaneous order', in Davis, J.B. Wade Hands, D. and Mäki, U. (eds) *Handbook of Economic Methodology*, Cheltenham: Edward Elgar, pp. 477–84.

—— (2001) 'Sur l'antiphysicalisme de Hayek: essai d'élucidation', *Revue de Philosophie Economique*, 3(1): 67–112.

Petroni, A.M. (1995) 'What is right with Hayek's ethical theory', *Revue européenne des sciences sociales*, 33(100): 89–126.

Polanyi, M. (1951) *The Logic of Liberty: Reflections and Rejoinders*, Chicago: University of Chicago Press.

—— (1969) 'The determinants of social action', in Streissler, E. *et al.* (eds) *Roads to Freedom: Essays in Honour of Friedrich A. von Hayek*, London: Routledge and Kegan Paul, pp. 145–79.

Popper, K.R. (1976) *The Poverty of Historicism*, London: Routledge and Kegan Paul.

Radzicki, M.J. (1988) 'Institutional economics', *Journal of Economic Issues*, 22(3): 633–67.

Robbins, L. (1932) *An Essay on the Nature and Significance of Economic Science*, New York: New York University Press.

Steele, D.R. (1994) 'On the internal consistency of Hayek's evolutionary oriented constitutional economics: a comment', *Journal des Économistes et des Études Humaines*, 5(1): 157–64.

Streissler, E. (1994) 'Hayek on information and socialism', in Colonna, M., Hagemann, H. and Hamouda, O.F. (eds) *Capitalism, Socialism and Knowledge: The Economics of F.A. Hayek*, vol. II, Aldershot: Edward Elgar, pp. 47–75.

Vaughn, K. (1980) 'Economic calculation under socialism: the Austrian contribution', *Economic Theory*, 18: 535–54.

Wilber, C. and Harrison, R. (1978) 'The methodological basis of institutional economics – pattern models, story-telling and holism', *Journal of Economic Issues*, 12(1): 61–8.

Zappia, C. (1999) 'The economics of information, market socialism and Hayek's legacy', in Arena, R. (ed.) *Subjectivism, Information and Knowledge in Hayek's Economics*, History of Economic Ideas, VII(1–2): 105–38.

16 Hayek with Descartes and Durkheim

Reason and the individual

Ragip Ege

Introduction

We know that neither the Cartesian tradition nor the French sociology founded by Saint-Simon and Auguste Comte are popular with Hayek. Concerning Descartes and the Cartesian tradition he says: 'Such became the characteristic attitude of Cartesian constructivism with its contempt for tradition, custom, and history in general. Man's reason alone should enable him to construct society anew' (Hayek [1973–79] 1982: 10). Compared with the British philosophers who 'laid the foundations of a profound and essentially valid theory . . . the rationalist school (i.e. Cartesian tradition) was simply and completely wrong' (Hayek 1960: 56). And concerning the Saint-Simonian tradition, which constitutes his *bête noire*, Hayek formulates more severe judgements. He estimates that this tradition bears all defects, all the dogmatism and the totalitarianism of 'constructivist rationalism'. He characterizes the Saint-Simonian movement as the most eloquent illustration, the prototype of the constructivist attitude. He does not hesitate to affirm that Auguste Comte belongs to the 'enemies' of 'our civilization' (Hayek 1944: 12). Similar violent attacks are directed towards the Cartesian tradition.

In this chapter, I will first argue that, even from the standpoint of Hayek's proper epistemological and political vision, there is a serious logical inconsistency in his conceptual position when he opposes the Cartesian attitude. The logic, which governs the competitive market as a spontaneous order requires the Cartesian radical doubt as its precondition. The Cartesian doubt allows the individual to emancipate itself from the links and restrictions of tradition; it constitutes the logical precondition of the 'open society' as Hayek or Popper understand it.

Second, I will emphasize certain unexpected analytical affinities between Durkheim's and Hayek's enquiry on modern society. Durkheim is the most famous heir in France at the beginning of the twentieth century of the Saint-Simonian sociological tradition. But he never appears, in Hayek's work, as an interlocutor or an explicitly mentioned adversary. Probably, the author of the *Road to Serfdom* did not have occasion to read Durkheim's work. But we have ground to believe that Hayek would not have hesitated to rank Durkheim, also, among the representatives of 'constructivist rationalism'. In spite of Hayek's ideological opposition to the French sociological tradition, one can easily observe analytical similarities between Durkheim and Hayek in their respective studies on the characteristics of the individual in modern society.

Descartes

According to Hayek, Descartes is the most representative thinker of dogmatic rationalism. I will consider, first, the main arguments of Hayek's criticism of Descartes. I believe that a patient and thorough reading of the *Discourse on Method* reveals the partial character of this criticism. Hayekian judgements on Descartes tend to reduce the complexity of the Cartesian attitude. Moreover, this argument is also valid with regard to Hayek's judgements on some other continental thinkers such as Hegel. A close study of his texts demonstrates that Descartes did not ignore the risk that his position carries on the political level. But beyond the question of the relevance of Hayek's reading of Descartes, I believe that there is a logical inconsistency in his condemnation of the Cartesian concept of radical doubt. Therefore I will try to examine, second, the logical consequences of this condemnation.

Examination of Hayek's critical arguments on Descartes

Let us remember some of Hayek's judgements on Descartes and on the Cartesian tradition.

> The 'radical doubt' which made him [Descartes] refuse to accept anything as true which could not be logically derived from explicit premises that were 'clear and distinct', and therefore beyond possible doubt, deprived of validity all those rules of conduct which could not be justified in this manner . . . For those among his followers . . . the acceptance of anything which was based merely on tradition and could not be fully justified on rational grounds appeared as an irrational superstition. The rejection as 'mere opinion' of all that could not be demonstrated to be true by his criteria became the dominant characteristic of the movement which he started
>
> (Hayek [1973–79] 1982: 10)

This 'rationalist' approach, however, meant in effect a relapse into earlier, anthropomorphic modes of thinking. It produced a renewed propensity to ascribe the origin of all institutions of culture to invention or design. Morals, religion and law, language and writing, money and the market, were thought of as having been deliberately constructed by somebody, or at least as owing whatever perfection they possessed to such design. This internationalist or pragmatic account of history found its fullest expression in the conception of the formation of society by a social contract, first in Hobbes and then in Rousseau, who in many respects was a direct follower of Descartes.

(ibid.: 10)

It is necessary to free ourselves wholly from the erroneous conception that there can be first a society which then gives itself laws. This erroneous conception is basic to the constructivist rationalism which from Descartes and Hobbes through Rousseau and Bentham down to contemporary legal positivism has blinded students to the true relationship between law and government.

(ibid.: 95)

Let us now consider the Cartesian text. Are the reproaches of Hayek justified? Would Descartes really place at the origin of the institutions an omniscient consciousness which determines what is useful, and most beneficial for society?

In the second part of the *Discourse on Method* Descartes indeed says:

There is often less perfection in what has been put together bit by bit, and by different masters, than in the work of a single hand. Thus we see how a building, the construction of which has been undertaken and completed by a single architect, is usually superior in beauty and regularity to those that many have tried to restore by making use of old walls which had been built for other purposes ... In the same way I fancied that half-savage nations, who had gradually become civilized, but who had made their laws by degrees as the need arose to counter the harm done by crimes and disputes, could never be as well regulated as those who, from the beginning of their associations, had observed the decrees of some prudent lawgiver.

(Descartes 1637: 44–5)

Indisputably Descartes adopts here an explicit anti-evolutionist, rationalist, voluntarist, constructivist attitude. In fact, a little further we read also: 'it is almost impossible that our judgements should be as clear and as well-founded as they would have been if we had had the use of our reason from birth and had never been governed by anything else' (ibid.: 45–6). In other words, if we had never been children, our thoughts would never have displayed this disorderly and anarchistic sight, and we would have built a perfectly ordered and harmonious world. An author like Hayek who put a particular emphasis on the importance of the childhood and the principle of spontaneous mimetism which governs it, could be nothing but scandalized by such remarks. At this juncture of the *Discourse on Method*, the perfect world is imagined by Descartes as a world which is necessarily based on reason and seen, from that angle, Hayek is right in bearing Descartes a grudge for his rationalistic approach.

However, immediately after these constructivist considerations, Descartes notes:

> We do not, it is true, see people pulling down the houses of a whole town simply for the purpose of rebuilding them and rendering the streets more beautiful . . . With this as my example, I am convinced that . . . it would be truly absurd for an individual to undertake a reform of the State, by changing its foundations, and by overturning it in order to raise it up again, or to undertake a reform of the body of the sciences, or even of the established order of instruction in our schools . . . That is why I could in no way approve those cloudy and unquiet spirits who, being called neither by birth nor fortune to the handling of public affairs, are forever reforming the State in imagination; and, if I thought that there was the least thing in what I have written to bring me under suspicion of such folly, I should deeply regret its publication.
>
> (ibid.: 46)

We see that Descartes is particularly concerned with a possible misunderstanding and misinterpretation of his thinking. Hence, he carries on: 'My design has never stretched further than the attempted reform of my own thoughts and a reconstruction on foundations that belong only to me' (ibid.: 47). One can observe that Descartes is deeply aware of the danger that represents a *tabula rasa* attitude in the social and political field. Moreover, a few lines further, Descartes says that the radical doubt is a very risky and dangerous enterprise that must be undertaken only by those who are able to resist the mental shock it involves. The Cartesian doubt concerns basically opinions, convictions, beliefs, principles and values of an individual as 'subject', it does not concern the foundations of social institutions. As regards the desire to reform social and political institutions, Descartes has always recommended the greatest prudence and discretion. Hence, if we carefully read the Cartesian text – and that is evidently the first thing we should do to be authorized to pass a judgement on Descartes – by no means can we pretend that the author of the *Discourse on Method* was tempted to recommend a constructivist attitude with regard to the social and political institutions.

Logical inconsistency of Hayek's judgments on Descartes

Hayek remarks that thinkers who criticized Cartesian rationalism such as Mandeville and Hume

> insist that to make reason as effective as possible requires an insight into the limitations of the powers of conscious reason and into the assistance we

obtain from processes of which we are not aware, an insight which constructivist rationalism lacks.

(Hayek [1973–79] 1982: 29)

Let us examine this conception of reason as a limited faculty. Is it legitimate to
postulate such hypothesis on rationality? In accordance with the Hegelian description of consciousness, one can assert that reason is by definition what is always
going beyond any position. In other words, reason tends to go always beyond the
limits assigned to it at a given time, in a given context. Reason is the permanent
act of surpassing its limits, and when these limits are its own, it tends to go
beyond itself. Here the term 'itself' means a particular, hence limited, manifestation of reason. There is no fixed 'itself' for the reason, because reason acts continuously out of itself. Therefore, on a logical level, one cannot formulate any
finite definition of reason, insofar as each definition is a particular proposal,
necessarily limited, hence falling short of reason. No definition can exhaust
reason. Hegel says:

> Consciousness, however, is explicitly the *Notion* of itself. Hence it is some-
> thing that goes beyond limits, and since these limits are its own, it is some-
> thing that goes beyond itself . . . Thus consciousness suffers this violence at
> his own hands; it spoils its own limited satisfaction. When consciousness
> feels this violence, its anxiety may well take retreat from the truth, and
> strive to hold on to what it is in danger of losing. But it can find no peace . . .
> Or, if it entrenches itself in sentimentality, which assures us that it finds
> everything to be *good in its kind*, then this assurance likewise suffers violence
> at the hands of Reason, for, precisely in so far as something is merely a kind,
> Reason finds it *not* to be good [*diese Versicherung leidet ebenso Gewalt von der Ver-
> nunft, welche gerade darum etwas nicht gut findet, insofern es eine Art ist*].
>
> (Hegel 1807: 51–2)

This means that any rational explanation is proved immediately insufficient,
partial and limited, precisely because reason exceeds this particular explanation.
Consequently, as beings endowed with reason, we go always beyond ourselves
(our ideas, our assurances, our convictions, our representations, our opinions,
etc.). I believe that Hayek's misunderstanding of the Cartesian or Hegelian
undertaking can be explained by the fact that he does not pay sufficient attention
to the condition of man as a being tending always to stretch beyond himself. As a
being endowed with reason, man is 'restless in his quest for the infinite'. It is this
'restlessness' which prevents him from being satisfied with a finite or limited definition of reason.

Moreover, when we examine closely the logic that governs the Hayekian
philosophy of history, we observe that the Cartesian doubt must constitute an

essential moment or stage of all this construction. Let us examine Hayek's considerations on the advent of the 'Great Society', as Adam Smith called it:

> The Great Society arose through the discovery that men can live together in peace and mutually benefiting each other without agreeing on the particular aims which they severally pursue. The discovery that by substituting abstract rules of conduct for obligatory concrete ends made it possible to extend the order of peace beyond the small groups pursuing the same ends, because it enables each individual to gain from the skill and knowledge of others whom he need not even know and whose aims could be wholly different from his own.
>
> (Hayek [1973–79] 1982: 109)

In other words, till the advent of the Great Society, men lived under the constraint of *concrete aim-pursuing rules*, laid down by a transcendent authority or legitimized by reference to the tradition. The citizens of modern society are individuals who learned to challenge this constraint, and to resist the prescriptions of the custom and the authority of the tradition. They became emancipated from the constraint of archetypal models and asserted themselves as free individuals. On every occasion, Hayek reminds us that the fundamental moral and political value of modernity is the freedom and autonomy of the individual. Modernity, that is to say the Great Society, represents the emancipation of men from the repression of tradition. Individual liberty of action is the *sine qua non* condition of the competitive market, the development of which gives rise to the Great Society. Hayek defines freedom as follows:

> It [freedom] meant always the possibility of a person's acting according to his own decisions and plans, in contrast to the position of one who was irrevocably subject to the will of another, who by arbitrary decision could coerce him to act or not to act in specific ways. The time-honoured phrase by which this freedom has often been described is therefore 'independence of the arbitrary will of another.'
>
> (Hayek 1960: 12)

In other words, modernity is the reign of individualism; more precisely, modernity is the space of the constitution of individual liberty. The archaic or traditional society is, on the other hand, a rigorously hierarchical structure within which men are relating to each other according to a logic of domination and servitude. Great Society, the space of the emancipation of free and autonomous individuals, breaks up precisely with this structure of subordination.

Now if we try to identify the power that allowed modern man to defy ancient society, we cannot but turn our attention to the Cartesian doubt. It is actually this radical doubt which confers upon the individual the capacity to resist the constraints and repression of tradition. Only such an attitude, supported by the critical reason, which poses itself as the sovereign authority of evaluation of the world, can resist the self-evident authority of tradition. Modern society, the space of emancipation of the individual, necessarily needs the Cartesian doubt as its precondition, not as contingency but as logical requirement. Our preceding assertion that the Cartesian doubt represents a constitutive stage or moment of the Hayekian system is to be understood in this sense. The Cartesian concept of doubt constitutes an essential condition supporting the logical consistency of this system.

The foregoing considerations invite us to reconsider the consistency of the Hayekian system as an evolutionary process. Thinking it over, one must admit that the advent of modern society as described in the Hayekian historical analysis necessitates logically the hypothesis of the eruption of a radical discontinuity in human history. The refusal of the individual to conform his behaviour and his mind to the requisites of canonical and traditional models constitutes precisely this radical discontinuity. One cannot accede to liberty, defined as individual autonomy, through a trial and error process. Individual opposition to the authority of tradition presupposes a voluntary act of insubordination to the 'concrete aim pursuing rules'. In other words, one cannot have an authentic comprehension of modernity without an explicit reference to the Cartesian moment.

Durkheim

I already said that Hayek never discussed explicitly Durkheim's sociological theses or arguments in his work. But I believe that Hayek would probably have ranked Durkheim in the constructivist tradition, which, according to him, descends from Saint-Simon's work. The feature, which would probably greatly irritate Hayek in Durkheim's work, is the sympathy of the French sociologist for the socialist movement. It is nevertheless true that Durkheim never embraced the radical or Marxist forms of socialism; he even severely criticized them. But, as Marcel Mauss notices, the problems Durkheim tackled at the beginning of his career dealt with the social question (Durkheim 1928, Preface: 27). And his famous work on socialism constitutes the first part, devoted primarily to Saint-Simonism, of a great project on the socialist movement. For Hayek, a will of repression and domination of the individual and personal freedom animates all socialists, and in general, all anti-liberals, whereas Durkheim depicts socialism as a 'cry of pain, and sometimes of anger, screamed by men who felt strongly our collective misfortune' (ibid.: 37). Even when he criticizes it, Durkheim approaches socialism as a social phenomenon with affection and respect. For Hayek, on the contrary, socialism is the greatest enemy of the occidental civilization.

However, in spite of this radical difference on the moral and political level, there are striking analytical affinities between our two authors. I will try to identify and specify these similarities. It will be shown, on this occasion, that the sociological analyses of Durkheim, in particular, in his work *The Division of Labour in Society*, are not too far from certain major Hayekian concepts (cf. Birner and Ege 1999).

Segmentary society and tribal society

On the methodological level we can observe a similarity between Durkheim and Hayek. They both construct a fictitious, imaginary primitive society – Durkheim speaks of 'segmentary society', Hayek of 'tribal society' – in order to analyse, comparatively, the specificity of modern society. From a rigorous historical point of view, no concrete reality corresponds to these concepts. And neither in Hayek's work nor in Durkheim's have we any concrete historical fact liable to illustrate the primitive society. The concern of both authors is the knowledge of the specificity of modern society and not the intelligence of the hypothetical original society.

According to Durkheim, the so-called 'repressive law' rules the segmentary society. Such a law supposes the existence of a strong collective conscience borne by all the individuals who compose the society:

> The totality of beliefs and sentiments common to average citizens of the same society forms a determinate system which has its own life; one may call it the *collective* or *common conscience*. No doubt, it has not a specific organ as a substratum; it is, by definition, diffuse in every reach of society.
>
> (Durkheim 1893: 79)

Repressive law sanctions the acts which offend collective feelings, which transgress common rules shared entirely by all the community. Therefore such a penal law is operating in a society where there is no need to codify or to draw up a list of criminal acts. These criminal acts are rigorously registered or consigned in the collective memory that each individual of the group bears.

> We must not say that an action shocks the common conscience because it is criminal, but rather that it is criminal because it shocks the common conscience . . . A sentiment, whatever its origin and end, is found in all consciences with a certain degree of force and precision, and every action which violates it is a crime.
>
> (ibid.: 81–2)

In a segmentary society, collective conscience invades quite totally individual conscience; this invasion does not leave any place for particular forms of existence which can break away from canonical ones. That is the reason why Durkheim calls 'solidarity through likeness' the kind of solidarity prevailing in the traditional society. Individuals are integrated in the group through juxtaposition and not through specific functions they assume. Here we have the meaning of the well-known Durkheimian term: 'mechanical solidarity'. Defining traditional society as a 'segmentary society' means that each element of it can substitute for another. Each segment is carrying the same strong feelings, ancestral values and principles of life, the same social rules the transgression of which justifies, without any further enquiry, the most severe punishment. On the socioeconomic level, segments are carrying the same knowledges, know-how and technology. They correspond, therefore, to the autarkic socio-economic unites (just like *the oikoi* of the ancient Greece, cf. Vernant 1965 and Vidal-Naquet 1965), which are able to satisfy the needs of their members by their own means, without having recourse to resort to the technological resources of other segments.

The individual of a segmentary society is literally wrapped up (*'absorbé'*) (Durkheim 1893: 170) in the group. The concept of individual personality cannot emerge in a social structure where the individual conscience is to such an extent invaded by the collective conscience. It is important to notice that for Durkheim the lack of individual personality is not due to a strong centralization of the power in primitive society, as Spencer believes. The representation of the primitive society as a structure where the individuals are absolutely submissive to a strongly centralized and coercive authority is wrong. In a segmentary society there is no place for a clear and distinct feeling of individuality and subjectivity. Actually Durkheim writes:

> This effacement of the individual has as its place of origin a social type which is characterized by a complete absence of all centralization. It is a product of that state of homogeneity, which distinguishes primitive societies. If the individual is not distinct from the group, it is because the individual conscience is hardly at all distinguishable from the collective conscience.
>
> (ibid.: 193–4)

And a little further we still read: 'If in lower societies so small a place is given to individual personality, that is not because it has been restrained or artificially suppressed. It is simply because, at that moment of history, *it did not exist.*' (ibid.: 194). Therefore if the primitive society's individual conforms absolutely to the collective moral rules and to the canonical forms of behaviour laid down by the tradition, it is not because he would be coerced by the explicit repression of a despotic power. In other words, he assents to it spontaneously, since he does not know any other modality of existence than the one instituted by the group. In short, one finds here Louis Dumont's concept of 'holism' (Dumont 1977).

Hayek does not devote in his work a systematic analysis to what he calls 'tribal society', as does Durkheim. But he often insists on the fact that traditional society is essentially governed by *concrete rules of conduct*. In opposition to the *abstract rules of conduct*, the rules that the tribal society imposes upon individuals are a set of common goals that nobody can refuse to pursue. One cannot refuse to obey these constraints. Tribal society coerces its members to pursue the same aims and to conform in their behaviour to the same ancestral pattern. Members of this kind of society are governed by so-called gregarious instincts. In this sense, the community overcomes the tribal man and all acts of transgression of rules are severely punished by his own community. In other words, tribal society is a social structure where concrete rules of conduct prescribe to the individual what he should do, in opposition to the abstract rules of conduct, which prescribe what he should not do. With regard to the logic of the Hayekian system, the difference between rules of a negative nature and rules of a positive nature is fundamental. The first kind of rules leave an undefined field of the possible, forbidding only a sequence of this one, whereas the second kind of rules close the field of the possible, coercing the individual to adopt an archetypal behaviour. In this sense, Hayek believes, like Durkheim, that tribal society cannot give birth to the personal individuality. In Hayek's terminology we can express this idea saying that all the members of tribal society are carrying the same set of informations or knowledge. We find here again the Durkheimian concept of 'solidarity through likeness'. Because of the preponderance of concrete rules of conduct in tribal society, individual actions are all directed towards similar common aims; that, in turn, puts a serious brake on the development of individual talents and skills in society. One can assert that tribal society is a structure, which hinders the emergence and development of innovation. These considerations lead Durkheim and Hayek to enquire on the theoretical conditions of individualism in history.

The advent of the individualism

According to Durkheim, individualism develops in parallel with the progressive substitution of the 'restitutive law' for the 'repressive law'. From the Hayekian point of view the progressive adoption and development of abstract rules of conduct by the society carry out this process. 'Co-operation' represents, in Durkheim's work, the new mode of interaction between individuals of the modern society. The division of labour gets an extraordinary development – incommensurate with the elementary complexity of the economic and social organization of traditional society – thanks to this new form of solidarity. In the case of Hayek, the emancipation of individuals from the despotism of common goals makes possible, in society, the constitution of a space, namely the competitive market where individual actions are spontaneously co-ordinated without any intervention of a planning consciousness.

Durkheim observes that modern society, as opposed to the segmentary one, is governed by 'organic solidarity'. Such a society is 'constituted, not by a repetition of similar, homogeneous segments, but by a system of different organs each of which has a special role, and which are themselves formed of differentiated parts' (Durkheim 1893: 181). In other words, industrial society appears essentially as a scene of huge diversity and differentiation, rigorously unfamiliar to the segmentary society. Elements or components of modern society are 'not juxtaposed linearly as the rings of an earthworm, nor entwined one with another, but co-ordinated and subordinated one to another around the same central organ which exercises a moderating action over the rest of the organism' (ibid.: 181). They are integrated into society with respect to a hierarchical logic. But this hierarchy or subordination is essentially different from the passive submission of the primitive man to moral prescriptions of his society. Primitive society's individuals are, to a great extent, interchangeable, seeing that they are carrying the same set of informations, know-how and techniques while individuals of modern society are highly irreplaceable because of specific functions they assume, even if they are called to obey a lot of organizational principles:

> Individuals are here grouped, no longer according to their relations of lineage, but according to the particular nature of the social activity to which they consecrate themselves. Their natural milieu is no longer the natal milieu, but the occupational milieu.
>
> (ibid.: 182)

The law prevailing in modern society is so-called restitutive law. Unlike the penal sanction, the restitutive sanction 'is not expiatory, but consists of a simple *return in state* . . . If certain things were done, the judge reinstates them as they would have been. He speaks of law; he says nothing of punishment' (ibid.: 111). And 'while repressive law tends to remain diffuse within society, restitutive law creates organs which are more and more specialized' (ibid.: 113). In other words, restitutive law operates beyond the collective conscience seeing that it tackles in increasingly specific and increasingly exceptional situations. When in segmentary society an interdict or a law is transgressed, such an act becomes the concern of the whole of community and through the punishment the community takes its revenge on a criminal who dared disturb its immutable order. To put it differently, legal proceedings instituted in the sphere of the restitutive law concern conflicts, disturbances or disorders so specific that they are totally ignored by the majority of the population. The increasingly technical character of restitutive law evolves in parallel with the development of the social division of labour. The more functions diversify in society, the more the problems generated by the co-ordination of these functions become subjects of particular knowledges. One can assert that, if the science of law has achieved great progress in modern society, this is due to the spectacular development of the social division of labour required for the invention of a great number of rules in order to administer the complex relations between extremely specialized functions.

We can observe that Durkheim's vision of the social division of labour with its logical corollary, i.e. the development of restitutive law, reveals great similarities with Hayekian analyses concerning the development of individualism. In fact, the individual personality can appear and develop only in a society where individuals enjoy material and spiritual conditions which allow them to act beyond the collective conscience. In other words, individuals can develop their subjectivity only in a society where those who dare to challenge common values and feelings are not immediately penalized. Here Durkheim's position is closest to the Hayekian one. Indeed, according to Hayek, the Great Society can emerge only when individuals can escape the prescriptions of common morality and can learn by experience a form of existence that is oriented by the pursuit of particular and exclusive objectives. In the Hayekian terminology, the condition of the possibility of the so-called 'catallaxy' lies in the adoption by the community of abstract rules of conduct. This learning by experience of a pacific collective existence without any agreement by individuals on common goals requires, on the part of the community, a capacity to assume a great risk, namely trust in the existence of spontaneous, unplanned co-ordination mechanisms of scattered actions. Men must learn to renounce a form of social cohesion or solidarity, which is supposed to be realized by the adoption of common aims and objectives. This renunciation allows individuals to escape the responsibility of social solidarity (henceforward social solidarity is considered a spontaneous phenomenon) and to learn to rely on the operation of the 'invisible hand'. But just as in the case of Durkheim's assumption of the transition from repressive law to restitutive law, the renunciation of concrete rules of conduct is risky, as we have already noted, i.e. the prospect of the disintegration of society. Individualism requires as a *sine qua non* that society can assume such a risk. We find here, once again, the problematic of Cartesian doubt. While according to Durkheim individual personality, i.e. individual diversity, develops in proportion to the development of the social division of labour and of the restitutive law, according to Hayek, the development of the individual personality requires the development of the competitive market.

Conclusion

We can easily imagine Hayek's objection to the foregoing. Probably Hayek would not have contested the relevance of the connection we have made between his conception of the advent of individualism and Durkheim's. But he would undoubtedly have drawn our attention to the limits of such a connection. The great reproach Hayek addresses to socialism concerns its incapacity to renounce the necessity of a unifying authority in the organization of society. Socialism is incapable of renouncing the necessity for an intervention by an external conscience representing community's unity or general interest, in order to establish social cohesion. Otherwise, this unity is severely threatened by the excessive development of individualism. According to Hayek, socialism – which for him includes the Cartesian tradition as well as the socialist movement, and particularly the Saint-Simonian tradition – could never believe in the spontaneous, self-organizational capacity of society to assure its cohesion. However, also on this point, some reflections of Durkheim at the end of his work could have surprised Hayek.

In the third book of his work Durkheim examines Comte's theoretical fear. In fact, Comte says:

> Since all such decomposition (the division of labour pushed further) necessarily has the tendency to determine a corresponding dispersion, the fundamental partition of human labour cannot avoid evoking, in a proportionate degree, individual divergences, both intellectual and moral, whose combined influence must, in the same measure, demand a permanent discipline able to prevent or unceasingly contain their discordant flight . . . The social destiny of government appears to me to consist particularly in sufficiently containing, and preventing, so far as possible, this fatal disposition towards a fundamental dispersion of ideas, sentiments, and interests . . . It is clear, in effect, that the only real means of preventing such a dispersion consists in this indispensable reaction in a new and special function, susceptible of fittingly intervening in the habitual accomplishment of all the diverse functions of social economy, so as to recall to them unceasingly the feeling of unity and the sentiment of common solidarity.
>
> (A. Comte, quoted by Durkheim 1893: 357–9)

However, Durkheim does not share the Comtian pessimism. When we closely examine the organization of modern society, we can see that organic solidarity is perfectly endowed by a spontaneous mechanism of regulation and cohesion. The problem is the following: the transition of society from mechanical solidarity to organic solidarity was carried out so quickly that there was not enough time to draw up new specific rules to resolve particular conflicts which occur among new functions. This delay explains crises and anomalies in modern society. But, according to Durkheim, spontaneous mechanisms will work and the negativity generated by the organic division of labour will be overcome. He writes:

> We may say that the division of labour produces solidarity only if is spontaneous. But by spontaneity we must understand not simply the absence of all express violence, but also of everything that can even indirectly shackle the free unfolding of the social force that each carries himself. It supposes, not only that individuals are not relegated to determinate functions by force, but

also that no obstacle, of whatever nature, prevents them from occupying the place in the social framework, which is compatible with their faculties. In short, labour is divided spontaneously only if society is constituted in such a way that social inequalities exactly express natural inequalities.

(ibid.: 377)

We can observe here how Durkheim's position is closed to Hayekian one.

Hayek always insisted on two kinds of individualism: the 'true' and the 'false'. The 'true individualism' was inaugurated by John Locke, Bernard Mandeville and David Hume and carried on by Josiah Tucker, Adam Ferguson, and Adam Smith. The 'false individualism' was, on the other hand, represented

> by French and other Continental writers – a fact due, I believe, to the dominant role which Cartesian rationalism plays in its composition. The outstanding representatives of this tradition are the Encyclopedists, Rousseau, and the physiocrats; and . . . this rationalistic individualism, always tends to the opposite of individualism, namely, socialism and collectivism.

(Hayek 1949: 4)

I believe that this brutal and Manicheistic opposition between two traditions is a very hasty verdict. We observed that the authors considered by Hayek as belonging to the bad side of the opposition are by no means unfamiliar with the problematic of 'spontaneous order'. On the contrary, they are greatly attentive to the spontaneous mechanisms and regularities, which govern human historical evolution. Nevertheless, in the final analysis, Descartes and Hayek are 'constructivists'. In other words, they believe that the concept of individual autonomy or independence is closely associated with the concept of reason and rationality. Individualism and reason are indissolubly linked each other. This is a logical and necessary consequence of a rigorous and coherent analysis of the emergence of historical conditions of individualism. A scrupulous comparative examination of the logic, which rules the arguments of the 'Cartesian rationalism's' authors and the Hayekian ones reveals that the whole philosophical structure of the author of the *Road to Serfdom* necessarily requires a constitutive moment of discontinuity (what I called the Cartesian moment), i.e. a constructivist dimension.

References

Birner, J. and Ege, R. (1999) 'Two views on social stability: an unsolved question', *American Journal of Economics and Sociology*, 58(4): 749–80.

Descartes, R. (1637) *Discourse on Method*, trans. A. Wollaston, 1966, Pittsburgh: Penguin Books.

Durkheim, E. (1893) *The Division of Labor in Society*, trans. G. Simpson, 1969, Houndsmills: The Free Press, Collier-Macmillan Limited.

—— (1928) *Le Socialisme: Sa définition – ses débuts. La doctrine saint-simonienne*, 1992, Paris: Quadrige, PUF.

Dumont, L. (1977) *From Mandeville to Marx: The Genesis and Triumph of Economic Ideology*, Chicago: University of Chicago Press.

Ege, R. (1992) 'Emergence du marché concurrentiel et évolutionnisme chez Hayek', *Reveuue Economique*, 43(6), November: 1007–36.

Hayek, F.A. ([1944] 1976) *The Road to Serfdom*, Chicago: University of Chicago Press.

—— (1949) *Individualism and Economic Order*, London: Routledge and Kegan Paul.

—— ([1960] 1993) *The Constitution of Liberty*, London: Routledge.

—— ([1973–79] 1982) *Law, Legislation and Liberty*, London: Routledge and Kegan Paul.

Hegel, G.W.F. ([1807] 1977) *Phenomenology of Spirit*, trans. A.V. Miller, Oxford: Oxford University Press.

Vernant, J.-P. ([1965] 1974) *Mythe et pensée chez les Grecs*, Paris: François Maspero, vol. 2.

Vidal-Naquet, P. ([1965] 1990) 'Economie et société dans la Grèce ancienne: l'œuvre de Moses I. Finley', in *La Démocratie grecque vue d'ailleurs*, Paris: Flammarion, pp. 55–94.

Index